ANNUAL EDITIONS

Education
Thirty-third Edition

06/07

EDITOR

Fred Schultz

University of Akron (Retired)

Fred Schultz, former professor of education at the University of Akron, attended Indiana University to earn a B.S. in social science education in 1962, an M.S. in the history and philosophy of education in 1966, and a Ph.D. in the history and philosophy of education and American studies in 1969. His B.A. in Spanish was conferred from the University of Akron in May 1985. He is actively involved in researching the development and history of American education with a primary focus on the history of ideas and social philosophy of education. He also likes to study languages.

**SCHOOL OF EDUCATION
CURRICULUM LABORATORY
UM-DEARBORN**

Mc Graw Hill **Contemporary Learning Series**

2460 Kerper Blvd., Dubuque, IA 52001

Visit us on the Internet
http://www.mhcls.com

Credits

1. **How Others See Us and How We See Ourselves**
   Unit photo—© CORBIS/Royalty-Free.
2. **Rethinking and Changing the Educative Effort**
   Unit photo—White House Photo by Paul Morse
3. **Striving for Excellence: The Drive for Quality**
   Unit photo—© Getty Images/Photodisc.
4. **Morality and Values in Education**
   Unit photo—© CORBIS/Royalty-Free.
5. **Managing Life in Classrooms**
   Unit photo—© Getty Images/Doug Menuez.
6. **Cultural Diversity and Schooling**
   Unit photo—© CORBIS/Royalty-Free.
7. **Serving Special Needs and Concerns**
   Unit photo—Photo courtesy of Sandy Wille.
8. **The Profession of Teaching Today**
   Unit photo—© CORBIS/Royalty-Free.
9. **For Vision and Hope: Alternative Visions of Reality**
   Unit photo—© Getty Images/Ryan McVay.

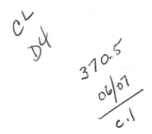

Copyright

Cataloging in Publication Data
Main entry under title: Annual Editions: Education. 2006/2007.
1. Education—Periodicals. I. Schultz, Fred, *comp.* II. Title: Education.
ISBN 0–07–354580–5   658'.05   ISSN 0272–5010

Thirty-third Edition

Cover image © Ryan McVay/Getty Images and Creatas/PunchStock
Printed in the United States of America   1234567890QPDQPD98765   Printed on Recycled Paper

Editors/Advisory Board

Members of the Advisory Board are instrumental in the final selection of articles for each edition of ANNUAL EDITIONS. Their review of articles for content, level, currentness, and appropriateness provides critical direction to the editor and staff. We think that you will find their careful consideration well reflected in this volume.

Preface

In publishing ANNUAL EDITIONS we recognize the enormous role played by the magazines, newspapers, and journals of the public press in providing current, first-rate educational information in a broad spectrum of interest areas. Many of these articles are appropriate for students, researchers, and professionals seeking accurate, current material to help bridge the gap between principles and theories and the real world. These articles, however, become more useful for study when those of lasting value are carefully collected, organized, indexed, and reproduced in a low-cost format, which provides easy and permanent access when the material is needed. That is the role played by ANNUAL EDITIONS.

We face a situation with reference to our educational policy priorities not unfamiliar in our history as a nation, the options open to us are divided and not easily resolved. On the one hand, we are to have "highly qualified teachers"; on the other hand, we leave it to state politicians and the local school authority as to what constitutes "highly qualified teachers." This is a typical enigmatic dilemma in the history of American education, and one we will soon regret. If we are not to leave any student behind, really and sincerely, can we come to grips with what it means to have a "highly qualified teacher?" As has been the case throughout the history of American education, the politicians will decide what we will do with this situation. We will deal with it as a profession, knowing full well that this is about as much as we can do.

Issues regarding the purposes of education as well as the appropriate methods of educating have been debated throughout all generations of literate human culture. This is because the meaning of the word "educated" shifts within ideological realms of thought and cultural belief systems. There will always be debates over the purposes and the ends of "education" as it is understood in any time or place. This is because each generation must continuously reconstruct the definition of "education" based upon its understanding of "justice," "fairness," and "equity" in human relations, and each generation must locate and position their understanding of social and personal reality.

In the twenty-first century, educators are presented with many new challenges caused by many forces at work in human society. We must decide really what knowledge is of most worth and what basic skills and information each child, of whatever heritage, needs to know. We must face this question once and for all. It is no longer a choice; it is a duty if we are disciplined persons interested in the well being of our children and adolescents. We have before us a great qualitative challenge, our response to which will determine the fate of future generations of our society.

The technological breakthroughs now developing in the information sciences will have an amazing impact on how people learn. The rates of change in how we learn and how we obtain information is already increasing at a very rapid pace that will assuredly continue.

The public conversation on the purposes and future directions of education is lively as ever. Alternative visions and voices regarding the broad social aims of schools and the preparation of teachers continue to be presented. *Annual Editions: Education 06/07* attempts to reflect current mainstream as well as alternative visions as to what education ought to be. Equity issues regarding what constitutes equal treatment of students in the schools continue to be addressed. This year's edition con- tains articles on gender issues in the field and on the application of research in multicultural education to the areas of teacher preparation and the staff development of teachers already in the schools. The debate over whether all public monies for education should go to the public schools or whether these funds should follow the student into either public or private schools has again intensified.

Communities are deeply interested in local school politics and school funding issues. There continues to be healthy dialogue about and competition for the support of the various "publics" involved in public schooling. The articles reflect spirited critique of our public schools. There are competing, and very differing, school reform agendas being discussed. All of this occurs as the United States continues to experience fundamentally important demographic shifts in its cultural makeup.

Compromise continues to be the order of the day. The many interest groups within the educational field reflect a broad spectrum of viewpoints ranging from various behaviorist and cognitive developmental perspectives to humanistic, postmodernist, and critical theoretical ones.

In assembling this volume, we make every effort to stay in touch with movements in educational studies and with the social forces at work in schools. Members of the advisory board contribute valuable insights, and the production and editorial staffs at the publisher, McGraw-Hill Contemporary Learning Series, coordinate our efforts. Through this process we collect a wide range of articles on a variety of topics relevant to education in North America.

The readings in *Annual Editions: Education 06/07* explore the social and academic goals of education, the current conditions of the nation's educational systems, the teaching profession, and the future of American education. In addition, these selections address the issues of change and the moral and ethical foundations of schooling. As always, we would like you to help us improve this volume. Please rate the material in this edition on the postage-paid *article rating form* provided at the back of this book and send it to us. We care about what you think. Give us the public feedback that we need.

Fred Schultz

Fred Schultz
Editor

iv

Contents

UNIT 1
How Others See Us and How We See Ourselves

The concepts in bold italics are developed in the article. For further expansion, please refer to the Topic Guide and the Index.

UNIT 2
Rethinking and Changing the Educative Effort

The concepts in bold italics are developed in the article. For further expansion, please refer to the Topic Guide and the Index.

UNIT 3
Striving for Excellence: The Drive for Quality

The concepts in bold italics are developed in the article. For further expansion, please refer to the Topic Guide and the Index.

UNIT 4
Morality and Values in Education

UNIT 5
Managing Life in Classrooms

The concepts in bold italics are developed in the article. For further expansion, please refer to the Topic Guide and the Index.

UNIT 6
Cultural Diversity and Schooling

UNIT 7
Serving Special Needs and Concerns

The concepts in bold italics are developed in the article. For further expansion, please refer to the Topic Guide and the Index.

UNIT 8
The Profession of Teaching Today

UNIT 9
For Vision and Hope: Alternative Visions of Reality

The concepts in bold italics are developed in the article. For further expansion, please refer to the Topic Guide and the Index.

The concepts in bold italics are developed in the article. For further expansion, please refer to the Topic Guide and the Index.

Topic Guide

This topic guide suggests how the selections in this book relate to the subjects covered in your course. You may want to use the topics listed on these pages to search the Web more easily.

On the following pages a number of Web sites have been gathered specifically for this book. They are arranged to reflect the units of this *Annual Edition.* You can link to these sites by going to the student online support site at *http://www.mhcls.com/online/.*

ALL THE ARTICLES THAT RELATE TO EACH TOPIC ARE LISTED BELOW THE BOLD-FACED TERM.

Internet References

The following internet sites have been carefully researched and selected to support the articles found in this reader. The easiest way to access these selected sites is to go to our student online support site at *http://www.mhcls.com/online/*.

AE: Education 06/07

The following sites were available at the time of publication. Visit our Web site—we update our student online support site regularly to reflect any changes.

General Sources

Education Week on the Web
http://www.edweek.org

At this *Education Week* home page, you will be able to open its archives, read special reports on education, keep up on current events in education, look at job opportunities, and access articles relevant to educators today.

Educational Resources Information Center
http://www.eric.ed.gov

This invaluable site provides links to all ERIC sites: clearinghouses, support components, and publishers of ERIC materials. You can search the ERIC database, find out what is new, and ask questions about ERIC.

National Education Association
http://www.nea.org

Something about virtually every education-related topic can be accessed via this site of the 2.3-million-strong National Education Association.

National Parent Information Network/ERIC
http://npin.org

This is a clearinghouse of information on elementary and early childhood education as well as urban education. Browse through its links for information for parents and for people who work with parents.

U.S. Department of Education
http://www.ed.gov

Explore this government site for examination of institutional aspects of multicultural education. National goals, projects, grants, and other educational programs are listed here as well as many links to teacher services and resources.

UNIT 1: How Others See Us and How We See Ourselves

Charter Schools
http://www.edexcellence.net/topics/charters.html

Open this site for news about charter schools. It provides information about charter school research and issues, links to the U.S. Charter Schools Web site, and Best on the Web charter school sites.

Pathways to School Improvement
http://www.ncrel.org/sdrs/pathwayg.htm

This site of the North Central Regional Educational Laboratory leads to discussions and links about education, including the current state of education, reform issues, and goals and standards. Technology, professional development, and integrated services are a few of the subjects also discussed.

UNIT 2: Rethinking and Changing the Educative

Effort

The Center for Innovation in Education
http://www.center.edu

The Center for Innovation in Education, self-described as a "not-for-profit, nonpartisan research organization" focuses on K–12 education reform strategies. Click on its links for information about and varying perspectives on school privatization and other reform initiatives.

Colorado Department of Education
http://www.cde.state.co.us/index_home.htm

This site's links will lead you to information about education-reform efforts, technology in education initiatives, and many documents of interest to educators, parents, and students.

National Council for Accreditation of Teacher Education
http://www.ncate.org

The NCATE is the professional accrediting organization for schools, colleges, and departments of education in the United States. Accessing this page will lead to information about teacher and school standards, state relations, and developmental projects.

Phi Delta Kappa International
http://www.pdkintl.org

This important organization publishes articles about all facets of education—from school vouchers and charter schools to "new dimensions" in learning.

UNIT 3: Striving for Excellence: The Drive for Quality

Awesome Library for Teachers
http://www.awesomelibrary.org

Open this page for links and access to teacher information on everything from educational assessment to general child development topics.

Education World
http://www.education-world.com

Education World provides a database of literally thousands of sites that can be searched by grade level, plus education news, lesson plans, and professional-development resources.

EdWeb/Andy Carvin
http://edwebproject.org

The purpose of EdWeb is to explore the worlds of educational reform and information technology. Access educational resources around the world, learn about trends in education policy and information infrastructure development, examine success stories of computers in the classroom, and much more.

Kathy Schrock's Guide for Educators
http://www.discoveryschool.com/schrockguide/

This is a classified list of sites on the Internet found to be useful for enhancing curriculum and teacher professional growth. It is updated daily.

www.mhcls.com/online/

Teacher's Guide to the U.S. Department of Education
http://www.ed.gov/pubs/TeachersGuide/

Government goals, projects, grants, and other educational programs are listed here as well as many links to teacher services and resources.

UNIT 4: Morality and Values in Education

Association for Moral Education
http://www.amenetwork.org/

AME is dedicated to fostering communication, cooperation, training, curriculum development, and research that links moral theory with educational practices. From here it is possible to connect to several sites on ethics, character building, and moral development.

Child Welfare League of America
http://www.cwla.org

The CWLA is the United States' oldest and largest organization devoted entirely to the well-being of vulnerable children and their families. This site provides links to information about issues related to morality and values in education.

Ethics Updates/Lawrence Hinman
http://ethics.acusd.edu

This site provides both simple concept definition and complex analysis of ethics, original treatises, and sophisticated search engine capability. Subject matter covers the gamut from ethical theory to applied ethical venues. There are many opportunities for user input.

The National Academy for Child Development
http://www.nacd.org

This international organization is dedicated to helping children and adults reach their full potential. Its home page presents links to various programs, research, and resources into such topics as ADD.

UNIT 5: Managing Life in Classrooms

Classroom Connect
http://www.classroom.com

This is a major Web site for K–12 teachers and students, with links to schools, teachers, and resources online. It includes discussion of the use of technology in the classroom.

Global SchoolNet Foundation
http://www.gsn.org

Access this site for multicultural educational information. The site includes news for teachers, students, and parents, as well as chat rooms, links to educational resources, programs, and contests and competitions.

Teacher Talk Forum
http://education.indiana.edu/cas/tt/tthmpg.html

Visit this site for access to a variety of articles discussing life in the classroom. Clicking on the various links will lead you to electronic lesson plans covering a variety of topic areas from Indiana University's Center for Adolescent Studies.

UNIT 6: Cultural Diversity and Schooling

American Scientist
http://www.amsci.org/amsci/amsci.html

Investigate this site to access a variety of articles and to explore issues and concepts related to race and gender.

American Studies Web
http://www.georgetown.edu/crossroads/asw/

This site provides links to a wealth of resources on the Internet related to American studies, from gender studies to race and ethnicity. It is of great help when doing research in demography and population studies.

National Institute on the Education of At-Risk Students
http://www.ed.gov/offices/OERI/At-Risk/

The At-Risk Institute supports research and development activities designed to improve the education of students at risk of educational failure due to limited English proficiency, race, geographic location, or economic disadvantage.

Prospects: The Congressionally Mandated Study of Educational Growth and Opportunity
http://www.ed.gov/pubs/Prospects/index.html

This report analyzes cross-sectional data on language-minority and LEP students in the United States and outlines what actions are needed to improve their educational performance. Family and economic situations are addressed. Information on related reports and sites is provided.

UNIT 7: Serving Special Needs and Concerns

Constructivism: From Philosophy to Practice
http://www.stemnet.nf.ca/~elmurphy/emurphy/cle.html

Here is a thorough description of the history, philosophy, and practice of constructivism, including quotations from Socrates and others, epistemology, learning theory, characteristics, and a checklist.

National Association for Gifted Children
http://www.nagc.org/home00.htm

NAGC, a national nonprofit organization for gifted children, is dedicated to developing their high potential.

National Information Center for Children and Youth With Disabilities (NICHCY)
http://www.nichcy.org/index.html

NICHCY provides information and makes referrals in areas related to specific disabilities, early intervention, special education and related services, individualized education programs, and much more. The site also connects to a listing of Parent's Guides to resources for children and youth with disabilities.

UNIT 8: The Profession of Teaching Today

Canada's SchoolNet Staff Room
http://www.schoolnet.ca/home/e/

Here is a resource and link site for anyone involved in education, including special-needs educators, teachers, parents, volunteers, and administrators.

Teachers Helping Teachers
http://www.pacificnet.net/~mandel/

This site provides basic teaching tips, new teaching methodology ideas, and forums for teachers to share their experiences. Download software and participate in chat sessions. It features educational resources on the Web, and new ones are added each week.

The Teachers' Network
http://www.teachers.net

Bulletin boards, classroom projects, online forums, and Web mentors are featured on this site, as well as the book *Teachers' Guide to Cyberspace* and an online, 4-week course on how to use the Internet.

Teaching with Electronic Technology

http://www.wam.umd.edu/~mlhall/teaching.html

Michael Hall's Web site leads to many resources of value to those contemplating the future of education, particularly regarding the role of technology in the classroom and beyond.

UNIT 9: For Vision and Hope: Alternative Visions of Reality

Goals 2000: A Progress Report

http://www.ed.gov/pubs/goals/progrpt/index.html

Open this site to survey a progress report by the U.S. Department of Education on the Goals 2000 reform initiative. It provides a sense of what goals educators are reaching for as they look toward the future.

Mighty Media

http://www.mightymedia.com

The mission of this privately funded consortium is to empower youth, teachers, and organizations through the use of interactive communications technology. The site provides links to teacher talk forums, educator resources, networks for students, and more.

Online Internet Institute

http://www.oii.org

A collaborative project among Internet-using educators, proponents of systemic reform, content-area experts, and teachers who desire professional growth, this site provides a learning environment for integrating the Internet into educators' individual teaching styles.

We highly recommend that you review our Web site for expanded information and our other product lines. We are continually updating and adding links to our Web site in order to offer you the most usable and useful information that will support and expand the value of your Annual Editions. You can reach us at: *http://www.mhcls.com/annualeditions/*.

UNIT 1

How Others See Us and How We See Ourselves

Unit Selections

Key Points to Consider

- Describe the change in American population statistics between 1950 and the present. How have these changes affected education?

- What can teachers do about the unhealthy dietary practices of children and adolescents?

- How can we most accurately assess public perceptions of the educational system?

- What is the fundamental effect of public opinion on national public policy regarding educational development?

Student Website

www.mhcls.com/online

Internet References

Further information regarding these websites may be found in this book's preface or online.

Charter Schools
http://www.edexcellence.net/topics/charters.html

Pathways to School Improvement
http://www.ncrel.org/sdrs/pathwayg.htm

There are many ways in which children and youth are educated. The social, racial, and cultural landscape in the United States is becoming more and more diverse and multifaceted. How youth respond to current issues is a reflection of their perceptions as to how older citizens respond to social reality. How to improve the quality of educational services remains a concern of the general public. Public perceptions of the nation's efforts in the education of its youth are of great importance to those who work with children and youth. We must be attentive to the peoples' concerns; we cannot ignore them.

How the people served by a nation's schools perceive the quality of the education they received is of great interest, because public perceptions can translate into either increased or decreased levels of support for a nation's educational system. Achieving a public consensus as to what the aims or purposes of education ought to be can be difficult. Americans debate what the purposes of education should be in every generation. Many different sorts of schools exist at both the elementary and the secondary levels. Many different forms of "charter" schools are attracting the interest of parents; some of these charter schools are within public school systems and some are private ones. Parents wish to have choices as to the types of schools their children attend.

Schools need to be places where students and teachers feel safe, places that provide hope and that instill confidence in the prospects for a happier and better future for all. The safety of students and teachers in schools is a matter of concern to many persons due to tragic events in the recent past. Schools also need to be places where students can dream, hope, and work to inform themselves in the process of building their futures. Schools need to help students learn to be inquiring persons.

There are several major policy issues regarding the content and form of schooling that are being debated. We are anticipating greater ranges of choice in the types and forms of schooling that will become available to our children and youth. The United States has great interest in policy issues related to increased accountability to the public for what goes on in schools. Also, we are possibly the most culturally pluralistic nation in the world, and we are becoming even more diverse.

We may be approaching a historic moment in our national history regarding the public funding of education and the options parents might be given for the education of their children. Some of these options and the lines of reasoning for them are explored in this volume. Financial as well as qualitative options are being debated. Scholars in many fields of study as well as journalists and legislators are asking how we can make our nation's schools more effective as well as how we might optimize parents' sense of control over how their children are to be educated.

Young people "read" certain adult behaviors well; they see it as hypocrisy when the adult community wants certain standards and values to be taught in schools but rewards other, often opposite behaviors in society. Dialogue regarding what it means to speak of "literacy" in democratic communities continues. Our students read much from our daily activities and our many information sources, and they form their own shrewd analyses of what social values actually do prevail in society. How to help young people develop their intellectual potential and become perceptive students of and participants in democratic traditions are major public concerns.

There is serious business yet to be attended to by the social service and educational agencies that try to serve youth. People are impatient to see some fundamental efforts made to meet the basic educational needs of young people. The problems are the greatest in major cities and in more isolated rural areas. Public perceptions of the schools are affected by high levels of economic deprivation among large sectors of the population and by the economic pressures that our interdependent world economy produces as a result of international competition for the world's markets.

Studies conducted in the past few years, particularly the Carnegie Corporation's studies of adolescents in the United States,

document the plight of millions of young persons in the United States. Some authors point out that although there was much talk about educational change in the 1990s, those changes were only marginal and cosmetic at best. States responded by demanding more course work and tougher exit standards from schools. With still more than 25 percent of schoolchildren in the United States living at or below the poverty level, and almost a third of them in more economically and socially vulnerable nontraditional family settings, the overall social situation for many young people continues to be difficult. The public wants more effective responses to public needs.

So, in the face of major demographic shifts and of the persistence of many long-term social problems, the public watches how schools respond to new as well as old challenges. In recent years, these challenges have aggravated rather than allayed much public concern about the efficacy of public schooling. Various political, cultural, corporate, and philanthropic interests continue to articulate alternative educational agendas. At the same time the incumbents in the system respond with their own educational agendas, which reflect their views from the inside.

The Biology of Risk Taking

For help in guiding adolescents into healthy adulthood, educators can look to new findings in the fields of neuroscience and developmental psychology.

Lisa F. Price

I celebrate myself,

And what I assume you shall assume,

For every atom belonging to me as good belongs to you.

　　—Walt Whitman, *Leaves of Grass*

Adolescence is a time of excitement, growth, and change. Whitman's words capture the enthusiasm and passion with which teenagers approach the world. Sometimes adolescents direct this passion toward a positive goal, such as a creative essay, an art project, after-school sports, or a healthy romance. At other times, they divert their passions to problematic activities, such as drug experimentation, reckless driving, shoplifting, fights, or school truancy.

Why do adolescents take risks? Why are teens so passionate? Are adolescents just young adults, or are they fundamentally different? Advances in developmental psychology and neuroscience have provided us with some answers. We now understand that adolescent turmoil, which we used to view as an expression of raging hormones, is actually the result of a complex interplay of body chemistry, brain development, and cognitive growth (Buchanan, Eccles, & Becker, 1992). Moreover, the changes that teenagers experience occur in the context of multiple systems—such as individual relationships, family, school, and community—that support and influence change.

Educators are in a pivotal position to promote healthy adolescent growth. Understanding the biological changes that adolescents undergo and the behaviors that result can provide the foundation for realistic expectations and effective interventions.

The Impact of Puberty

The hormonal changes of adolescence are often considered synonymous with puberty. The word *puberty* comes from the Latin term *pubertas*, meaning "age of maturity." As implied by the word's etymology, the changes of puberty have long been understood to usher in adulthood; in many cultures, puberty and the capacity to conceive continue to mark entry into adulthood. In contrast, puberty in modern Western culture has become a multistep entry process into a much longer period of adolescence (King, 2002).

Hormonal changes of adolescence include adrenarche, gonadarche, and menarche (Dahl, 2004; King, 2002). Adrenarche refers to the increased production of adrenal hormones and occurs as early as age 6-8. These hormones influence skeletal growth, hair production, and skin changes. Gonadarche refers to the pulsatile production of a cascade of hormones and contributes to driving the growth spurt and genital, breast, and pubic hair development. Menarche refers to the beginning of girls' menses, which generally occurs late in girls' pubertal development.

The Stages and Ages of Puberty

The clinician J. M. Tanner developed a system for classifying male and female pubertal growth into five stages (Tanner I-V). In the 1960s, he identified a trend of progressively earlier age at menarche across cultures (1968). Since then, investigators have identified similar trends of earlier arrival of other markers of puberty, such as breast and pubic hair development (Herman-Giddens et al., 1997). These trends have diverged across race in the United States, with proportionately more African American girls experiencing earlier-onset puberty than white girls. The implications of these trends have ranged from debates over the threshold for premature puberty to investigations into factors that contribute to earlier-onset puberty (Kaplowitz & Oberfield, 1999).

Boys who enter puberty at an earlier age experience certain advantages, including higher self-esteem, greater popularity, and some advances in cognitive capabilities (King, 2002). These same boys may also be more likely to engage in risk-taking behavior, possibly because they often socialize with older boys (Steinberg & Morris, 2001). Girls, on the other hand, often have more problems associated with earlier entry into puberty, including lower self-esteem and elevated risk for anxiety, depression, and eating disorders. These girls are also more likely to engage in risk-taking behaviors, including earlier sexual intercourse.

Don't Blame It On Hormones

In the past, hormones were believed to be in a state of great flux, which presumably caused adolescents to be dramatic, erratic, intense, and risk-prone. Evidence suggests, however, that only minimal association exists between adolescent hormone levels and emotional/behavioral problems (Buchanan et al., 1992; King, 2002). Youth with higher levels of hormones do not appear to be at higher risk for emotional or behavioral problems (Dahl, 2004).

Adolescence is a time of excitement, growth, and change.

Today, adolescent specialists view emotional intensity and sensation-seeking as normative behaviors of adolescence that are more broadly linked to pubertal maturation than to hormone levels. Pubertal stage rather than chronological age is linked to romantic and sexual pursuits, increased appetite, changes in sleep patterns, and risk for emotional disorders in girls. One group of investigators studying teen smoking and substance use found that increased age had no correlation with increased sensation-seeking or risky behavior (Martin et al., 2002). Instead, they determined that pubertal maturation was correlated with sensation-seeking in boys and girls, which, in turn, led to a greater likelihood of cigarette smoking and substance use.

Pubertal stage was clearly linked to difficulties that Derek began experiencing in school. He had been a solid student in 6th grade who scored in the average range and generally turned his homework in on time. He socialized with a group of same-age friends and was teased occasionally because he was skinnier and shorter than his peers. By 7th grade, however, he had begun his growth spurt. He was now a few inches taller and had developed facial hair. Although he appeared more confident, he also seemed more aggressive and was involved in several fights at school. He began to spend part of his time with a few 8th grade boys who were suspected of writing graffiti on a school wall.

A teacher who had a good relationship with Derek took him aside and spoke with him about the change in his behavior from 6th to 7th grade. Derek was able to talk about his own surprise at the changes, his wish for more respect, and his ambivalence about entering high school—he was worried about what teachers would

expect of him. Derek and the teacher agreed to talk periodically, and the teacher arranged for Derek to meet with the school counselor.

The Adolescent Brain

Neuroscientists used to believe that by the time they reached puberty, youth had undergone the crucial transformations in brain development and circuitry. Data obtained through available technology supported this view, identifying similar brain structures in children and adults. The adolescent brain seemed entirely comparable to the adult brain.

This view of adolescent brain development has undergone a radical shift during the last decade, with the identification of ongoing brain changes throughout adolescence, such as synaptic pruning and myelination. People have the mature capacity to consistently control behavior in both low-stress and high-stress environments only after these neurobiological developments are complete. This maturation does not take place until the early 20s.

Synaptic pruning refers to the elimination of connections between neurons in the brain's cortex, or gray matter. In the 1990s, researchers determined that during adolescence, up to 30,000 synapses are eliminated each second (Bourgeois & Rakic, 1993; Rakic, Bourgeois, & Goldman-Rakic, 1994). The removal of these redundant synaptic links increases the computational ability of brain circuits, which, in turn, enhances a function intricately connected to risk taking: the capacity to regulate and rapidly stop activity. Myelination, which refers to the wrapping of glial cell membranes around the axon of neurons, results in increased speed of signal transmission along the axon (Luna & Sweeney, 2004). This facilitates more rapid and integrated communication among diverse brain regions.

Synaptic pruning and myelination, along with other neurobiological changes, facilitate enhanced cognitive capacity as well as behavioral control, also known as *executive function*. Executive function is the ability to interact in a self-directed, appropriate, organized, and purpose-

ful manner. The prefrontal cortex plays a vital role in guiding executive function, which is also influenced by such areas of the brain as the hippocampus (which coordinates memory), the amygdala (which coordinates emotional processing), and the ventral striatum (which coordinates reward-processing). The prefrontal cortex is less mature, however, in young adolescents than in adults.

Given these three factors—an inability to completely regulate and refrain from certain activities, an absence of fully integrated communication among the various regions of the brain, and a less developed prefrontal cortex—it is not surprising that adolescents biologically do not have the same capacities as adults to inhibit their impulses in a timely manner.

Biology and Thrill-Seeking

By their mid-teens, adolescents appear to have achieved many decision-making abilities seen in adults (Steinberg & Cauffman, 1996). In fact, studies have found that teens can identify the same degree of danger in risky activities that adults can—driving while intoxicated, for example (Cauffman, Steinberg, & Woolard, 2002). However, certain methodological flaws in studies of adolescents may have prevented investigators from accurately assessing adolescent risk taking (Steinberg, 2004). These flaws include evaluating teens individually rather than in the context of a group, within which most risk-taking behavior occurs; asking teens to evaluate theoretical situations, which may not sufficiently represent the challenges of actual situations; and evaluating teens in settings that reduce the influence of emotion or induce anxiety rather than generate the exhilaration associated with risk taking.

One result of these flaws may be that measures of adolescents' cognitive abilities—particularly their evaluation of risk—do not adequately reflect their actual cognitive and emotional processes in real time. Consequently, teens *appear* to have the cognitive capacities of adults yet continue to engage in more risky behaviors.

The emotional lives of adolescents also appear to shift during these years. Adolescents seek more intense emotional experiences than children and adults do. They appear to need higher degrees of stimulation to obtain the same experience of pleasure (Steinberg, 2004). Developments in an area of the brain called the limbic system may explain this shift in pursuit and experience of pleasure (Spear, 2000).

> **Teenagers generally thrive in reasonable, supportive environments that have a predictable, enforced structure.**

Ongoing cognitive development and emotional shifts result in a biologically based drive for thrill-seeking, which may account for adolescents' continued risk taking despite knowledge of the accompanying hazards. Some interventions attempt to reduce the potential for risky behavior through external means—laws and rules, for example—rather than placing sole emphasis on the practice of educating teens in risk assessment (Steinberg, 2004). Others have considered teens' ability to reason well in "cool" circumstances but their failure to do so when in "hot" situations that arouse the emotions. Providing adolescents with sufficient scaffolding, or a good balance of support and autonomy, may be particularly important (Dahl, 2004).

This kind of scaffolding would be especially effective with a student like Shauna. Shauna raised the concerns of school faculty soon after she started 9th grade. Her attendance, class participation, and assignment completion were erratic. She had also run away from home during the summer and received a warning for shoplifting. The school counselor learned that Shauna's parents had separated over the summer and that her mother was struggling to set limits in the absence of Shauna's father. The school counselor, several teachers, and the vice principal decided to meet with both of Shauna's parents.

Although tension between the parents was evident, both parents agreed that Shauna should come home immediately after school instead of going to the mall, which she had recently started to do. Both parents also felt strongly that she needed to regularly attend school and complete assignments. The parents arranged to meet with Shauna together to discuss their shared expectations for her. The parents and teachers agreed to stay in contact with one another regarding Shauna's attendance and homework. The group also decided that a home-based reward system might encourage Shauna's success at school. The reward system would involve outings to the mall and to friends' homes, with incrementally less adult supervision and more autonomy as she continued to succeed.

The Role of Educators

These new findings suggest some beneficial approaches that educators might follow to guide adolescents into healthy adulthood.

- *Ensure that schools provide adolescents with vital support.* School bonding provides a protective influence for youth. The mentorship of a teacher can make the difference in a teen's course.
- *Keep a long view.* Researchers have found that the benefits of successful interventions may disappear for a few years in adolescence to reappear in later adolescence (Masten, 2004). Other teens are late bloomers whose troubled earlier years are followed by success.
- *Prioritize your concern.* The junior who has never been a problem and gets into trouble once is at a different level of risk than the 7th grader who has a long history of worrisome behaviors, such as fights, school truancy, mental illness, exposure to trauma, loss of important adult figures, or absence of stable supports. Act early for adolescents with long histories of risk taking.
- *Remember that puberty is not the same for all teens.* Some adolescents enter puberty earlier than others, giving them a perceived social advantage as well as possible disadvantages. There may be a biological drive to risk taking in teens, which is expressed by individual teens at different ages.
- *Remember that teens are not adults.* Having the scientific evidence to support the view that teens are not adults can be helpful to educators working with families, adolescents, or other professionals who may have unrealistic expectations for adolescents.
- *Take advantage of adolescent passion.* Direct adolescents' enthusiasm toward productive ends. A teen's passion can become a bridge to learning about such topics as music theory, history, politics, race relations, or marketing.
- *Reduce risk with firm structure.* Although teenagers dislike rules, they generally thrive in reasonable, supportive environments that have a predictable, enforced structure. For example, an authoritative stance in parenting—which reflects firmness coupled with caring—has repeatedly been found to be the most effective parenting strategy. Continue to maintain school rules and expectations, even when an adolescent continues to break the rules.
- *Collaborate to solve problems.* Working with risk-taking adolescents can be demanding, taxing, and worrisome. Talk regularly with colleagues for support. Contact appropriate consultants when your concern grows. Teens who see teachers collaborate with other adults benefit from these healthy models of problem solving.

It's important for educators to keep in mind that up to 80 percent of adolescents have few or no major problems during this period (Dahl, 2004). Remembering that most adolescents do well can encourage the positive outlook that educators need to effectively work with youth during this exciting and challenging time in their lives.

References

Bourgeois, J-P., & Rakic, P. (1993). Changes of synaptic density in the primary visual cortex of the macaque monkey from fetal to adult stage. *Journal of Neuroscience, 13*, 2801–2820.

Buchanan, C. M., Eccles, J. S., & Becker, J. B. (1992). Are adolescents the victims of raging hormones? *Psychological Bulletin, 111*, 62–107.

Cauffman, E., Steinberg, L., & Woolard, J. (2002, April 13). *Age differences in capacities underlying competence to stand trial.* Presentation at the Biennial Meeting of the Society for Research for Adolescence, New Orleans, Louisiana.

Dahl, R. E. (2004). Adolescent brain development: A period of vulnerabilities and opportunities. *Annals of the New York Academy of Science, 1021*, 1–22.

Herman-Giddens, M. E., Slora, E. J., Wasserman, R. C., Bourdony, C.J., Bhapkar, M. V., Koch, G. G., et al. (1997). Secondary sexual characteristics and menses in young girls seen in office practice. *Pediatrics, 99*, 505–512.

Kaplowitz, P. B., & Oberfield, S. E. (1999). Reexamination of the age limit for defining when puberty is precocious in girls in the United States. *Pediatrics, 104*, 936–941.

King, R. A. (2002). Adolescence. In M. Lewis (Ed.), *Child and adolescent psychiatry* (pp. 332–342). Philadelphia: Lippincott Williams & Wilkins.

Luna, B., & Sweeney, J. A. (2004). The emergence of collaborative brain function: fMRI studies of the development of response inhibition. *Annals of the New York Academy of Science, 1021*, 296–309.

Martin, C. A., Kelly, T. H., Rayens, M. K., Brogli, B. R., Brenzel, A., Smith, W. J., et al. (2002). Sensation seeking, puberty, and nicotine, alcohol, and marijuana use in adolescence. *Journal of the American Academy of Child and Adolescent Psychiatry, 41*, 1495–1502.

Masten, A. S. (2004). Regulatory processes, risk, and resilience in adolescent development. *Annals of the New York Academy of Science, 1021*, 310–319.

Rakic, P., Bourgeois, J-P., & Goldman-Rakic, P. S. (1994). Synaptic development of the cerebral cortex. *Progress in Brain Research, 102*, 227–243.

Spear, P. (2000). The adolescent brain and age-related behavioral manifestations. *Neuroscience and Biobehavioral Reviews, 24*, 417–463.

Steinberg, L. (2004). Risk taking in adolescence: What changes, and why? *Annals of the New York Academy of Science, 1021*, 51–58.

Steinberg, L., & Cauffman, E. (1996). Maturity of judgment in adolescence. *Law and Human Behavior, 20*, 249–272.

Steinberg, L., & Morris, A. S. (2001). Adolescent development. *Annual Review of Psychology, 52*, 83–110.

Tanner, J. M. (1968). Early maturation in man. *Scientific American, 218*, 21–27.

Lisa F. Price, *M.D., is the Assistant Director of the School Psychiatry Program in the Department of Psychiatry at Massachusetts General Hospital, 55 Fruit St., YAW 6900, Boston, MA 02114. She is also an Instructor in Psychiatry at Harvard Medical School.*

PARENTS BEHAVING BADLY

Inside the new classroom power struggle: what teachers say about pushy moms and dads who drive them crazy

By Nancy Gibbs

If you could walk past the teachers' lounge and listen in, what sorts of stories would you hear?

An Iowa high school counselor gets a call from a parent protesting the C her child received on an assignment. "The parent argued every point in the essay," recalls the counselor, who soon realized why the mother was so upset about the grade. "It became apparent that she'd written it."

A sixth-grade teacher in California tells a girl in her class that she needs to work on her reading at home, not just in school. "Her mom came in the next day," the teacher says, "and started yelling at me that I had emotionally upset her child."

A science teacher in Baltimore, Md., was offering lessons in anatomy when one of the boys in class declared, "There's one less rib in a man than in a woman." The teacher pulled out two skeletons—one male, the other female—and asked the student to count the ribs in each. "The next day," the teacher recalls, "the boy claimed he told his priest what happened and his priest said I was a heretic."

A teacher at a Tennessee elementary school slips on her kid gloves each morning as she contends with parents who insist, in writing, that their children are never to be reprimanded or even corrected. When she started teaching 31 years ago, she says, "I could make objective observations about my kids without parents getting offended. But now we handle parents a lot more delicately. We handle children a lot more delicately. They feel good about themselves for no reason. We've given them this cotton-candy sense of self with no basis in reality. We don't emphasize what's best for the greater good of society or even the classroom."

When our children are born, we study their every eyelash and marvel at the perfection of their toes, and in no time become experts in all that they do. But then the day comes when we are expected to hand them over to a stranger standing at the head of a room full of bright colors and small chairs. Well aware of the difference a great teacher can make—and the damage a bad teacher can do—parents turn over their kids and hope. Please handle with care. Please don't let my children get lost. They're breakable. And precious. Oh, but push them hard and don't let up, and make sure they get into Harvard.

"The parent doesn't know what you're giving and accepts what the child says. **Parents are trusting children before they trust us.** They have lost faith in teachers."

But if parents are searching for the perfect teacher, teachers are looking for the ideal parent, a partner but not a pest, engaged but not obsessed, with a sense of perspective and patience. And somehow just at the moment when the experts all say the parent-teacher alliance is more important than ever, it is also becoming harder to manage. At a time when competition is rising and resources are strained, when battles over testing and accountability force schools to adjust their priorities, when cell phones and e-mail speed up the information flow and all kinds of private ghosts and public quarrels creep into the parent-teacher conference, it's harder for both sides to step back and breathe deeply and look at the goals they share.

Ask teachers about the best part of their job, and most will say how much they love working with kids. Ask them about the most demanding part, and they will say dealing with parents. In fact, a new study finds that of all the challenges they face, new teachers rank handling parents at the top. According to preliminary results from the MetLife Survey of the American Teacher, made available exclusively to TIME, parent management was a bigger struggle than finding enough funding or maintaining discipline or enduring the toils of testing. It's one reason, say the Consortium for Policy Research in Education and the Center for the Study of Teaching and Policy, that 40% to 50% of new teachers leave the profession within five years. Even master teachers who love their work, says Harvard education professor Sara Lawrence-Lightfoot, call this "the most treacherous part of their jobs."

"You get so angry that you don't care what the school's perspective is. This is my child. And you did something that negatively impacted my child. I don't want to hear that you have 300 kids."

"Everyone says the parent-teacher conference should be pleasant, civilized, a kind of dialogue where parents and teachers build alliances," Lawrence-Lightfoot observes. "But what most teachers feel, and certainly what all parents feel, is anxiety, panic and vulnerability." While teachers worry most about the parents they never see, the ones who show up faithfully pose a whole different set of challenges. Leaving aside the monster parents who seem to have been born to torment the teacher, even "good" parents can have bad days when their virtues exceed their boundaries: the eager parent who pushes too hard, the protective parent who defends the cheater, the homework helper who takes over, the tireless advocate who loses sight of the fact that there are other kids in the class too. "I could summarize in one sentence what teachers hate about parents," says the head of a private school. "We hate it when parents undermine the education and growth of their children. That's it, plain and simple." A taxonomy of parents behaving badly:

• **THE HOVERING PARENT**
It was a beautiful late morning last May when Richard Hawley, headmaster at University School in Cleveland, Ohio, saw the flock of mothers entering the building, eager and beaming. "I ask what brings them to our halls," he recalls. "They tell me that this is the last day the seniors will be eating lunch together at school and they have come to watch. To watch their boys eat lunch? I ask. Yes, they tell me emphatically. At that moment, a group of lounging seniors spot their mothers coming their way. One of them approaches his mother, his hands forming an approximation of a crucifix. 'No,' he says firmly to his mother. 'You can't do this. You've got to go home.' As his mother draws near, he hisses in embarrassment, 'Mother, you have no life!' His mother's smile broadens. 'You are my life, dear.'"

Parents are passionate, protective creatures when it comes to their children, as nature designed them to be. Teachers strive to be dispassionate, objective professionals, as their training requires them to be. Throw in all the suspicions born of class and race and personal experience, a culture that praises teachers freely but pays them poorly, a generation taught to question authority and a political climate that argues for holding schools ever more accountable for how kids perform, and it is a miracle that parents and teachers get along as well as they do. "There's more parent involvement that's good—and bad," notes Kirk Daddow, a 38-year veteran who teaches Advanced Placement history in Ames, Iowa. "The good kind is the 'Make yourself known to the teacher; ask what you could do.' The bad kind is the 'Wait until something happens, then complain about it and try to get a grade changed.'" Overall, he figures, "we're seeing more of the bad."

Long gone are the days when the school was a fortress, opened a couple of times a year for parents' night and graduation but generally off limits to parents unless their kids got into trouble. Now you can't walk into schools, public or private, without tripping over parents in the halls. They volunteer as library aides and reading coaches and Mentor Moms, supplement the physical-education offerings with yoga and kickboxing, sponsor faculty-appreciation lunches and fund-raising barbecues, supervise field trips and road games and father-daughter service projects. Even the heads of boarding schools report that some parents are moving to live closer to their child's school so that they can be on hand and go to all the games. As budgets shrink and educational demands grow, that extra army of helpers can be a godsend to strapped schools.

In a survey, **90%** of new teachers agreed that **involving parents in their children's education** is a priority at their school, but only **25%** described their experience working with parents as "very satisfying." When asked to choose **the biggest challenge they face, 31%** of them cited involving parents and communicating with them as their top choice. **73%** of new teachers said too many **parents treat schools and teachers as adversaries.**

But parents, it turns out, have a learning curve of their own. Parents who are a welcome presence in elementary school as library helpers need to learn a different role for junior high and another for high school as their children's needs evolve. Teachers talk about "helicopter parents," who hover over the school at all times, waiting to drop in at the least sign of trouble. Given these unsettled times, if parents feel less in control of their own lives, they try to control what they can, which means everything from swooping down at the first bad grade to demanding a good 12 inches of squishy rubber under the jungle gym so that anyone who falls will bounce right back. "The parents are not the bad guys," says Nancy McGill, a teacher in Johnston, Iowa, who learned a lot about handling parents from being one herself. "They're mama grizzly bears. They're going to defend that cub no matter what, and they don't always think rationally. If I can remember that, it defuses the situation. It's not about me. It's not about attacking our system. It's about a parent trying to do the best for their child. That helps keep the personal junk out of the way. I don't get so emotional."

While it's in the nature of parents to want to smooth out the bumps in the road, it's in the nature of teachers to toss in a few more: sometimes kids have to fail in order to learn. As children get older, the parents may need to pull back. "I believe that the umbilical cord needs to be severed when children are at school," argues Eric Paul, a fourth- and fifth-grade teacher at Roosevelt Elementary School in Santa Monica, Calif. He goes to weekend ball games and piano recitals in an effort to bond with families but also tries to show parents that there is a line that shouldn't be crossed. "Kids need to operate on their own at school, advocate on their own and learn from each other. So in my class, parents' involvement is limited," he says.

"They'll misbehave in front of you. You see very little of that 'I don't want to get in trouble' attitude because **they know Mom or Dad will come to their defense**."

High schools, meanwhile, find themselves fending off parents who expect instant responses to every e-mail; who request a change of teacher because of "poor chemistry" when the real issue is that the child is getting a poor grade; who seek out a doctor who will proclaim their child "exceptionally bright but with a learning difference" that requires extra time for testing; who insist that their child take five Advanced Placement classes, play three varsity sports, perform in the school orchestra and be in student government—and then complain that kids are stressed out because the school doesn't do enough to prevent scheduling conflicts. Teachers just shake their heads as they see parents so obsessed with getting their child into a good college that they don't ask whether it's the right one for the child's particular interests and needs.

And what if kids grow so accustomed to these interventions that they miss out on lessons in self-reliance? Mara Sapon-Shevin, an education professor at Syracuse University, has had college students tell her they were late for class because their mothers didn't call to wake them up that morning. She has had students call their parents from the classroom on a cell phone to complain about a low grade and then pass the phone over to her, in the middle of class, because the parent wanted to intervene. And she has had parents say they are paying a lot of money for their child's education and imply that anything but an A is an unacceptable return on their investment.

These parents are not serving their children well, Sapon-Shevin argues. "You want them to learn lessons that are powerful but benign. Your kid gets drunk, they throw up, feel like crap—that's a good lesson. They don't study for an exam, fail it and learn that next time they should study. Or not return the library book and have to pay the fine. But when you have a kid leave their bike out, it gets run over and rusty, and you say, 'O.K., honey, we'll buy you a new one,' they never learn to put their bike away."

• THE AGGRESSIVE ADVOCATE

Marguerite Damata, a mother of two in Silver Spring, Md., wonders whether she is too involved in her 10-year-old son's school life. "Because he's not in the gifted and talented group, he's almost nowhere," she says. "If I stopped paying attention, where would he be?" Every week she spends two hours sitting in his math class, making sure she knows the assignments and the right vocabulary so that she can help him at home. And despite all she sees and all she does, she says, "I feel powerless there."

"With the oldest, **I think I micromanaged things.** I had to come to a point where I said, 'These are his projects. They're not my projects. I'm not helping him.'"

Parents understandably argue that there is a good reason to keep a close watch if their child is one of 500 kids in a grade level. Teachers freely admit it's impossible to create individual teaching programs for 30 children in a class. "There aren't enough minutes in the day," says Tom Loveless, who taught in California for nine years and is now director of the Brown Center on Education Policy at the Brookings Institution. "You have to have kids tackling subject matter together as a group. That's a shoe that will pinch for someone." Since the passage of the No Child Left Behind Act, which requires schools to show progress in reading and math test scores in Grades 3 through 8 across all racial and demographic groups, parents are worried that teachers will naturally focus on getting as many students as possible over the base line and not have as much time to spur the strongest kids or save the weakest. Some educators argue that you can agree on the goals of accountability and achievement, but given the inequalities in the system, not all schools have the means to achieve them. "A really cynical person who didn't want to spend any more money on an educational system might get parents and teachers to blame each other and deflect attention away from other imperfect parts of the system," observes Jeannie Oakes, director of the Institute for Democracy, Education and Access at UCLA.

Families feel they have to work the system. Attentive parents study the faculty like stock tables, looking for the best performer and then lobbying to get their kids into that teacher's class. "You have a lot of mothers who have been in the work force, supervising other people, who have a different sense of empowerment and professionalism about them," notes Amy Stuart Wells, professor of sociology and education at Columbia University's Teachers College. "When they drop out of the work force to raise their kids, they see being part of the school as part of their job." Monica Stutzman, a mother of two in Johnston, Iowa, believes her efforts helped ensure that her daughter wound up with the best teacher in each grade. "We know what's going on. We e-mail, volunteer on a weekly basis. I ask a lot of questions," she says. "I'm not there to push my children into things they're not ready for. The teachers are the experts. We've had such great experiences with the teacher because we create that experience, because we're involved. We don't just get something home and say, 'What's this?'"

"Most teachers will do what they need to, but there are teachers who are uncomfortable, who turn their backs or close their eyes or ears because they do not want what they perceive might be a confrontation."

Parents seeking to stay on top of what's happening in class don't have to wait for the report card to arrive. "Now it's so easy for the parents through the Internet to get ahold of us, and they expect an immediate response," notes Michael Schaffer, a classroom veteran who teaches AP courses at Central Academy in Des Moines, Iowa. "This e-mail—'How's my kid doing?'—could fill my day. That's hyperbole. But it's a two-edged sword here, and unfortunately it's cutting to the other side, and parents are making demands on us that are unreasonable. Yeah, they're concerned about their kids. But I'm concerned about 150 kids. I don't have time during the day to let the parent know when the kid got the first B." As more districts make assignments and test scores available online, it may cut down on the "How's he doing" e-mails but increase the "Why did she get a B?" queries.

Beneath the ferocious jostling there is the brutal fact that outside of Lake Wobegon, not all children are above average. Teachers must choose their words carefully. They can't just say, "I'm sorry your child's not as smart as X," and no parent wants to hear that there are five other kids in the class who are a lot smarter than his or hers. Younger teachers especially can be overwhelmed by parents who announce on the first day of school that their child is going to be the smartest in the class and on the second day that he is already bored. Veteran teachers have learned to come back with data in hand to show parents who boast that their child scored in the 99th percentile on some aptitude test that 40 other students in the class did just as well.

It would be nice if parents and teachers could work together to improve the system for everyone, but human nature can get in the way. Both sides know that resources are limited, and all kinds of factors play into how they are allocated—including whose elbows are sharpest. Many schools, fearful of "bright flight," the mass departure of high-achieving kids, feel they have no choice but to appease the most outspoken parents. "I understand, having been a parent, the attitude that 'I don't have time to fix the whole system; I don't have time and energy to get rid of systemic injustice, racism, poverty and violence; I have to get what's right for my kid,'" says Syracuse's Sapon-Shevin. "But then the schools do educational triage. They basically attend to the most vocal, powerful people with more resources. They say, 'Don't get angry. We'll take care of this issue.' And they mean, 'We'll take care of it for your child. We'll get your kid out of the class with the bad teacher and leave the other kids in there.'"

At the deepest level, teachers fear that all this parental anxiety is not always aimed at the stuff that matters. Parents who instantly call about a grade or score seldom ask about what is being taught or how. When a teacher has spent the whole summer brightening and deepening the history curriculum for her ninth-graders, finding new ways to surprise and engage them, it is frustrating to encounter parents whose only focus is on test scores. "If these parents were pushing for richer, more meaningful instruction, you could almost forgive them their obnoxiousness and inattention to the interests of all the other children," says Alfie Kohn, a Boston-based education commentator and author of *Unconditional Parenting*. But "we have pushy parents pushing for the wrong thing." He argues that test scores often measure what matters least—and that even high test scores should invite parents to wonder what was cut from the curriculum to make room for more test prep.

"It's a challenge to be a good parent of a high school student. You want to help our kids without putting too much pressure on."

Kohn knows a college counselor hired by parents to help "package" their child, who had perfect board scores and a wonderful grade-point average. When it was time to work on the college essay, the counselor said, "Let's start with a book you read outside of school that really made a difference in your life." There was a moment of silence. Then the child responded, "Why would I read a book if I didn't have to?" If parents focus only on the transcript—drive out of children their natural curiosity, discourage their trying anything at which they might fail—their definition of success will get a failing grade from any teacher watching.

• THE PUBLIC DEFENDERS

By the time children turn 18, they have spent only 13% of their waking lives in the classroom. Their habits of mind, motivation and muscles have much more to do with that other 87%. But try telling that to an Ivy-educated mom and dad whose kids aren't doing well. It can't be the genes, Mom and Dad conclude, so it must be the school. "It's the bright children who aren't motivated who are most frustrating for parents and teachers," says Nancy McGill, a past president of the Iowa Talented and Gifted Association. "Parents don't know how to fix the kid, to get the kid going. They want us to do it, and discover we can't either." Sometimes bright kids intentionally work just hard enough to get a B because they are trying to make a point about what should be demanded of them, observes Jennifer Loh, a math teacher at Ursuline Academy in Dallas. "It's their way of saying to Mom and Dad, 'I'm not perfect.'" Though the best teachers work hard to inspire even the most alienated kids, they can't carry the full burden of the parents' expectations. In his dreams, admits Daddow, the Iowa history teacher, what he would like to say is "Your son or daughter is very, very lazy." Instead, he shows the parents the student's work and says, "I'm not sure I'm getting Jim's best effort."

When a teacher asks parents to be partners, he or she doesn't necessarily mean Mom or Dad should be camping in the classroom. Research shows that though students benefit modestly from having parents involved at school, what happens at home matters much more. According to research based on the National Education Longitudinal Study, a sample of nearly 25,000 eighth-graders, among four main areas of parental involvement (home discussion, home supervision, school communication and school participation), home discussion was the most strongly related to academic achievement.

Any partnership requires that both sides do their part. Teachers say that here again, parents can have double standards: Push hard, but not too hard; maintain discipline, but don't punish my child. When teachers tell a parent that a child needs to be reprimanded at home, teachers say they often get the response, "I don't reprimand, and don't tell me how to raise my child." Older teachers say they are seeing in children as young as 6 and 7 a level of disdain for adults that was once the reserve of adolescents. Some talk about the "dry-cleaner parents" who drop their rambunctious kids off in the morning and expect them to be returned at the end of the day all clean and proper and practically sealed in plastic.

At the most disturbing extreme are the parents who like to talk about values but routinely undermine them. "You get savvier children who know how to get out of things," says a second-grade teacher in Murfreesboro, Tenn. "Their parents actually teach them to lie to dodge their responsibilities." Didn't get your homework done? That's O.K. Mom will take the fall. Late for class? Blame it on Dad. Parents have sued schools that expelled kids for cheating, on the grounds that teachers had left the exams out on a desk and made them too easy to steal. "Cheating is rampant," says Steve Taylor, a history teacher at Beverly Hills High School in California. "If you're not cheating, then you're not trying. A C means you're a loser." Every principal can tell a story about some ambitious student, Ivy bound, who cheats on an exam. Teacher flunks her. Parents protest: She made a mistake, and you're going to ruin her life. Teachers try to explain that good kids can make bad decisions; the challenge is to make sure the kids learn from them. "I think some parents confuse advocating on behalf of their student with defending everything that the student does," says Scott Peoples, a history teacher at Skyview High School outside Denver.

"I called the parents on a discipline issue with their daughter. **Her father called me a total jerk.** Then he said, "Well, do you want to meet someplace and take care of this man to man?"

Student-teacher disputes can quickly escalate into legal challenges or the threat of them. The fear of litigation that has given rise to the practice of defensive medicine prompts educators to practice defensive teaching. According to Forrest T. Jones Inc., a large insurer of teachers, the number of teachers buying liability insurance has jumped 25% in the past five years. "A lot of teachers are very fearful and don't want to deal with it," says Roxsana Jaber-Ansari, who teaches sixth grade at Hale Middle School in Woodland Hills, Calif. She has learned that everything must be documented. She does not dare accuse a student of cheating, for instance, without evidence, including eyewitness accounts or a paper trail. When a teacher meets with a student alone, the door always has to be open to avoid any suspicion of inappropriate behavior on the teacher's part. "If you become angry and let it get to you, you will quit your job," says Jaber-Ansari. "You will hate what you do and hate the kids."

• THE CULTURE WARRIORS

Teachers in schools with economically and ethnically diverse populations face a different set of challenges in working with parents. In less affluent districts, many parents don't have computers at home, so schools go to some lengths to make contact easier. Even 20 minutes twice a year for a conference can be hard for families if parents are working long hours at multiple jobs or have to take three buses to get to the school. Some teachers visit a parent's workplace on a Saturday or help arrange language classes for parents to help with communication. Particularly since a great goal of education is to level the playing field, teachers are worried that the families that need the most support are least able to ask for it. "The standards about what makes a good parent are always changing,"

> ## TEACHER'S PESTS
>
> Some parents ask too much of the school or too little of their kids
>
> ## HELICOPTER PARENTS
>
> In order to grow, kids need room to fail; the always hovering parent gets in the way of self-reliance
>
> ## MONSTER PARENTS
>
> The lurking moms and dads always looking for reasons to disagree are a teacher's worst nightmare
>
> ## DRY-CLEANER PARENTS
>
> They drop their rambunctious kids off and want them all cleaned up and proper by the end of the day

notes Annette Lareau, a professor of sociology at Temple University, who views all the demand for parent involvement as a relatively recent phenomenon. "And it's middle-class parents who keep pace."

Lareau also sees cultural barriers getting in the way of the strong parent-teacher alliance. When parents don't get involved at school, teachers may see it as a sign of indifference, of not valuing education—when it may signal the reverse. Some cultures believe strongly that school and home should be separate spheres; parents would no more interfere with the way a teacher teaches than with the way a surgeon operates. "Working-class and poor families don't have a college education," says Lareau. "They are looking up to teachers; they respect teachers as professionals. Middle-class parents are far less respectful. They're not a teacher, but they could have been a teacher, and often their profession has a higher status than teachers'. So they are much more likely to criticize teachers on professional grounds."

And while she views social class as a major factor in shaping the dynamic, Lareau finds that race continues to play a role. Middle-class black parents, especially those who attended segregated schools, often approach the teacher with caution. Roughly 90% of teachers are white and middle class, and, says Lareau, many black parents are "worried that teachers will have lowered expectations of black children, that black boys will be punished more

than white boys. Since teachers want parents to be positive and supportive, when African-American parents express concerns about racial insensitivity, it can create problems in their relationship."

Finally, as church-state arguments boil over and principals agonize over what kids can sing at the Winter Concert, teachers need to be eternally sensitive to religious issues as well. This is an arena where parents are often as concerned about content as grades, as in the debate over creationism vs. evolution vs. intelligent design, for instance. Teachers say they have to become legal scholars to protect themselves in a climate where students have "rights." Jaber-Ansari was challenged for hanging Bible quotes on her classroom walls. But she had studied her legal standing, and when she was confronted, "the principal supported me 100%," she says.

Perhaps the most complicated part OF the conversation—beyond all the issues of race and class and culture, the growing pressures to succeed and arguments over how success should be defined—is the problem of memory. When they meet in that conference, parent and teacher bring their own school experiences with them—what went right and wrong, what they missed. They are determined for it to be different for the child they both care about. They go into that first-grade room and sit in the small chairs and can easily be small again themselves. It is so tempting to use the child's prospects to address their own regrets. So teachers learn to choose their words with care and hope that they can build a partnership with parents that works to everyone's advantage and comes at no one's expense. And parents over time may realize that when it comes to their children, they still have much to learn. "I think that we love our children so much that they make us a little loony at times," says Arch Montgomery, head of the Asheville School in North Carolina. He winces at parents who treat their child as a cocktail-party trophy or a vanity sticker for the window of their SUV, but he also understands their behavior. "I think most parents desperately want to do what is right for their kids. This does not bring out the better angels of our natures, but it is understandable, and it is forgivable."

—With reporting by Amanda Bower, New York, Melissa August, Washington, Anne Berryman, Athens, Cathy Booth Thomas, Dallas, Rita Healy, Denver, Elizabeth Kauffman, Nashville, Jeanne McDowell, Los Angeles and Betsy Rubiner, Des Moines

---

METAPHORS OF HOPE

Refusing to be disheartened by all the negative press surrounding education today, Ms. Chenfeld travels the country and encounters one inspiring educator after another. She tells four of their stories here.

MIMI BRODSKY CHENFELD

ON the Big Island of Hawaii, there's a forest of lava-crusted hills and bare corpses of trees called Devastation Trail. Old volcanic eruptions burnt the Ohia trees and left this once-lush terrain barren and ashen.

Walking on the wooden paths through the devastation, one could easily miss the tiny flowers remarkably pushing through the charred earth. The markers that identify these flowers read: Thimbleberry, Swordfern, Creeping Dayflower, and Nutgrass. While others aimed their cameras at the stark, mysterious lava hills, I focused on the flowers. In the midst of such a desolate scene, these perky "signs of life" seemed to be symbols of courage and persistence.

Reading daily the bleak headlines and articles that stress the stress by focusing on bullying, violence, gangs and cliques, and numerous random acts of unkindness and hostility in our seemingly devastated educational landscape, one could easily sink into despair. However, as a stubborn optimist, I always search for markers of thimbleberry, swordfern, creeping dayflower, and nutgrass—metaphors of hope!

When Mr. T (also known as Tom Tenerovich) was moved upstairs after years of teaching kindergarten classes, he observed that second-graders were more vocal, more argumentative, more opinionated! A voracious reader of books about education, he was familiar with many theories and pro-

grams. *But reading about ideas is different from doing.*

One idea that intrigued Mr. T was that of Town Meeting. He and his students discussed building a structure that would enable all voices to be heard, problems to be solved, and good listening habits to be formed.[1]

The class added mayor and assistant mayor to the list of jobs on their classroom helpers board. During the year, every student would be assigned to these jobs for a one-week term of office.

The Town Meeting works this way: each week, the mayor and assistant mayor, along with Tom, write an agenda for two, 30- to 40-minute Town Meetings. Any student can submit a proposal for discussion, but it has to be written and include name, date, and the issue to be discussed. Some of the issues concerning the students have included changing seats, playground rules, classmates being hurtful, picking team members, and activities for "Fun Fridays."

At the Town Meeting, the class discusses the topic and votes to resolve the issue. "Even if they disagree, it's so sweet to hear how they disagree," Tom reports. "They're really beginning to listen to each other." He continues,

It's amazing the way it works out. None of the kids are bossy when they become mayor. Even our most timid children became good mayors. Believe it or not, one of my most high-maintenance tough kids

was the best mayor! He took charge in a fair way—he knew what to do—he behaved appropriately.

Even I became an agenda issue! One of the kids reminded me that I hadn't done something I promised. That was important to the children, and I had to remedy it.

Committees formed from discussions: academic committees, playground committees (to see that no students were left out of games or weren't chosen for teams), and classroom improvement committees. Tom was thrilled to see how the twice-weekly Town Meetings honoring the feelings and agendas of the students carried over into the everyday life of the group. "This really is democracy in action! Points of view are freely expressed. All opinions are valued and respected. You can see and feel the increase of courtesy and kindness."

The school mascot is a bobcat. Tom and his second-graders added the idea of Bobcat Purrs to their Town Meeting. Like "warm fuzzies," pats on the back, recognition of positive acts, observations of improvements, Bobcat Purrs were "built into our meetings," Tom explains, "and became part of our culture. Children wrote up a 'purr,' decorated it, and handed it to the mayor, who read it and presented it. No one was ever left out. We promised *not* to just recognize our best friends. Children looked for what their classmates were doing well. They were very specific."

One student, who had experienced alienation, low self-image, and loneliness in earlier years and whose posture defined his feelings, received a Bobcat Purr during a Town Meeting that stated how proudly he was standing. He was standing up straight! The boy beamed!

Another student who had difficulty finishing her work received a Bobcat Purr from a classmate honoring her for finishing *all* of her work. Everyone rejoiced.

When children live in a climate that accentuates the positive, their eagle eyes catch the flickering light of flames that are almost burnt out.

The picture I want to snap for my Album of Hope is of a proud second-grader standing up straight with the mayor, assistant mayor, his teacher, and all of his classmates honoring him with a Bobcat Purr during the Town Meeting.[2]

SWORDFERN: CATHY

Cathy Arment and her first-graders are not involved in the building of structures like Town Meetings. With their teacher, this group of students from diverse cultures, races, and religions works hard and plays hard together. Cathy described a memorable scene in a telephone message: "I was reading the children Jonathan London's *Froggy's First Kiss*—you know, for Valentine week. Mim, I looked up from the story to see the children sitting in clusters, their arms around each other, their eyes wide as I turned the pages, so totally involved. I almost began to weep at the sight of their beauty."

> *Here we have students with Ethiopian, Mexican, Appalachian, Southeast Asian, and African American backgrounds. How did such a diverse group of children learn to love one another?*

Here we have students with Ethiopian, Mexican, Appalachian, Southeast Asian, and African American backgrounds—children who are newcomers, some from dysfunctional homes, some from foster homes, some with hardship home lives, some at risk. How did such a diverse group of children learn to love one another?

Cathy and I talked at length. With all the realities of alienation, anxiety, insecurity, and mean-spiritedness that these students face, *how is such a warm and loving environment created?* What is the strategy? What are the techniques? Cathy thought long and hard about these questions. She realized that she did not have a preconceived plan for helping her students build positive classroom relationships. She hadn't adopted a program specifically aimed at such outcomes. Nowhere in her plan book were consciously chosen activities based on proven behavior management theories. *She just did what she did because of who she was and what she believed.* Reviewing her ideas, she said:

> All I can think of is that from day one, we are together. We verbalize feelings—good and bad. We're not afraid to share. From our first moment together, we talked about respecting everyone. Some of my children have heavy accents. They are "different." Many of them have been made fun of. We talk about how hurtful it is to be teased, to put people down and to be put down. We begin to listen to each other. To care about each other. *My children never, ever tease!* And—I'm a human being, too—I share with them. They'll ask me, "Teacher, what did YOU read? What did YOU do over the weekend? Did YOU have a fun holiday?" When a child has a low day, we all try to cheer that child. Sometimes I have a gray day. The kids will go out of their way to brighten me. They know we stick together, that I care for them very deeply. They know that we are all safe in our room.

When the children wrote and illustrated their "I Have A Dream" papers inspired by Dr. Martin Luther King, Jr.'s famous speech, many of them expressed the warm feelings they experienced in the classroom and wrote dreams like these: "I have a dream to be with my family and to give love to everybody and to care about everybody" (Abigail). "I have a dream that people would be nice to other people and, if people are hurt, other people could help them just like other people help me" (Carissa).

The Israeli-Yemenite dancer Margolith Ovid once said, "The greatest technique in the universe is the technique in the human heart."

The picture I would snap for my Album of Hope is of Cathy's kids, arms around each other, sitting in clusters, listening to Froggy's First Kiss.[3]

CREEPING DAYFLOWER: MS. GIBSON

Before the new school year even begins, Dee Gibson sends warm *Welcome to the Family* cards to her future students! These fortunate first-graders know—from everything said and done, from words and actions, activities and discussions, planning and projects—that their class is a second family in which each and every family member is important and connected to everyone else. This is not a theme or a curriculum item or a subject area—*it's the way it is* in Ms. Gibson's class. Because she is passionate, articulate, and committed to creating, with her children and families, a safe, encouraging, caring community that really is a second family (and for some children over the years, a first family!), the experiences of her students are very special. They help one another. They cooperate. They plan and talk together. They are totally involved in the life they share together in this home away from home.

> *We can't take the environment for granted. We are the architects of the culture of the school, of the program.*

When the children were asked such questions as "What is it like being in this kind of class family? What do you do? How do you feel?" the responses were honest and forthcoming:

> We're all together. We get in pods.
> We work together. If two kids are

having an argument, the whole class stops till we work it out. We really feel like everyone cares about each other.—*Jay*

* * *

We're like teamwork. We help each other with work and to pick up. Everyone here sticks together —*Lauri*

* * *

All the kids are friends. Arguing doesn't really happen much— everyone cooperates.—*Ryan*

* * *

Our teacher treats people fair. The other kids act very kind together. She teaches us how to work together.—*Barrett*

* * *

We don't really get in fights!—*Nikki*

* * *

Everybody is nice to each other, and they act like a family. Ms. Gibson is like one of the family.—*Danielle*

The language in this class is the language of respect, acceptance, courtesy, responsibility, and cooperation. It's not limited to a week's celebration of a theme! It's the vocabulary of a close-knit family. That's an everyday reality.

The picture I want to take for my Album of Hope is of the children holding up their summer "Welcome to the Family" cards. A sequel to that picture is of children discovering that the welcome cards were not a gimmick! They were the real thing.[4]

NUTGRASS: ANNE AND CLAUDETTE

Partners in Educating All Children Equally (PEACE), Anne Price and Claudette Cole travel to schools, programs, and conferences, spreading very simple messages—especially to administrators who too often don't attend workshops that are aimed directly at the heart. Anne and Claudette remind those directors, managers, principals, and superinten-

dents that their influence in the creation of positive, life-affirming school climates is immeasurable. They *really can* make the difference between the life and death of an entire program or school.

Claudette and Anne discuss ways of helping teachers to develop positive relationships with their students and to motivate the students to develop caring and respectful relationships with one another. What are some suggestions for doing so? Usually, without hesitation, most of the administrators offer such actions as recognizing students, paying attention to them, appreciating their talents and efforts, encouraging them to cooperate with and be considerate of one another, and inviting students to share ideas and input so that they are directly involved in the success of the school.

Claudette and Anne gently turn these ideas around, directing them to the administrators. "Just as we advocate developmentally appropriate practices for teaching children, so we have to apply those ideas to our staff." Anne explains their simple, direct approach: "It's our responsibility to pay attention to the needs of staff so they can meet the children's needs."

What are some of the greatest trouble spots in the dynamics of any school or program? Absenteeism, turnover, bullying, discipline problems, low morale, lack of trust, miscommunication—to name just a few. It's so obvious to Anne and Claudette that these problems, often reflecting a disconnected and resentful staff, carry over to the students and poison the atmosphere. (Think lava!)

Think of ways to inspire and create a healthy workplace for all who spend time there. Claudette asks, "Does the staff feel appreciated? Respected? Do they feel they have ownership of and an investment in the success of the program? Are their efforts and contributions valued? Do we keep all avenues of communication open? Do we trust enough to be honest with each other without fear of reprisal?"

Anne reminds participants in her workshops that we can't take the environment for granted. *We are the architects of the culture of the school, of the program.* "You'll see the difference in an environment where children, staff, fami-

lies, and communities are nurtured and respected. Ideas flow freely, teamwork flourishes, staff feels open and trusting with each other and with the administration—now, will the turnover be as great? The absenteeism? The low morale?" She challenges her groups to talk honestly about these vital components that make for a healthy, positive school culture.

"And," she warns, "you can't give it if it's not in you to give. That's why we constantly have to think about our commitments, beliefs, and goals. How we feel about those deeper questions will generate our behavior."

Claudette and Anne inspire those who lead to look deeply into their own hearts and souls and honestly find whether their beliefs, actions, and words are in harmony. Their decisions will shape the culture of their schools, affecting children, staff, families, and neighbors.

The image for my Album of Hope is a group of administrators exchanging ideas and experiences, sharing feelings, and being energized by the process and promise of making a real difference in the lives of those they guide.[5]

These are just four examples of courageous, confident, hopeful educators who, like our four brave little flowers, insist on growing through hardened and lava-crusted times! I must tell you, I have gathered hundreds and hundreds of examples of educators throughout the land who inspire and nurture caring, compassionate communities of learners.

All of them give themselves wholly to this "holy" process. Their words aren't slogans. Their promises are not bulletin-board displays or mottos. Their commitments are demonstrated every day by how they meet and greet, listen and talk, share and care in their numerous interactions with children and adults.

They know that nothing is to be taken for granted. Tom's Town Meeting is not guaranteed to succeed. A teacher who does not teach in the "key of life," who doesn't listen to or respect the students, who is rigid and devoid of joy and humor, can follow the recipe for a Town Meeting to the last syllable, but it will yield nothing that will teach the children, *through doing*, the art of building positive classroom relationships.

> *I have gathered hundreds and hundreds of examples of educators throughout the land who inspire and nurture caring, compassionate communities of learners.*

Cathy didn't adopt a specific program. She and her children *are* the program, and their mutuality, kindness, and concern for one another are expressed in everything they do. There is no place for bullying in the safe place of Cathy's classroom. She teaches by heart!

Unless one believes it deeply and demonstrates that belief in everything he or she does (from the smallest acts to the largest), even a stellar concept like *family* will be another act of betrayal. Dee Gibson truly believes in establishing a second family with her children. This is not a once-a-month, set-aside time slot; it's the air they breathe and everything they do. Children are acutely alert to hypocrisy. They know when their teachers speak empty words. Lip service is disservice! They learn those lessons well.

Anne and Claudette, in their workshops, invite administrators to examine their own beliefs, motivations, and actions. Joanne Rooney, in her excellent article "Principals Who Care: A Personal Reflection," wrote:

> Good principals model care. Their words and behavior explicitly show that caring is not optional. Nothing can substitute for this leadership. Phoniness doesn't cut it. No principal can ask any teacher, student, or parent to travel down the uncertain path of caring if the principal will not lead the way.[6]

The way through these often grim times is through dedication and commitment, courage, persistence and fierce optimism. Just as Swordfern, Nutgrass, Creeping Dayflower, and Thimbleberry push their bright colors through seemingly solid lava, countless teachers and administrators shine their lights—brightening the sacred spaces they influence, dotting the charred landscape with blossoms of hope.

Notes

1. Tom was inspired by A. S. Neill, *Summerhill School* (New York: St. Martin's Griffin, 1992).
2. Tom Tenerovich and his second-graders enjoyed their Town Meetings at the Royal Palm Beach Elementary School, Royal Palm Beach, Fla. Tom currently teaches second grade at Equestrian Trails Elementary school in Wellington, Fla.
3. Cathy Arment and her loving first-graders listened to *Froggy's First Kiss* at the Etna Road School, Whitehall-Yearling Public Schools, Whitehall, Ohio, where she was voted Teacher of the Year 2004.
4. Dee Gibson and her family of first-graders thrive in the Walden School, Deerfield Public Schools, Deerfield, Ill. Dee was featured in my guest editorial, "Welcome to the Family," *Early Childhood Education Journal*, Summer 2003, pp. 201–2.
5. Anne Price and Claudette Cole are PEACEmakers in Cleveland, Ohio. You can contact Anne and Claudette at www.peaceeducation.com.
6. Joanne Rooney, "Principals Who Care: A Personal Reflection," *Educational Leadership*, March 2003, p. 77.

MIMI BRODSKY CHENFELD *began teaching in 1956. She works and plays with people of all ages and grade levels throughout the country. Among her books are* Teaching in the Key of Life *(National Association for the Education of Young Children, 1993),* Teaching by Heart *(Redleaf Press, 2001), and* Creative Experiences for Young Children, *3rd ed. (Heinemann, 2002). She lives in Columbus, Ohio. She dedicates this article to the memory of Pauline Gough, whose life's work, brightening the way for educators and children, is a stellar example of metaphors of hope.*

Pell Grants vs. Advanced Placement

"Under a Pell grant program ... a low-income student who might be particularly gifted in computers could take computer science course at a local junior college–an option he or she would not enjoy in most AP programs."

Kirk A. Johnson

IN HIS 2004 State of the Union address, Pres. George W. Bush proposed to "expand Advanced Placement programs in low-income schools." The President's subsequent budget for fiscal year 2005 calls for $28,000,000 in additional funding for the Advanced Placement Incentive Program. This would allocate some $52,000,000 in 2005 to establish Advanced Placement programs in low-income areas and prepare more teachers to instruct these rigorous classes.

While increasing college-level educational opportunities for low-income students is a worthy goal, there are more efficient and cost effective ways to achieve this aim. Specifically, the President and Congress should divert the proposed $52,000,000 to the Pell grant program and aim these funds specifically at bright, low-income high school students who could use the grants to attend classes at a community college or state university in the U.S.'s extensive network of higher education institutions.

Such a program could enable over 43,000 high school students nationwide to attend one college class per semester. There are two basic ways that especially intelligent high school students can perform college-level work. First, they may enroll in Advanced Placement or International Baccalaureate classes. More than 14,000 institutions—about 60% of the high schools in the nation—offer at least one AP class. These courses are an extremely challenging way for students to experience the rigors of college while still in high school.

At the end of an AP class, the student is eligible to take a test administered by the College Board (the organization responsible for the SAT and a number of other exams). If he or she achieves a sufficiently high score, most colleges and universities will award the student a certain amount of credit toward a bachelor's degree.

The second way to get college credit while still in high school simply is to take one or more classes at a community college or state university. Virtually all states have some program that allows high school students to take such courses, subject to various admission requirements and regulations.

Federal initiatives clearly have favored the establishment of AP courses. One of the declared purposes of the No Child Left Behind Act was "to increase the number of individuals that achieve a baccalaureate or advanced degree and to decrease the amount of time such individuals require to attain such degrees."

To that end, the No Child Left Behind legislation authorized Advanced Placement Incentive Program grants, which provided roughly $24,000,000 annually to state and local education agencies to fund Advanced Placement and pre-AP programs in low-income communities. Although there are many allowable uses for these grants—including tutoring lessons and faculty in-service activities—the intent of the law clearly is to funnel more students into high school-based AP programs.

Pres. Bush's additional funding for FY2005 was proposed to "provide teacher training to expand the pool of instructors qualified to teach AP classes at schools that serve large populations of low-income students."

Generally speaking, AP courses are far more expensive to operate than regular high school classes because of the higher salaries given to teachers who are qualified to instruct these subjects, the smaller class size that is typical of AP programs, and the higher cost of AP books and other materials. For instance, a typical high school math instructor (who might teach, for example, algebra or geometry) has, at a minimum, a bachelor's degree in mathematics or math education and some teaching credential. In contrast, because an AP calculus class would require a higher understanding of complex mathematical concepts, a qualified AP math teacher typically would have a master's degree or perhaps even a Ph.D.

In 2002, an entry-level teacher with a bachelor's degree, teaching in a large urban school district, earned an average of $31,567 per year. Yet, a highly educated teacher with a master's degree and additional graduate training—a likely candidate to teach AP courses—might earn as much as $53,248 per year.

AP classes also are more expensive to operate because the average size (17 students) is smaller than the standard high school class (24 pupils). Additionally, as noted by the President, many high school teachers need supplementary training to achieve the competency needed to teach AP. Indeed, most of the proposed $28,000,000 increase would be designated for teacher-training activities.

In the end, the cost of the typical AP class is more than twice that of the average non-AP high school class. Nevertheless, increasing numbers of low-income students have taken AP tests in recent years. This is due, in part, to the Advanced Placement Incentive Program grants and the Advanced Placement Test Fee Program (which pays a portion of the AP test fee), as well as to various state and local incentives.

In 1999, fewer than 93,000 low-income students took AP tests; by 2002, that figure had increased to more than 140,000. Even so, this represents only about nine percent of the total AP tests administered in 2002. Compared with higher-income peers, far fewer low-income students are taking AP tests.

This discrepancy likely is the result of two factors. First, there is a well-documented academic achievement gap between low-income students and their more affluent peers. For example, according to the National Assessment of Educational Progress, in 2002, one percent of the 12th-grade students who qualified for free or reduced-price lunches exhibited an advanced level of proficiency in reading, compared to nearly five percent of students from higher-income families. These high-achieving students would be the most likely to benefit from rigorous college-level studies.

A second, and related, reason is that the demand for AP classes in low-income areas may not be sufficient to justify the costs of their implementation at individual schools. In these areas, only a few students may have the aptitude necessary to benefit from an AP regimen. Cost concerns are augmented by the fact that, in low-income schools, even fewer students may be sufficiently advanced to qualify for AP classes, thereby increasing the per-pupil expenditures.

Another drawback is that these courses may duplicate classes that currently are being offered in institutions of higher education. Indeed, the point of the AP program, according to the College Board, is to "get a head start on exactly the sort of work you will confront in college." Classes similar to the ones in the AP program can be found at virtually all of the nearly 2,100 community colleges and state universities across the U.S.

For the most part, these institutions already have the infrastructure to offer these types of classes, and they exist in close proximity to high school students—especially those in low-income urban areas. Consequently, these AP programs would tend to duplicate the kinds of classes that already are available at a broad range of colleges and universities.

A final—and key—policy question in evaluating the AP Incentive Program versus other alternatives is: How many students does the program serve? A corollary question is: How far is the reach of the program in terms of the potential population of students served?

There is reason to believe that estimates have been overstated. They are based on the assumption that the program would benefit two groups: those who directly are served through newly formed AP classes and those who are not in the AP classes but would profit indirectly through the increased teacher training provided by the program. Estimates from the Department of Education peg the total number of beneficiaries at approximately 370,000 students attending 550 middle schools and high schools.

This assumes that all students in a given school benefit from the existence of AP classes. Applying this premise, a remedial

student is counted as a beneficiary of the program, as is an advanced student enrolled in an AP course. This clearly overstates the program's reach.

Currently, the AP Incentive Program initiative offers tutoring and summer enrichment programs for students, as well as teacher training. Overall, however, it has a limited reach because of the program's relatively small dollar funding. During 2002–03, the AP Incentive Program funded a mere 35 projects, with most of the money going to individual school districts and a few state education agencies.

As an alternative to the AP system, Pell grants could be offered to bright, low-income high school students as a fiscally responsible way to expand their access to college-level classes. These grants could be used to take classes at any community college or university that would admit a high school student for the purpose of taking advanced, college-level classes.

Using the $24,000,000 the Federal government currently spends on the Advanced Placement Incentive Program every year, more than 18,500 low-income students could be given $1,200 Pell grants, enabling them to take one class in both the fall and spring semesters. If program funding is increased to $52,000,000, more than 43,000 low-income high school students could take college classes.

Six hundred dollars per class should be adequate to cover the tuition costs for most public colleges and universities. According to the College Board, the average price for full-time tuition at four-year public colleges is $4,694; therefore, $1,200 Pell grants would cover the tuition for a single class each semester.

"One possible criticism of the expanded Pell grant proposal may be that states, some of which already have higher education programs for high school students, might shift money away from such initiatives if they can receive Federal funding."

Moreover, there would be the ancillary benefit of allowing students to choose from a wider variety of classes than what might be offered in a limited, school-based AP program. Schools with an AP program are most likely to offer English literature/composition, calculus, and American his-

tory. Fewer than half of high school AP programs have courses such as biology, English, chemistry, or Spanish.

The typical multidisciplinary college boasts all of these classes and a broad range of others. Under a Pell grant program, for example, a low-income student who might be particularly gifted in computers could take computer science courses at a local junior college—an option he or she would not enjoy in most AP programs.

In 2000, Bush (then a presidential candidate) proposed a program in which high school students could use what he called "enhanced Pell grants" to receive up to $1,000 for the purpose of taking advanced math and science classes at college. In practice, such a program would be very similar to the one recommended here.

Such grants also could be used for other AP alternatives. For example, certain enterprising firms have begun to offer AP classes over the Internet or via home study/correspondence courses.

One possible criticism of the expanded Pell grant proposal may be that states, some of which already have higher education programs for high school students, might shift money away from such initiatives if they can receive Federal funding. Several states already have programs that allow intelligent high school students into college courses without paying tuition fees. For example, Washington has had a program since 1992 called "Running Start" that encourages 11th- and 12th-graders to try college-level courses at community colleges and a few state universities. This dual enrollment gives individuals high school and college credit simultaneously.

Similar programs are peppered throughout the nation. Individual school districts and/or states that permit high school students to take college classes for free would be reimbursed for the class cost, up to $600 per class each semester. Those states could not, however, receive Federal money unless they expanded the program to include more students. Therefore, any legislation authorizing this expanded version of Pell grants should have a "supplement, not supplant" clause.

Kirk A. Johnson is a senior policy analyst in the Center for Data Analysis at The Heritage Foundation, Washington, D.C.

How Smart Is AP?

**As ambitious students load up on
Advanced Placement classes, critics question their quality**

CLAUDIA WALLIS and
CAROLINA A. MIRANDA

It's 8:30 in the morning, and the day is cold and rainy—conditions that, biologically, make it nearly impossible for the average teenager to function. Yet the 10 boys and eight girls who pour into the first-period Advanced Placement (AP) Calculus class at McNair Academic High School in Jersey City, N.J., seem remarkably alert. Maybe it's the influence of Victorina Wasmuth, their peppy, diminutive math teacher, who exudes a boundless enthusiasm as she introduces a lesson on Rolle's theorem and the extreme-value theorem, which, she explains, are key underpinnings of calculus. Wasmuth tosses out problems for her students to solve and then roves the room, examining their work. "You're all very smart!" she exclaims. "You're all capable of coming up with these theorems on your own."

Adam Capulong, 17, who sports the collared shirt and tie required for boys at this racially diverse urban magnet school, adores the class. "It brings all aspects of math together," says the straight-A student, who is hoping to go to Harvard. But the challenging college-level course is just one small serving on an academic plate that he has heaped with five additional AP courses, including AP French, AP English Literature and AP Art History. That's on top of the three AP courses he took as a junior and one as a sophomore. Capulong's fellow senior Nayla Scaramello, 17, carries a similar load, and she got an even earlier start on her nine AP courses. As a ninth-grader, she took AP U.S. History, with its daunting college-level reading list. "College is so competitive," she explains, "and you want to stand out. I want my transcript to reflect that I'm a hard worker."

There are **34 DIFFERENT AP TESTS** today, compared with 11 when they were introduced in 1955 ■ **1.1 MILLION** students, including nearly **140,000** freshman and sophomores, took **1.9 MILLION AP EXAMS** last May ■ **14,904 HIGH SCHOOLS** offer AP, compared with 10,863 that did so 10 years ago

Capulong and Scaramello may be hard-core overachievers, but they're part of a national trend. The thirst to stand out in the brutal college-admissions game is driving a kind of AP-mania all across the U.S. Last May 1.9 million AP exams were taken by 1.1 million U.S. high school students—more than double the number who took them in 1994 and more than six times the number who took them 20 years ago. During the past decade, the number of high schools offering AP classes has grown a third, to 14,904, or 60% of all U.S. high schools.

To feed the demand, the College Board, the New York City-based company best known for administering the SAT, keeps creating new AP courses and exams. Back in 1955, when AP was introduced, there were 11 courses. By 1990 there were 29. Today there are 34, ranging from Music Theory to Computer Science. Next fall there will be three more: Italian, Russian and Chinese. It's a booming business for the nonprofit College Board, which sells teaching guides and seminars to instructors, study guides and practice exams to students, and charges $82 for an AP exam. (Much of this covers the costs of paying high school teachers and college professors to grade the exams, which include essays as well as multiple-choice questions.)

All this growth is generally viewed as good news by the many fans of AP programs, who include parents, college-admissions officers and school administrators, as well as politicians on both sides of the aisle, who have called for additional funding to make AP courses more available to low-income students. A large selection of AP courses attended by a broad swath of the student body is widely seen as a measure of excellence for U.S. high schools and figures prominently in formulas that attempt to rank public high schools. The more active the AP program, the higher the rank and, often, the higher the school district's real estate values.

But in some quarters, educators are worried that AP, which was created as a way to give bright high school seniors a taste of college, is turning into something it was never meant to be: a kind of alternative high school curriculum for ambitious students that teaches to the test instead of encouraging the best young minds to think more creatively. And as AP expands, some educators have begun to question the integrity of the programs and ask whether the classes are truly offering students an extra boost or merely giving them filigree for their college applications.

To be sure, many AP programs are first rate. Calculus, especially in the hands of a gifted teacher like Wasmuth, is widely considered to be one of the best-thought-out AP programs, as is AP English Language and Composition, which teaches students how to critically analyze literary works. Two years ago, when the Center for Education at the National Academy of Sciences conducted one of the few serious studies of the AP curriculum ever done, it praised the AP Calculus program for achieving "an appropriate balance between breadth and depth."

But the balance was off for the three other courses examined. AP Chemistry, Biology and Physics were found to be too sweeping in scope, lacking the depth of a good college course. The study's authors concluded that the practice and understanding of laboratory work—a critical piece of college-level science—was given short shrift both in the AP teacher's manuals and on the exams. They lamented that a "significant number of examination questions ... appear to require only rote learning" rather than a deeper understanding of science.

The emphasis of breadth over depth is a charge commonly leveled at AP history courses as well. Teachers who oversee the U.S.- and European-history classes frequently complain that there is little time for discussion or debate in these fast-paced romps through a half-millennium or more of names, dates and battles. Dennis Kenny, who teaches the AP U.S. History course at McNair, has to keep an eye on the clock and calendar to make sure he covers the sprawling curriculum in time for the May exam. "We're usually struggling the last few weeks just to get to the Reagan years," he says. This fall, with a presidential campaign under way, Kenny would have loved to draw some lessons from current

events, but, he laments, "there's no time. The kids love when we break away and talk about today's election, but I'm looking at the clock—and that's not a good thing."

It was the pell-mell nature of AP history classes in particular that prompted the Ethical Culture Fieldston School, a top private school in New York City, to drop all AP courses four years ago. Last year the Montclair Kimberley Academy in New Jersey decided to drop AP U.S. History. A number of other top private schools, including Phillips Exeter Academy in New Hampshire, have always steered clear of AP courses. Myra McGovern, a spokeswoman at the National Association of Independent Schools, discerns "a movement from a small group of independent schools that have said no to AP courses," preferring to offer high-level classes that are more focused, less test-driven and perhaps more engaging. "Learning is about having a passion," observes McGovern. "The threat is that students are so concerned with how they appear to the colleges that they pack in all sorts of AP courses that may not even interest them."

To its credit, the College Board has taken its detractors seriously. The National Academy of Sciences report offered "really good criticism," says Trevor Packer, executive director of AP programs. In response, Packer says the company has sought funds from the National Science Foundation to improve its biology, physics and chemistry courses. A retooling of the U.S. History program is also under way. But those changes will fix only part of the problem. AP courses and exams are created by teams of university professors who periodically revisit the curriculums, but the program information they send out is simply a guideline for classroom instructors. There is no mandated curriculum, nor is there any required training of teachers for AP classes, which is why the quality of the courses can vary widely from school to school. "Ultimately, our quality control is in the exam," concedes Packer.

It's not a perfect tool. As a 10th-grader, Todd Rosenbaum, now a junior at the University of Virginia, took a biology course that met just twice a week and offered no labs, but he crammed so successfully for the AP exam that he earned a 5 (tops on AP's 5-point scale). That score allowed the high school valedictorian to skip introductory biology at the university, but he found himself woefully unprepared for an upper-level course. "Pretty much as soon as I got in, I realized that there was no way I'd survive," says Rosenbaum. He withdrew from the course and wrote an essay for the college paper urging the university "to take a more skeptical approach in accepting AP scores."

At least Rosenbaum took the AP test (actually, he took 16 of them). About one-third of students who proudly list AP courses on their transcripts never take the exams, which are optional. Many top universities, including Harvard and M.I.T., have tightened their terms for granting credit or advanced standing on the basis of AP scores. They recognize that an exam-oriented class taken by 10th- and 11th-graders, no matter how bright and hardworking, is generally not the equivalent of a rigorous college course. "If you're being told that this is a college course, you're being told things that are not true," says Douglas Taylor, who chairs the University of Virginia biology department.

But even as some college department heads downgrade the value of APs, admissions officers continue to regard them as a hallmark of the student who enjoys a challenge. "If the school offers APs, we expect that the students are taking them," says Marilee Jones, dean of admissions at M.I.T.

"This is not a case of whoever has the most APs wins," insists Stanford director of undergraduate admissions Anna Marie Porras. But as kids like Adam Capulong and Nayla Scaramello know, it certainly doesn't hurt. This fall 424 students at McNair Academic signed up for AP courses. That's three-quarters of the student body.

Sobriety Tests Are Becoming Part of the School Day

By PATRICK O'GILFOIL HEALY

EAST HAMPTON, N.Y.— For years, schools across the country have deployed breath analyzers at proms, pep rallies and other after-school events to catch students who arrived drunk or smuggled in alcohol.

After some resistance and fevered debate, student advocates and even lawyers gradually came to accept that schools were within their rights to use every means to ensure that students were not toting six-packs and liquor bottles to after-school, night and weekend events.

Quietly though, a few districts around the country, from Indiana to Connecticut to Long Island, have begun to integrate breath-testing devices into the regular school day, a move that adds a new wrinkle to the ongoing struggle between students' privacy rights and a school's duty to limit drug and alcohol abuse.

Schools say they need to ensure that no students are drinking in class. Civil rights lawyers worry that high school students pulled out of class and forced to take a breath-alcohol test could be unfairly stigmatized for goofy or strange behavior.

Manufacturers of breath analyzers say they have sold their devices to thousands of schools across the country, but it is impossible to say how many districts have started using breath-alcohol tests during the school day. Officials with the Office of National Drug Control Policy and the National School Boards Association said they knew of no statistics tracking schools' use of breath analyzers. But lawyers who argue cases involving students' civil liberties said that tests during the school day are rare, and represent untested ground for most districts.

On the East End of Long Island, the East Hampton School District is venturing into this terrain with a proposal to use breath analyzers on students suspected of being intoxicated in high school.

District officials said they grew concerned after hearing of rampant student drinking. Teenagers were caught drinking on school trips to Costa Rica and Italy. A drunk student vomited on a bus on the way to a field trip. Then there were students showing up in class drunk, sometimes after having alcohol at lunch.

Things seemed to be getting out of hand, even for East Hampton, a summer oasis for wealthy New Yorkers that reverts to a rural small town in the off-season where teenagers can get away with holding beach bonfire parties where alcohol flows freely, and year-round residents describe 16 as the de facto drinking age.

So, to stop what seemed like a swell of student drinking, school administrators this winter proposed administering breath analyzers to students while high school is in session. Any student suspected of being drunk in class would be tested by a trained staff member, and not a police officer, board officials said. Results showing alcohol consumption would mean suspension. Refusing to take a test would be seen as an admission of guilt.

In central Connecticut, officials in the Avon School District are writing a plan similar to East Hampton's. A school district near South Bend, Ind. has had the policy in place for several years. Other districts around the country may well use their breath analyzers during the school day, even if their policies were originally intended for events outside of school.

But on Long Island, only one other school district—the Sayville School District—already has an in-school breath-alcohol test policy, and in that case administrators say they have not tested a single student in the seven years it has been in effect. Still, they say it has merit. "It's really preventative," said Geri Sullivan-Keck, Sayville's assistant superintendent for curriculum.

Prof. Bernard James of Pepperdine University, who specializes in constitutional law, said such policies easily survive legal challenges, but often crumple under community opposition. "In policy, it's an extraordinarily controversial issue," he said.

News of the plan has roiled East Hampton. Last month, parents and teachers crowded a school board meeting to cheer the proposal. The op-ed pages of The East Hampton Star overflowed with letters, many of them calling the plan heavy-handed and invasive.

Wendy Hall, the school board president, said the seven-member board would probably approve the plan at a meeting in early April. She called the plan gutsy and said it was one of several efforts the district had undertaken to restrict student drinking.

The proposal has forced students, teachers and parents to focus on drinking in East Hampton. The high school is a drab, boxy building set among the town's cedar-shingled homes. It spends $16,000 per student per year, and 80 percent of its 1,000 students graduate with a Regents diploma. Right now, students are preparing for spring break and Advanced Placement Tests, but the breath analyzer plan is what really drives conversation, residents said.

Daniel Otto, a senior at East Hampton High, mulled it over one night in his kitchen, as he sipped Coors Light. It was Thirsty Thursday, the night he and a few friends play poker and drink. Mr. Otto said the plan was ridiculous.

"I think they're trying to fix a problem they can't fix," he said. "Everybody drinks. It's the way East Hampton kids are."

Claudia Pilato Maietta, the president of the Parent Teacher Student Association, said the breath analyzer proposal had come after a rash of complaints about student drinking. In addition to complaints about drinking at pep rallies and at a beach at lunch, there was one complaint in October from a parent who e-mailed the principal photos of East Hampton students drinking at parties. Officials alerted the students' parents, and suspended some of the students from extracurricular activities.

Kevin Flaherty, a senior in the pictures who was not among those drinking, said that the incident had helped pave the way for the testing, which he called an over-reaction. "I know the whole senior class," he said, "and no one drinks at school."

He and other students expressed concern that students with past problems would be targeted and those who were zany, tired or rowdy would be misjudged as being drunk.

In Indiana, at Penn High School in Mishawaka, which has a similar policy, the principal was forced to apologize to a student who had been pulled out of class by a police officer last year and given three breath tests, all of which were negative.

But school officials in East Hampton insist they would use the tests fairly and discreetly. Scott Farina, the principal, said the school would call parents before giving the test, and would make sure students were safe if the results came out positive.

"This is just one way that we're trying to be proactive," he said.

One of the few students unfazed by the proposal was James Westfall, a senior, who said he had smuggled alcohol to school in a Gatorade bottle just before Christmas vacation. He was caught that day by school officials, he said, even without a breath analyzer, and said the school should have carte blanche to keep students from drinking.

"They're trying to keep it out of school," he said. "They're right to do that."

Spinning the Message On NCLB

ANNE C. LEWIS

THIS COLUMN is about a city with two tales—one of spin and the other of sputter. No matter who occupies the White House for the next four years, the past four have borne witness to some of the most ludicrous uses of taxpayer money ever, as the U.S. Department of Education (ED) has tried to spin its message on No Child Left Behind (NCLB) across the country. What was amusing ineptness at first finally became hard-ball strategy and put the department in the same league as other federal agencies in its efforts at manipulating the media.

As a former president of the Education Writers Association, I suppose I could be justifiably sensitive about what has been happening. Education coverage at the federal level used to be somewhat benign. Education was viewed as an important issue—but not nearly as critical as, say, national security or the affairs of the Department of State. It was a low priority. The way ED has shaped its media policies, however, has shoved education up a notch or two in status and importance. Education reporters now have a feel for what the conservative columnist William Safire wrote about this fall. Always quick to defend the Bush White House, Safire nevertheless said: "The fundamental right of Americans, through our free press, to penetrate and criticize the workings of our government is under attack as never before."

It seems that the Education Department paid a public relations firm a tidy sum to rate media coverage of NCLB. Lumping news stories and editorials together, the analysis gave points to articles, reporters, and states according to how positive or negative the coverage of NCLB. (Secretary of Education Rod Paige himself got a grade of 95% for an op-ed in the *Seattle Times*; he failed to attain a perfect 100% because the paper was deemed a local and not a national newspaper). The purpose of the analysis, according to a spokesperson for the public relations firm, was to further "educate" reporters who scored low.

Since reporters are naturally cynical, their reaction to news of the rating project was more irreverent than acquiescent. Reporters who rated high scores were apologizing and trying to understand why covering a press conference about NCLB put them high on the list. Those who needed "educating" were more inclined to brag about their standing or to call the raters "idiots."

The PR firm also produced videos made to look like press conferences (as had already been done by the Department of Health and Human Services to convey positive messages about changes in Medicare). The NCLB videos were withdrawn, and so were the HHS videos when the Government Accountability Office said their obvious plugging of President Bush's political agenda represented illegal use of taxpayers' money.

The signs of heightened spin came early in the Paige tenure at ED. In the initial months of the implementation of NCLB—when state and district leaders were begging for clarification of the law and for timely regulations— Paige was on a photo-op tour of the country promoting certain aspects of the law, especially parental choice. His appearances were made that much jollier by the singing of a little song praising NCLB—a song also paid for by taxpayers.

Reporters found that they had to funnel all queries to ED through a single person, the communications director who managed Paige's media contacts in the Houston school district, where the secretary had been superintendent. Giving workshops especially for the communications staffs of big-city districts, this person, who is now back in Houston, describes how he measures, in inches, all media coverage of the schools and judges it as either negative or positive. Investigative reporters responsible for too much negative coverage have had trouble getting their phone calls answered. He also advises that communications staff members allow their superintendents to speak to the press only when they have good news, as was his policy with Paige.

Education coverage at the federal level used to be somewhat benign. Education was viewed as important—but not nearly as critical as, say, national security. The way ED has shaped its media policies, however, has shoved education up a notch or two in status.

The press releases from the Department of Education and Paige's appearances around the country have continued this little tradition. They are so full of good news that they are more irritating than useful. ED's media strategy plays to the audiences it wishes to reassure. The most recent issue of a regular electronic newsletter from the Office of Innovation and Improvement, for example, carried only stories about Bush Administration priorities—choice, charters, alternative teacher certification, and so on.

For policy makers and district and community leaders trying their best to implement NCLB and to deal with some of its irrational mandates, this Pollyannaish leadership on an incredibly complicated and challenging piece of legislation makes the work even more difficult. The Center for Community Solutions in Ohio, for example, issued a report this fall on the implementation of NCLB in that state. The report criticized Paige's "blemish-free impression of NCLB." The leaders of the Ohio districts cited in the report support the law's goals and the need for schools to be accountable, but they "had a difficult time finding additional positive elements of NCLB. This is in direct contrast to what the U.S. Department of Education and Congressman [John] Boehner's office continue to communicate to the public," the report said. (Boehner is chair of the House Committee on Education and the Workforce.)

Spin has been allowed to invade the traditionally bland and noncontroversial area of communications on education policy because sputtering has characterized the effort for years. Education policy has always been vulnerable to becoming educational political policy. Across the land, there are deep and critical communication problems with regard to NCLB and education policy in general. In a forthcoming report, the Public Education Network (PEN) will probably identify this as a major finding of its series of hearings on NCLB, which were held earlier this year.

Many years ago there was a hastily conceived request for a proposal to establish a federally funded center to examine the dissemination of educational research to the public and to look at communication issues in general. I served on the review panel, which rejected all of the proposals because none—even those from some of our most eminent research universities—had a good grasp of the problem or of what questions to try to answer.

The PEN hearings have revealed that policy makers and education officials still do not know—or care much about—how to involve the public in their work. Nor do they know much about how to help parents, teachers, and students place their very personal experiences with the schools in the larger context where the problems that NCLB is trying to address are played out. That will require that the public trust the message, and that is something that the spin masters cannot deliver.

ANNE C. LEWIS *is a national education policy writer living in the Baltimore area (email:* anneclewis@earthlink.net).

Choice Struggles On

The progress of a great and necessary idea

CLINT BOLICK

THE year 2004 will be remembered as a pivotal year for the school-choice movement for multiple reasons, not least of which is that this was the year the president of the United States endorsed school choice.

Not George W. Bush—he's been a backer for years. Rather, it was Jed Bartlet, the liberal president on TV's *The West Wing*, whose grudging endorsement of school choice in Washington, D.C., was symbolically significant. If even Hollywood recognizes the importance of this educational reform, can the rest of the nation be far behind?

The *West Wing* episode was a case of art imitating life. In September, more than 1,000 D.C. children were able to attend private schools using publicly funded vouchers. The program resulted from an impressive coalition, one that joined the Bush administration and congressional Republicans with D.C. mayor Anthony Williams, City Council member Kevin Chavous, and school-board president Peggy Cooper Cafritz. In the coming year, school-choice legislation will be in play in more states than ever before. Depending on state election results this fall, serious efforts could be mounted in a dozen or more states.

Predictably, teachers' unions have shifted into high gear to defeat the one reform that threatens their monopoly vise-grip on public education. Earlier this year, the National Education Association announced new partnerships with ACORN and MoveOn.org—two of the nation's most sophisticated grassroots organizing groups—in a campaign to "protect" public schools.

At its most recent national convention, the NEA introduced a $1-per-member increase in dues for each of the next five years, which will generate $40 million for political activity. (By contrast, the Alliance for School Choice, the leading national pro-school-choice organization, has an annual budget of $6 million, which must be raised from voluntary contributions.) In Washington state, unions are trying a new tactic: bankrolling a referendum to repeal the state's newly enacted charter-school law. If it passes, expect similar ballot efforts to become a staple of the anti-school-choice arsenal.

Despite the validation of school choice two years ago by the U.S. Supreme Court in *Zelman* v. *Simmons-Harris*, union-backed legal challenges continue to vex school-choice programs. This year, the Colorado supreme court struck down that state's voucher program for poorer children under the state constitution's local-control provision. Meanwhile, a Florida appeals court invalidated a similar program under the state's Blaine Amendment, which forbids direct or indirect aid to religious schools. (So far, the U.S. Supreme Court has ducked the issue of whether state-court decisions that discriminate against religious options violate the First Amendment's guarantee of religious liberty.)

But school-choice forces are growing more sophisticated. Several organizations merged in May to lead the national school-choice effort, forming the Alliance for School Choice and its sister lobbying group, Advocates for School Choice. Together with the Black Alliance for Educational Options, the Hispanic Council for Reform and Educational Options, and the Milton and Rose D. Friedman Foundation, the national groups are pumping resources and lobbying acumen into states to create school-choice programs and protect them against attacks from unions and groups such as People for the American Way.

The movement has also developed a political arm. Two national groups, All Children Matter and LEAD, are carefully targeting state elections to improve legislative prospects for school choice. The groups scored impressive wins in primaries this year in South Carolina, Missouri, Florida, and elsewhere. But their biggest win was in Utah, where

Gov. Olene Walker, who had vetoed a school-choice program for disabled children, was defeated for the Republican nomination by Jon Huntsman almost entirely on the issue of school choice. The teachers' unions can't point to a single candidate for office who was defeated because of *support* for choice.

Still, politicians and political parties lag behind on the school-choice issue. Only a handful of Republicans, such as Tommy Thompson and Jeb Bush, recognize that school choice is a powerful way to attract minority voters. Most Democrats, beholden to unions, cannot match what Republicans have to offer on the issue of most tangible concern to inner-city families: the chance for a decent education for their children.

Likewise, only a few Democrats, such as Sens. Joe Lieberman and Dianne Feinstein and former Milwaukee mayor John Norquist, recognize that their party is in danger of losing education—one of its most important issues—if Republicans ever get a clue about the political potential of school choice.

Sadly, the best thing going for the school-choice movement is the abysmal and declining quality of public education, particularly for minority children. Fifty years after *Brown* v. *Board of Education*, the racial academic gap suggests we are nowhere close to achieving true equality of educational opportunity. Nearly 50 percent of black and Hispanic students drop out of high school, and 27 percent of all 20- to 29-year-old black men who dropped out are in jail. Despite high attrition rates, the average black high-school senior achieves at a level four academic years behind the average white senior—a gap that has *increased* by one-third over the past decade.

School-voucher programs have shown the potential to close the racial academic gap by between one-fourth and one-third over four years. Perhaps more significant, competitive pressure from school-choice programs forces public schools to buck union pressure and adopt long-overdue reforms. Harvard economist Caroline Hoxby has found that public schools consistently improve when faced with competition from viable school-choice programs.

The best case in point is Florida, where public schools that earn an "F" grade from the state for two years face two consequences: state intervention and an opportunity-scholarship program that allows students to transfer to better-performing public schools or receive scholarships to private schools. In the program's first year, only two public schools qualified for the program (factoring in grades from previous years), but approximately 75 other schools had one "F," meaning that another failing grade would trigger vouchers.

Over that year, *every* failing school in the state lifted itself from the "F" list, taking steps they should have been taking for years: spending more resources in the classroom, moving to year-round schooling, and hiring tutors for failing students. Records obtained by the Institute of Justice through the Freedom of Information Act revealed that school-board officials referred to the threat of vouchers as a motivation for adopting remedial measures. Researcher Jay Greene found improved test scores state-wide for the poorest-performing students.

Right now, children in publicly funded school-choice programs account for fewer than 0.2 percent of American schoolchildren. Yet the potential is boundless. School choice is the nation's most urgent civil-rights issue. We cannot tolerate, or afford, the current racial gap in education if we are to continue to be a great nation.

Mr. Bolick is president and general counsel of the Alliance for School Choice, and author of Voucher Wars: Waging the Legal Battle Over School Choice.

The 36th Annual
Phi Delta Kappa/Gallup Poll
of the Public's Attitudes Toward the Public Schools

By Lowell C. Rose and Alec M. Gallup

THE 36TH ANNUAL Phi Delta Kappa/Gallup Poll of the Public's Attitudes Toward the Public Schools continues the previous poll's focus on the No Child Left Behind (NCLB) Act because of that act's potential for improving student achievement and because of last year's finding that the strategies employed by NCLB at that time lacked the public support necessary to bring success. While some critics may question the appropriateness of the expanded federal presence in the area of K–12 education and others may believe that the federal mandate of NCLB is inadequately funded, this poll focuses on whether the public supports the strategies used in NCLB, strategies that are crucial to its primary goals of improving student achievement and simultaneously closing a minority achievement gap that has plagued our society for years. Without public support for these strategies, the goals of NCLB are not likely to be accomplished.

Executive Summary

The public's attitudes toward the public schools shape the initiatives and strategies that can be brought to bear to improve those schools so that they can meet the changing needs of our society. As this poll has evolved over 35 years, its primary purpose has become that of tracing and interpreting the public's view of its schools. This, the 36th poll in the series, continues that effort. However, readers are encouraged to do their own take on the data, to measure the authors' interpretations of the data against their own, and to draw their own conclusions. If the information provided here advances the discussion of the issues, the poll's purpose will have been served.

The federal No Child Left Behind Act dominates the public education scene. It is inextricably linked to the effort to improve overall student achievement while simultaneously moving to close the achievement gap. Closely tied to this effort is the debate over the appropriate role of standardized testing. The poll

addresses these issues against the background of the public's assessment of the public schools. It then turns to questions about the appropriate venue for pursuing change and how the public views selected proposals for change. Finally, the poll explores the public's opinion of the two political parties' relationship to public education and how that thinking is likely to affect the November election.

We begin this report with 16 conclusions that the authors believe capture the poll's most significant findings. Rationales are provided, and the tables containing the data on which the conclusions are based are referenced by number.

1. The trend line showing that the public in general gives reasonably high marks to the public schools continues. Those marks go higher when parents do the rating and even higher when parents rate the school their oldest child attends. This year 47% of all respondents give the schools in their community an A or a B; 61% of parents give the schools in their community an A or a B; and 70% of parents give the school attended by their oldest child an A or a B. (See Tables 1 and 3.)

2. It is important to distinguish between the schools in the community and the schools nationally, since the marks vary greatly. It is the latter schools that traditionally receive low grades. Schools nationally receive a total of 26% A's and B's in this year's poll. (See Table 2.) Respondents have no direct knowledge of these schools, and it would seem that public policy should be based on judgments of schools that are familiar to those doing the assessing.

3. Lack of financial support is now firmly established in the public's mind as the major problem facing the public schools. Issues related to discipline and drugs dominated the poll as the major concern until 2000, when lack of financial support rose to the top. In 2001, it was tied for first place; in each subsequent year it has stood alone at the top. Twenty-one percent in this year's poll mention finance as the number-one problem. (See Table 4.) No other problem exceeds 10%.

4. As it has indicated in every poll since 1999, the public expects change in the public schools to come through reforming the existing system, not through seeking an alternative. Given the choice of reforming the existing system or finding an alternative system, 66% choose reform of the existing system while 26% point to seeking an alternative. (See Table 5.)

5. The public lacks the information it believes it would need to form an opinion about NCLB.

- Last year, 76% of respondents said they knew little or nothing about NCLB; this year, that figure is 68%. (See Table 6.)
- Last year, 78% of public school parents said they knew little or nothing about NCLB; this year, that figure is 62%. (See Table 6.)
- Last year, 69% of respondents said they did not know enough about NCLB to say whether their view was favorable or unfavorable; this year, that figure is 55%. (See Table 7.)

6. The public disagrees with the major strategies NCLB uses to determine whether a school is or is not in need of improvement. Unless these strategies are modified, there is little reason to change last year's conclusion that greater familiarity with NCLB is unlikely to bring approval.

- Sixty-seven percent say the performance of a school's students on a single test is not sufficient for judging whether the school is in need of improvement. (See Table 8.)
- Eighty-three percent say testing in English and math only will not yield a fair picture of a school. (See Table 9.)
- Seventy-three percent say it is not possible to judge a student's proficiency in English and math on the basis of a single test. (See Table 10.)
- Eighty-one percent are concerned that basing decisions about schools on students' performance in English and math only will mean less emphasis on art, music, history, and other subjects. (See Table 11.)
- If a school is found to be in need of improvement, 80% would favor keeping students in that school and making additional efforts to help them, while 16% would favor permitting students to transfer to a school not in need of improvement. (See Table 12.)
- If a school is found to be in need of improvement, 55% would prefer to have students tutored by teachers in that school as compared to 40% who would prefer tutoring to be provided by an outside agency. (See Table 13.)

7. At this time the public does not support the separate reporting of test data mandated by NCLB and does not support the inclusion of special education students on the same basis as all other students. Fifty-two percent of respondents oppose separating test scores by race and ethnicity, disabled status, English-speaking ability, and poverty level; 61% oppose requiring special education students to meet the same standards as other students; 57% oppose including special education scores in determining whether a school is in need of improvement; and 56% oppose designating a school as in need of improvement based on special education scores alone. (See Tables 14–17.)

8. There is still time to make the changes that must be made in NCLB if it is to improve student achievement while contributing to closing the achievement gap. Despite the problems NCLB has encountered, 56% of respondents believe the goal of having a highly qualified teacher in every classroom by the end of 2005-06 is likely to be met, and 51% believe the act will improve student achievement in their local schools. (See Tables 18 and 19.)

9. Despite the controversy that has accompanied the increasing use of standardized tests for high-stakes purposes, there is majority support for at least the current level of testing. Forty percent say there is about the right amount of emphasis on standardized tests, 32% say there is too much emphasis, and 22% say there is too little emphasis. The percentage saying there is too much emphasis is up 12% since 1997. (See Table 20.)

10. The public is divided regarding the use of standardized tests for high-stakes purposes. This poll queried respondents about the use of standardized tests for deciding whether to grant a high school diploma and for judging the quality of teachers and principals.

- Fifty-one percent of respondents favor using a single standardized test as the basis for awarding a diploma; 47% oppose. (See Table 21.)
- Forty-nine percent say students' performance on standardized tests should be one of the measures used in judging teacher quality; 47% say student test scores should not be used. (See Table 22.)
- As to judging principals, 47% say standardized test scores of students in the school should be one measure of quality; 50% say test scores should not be used for this purpose. (See Table 23.)

11. The public believes strongly that the achievement gaps that separate white students from black and other minority students must be closed. Though respondents do not attribute the gap to schools, they believe the schools must close it. Eighty-eight percent say that it is important that the achievement gap be closed. Although 74% attribute the gap to factors other than schooling, 56% say it is the responsibility of the schools to close it. (See Tables 24–26.)

12. The public gives strong support to a variety of measures mentioned as possibilities for closing the gap. Six strategies that are among those frequently mentioned as possibilities for closing the gap all draw strong support. Strategies supported by more than 90% of respondents include encouraging more parent involvement, providing more instructional time for low-performing students, and strengthening remedial programs for low-performing students. (See Table 27.)

13. The idea of allowing parents to choose a private school for their child to attend at public expense continues to lack majority support. Fifty-four percent of respondents oppose this choice option, as compared to 42% who favor it. (See Table 30.) The other choice-related questions suggest that religious reasons would be the major factor in causing people to use a voucher to attend a nonpublic school. This conclusion applies whether the voucher covers all or half of the tuition. (See Tables 31 and 32.)

14. The public supports adding rigor to the high school curriculum and supports mandatory attendance until age 18. Seventy-eight percent of respondents favor requiring students to complete four years of English, math, and science in order to receive a diploma, and 66% would increase the mandatory attendance age to 18. (See Tables 34 and 35.)

15. While a plurality of respondents believe the Democratic Party is more interested in improving public education, the Republican Party continues to narrow the gap. Forty-two percent of respondents identify the Democratic Party as more interested in education, while 35% identify the Republican Party. The gap narrowed by 5 percentage points from 1996 to 2000 and by 5 percentage points from 2000 to 2004. (See Table 38.)

16. A dead heat results when respondents are asked which of the Presidential candidates they would support if they were voting solely on education issues. John Kerry and George Bush each draw support from 41% of respondents. (See Table 39.)

Assessment, Problems, and Change

Grading the Public Schools

Tables 1, 2, and 3 report the trend questions used to track the public's assessment of the public schools. Adding this year's 33% of respondents who give the schools a C to the 47% who give the schools an A or a B brings the total to 80%. For public school parents, the percentage who assign the top three grades is 85%.

TABLE 1. Students are often given the grades of A, B, C, D, and FAIL to denote the quality of their work. Suppose the public schools themselves, in your community, were graded in the same way. What grade would you give the public schools here—A, B, C, D, or FAIL?

	National Totals		No Children In School		Public School Parents	
	'04 %	'03 %	'04 %	'03 %	'04 %	'03 %
A & B	47	48	42	45	61	55
A	13	11	11	8	17	17
B	34	37	31	37	44	38
C	33	31	37	30	24	31
D	10	10	9	10	10	10
FAIL	4	5	3	7	5	3
Don't know	6	6	9	8	*	1

*Less than one-half of 1%.

TABLE 2. How about the public schools in the nation as a whole? What grade would you give the public schools nationally—A, B, C, D, or FAIL?

	National Totals		No Children In School		Public School Parents	
	'04 %	'03 %	'04 %	'03 %	'04 %	'03 %
A & B	26	26	28	26	22	26
A	2	2	2	1	3	5
B	24	24	26	25	19	21
C	45	52	45	52	44	49
D	13	12	13	11	13	13
FAIL	4	3	3	4	6	2
Don't know	12	7	11	7	15	10

TABLE 3. Using the A, B, C, D, FAIL scale again, what grade would you give the school your oldest child attends?

	Public School Parents	
	'04 %	'03 %
A & B	70	68
A	24	29
B	46	39
C	16	20
D	8	8
FAIL	4	4
Don't know	2	*

* Less than one-half of 1%.

The Biggest Problem

Table 4 provides responses to an open-ended question for which the public initiates the answers. The question is also the only one to have appeared in all 35 previous polls. The major problem has varied with the times and has included discipline, use of drugs, lack of financial support, and gangs and violence. For the moment, the public is firmly settled on lack of financial support as the biggest problem.

TABLE 4. What do you think are the biggest problems the public schools of your community must deal with?

	National Totals			No Children In School			Public School Parents		
	'04 %	'03 %	'02 %	'04 %	'03 %	'02 %	'04 %	'03 %	'02 %
Lack of financial support/ funding/money	21	25	23	22	26	23	20	24	23
Lack of discipline, more control	10	16	17	10	17	18	8	13	13
Overcrowded schools	10	14	17	9	12	14	13	16	23
Use of drugs/dope	7	9	13	7	10	14	7	7	11
Fighting/ violence/gangs	6	4	9	6	3	9	6	5	9

The Means of Improving Public Education

Starting in 2000, the poll began to ask the public how it expected improvement in schooling to come about. The choices offered were reforming the existing system or finding an alternative system. The public has consistently opted for improving the existing system.

TABLE 5. In order to improve public education in America, some people think the focus should be on reforming the existing public school system. Others believe the focus should be on finding an alternative to the existing public school system. Which approach do you think is preferable—reforming the existing public school system or finding an alternative to the existing public school system?

	National Totals					No Children In School					Public School Parents				
	'04 %	'03 %	'02 %	'01 %	'00 %	'04 %	'03 %	'02 %	'01 %	'00 %	'04 %	'03 %	'02 %	'01 %	'00 %
Reforming existing system	66	73	69	72	59	63	73	69	73	59	72	73	69	73	60
Finding alternative system	26	25	27	24	34	28	24	26	23	34	21	25	27	25	34
Don't know	8	2	4	4	7	9	3	5	4	7	7	2	4	2	6

No Child Left Behind Act

Information and Attitudes

More than two years after the passage of NCLB and despite the publicity it has received, the public continues to regard itself as insufficiently informed to comment on the law. The data in Table 6 indicate that public school parents have gained the most knowledge in the past year: the percentage saying they know very little or nothing at all about NCLB has dropped from 78% to 62%. Table 7, which reports on attitudes toward NCLB, summarizes separately the results for those saying they know "a great deal" or "a fair amount" about the law and those saying they know "very little" or "nothing at all" about it. In the groups claiming knowledge, a greater number of respondents indicate a favorable attitude toward NCLB, while a somewhat smaller number indicate an unfavorable attitude. The division between favorable and unfavorable opinions is smaller among those saying they know "very little" or "nothing at all." Note, however, that a large percentage of those in this group do not feel they know enough to express an opinion.

TABLE 6. Now, here are a few questions about the No Child Left Behind Act. How much, if anything, would you say you know about the No Child Left Behind Act—the federal education bill that was passed by Congress in 2001—a great deal, a fair amount, very little, or nothing at all?

	National Totals		No Children In School		Public School Parents	
	'04 %	'03 %	'04 %	'03 %	'04 %	'03 %
Great deal + fair amount	31	24	28	25	37	22
A great deal	7	6	6	5	8	7
A fair amount	24	18	22	20	29	15
Very little	40	40	41	37	38	44
Nothing at all	28	36	30	38	24	34
Don't know	1	*	1	*	1	*
Very little + nothing at all	68	76	71	75	62	78

*Less than one-half of 1%.

TABLE 7. From what you know or have heard or read about the No Child Left Behind Act, do you have a very favorable, somewhat favorable, somewhat unfavorable, or very unfavorable opinion of the act—or don't you know enough about it to say?

	National Totals		Those Knowing Great Deal	Those Knowing Fair Amount	Those Knowing Very Little	Those Knowing Nothing At All
	'04 %	'03 %	'04 %	'04 %	'04 %	'04 %
Very favorable + somewhat favorable	24	18	50	47	19	5
Very favorable	7	5	27	9	5	2
Somewhat favorable	17	13	23	38	14	3
Somewhat unfavorable	12	7	10	26	11	1
Very unfavorable	8	6	31	11	6	3
Don't know enough to say	55	69	8	14	64	89
Don't know	1	*	1	2	*	2
Somewhat unfavorable + very unfavorable	20	13	41	37	17	4

*Less than one-half of 1%.

Reaction to NCLB Strategies

Tables 8 through 13 focus on specific NCLB strategies, some of which are used to determine if a school is in need of improvement and others that come into play after such a determination has been made. In Table 8 respondents reject the use of a single statewide test for determining a school's status. In Table 9 they reject basing that decision on English and math only. In Table 10 they reject using a single test as the basis for judging student proficiency in English and math. Table 11 data reflect the public's concern over the negative impact the emphasis on English and math will have on other subjects. The data in Table 12 show that parents prefer helping students in the school over allowing students to transfer out. Table 13 indicates that parents prefer tutoring by teachers in their child's school over tutoring by an outside agency. And those claiming knowledge of NCLB are as critical of its strategies as those claiming little knowledge and in some cases more critical.

TABLE 8. According to the NCLB Act, determining whether a public school is or is not in need of improvement will be based on the performance of its students on a single statewide test. In your opinion, will a single test provide a fair picture of whether or not a school needs improvement?

	National Totals		No Children In School		Public School Parents		Those Knowing Great Deal/Fair Amount	Those Knowing Very Little/ Nothing At All
	'04 %	'03 %	'04 %	'03 %	'04 %	'03 %	'04 %	'04 %
Yes	31	32	33	32	28	31	28	32
No	67	66	64	67	70	66	71	65
Don't know	2	2	3	1	2	3	1	3

TABLE 9. According to the NCLB Act, the statewide tests of students' performance will be devoted to English and math only. Do you think a test covering only English and math would provide a fair picture of whether a school in your community is or is not in need of improvement, or should the test be based on other subjects also?

	National Totals		No Children In School		Public School Parents		Those Knowing Great Deal/Fair Amount	Those Knowing Very Little/ Nothing At All
	'04 %	'03 %	'04 %	'03 %	'04 %	'03 %	'04 %	'04 %
Test covering only English and math would provide a fair picture of whether a school is in need of improvement	16	15	15	14	18	18	20	14
Test should be based on other subjects also	83	83	84	84	81	81	79	85
Don't know	1	2	1	2	1	1	1	1

TABLE 10. In your opinion, is it possible or not possible to accurately judge a student's proficiency in English and math on the basis of a single test?

	National Totals		No Children In School		Public School Parents		Those Knowing Great Deal/ Fair Amount	Those Knowing Very Little/ Nothing At All
	'04 %	'03 %	'04 %	'03 %	'04 %	'03 %	'04 %	'04 %
Yes, possible	25	26	26	27	24	22	27	24
No, not possible	73	72	72	71	75	77	72	74
Don't know	2	2	2	2	1	1	1	2

TABLE 11. How much, if at all, are you concerned that relying on testing for English and math only to judge a school's performance will mean less emphasis on art, music, history, and other subjects? Would you say you are concerned a great deal, a fair amount, not much, or not at all?

	National Totals		No Children In School		Public School Parents		Those Knowing Great Deal/Fair Amount	Those Knowing Very Little/ Nothing At All
	'04 %	'03 %	'04 %	'03 %	'04 %	'03 %	'04 %	'04 %
A great deal + a fair amount	81	80	81	80	85	82	84	81
A great deal	37	40	35	38	43	45	42	35
A fair amount	44	40	46	42	42	37	42	46
Not much	13	14	13	13	11	15	10	14
Not at all	4	6	4	7	3	3	4	5
Don't know	2	*	2	*	1	*	2	0

* Less than one-half of 1%.

TABLE 12. Assume you had a child attending a school identified as in need of improvement by the NCLB Act. Which would you prefer, to transfer your child to a school identified as NOT in need of improvement or to have additional efforts made in your child's present school to help him or her achieve?

	National Totals		No Children In School		Public School Parents		Those Knowing Great Deal/ Fair Amount	Those Knowing Very Little/ Nothing At All
	'04 %	'03 %	'04 %	'03 %	'04 %	'03 %	'04 %	'04 %
To transfer child to school identified as not in need of improvement	16	25	16	24	14	25	18	15
To have additional efforts made in child's present school	80	74	79	75	85	74	81	80
Don't know	4	1	5	1	1	1	1	5

TABLE 13. Now, let's assume that your child was failing in his or her school. Which kind of tutoring would you prefer—tutoring provided by teachers in your child's school or tutoring provided by an outside agency that you would select from a state-approved list?

	National Totals		No Children In School		Public School Parents		Those Knowing Great Deal/ Fair Amount	Those Knowing Very Little/ Nothing At All
	'04 %	'03 %	'04 %	'03 %	'04 %	'03 %	'04 %	'04 %
Tutoring provided by teachers in child's school	55	52	53	52	60	54	53	56
Tutoring provided by outside agency	40	45	42	46	34	42	41	39
Don't know	5	3	5	2	6	4	6	5

Reaction to NCLB's Separate Reporting of Data

The findings in Table 14 are the most surprising and should be of most concern for the supporters of NCLB. The separate reporting of test data would appear to have brought much-needed attention to the existing achievement gap. Nonetheless, Table 14 data indicate that a divided public rejects this strategy. The data in Tables 15 through 17 may be part of the problem, since they indicate that the public rejects holding special education students to the same grade-level standards as other students, rejects their inclusion in the base for determining if a school is in need of improvement, and rejects deciding a school's status on the basis of special education students' performance alone. This issue may prove difficult to resolve, since many in the special education community believe special education students should be included and judged according to the same standards as all other students.

TABLE 14. The No Child Left Behind Act requires that test scores be reported separately by students' race and ethnicity, disability status, English-speaking ability, and poverty level. Do you favor or oppose reporting test scores in this way in your community?

	National Totals %	No Children In School %	Public School Parents %	Those Knowing Great Deal/ Fair Amount %	Those Knowing Very Little/ Nothing At All %
Favor	42	41	45	47	41
Oppose	52	53	53	51	53
Don't know	6	6	2	2	6

TABLE 15. In your opinion, should students enrolled in special education be required to meet the same standards as all other students in the school?

	National Totals		No Children In School		Public School Parents	
	'04 %	'03 %	'04 %	'03 %	'04 %	'03 %
Yes, should	36	31	37	31	35	31
No, should not	61	67	59	66	63	68
Don't know	3	2	4	3	2	1

TABLE 16. In your opinion, should the standardized test scores of special education students be included with the test scores of all other students in determining whether a school is in need of improvement under NCLB or not?

	National Totals %	No Children In School %	Public School Parents %
Yes, should	39	40	40
No, should not	57	56	57
Don't know	4	4	3

TABLE 17. In your opinion, should a school be designated in need of improvement if the special education students are the only group in that school that fails to make state goals or not?

	National Totals %	No Children In School %	Public School Parents %
Yes, should	39	40	39
No, should not	56	54	58
Don't know	5	6	3

Some Good News About NCLB

The findings in Table 18 indicate that a majority of respondents believe that the NCLB goal of having a highly qualified teacher in every classroom by the end of the 2005–06 school year is likely to be achieved. The findings in Table 19 show that 51% believe NCLB is likely to improve achievement in schools in the community, while 32% believe it will not. Given the fact that so many have not made up their minds about NCLB, these findings suggest that there is still time to deal with the strategy issues that appear, at this time, to be hampering NCLB.

TABLE 18. NCLB requires that there be a highly qualified teacher in each classroom by the end of the 2005–06 school year. What do you think is the likelihood of this happening in the public schools in your community by that time?

	National Totals %	No Children in School %	Public School Parents %	Those Knowing Great Deal/Fair Amount %	Those Knowing Very Little/ Nothing At All %
Very likely	19	17	24	26	17
Somewhat likely	37	36	41	37	37
Not very likely	31	33	25	25	34
Not at all likely	11	11	10	12	10
Don't know	2	3	*	*	2

———
* Less than one-half of 1%.

TABLE 19. From what you have seen or heard about the No Child Left Behind Act, how much do you think it will help to improve student achievement in the public schools in your community?

	National Totals %	No Children in School %	Public School Parents %	Those Knowing Great Deal/ Fair Amount %	Those Knowing Very Little/ Nothing At All %
Great deal + fair amount	**51**	**49**	**57**	**53**	**51**
A great deal	21	19	25	20	21
A fair amount	30	30	32	33	30
Not very much	23	23	21	32	19
Not at all	9	11	7	13	8
Don't know	17	17	15	2	22
Not very much + not at all	**32**	**34**	**28**	**45**	**27**

======

Appropriate Uses of Standardized Tests

How Much and for What Purpose

Standardized tests have become a flash point as they are used more frequently to support high-stakes decisions related to efforts to improve achievement and close the achievement gap. The data in Table 20 indicate that, while a good majority continue to believe that the amount of testing is about right or not enough, the percentage saying "too much" has gone up 12% since 1997. Tables 21 through 23 may help to explain this since they show a public that is divided regarding the use of standardized tests to make high-stakes decisions related to graduation and the quality of educators.

TABLE 20. Now, here are some questions about testing. In your opinion, is there too much emphasis on achievement testing in the public schools in this community, not enough emphasis on testing, or about the right amount?

	National Totals					No Children In School					Public School Parents				
	'04 %	'02 %	'01 %	'00 %	'97 %	'04 %	'02 %	'01 %	'00 %	'97 %	'04 %	'02 %	'01 %	'00 %	'97 %
Too much	32	31	31	30	20	30	30	29	28	20	36	32	36	34	19
Not enough	22	19	22	23	28	23	20	22	26	28	20	14	20	19	26
About the right amount	40	47	44	43	48	40	46	45	41	46	43	54	43	46	54
Don't know	6	3	3	4	4	7	4	4	5	6	1	*	1	1	1

* Less than one-half of 1%.

TABLE 21. Do you favor or oppose using a single standardized test in the public schools in your community to determine whether a student should receive a high school diploma?

	National Totals %	No Children In School %	Public School Parents %
Favor	51	50	52
Oppose	47	47	45
Don't know	2	3	3

TABLE 22. In your opinion, should one of the measurements of a teacher's ability be based on how well his or her students perform on standardized tests or not?

	National Totals %	No Children In School %	Public School Parents %
Yes, should	49	50	49
No, should not	47	45	49
Don't know	4	5	2

TABLE 23. How about school principals? In your opinion, should one of the measurements of a principal's quality be based on how well the students in his or her school perform on standardized tests or not?

	National Totals %	No Children In School %	Public School Parents %
Yes, should	47	47	48
No, should not	50	50	51
Don't know	3	3	1

The Achievement Gap

Closing the Achievement Gap

The data in Table 24 indicate that the public has consistently given high priority to closing the achievement gap between white students and minority students. The public is equally consistent, as indicated in Table 25, in its belief that the gap results from factors other than schooling. In last year's poll, respondents indicated that the three most important factors in creating the gap were lack of parent involvement, home life and upbringing, and lack of interest on the part of the students themselves. Although the public does not believe that the gap is

related to schooling, the data in Table 26 indicate that the public believes the schools must close it. The data in Table 27 reflect strong public support for six strategies for closing the gap. A 1978 question found 80% expressing the view that educational opportunities for whites and minorities were the same. The data in Table 28 indicate that this view is unchanged. The data in Table 29 suggest that the public places the responsibility for how well students learn primarily on parents. This view is in line with last year's finding that a lack of parent involvement is crucial to creating the gap.

TABLE 24. Black and Hispanic students generally score lower on standardized tests than white students. In your opinion, how important do you think it is to close this academic achievement gap between these groups of students?

	National Totals				No Children In School				Public School Parents			
	'04 %	'03 %	'02 %	'01 %	'04 %	'03 %	'02 %	'01 %	'04 %	'03 %	'02 %	'01 %
Very + somewhat important	88	90	94	88	89	91	93	89	89	88	96	87
Very important	64	71	80	66	65	70	80	66	63	73	80	67
Somewhat important	24	19	14	22	24	21	13	23	26	15	16	20
Not too important	5	5	2	5	4	5	2	5	3	4	2	5
Not at all important	5	4	3	5	5	3	4	4	7	7	1	6
Don't know	2	1	1	2	2	1	1	2	1	1	1	2

TABLE 25. In your opinion, is the achievement gap between white students and black and Hispanic students mostly related to the quality of schooling received or mostly related to other factors?

	National Totals				No Children In School				Public School Parents			
	'04 %	'03 %	'02 %	'01 %	'04 %	'03 %	'02 %	'01 %	'04 %	'03 %	'02 %	'01 %
Mostly related to quality of schooling received	19	16	29	21	19	15	31	20	20	18	22	22
Mostly related to other factors	74	80	66	73	73	80	64	72	76	80	75	74
Don't know	7	4	5	6	8	5	5	8	4	2	3	4

TABLE 26. In your opinion, is it the responsibility of the public schools to close the achievement gap between white students and black and Hispanic students or not?

	National Totals		No Children In School		Public School Parents	
	'04 %	'01 %	'04 %	'01 %	'04 %	'01 %
Yes, it is	56	55	56	56	56	53
No, it is not	40	41	39	39	41	45
Don't know	4	4	5	5	3	2

TABLE 27. Numerous proposals have been suggested as ways to close the achievement gap between white, black, and Hispanic students. As I mention some of these proposals, one at a time, would you tell me whether you would favor or oppose it as a way to close the achievement gap.

	Favor %	Oppose %	Don't Know %
Encourage more parent involvement	97	2	1
Provide more instructional time for low-performing students	94	5	1
Strengthen remedial programs for low-performing students	92	6	2
Provide free breakfast and free lunch programs as needed	84	15	1
Provide state-funded preschool programs	80	18	2
Provide in-school health clinics	76	21	3

TABLE 28. In your opinion, do black children and other minority children in your community have the same educational opportunities as white children?

	National Totals			No Children In School			Public School Parents		
	'04 %	'01 %	'78 %	'04 %	'01 %	'78 %	'04 %	'01 %	'78 %
Yes, the same	78	79	80	76	78	78	82	80	86
No, not the same	20	18	14	22	17	15	16	18	11
Don't know	2	3	6	2	5	7	2	2	3

TABLE 29. In your opinion, who is most important in determining how well or how poorly students perform in school—the students themselves, the students' teachers, or the students' parents?

	National Totals %	No Children In School %	Public School Parents %
Students themselves	22	23	21
Students' teachers	30	31	29
Students' parents	45	42	48
Don't know	3	4	2

Vouchers and Other Proposals

We have already noted that the public expects improvement in the public schools to come through reforming the existing public school system. That does not preclude the consideration of alternatives such as vouchers. The following tables provide an update regarding public opinion on vouchers and other proposals for change.

The Public View of Vouchers

Support for vouchers ranged from 41% to 44% in the late 1990s but dropped to 39% in 2000 and 34% in 2001. Fluctuations in support are now the norm, with a jump of 12% between 2001 and 2002, followed by a decline of 8% in 2003 and an increase of 4% this year.

TABLE 30. Do you favor or oppose allowing students and parents to choose a private school to attend at public expense?

National Totals

	'04 %	'03 %	'02 %	'01 %	'00 %	'99 %	'98 %	'97 %
Favor	42	38	46	34	39	41	44	44
Oppose	54	60	52	62	56	55	50	52
Don't know	4	2	2	4	5	4	6	4

TABLE 31. Suppose you had a school-age child and were given a voucher covering full tuition that would permit you to send that child to any public, private, or church-related school of your choice. Which kind of school do you think you would choose?

	National Totals		No Children In School		Public School Parents	
	'04 %	'03 %	'04 %	'03 %	'04 %	'03 %
A public school	37	35	38	35	38	39
A church-related private school	36	38	33	37	40	38
A non-church-related private school	20	24	22	25	17	21
Don't know	7	3	7	3	5	2

TABLE 32. What if the voucher covered only half of the tuition, which do you think you would choose?

	National Totals		No Children In School		Public School Parents	
	'04 %	'03 %	'04 %	'03 %	'04 %	'03 %
A public school	46	47	46	45	50	55
A church-related private school	32	34	29	34	34	29
A non-church-related private school	16	17	18	19	11	15
Don't know	6	2	7	2	5	1

Other Proposals for Change

The next four tables report public opinion on a variety of suggestions for change that have surfaced at the state level this year. The data in Table 33 show that the public believes that an increased emphasis on English, math, and science will benefit a great many students. The data in Table 34 document strong support for requiring students to complete four years of English, math, and science in order to graduate from high school. The data in Table 35 show strong support for increasing the mandatory attendance age to 18. As reported in Table 36, the idea of eliminating the senior year of high school is soundly rejected. (This idea surfaced in a state facing a financial crisis.) Finally, Table 37 reports respondents' views on criteria that might be used to determine whether teachers should receive extra pay.

TABLE 33. Some states are now requiring the public schools to place greater emphasis at all grade levels on English, math, and science. Thinking about the needs of the public school students in your community, do you think this increased emphasis will serve all, most, some, or only a few of these students' needs?

	National Totals %	No Children In School %	Public School Parents %
All	29	28	29
Most	32	30	37
Some	28	30	25
Only a few	9	10	6
Don't know	2	2	3

TABLE 34. Some states are now requiring that high school students complete four years of English, math, and science in order to graduate from high school. Would you favor or oppose this requirement in the public schools in your community?

	National Totals %	No Children In School %	Public School Parents %
Favor	78	79	76
Oppose	20	20	22
Don't know	2	1	2

TABLE 35. Some people have proposed increasing the mandatory attendance age to 18 as a way to deal with the school dropout problem. Would you favor or oppose increasing the mandatory attendance age to 18 in your state?

	National Totals %	No Children In School %	Public School Parents %
Favor	66	66	68
Oppose	30	31	28
Don't know	4	3	4

TABLE 36. Some people have proposed eliminating the senior year of high school so that students could get an earlier start on getting a college education or on entering the work force. Would you favor or oppose using this plan in the high schools in your community?

	National Totals %	No Children In School %	Public School Parents %
Favor	24	23	25
Oppose	74	75	73
Don't know	2	2	2

TABLE 37. I am going to mention some possible reasons for awarding extra pay to a public school teacher. As I read each reason, would you tell me whether you think it should be used to determine whether or not a teacher receives extra pay?

	Should Be Used %	Should Not Be Used %	Don't Know %
Having an advanced degree such as a master's or a Ph.D.	76	23	1
High evaluations of the teacher by his or her principal and other administrators	70	28	2
Length of his or her teaching experience	71	28	1
High evaluations by other teachers in the teacher's school district	65	33	2
High evaluations by his or her students	64	34	2
High opinions from the parents of his or her students	59	39	2

The Political Component

Election-Year Issues

K–12 education has moved close to the top of the political agenda at both the state and federal levels, thereby adding importance to the political questions that this poll reserves for Presidential election years. The data in Table 38 show that the Republican Party has made progress in closing a gap that had Democrats enjoying a 17% advantage in 1996 as the party more interested in improving public education. The gap is now 7%. Table 39 shows John Kerry and George Bush in a dead heat when voters are asked to choose between them based on education issues alone. Four years ago, Al Gore and George Bush were also in a dead heat in this poll. Table 40 tends to verify the conventional wisdom regarding policies that the two major parties would be inclined to support. And Tables 41 and 42 suggest that supporting vouchers would give a slight edge to candidates nationally, while supporting NCLB would be a major plus.

TABLE 38. In your opinion, which of the two major political parties is more interested in improving public education in this country—the Democratic Party or the Republican Party?

	National Totals			No Children In School			Public School Parents		
	'04 %	'00 %	'96 %	'04 %	'00 %	'96 %	'04 %	'00 %	'96 %
Democratic Party	42	41	44	45	41	45	37	41	41
Republican Party	35	29	27	35	29	26	34	28	29
No difference volunteered	*	*	15	*	*	15	*	*	14
Don't know	23	30	14	20	30	14	29	31	16

* Less than one-half of 1%.

TABLE 39. Suppose you were voting solely on the basis of a desire to strengthen the public schools. Who would you vote for in the Presidential election this November—John Kerry or George W. Bush?

	National Totals %	No Children In School %	Public School Parents %
John Kerry	41	42	37
George W. Bush	41	41	41
Don't know	18	17	22

TABLE 40. I am going to mention several policies pertaining to the public schools in this country. As I mention each policy, would you tell me which political party—the Democratic Party or the Republican Party—you feel would be more sympathetic to that policy?

	Democratic Party %	Republican Party %	Don't Know %
Providing financial support for private or church-related schools	31	55	14
Privatizing such school services as transportation, food, maintenance, etc.	34	50	16
Improving student achievement in the nation's public schools	45	39	16
Closing the achievement gap between white students and black and Hispanic students	55	30	15

Closing Statement

Polling is now a high-stakes component in the effort to improve the public schools. The issues explored herein are shaping the daily decisions made in K–12 schools. Poll findings have

TABLE 41. Would knowing that a candidate for national office supports vouchers for parents to use to pay for private schools make you more likely or less likely to vote for that candidate?

	National Totals		No Children In School		Public School Parents	
	'04 %	'00 %	'04 %	'00 %	'04 %	'00 %
More likely	43	41	43	41	43	40
Less likely	37	44	37	45	36	44
Makes no difference	15	12	15	11	15	12
Don't know	5	3	5	3	6	4

TABLE 42. Would knowing that a candidate for national office supports the No Child Left Behind Act make you more or less likely to vote for that candidate?

	National Totals %	No Children In School %	Public School Parents %
More likely	53	53	53
Less likely	25	26	23
Makes no difference	15	15	14
Don't know	7	6	10

taken on added importance, and, given the inexact nature of data analysis, it is not surprising that this report and the interpretations we provide are always subject to a critical review. That is as it should be. The poll is intended to contribute to the ongoing debate regarding the public schools, and disagreement fuels that debate. The public does, however, have a way of getting it right with issues that are both complex and puzzling. And, right or wrong, public attitudes determine, over the long haul, how those issues can be addressed.

Research Procedure

The Sample. The sample used in this survey embraced a total of 1,003 adults (18 years of age and older). A description of the sample and methodology can be found at the end of this report.

Time of Interviewing. The fieldwork for this study was conducted during the period of 28 May to 18 June 2004.

Due allowance must be made for statistical variation, especially in the case of findings for groups consisting of relatively few respondents.

The findings of this report apply only to the U.S. as a whole and not to individual communities. Local surveys, using the same questions, can be conducted to determine how local areas compare with the national norm.

Sampling Tolerances

In interpreting survey results, it should be borne in mind that all sample surveys are subject to sampling error, i.e., the extent to which the results may differ from what would be obtained if the whole population surveyed had been interviewed. The size of such sampling error depends largely on the number of interviews. For details and tables showing the confidence intervals for the data cited in this poll, please visit the Phi Delta Kappa website at `http://www.pdkintl.org/kappan/kpoll0409sample.htm`.

Design of the Sample

For the 2004 survey the Gallup Organization used its standard national telephone sample, i.e., an unclustered, directory-assisted, random-digit telephone sample, based on a proportionate stratified sampling design.

The random-digit aspect of the sample was used to avoid "listing" bias. Numerous studies have shown that households with unlisted telephone numbers are different in important ways from listed households. "Unlistedness" is due to household mobility or to customer requests to prevent publication of the telephone number.

To avoid this source of bias, a random-digit procedure designed to provide representation of both listed and unlisted (including not-yet-listed) numbers was used.

Telephone numbers for the continental United States were stratified into four regions of the country and, within each region, further stratified into three size-of-community strata.

Only working banks of telephone numbers were selected. Eliminating nonworking banks from the sample increased the likelihood that any sample telephone number would be associated with a residence.

The sample of telephone numbers produced by the described method is representative of all telephone households within the continental United States.

Within each contacted household, an interview was sought with the household member who had the most recent birthday. This frequently used method of respondent selection provides an excellent approximation of statistical randomness in that it gives all members of the household an opportunity to be selected.

Up to three calls were made to each selected telephone number to complete an interview. The time of day and the day of the week for callbacks were varied so as to maximize the chances of finding a respondent at home. All interviews were conducted on weekends or weekday evenings in order to contact potential respondents among the working population.

The final sample was weighted so that the distribution of the sample matched current estimates derived from the U.S. Census Bureau's Current Population Survey (CPS) for the adult population living in telephone households in the continental U.S.

Composition of the Sample

Adults	%	Education	%
No children in school	67	Total college	57
Public school parents	29	College graduate	24
Nonpublic school parents	4	College incomplete	33
		Total high school	42
		High school graduate	35
		High school incomplete	7
Gender	%	**Income**	
Men	45	$50,000 and over	34
Women	55	$40,000–$49,000	10
		$30,000–$39,000	12
Race		$20,000–$29,000	12
White	81	Under $20,000	17
Nonwhite	15	Undesignated	15
Black	11		
Undesignated	3	**Region**	
		East	22
Age		Midwest	24
18–29 years	20	South	32
30–49 years	40	West	22
50 and over	38		
Undesignated	2	**Community Size**	
		Urban	27
		Suburban	47
		Rural	26

Conducting Your Own Poll

The Phi Delta Kappa Center for Professional Development and Services makes available PACE (Polling Attitudes of Community on Education) materials to enable nonspecialists to conduct scientific polls of attitude and opinion on education. The PACE manual provides detailed information on constructing questionnaires, sampling, interviewing, and analyzing data. It also includes updated census figures and new material on conducting a telephone survey. The price is $60. For information about using PACE materials, write or phone Jeanne Storm at Phi Delta Kappa International, P.O. Box 789, Bloomington, IN 47402-0789. Ph. 800/766-1156.

Lowell C. Rose is executive director emeritus of Phi Delta Kappa International. ALEC M. GALLUP is co-chairman, with George Gallup, Jr., of the Gallup Organization, Princeton, NJ.

UNIT 2

Rethinking and Changing the Educative Effort

Unit Selections

Key Points to Consider

- What are some issues in the debate regarding educational reform?

- Should the focus of educational reform be on changing the ways educators are prepared, on the changing needs of students, or on both of these concerns? Defend your answer.

- Compare American concepts about alternative schooling and the uses of public funds to the views of other countries on school choice issues.

Student Website
www.mhcls.com/online

Internet References
Further information regarding these websites may be found in this book's preface or online.

The Center for Innovation in Education
http://www.center.edu

Colorado Department of Education
http://www.cde.state.co.us/index_home.htm

National Council for Accreditation of Teacher Education
http://www.ncate.org

Phi Delta Kappa International
http://www.pdkintl.org

The "No Child Left Behind" (NCLB) legislation has sparked a major debate among the educational community in the United States. What constitutes a "highly qualified teacher?" How many of them do we have? Which students get them? The questions roll on and on. We are left to decide the equity issues involved in all of this. We are also left to decide the most fundamental question of all: What constitutes a "highly qualified teacher?" What educational background should the person have? What are the motivations to do this? How are we to assess this person's ability to take this role? All of these questions need to be addressed plus the question as to how "highly qualified teachers" are to be permitted to play their professional roles in the classrooms assigned to them. We are a democratic society committed to the free education of all our citizens.

Rethinking and re-directing the educational system of a nation requires intensive reflective and analytical effort. How to best restructure educational services is a question which requires considerable contemplation and forethought as to the consequences of our decision-making processes. The dialogical processes involved among citizens as they engage in this decision-making process will shape the forms of our educational futures.

American educators could have a much better sense of their own past as a profession, and the public could better understand the history of public education. In the United States, a fundamental cycle of similar ideas and practices reappears in school curricula every so many years. The decades of the 1970s and 1980s witnessed the rise of "behavioral objectives" and "management by objectives," and the 1990s brought us "outcome-based education" and "benchmarking" in educational discourse

within the public school system's leadership. These are related behavioral concepts focusing on measurable ways to pinpoint and evaluate the results of educational efforts. Why do we seem to "reinvent the wheel" of educational thought and practice every so many decades? This is an important question worth addressing. Many of our ideas about change and reform in educational practice have been wrongheaded. There is a focus on more qualitative, as opposed to empirical, means of assessing the outcomes of our educative efforts; yet many state departments of education still insist on objective assessments and verifications of students' mastery of academic skills. How does this affect the development of imaginative teaching in schools? All of us in the education system are concerned, and many of us believe that there really are some new and generative ideas to help students learn basic intellectual skills and content.

Our current realities in the field of education reflect differing conceptions of how schooling ought to change. It is difficult to generalize regarding school quality across decades because of several factors; high schools, for instance, were more selective in 1900, when only 7 percent of American youths graduated from them. Today we encourage as many students as possible to graduate. The social purposes of schooling have been broadened; now we want all youths to complete some form of higher education.

We have to consider the social and ideological differences among those representing opposing school reform agendas for change. The differences over how and in what directions change is to occur in our educational systems rest on which educational values are to prevail. These values form the bases for differing conceptions of the purposes of schooling. Thus the differing agendas for change in American education have to be positioned within the context of the different ideological value systems that underpin each alternative agenda for change.

There are several currently contending (and frequently conceptually conflicting) strategies for restructuring life in schools as well as options open to parents in choosing the schools that they want their children to attend. On the one hand, we have to find ways to empower students and teachers to improve the quality of academic life in classrooms. On the other hand, there appear to be powerful forces contending over whether control of educational services should be even more centralized or more decentralized (site-based). Those who favor greater parental and teacher control of schools support greater decentralized site management and community control conceptions of school governance. Yet the ratio of teachers to nonteaching personnel (administrators, counselors, school psychologists, and others) continues to decline as public school system bureaucracies become more and more "top heavy."

In this unit, we consider the efforts to reconceive, redefine, and reconstruct existing patterns of curriculum and instruction at the elementary and secondary levels of schooling and compare them with the efforts to reconceive existing conflicting patterns of teacher education. A broad spectrum of dialogue is developing in North America, the British Commonwealth, Russia, Central Eurasia, and other areas of the world about the redirecting of learning opportunities for all citizens.

Prospective teachers here are being encouraged to question their own individual educational experiences as part of this process. We must acknowledge that our values affect our ideas about curriculum content and the purpose of educating others. This is perceived as vitally important in the developing dialogue over liberating all students' capacities to function as independent inquirers. The dramatic economic and demographic changes in our society necessitate a fundamental reconceptualization of how schools ought to respond to the many social contexts in which they are located. This effort to reassess and reconceive the education of persons is a vital part of broader reform efforts in society as well as a dynamic dialectic in its own right. How can schools, for instance, better reflect the varied communities of interest that they serve? What must they do to become better perceived as just and equitable places in which all young people can seek to achieve learning and self-fulfillment?

Each of the essays in this unit relates to the tension involved in reconceiving how educational development should proceed in response to all the dramatic social and economic changes in society.

Tradeoffs, Societal Values, and School Reform

Ms. Rotberg looks at a constant of education reform: for every new approach, tradeoffs must be made. She reports on the choices that educators in various countries, often dealing with similar issues, have made in their efforts to bring about school improvement.

Iris C. Rotberg

THE POLITICAL rhetoric about school reform makes it sound easy. Apparently, whatever the proposed reform—testing, reduced class size, vouchers—there are no tradeoffs or "costs" to consider. Or the tradeoffs are judged to be so insignificant that they do not merit discussion. There is also an unspoken premise that countries with effective education systems (i.e., high test scores) have gotten it right without ever having had to make difficult choices or cope with negative consequences. The rest of us could do the same if we would only adopt some other country's system. Finally, the societal context of school reform is often ignored, despite the fact that a country's priorities, values, and economic status ultimately play a major role in determining whether reforms can be implemented as planned.

Balancing Change and Tradition in Global Education Reform, a book I recently edited on current education reforms in 16 countries, analyzes the trends in school reform and the fact that all countries' reforms require policy makers to choose among conflicting goals.[1] In every country, there are examples of tradeoffs, painful costs, and ironies. There are several benefits of knowing those tradeoffs.

- First, after identifying tradeoffs, policy makers may reconsider, or temper, the reform as not worth the negative consequences.

- Second, even if the reform is judged worthwhile, those negative consequences may be ameliorated by paying attention in advance to those disadvantaged by the change.
- Third, the very process of evaluating the reform and its probable consequences will help strengthen the implementation of the reform, eve n if some of the negative consequences remain.
- Fourth, we will be less likely to spin our wheels trying to implement a reform that is fundamentally at odds with deeply held value systems, financial capacity, or political structures.
- Finally, understanding the broader implications of education policies will help us make more realistic assessments of both the reforms proposed in the U.S. and the educational practices in other countries.

In this article, I focus on several key trends in global education reform: 1) strengthening educational equity, 2) reducing central control of education, 3) holding teachers accountable for student performance, 4) increasing the flexibility of learning environments, and 5) increasing access to education. I examine the tradeoffs countries faced as they attempted to implement each of these reforms, and I conclude with a discussion of the societal factors that both facilitate and constrain reform.

TRENDS AND TRADEOFFS

Strengthening educational equity. The most dramatic increases in educational equity in recent years have occurred in South Africa, where political and ideological changes in the past decade have led to a redistribution of educational resources that is among the most significant ever attempted. Under apartheid, per-pupil expenditures for whites were 10 times greater than those for blacks, who attended schools designed to perpetuate apartheid by providing students with only a minimal education and by employing a curriculum that advocated separatist policies. That system was considered intolerable; as a result, the education system has been transformed into one that distributes resources according to student enrollment rather than according to race and also provides additional funding to schools in high-poverty areas. But the redistribution, in turn, required the withdrawal of funds from affluent communities and schools—an action that many feared would cause middle-class families (now increasingly both black and white) to leave the public school system.

South Africa, therefore, was faced with the difficult choice between permitting families to make private contributions to their public schools—thereby enabling those schools to have facilities and services not available in less affluent neighborhoods—

> Systems that offer an elite academic track provide an incentive for affluent parents to keep their children in public school, but often at a "cost" to children in the lower tracks.

and taking the risk that large numbers of middle-class families would move to private schools if they were not permitted to increase the resources in their public schools. The public schools would then lose both the participation of these families and their advocacy for increased spending on public education. The decision, therefore, to permit affluent families to make private contributions to public schools was based on the expectation that the loss of the middle-class constituency from the public school system would inevitably have adverse consequences for the education of all children.

The type of decision that South Africa faced is repeated in different guises in countries throughout the world. The choice is often painful because it requires tradeoffs between deeply held value systems.

In the United States, for example, affluent parents in some communities wish to make substantial private contributions to their children's public schools in order to provide services or equipment that would not be available otherwise. As in South Africa, school superintendents are faced with a difficult choice between maintaining an equitable distribution of resources across schools and encouraging middle-class families to remain in the public school system by permitting them to contribute extra resources to their schools.

Both school choice plans and student-tracking plans raise similar issues. School systems that offer an elite academic track, for example, provide an incentive for affluent parents to keep their children in the public school system, but often at a "cost" to children in the lower tracks.

There are variations on this theme. Over the past generation, England has moved to a nonselective school system in place of its earlier reliance on selective "grammar schools," which served high-achieving children from both middle- and working-class families and we re successful in sending their students to prestigious universities. These selective schools, however, were abolished in an attempt to make the education system less stratified. But the expectation was not fulfilled, as middle-class families left the nonselective state schools

and chose private schools. As a result, the proportion of children from state schools attending prestigious universities has declined since the 1970s. The point is that well-intentioned "solutions" to perceived problems sometimes provide incentives (in this case, the incentive for increased private school attendance) that undermine the reform's initial purpose.

The tradeoffs implicit in the South African and English examples are repeated in other countries. Cities in the U.S., as in England, have education systems that are polarized, with many middle- and upper-class students from all racial and ethnic groups attending private schools, charter schools, schools that are part of voucher programs, or schools that select by achievement levels or special interests. Moreover, even students attending comprehensive schools are often tracked into different courses or programs within the school, depending on their level of achievement. Some of these approaches have been developed in order to prevent an exodus to private schools. But whatever the reason they were adopted, these approaches do create the potential for relegating the children "left behind" to mediocre schools and tracks and for increasing social stratification.

Germany also provides an interesting example. A country in which most students attend public schools, Germany tracks children into three separate types of schools beginning in grade 5: an academic track (*Gymnasium*), which is the major route to the university; a middle track (*Realschule*), which provides a less intensive education and generally leads to technical or vocational training and sometimes to the university; and a third track (*Hauptschule*) for the lowest- achieving students, which is intended to lead to vocational training but has high dropout rates, with many of its students unable to find either vocational training or employment.

Because socioeconomic status (SES) is highly correlated with academic achievement, middle- and upper- class students are disproportionately re p resented in the academic track, with the *Hauptschule* enrolling the highest proportion of children of migrant workers. The tracking system, therefore, magnifies the effects of SES and is consistent with the finding that the performance of German students correlates more strongly with SES than the performance of students in most other countries.[2]

Reducing central control. There has been a trend toward decentralization in many countries, often for quite different reasons.

France and Sweden, for example, have attempted to reduce central control in order to respond more effectively to increased student diversity; Israel, because of disappointment in the failure of its well-intentioned central plans to close the achievement gap between children of high and low SES; Turkey, because of general disillusionment about cumbersome bureaucracies. The U.S. has responded to a concern about the quality of public schools by encouraging decentralization through school choice, even as it tightens central control through testing requirements–which apply only to public schools.

Countries also reduce central control in the aftermath of political or economic upheaval, often at a time when national resources are scarce. Perhaps the most dramatic examples are Russia and China, which in less than a generation have decentralized their previously highly uniform education systems. As a result, both countries now have increasing inequalities in educational resources, a consequence of the economic disparities within each country.

In Russia, as certain regions or sectors of the society have become more affluent, they have invested in schools that specialize or innovate. Schools in less affluent communities face serious shortages of resources and have fallen further behind. The poorer communities are particularly vulnerable to inadequate and unpredictable funding from all levels of government as the issue of "who pays for what" and "who owes what to whom" remains unsettled.[3] The lowest-income communities and children are inevitably at the greatest disadvantage in the competition for scarce funds.

In China, although decentralization has "opened up" the school system to innovative educational practices, it has led at the same time to large funding inequalities from region to region. As economic differences within the country have grown, so too have gaps in innovation and in education funding, which now comes largely from local areas, many of which are extremely poor. Indeed, the central government has established different educational goals for each of the three economic development zones, with the richer economic zones expected to achieve higher educational levels than the poorer ones.[4] As in Russia, equality of educational resources has given way to the increasing economic disparities in the broader society.

Holding teachers accountable for student performance. Some countries have placed increased emphasis on teacher accountability. The most visible method is through student testing requirements; the test scores, in turn, are used as indicators of school quality. Test-based accountability has become central to federal education policy in the U.S. as a result of the No Child Left Behind Act. A few other countries (e.g., England, Australia, and New Zealand) have also placed greater emphasis on testing, sometimes in combination with publicly disseminated school rankings and increased reporting requirements, although most countries do not administer tests for the purpose of evaluating teacher performance.

The requirements for test-based accountability involve difficult tradeoffs, sometimes between quite different educational values and objectives. Those who support the requirements argue that they increase the emphasis on basic skills instruction by providing the structure and uniformity needed to raise achievement, particularly for inexperienced teachers and low-achieving students. Those opposed argue that the testing requirements narrow the curriculum and make schools a less attractive place for teachers to work, thereby discouraging qualified educators from remaining in the profession or from choosing to teach in low-income communities. There is also a concern that using student test scores to judge school quality will lead to unfair evaluations because of the methodological problems in making that link.

Increasing the flexibility of learning environments. Many countries are attempting to move from a strict reliance on didactic teaching and rote learning to the cultivation of learning environments that encourage student participation, problem solving, and critical analysis. Turkey, for example, has attempted to modernize its curricula and teaching methods, but it has found that implementation is progressing slowly, both because of a huge bureaucracy that is unresponsive to change and because of resistance from those teachers, parents, and students who believe that the reform efforts are inconsistent with their values and beliefs.

> Success in university entrance examinations has traditionally been the main route out of poverty in China.

In Singapore, reform is designed to link the goals of education with the perceived needs of the global economy by giving stu-

dents the broad set of educational experiences that will allow the country to be competitive in that economy. Yet the reform "takes place in a society that exerts a level of political and social control unique among wealthy nations. That control might be inconsistent with an education environment that encourages critical thinking and flexibility."[5]

In Japan, the purpose of increased flexibility is described as "cultivating Japanese people with 'rich humanity' and 'rich creativity' by letting individual abilities grow.'"[6] The difficulty is that encouraging children's individuality conflicts with the country's strong desire to maintain its traditional cultural and community values, which stress cooperation and consensus—a tradeoff that some feel will have a negative impact on the society as a whole.

The attempt to revise curricula and teaching methods is also limited because parents, students, and teachers do not accept changes that are perceived to be inconsistent with high test scores, particularly when the scores determine students' admission to universities. China, for example, which recently has been successful in implementing innovative education programs, has also revised its university entrance examinations to support changes in classroom practice that encourage students to integrate knowledge from diverse fields, rather than simply to memorize facts. A recent university entrance examination included a question on the increase of private cars in China; the response required students to draw on knowledge of statistics, comparative analysis, supply and production, urban traffic, pollution, and social studies.

Although a test like the new university entrance exam has clear substantive advantages over a test that relies primarily on rote memorization, many families and teachers fear serious adverse consequences in terms of social mobility. Success in university entrance examinations has traditionally been the main route out of poverty in China. High scores seem more attainable if they depend primarily on hard work and memorization. It is more difficult to prepare for test questions that require analysis—particularly when the new teaching approaches have not yet reached the majority of Chinese schools. And that fact, in turn, increases the gap between the affluent and the poor areas of the country.

As many countries throughout the world struggle to make a transition from

rote learning to school environments that emphasize a broader set of skills, the United States, which has a reputation for flexible teaching practices, appears to be moving in the opposite direction. There is an increasing emphasis on testing, more pressure on schools to raise scores, and strong incentives to "teach to the test."

Increasing access to education. Countries throughout the world have increased their people's access to education. China, for example, has made major gains in the expansion of basic education and has also increased enrollment in lower secondary education. In Turkey, the extension of compulsory education from five to eight years has increased school attendance and reduced the gap in school enrollment between boys and girls, which has been a particularly serious problem in rural areas. In South Africa, the average grade-level achievement has increased from approximately seven grades to 10 grades in less than a generation.

Most countries have also made substantial progress in expanding access to upper secondary schools and universities. France, for example, has added a vocational *baccalauréat* (certificate of secondary school graduation) in order to increase the number of students eligible to attend universities. England, which formerly provided advanced academic education to only a small proportion of its young people, has now opened up its education system. The U.S., with relatively high attendance rates in higher education, has made major gains over the past 30 years in increasing the diversity of the student body.

Expansion, too, has involved tradeoffs. Some policy analysts have argued that the continued expansion of higher education in industrialized countries has neither reduced social inequities nor increased economic growth, but has instead created new problems.[7] Access to higher education has not always kept pace with rising expectations; the quality of education sometimes suffers because funding limitations make it difficult to support the faculty and infrastructure needed to serve the increased numbers of students; students from low-SES backgrounds continue to have very limited access to certain "elite" universities; and some countries' economies are unable to provide adequate jobs for university graduates. Despite these problems, however, increased access has provided opportunities for many students who would not otherwise have had them.

THE SOCIETAL CONTEXT

Societal constraints. The potential effectiveness of any education reform is seriously limited by poverty and by a broad range of other societal problems, such as poor health and inadequate resources for education—all factors that are outside the control of schools. No country has found that educational practices alone have solved the broader problems of society or eliminated the gap in educational performance between children of high- and low-SES families, although certain practices may contribute to reducing or magnifying that gap. Although this point seems obvious, it has apparently not led to realistic expectations about what an education system can and cannot accomplish. And it certainly hasn't reduced the level of disillusionment, blame, and rhetoric that occurs when unrealistic expectations are not met.

The incidence of poverty varies widely among the countries I've alluded to here. In a few of them, a large proportion of children live in poverty. As shown by a wide array of evidence, poverty is a major predictor of low educational achievement, and differences in poverty levels account for a significant portion of the variance in achievement both within and between countries.[8] To a greater or lesser degree, all countries face an achievement gap based on SES, and many school reforms have been initiated in an attempt to reduce that gap.

Nonetheless, poverty's central role is often overlooked in interpretations of test-score rankings, which are assumed to indicate the "quality" of education. Whether nations or schools are compared, however, the test scores are strongly influenced by the SES of the children taking the test and are not simply a reflection of the impact of educational practices. The rhetoric surrounding test-score rankings ignores this reality and, in doing so, leads to the adoption of "quick fixes" that do nothing to address basic societal problems.

In addition to poverty, other societal problems constrain education reform. South Africa and Russia, for example, face serious health crises. In South Africa, the education system faces enormous human and financial problems arising from the high rates of HIV/AIDS among students, parents, and teachers. In Russia, chronic illness among children is a major contributor to low academic achievement; it is estimated that in some parts of the country as many as one-third to one-half of children in primary schools have "incapacitating" physical or mental conditions.[9]

The impact of poverty and poor health on achievement is magnified by inadequate educational resources. In some cases, resources are scarce because of low GDP or even temporary economic recessions; in others, the problem arises from the unequal distribution of resources. More over, these funding shortfalls are closely related to shortages of qualified teachers, particularly in low-income communities.

But the problems show up in different ways. In the United States, for example, schools in high-poverty communities often have to resort to "out-of-field" teaching because of teacher shortages that result, in part, from high attrition rates. In Russia, young people are discouraged from entering the teaching profession because of extremely low salaries, payment of which is sometimes delayed as much as nine months to a year, as well as difficult working conditions in some regions—poor facilities, inadequate textbooks, and uncertainties about the availability of even basic amenities such as heat and electricity. France, which has a system of assigning teachers throughout the country, has been only partially successful in ensuring that the poorer communities have access to experienced teachers. The reason is that the assignment system conflicts with the seniority system, which permits the more experienced teachers to have choice with regard to where they teach. Not surprisingly, they choose the more affluent communities, like Paris or the Riviera.

> All countries face an achievement gap based on SES, and many school reforms have been initiated in an attempt to reduce that gap.

Each of these factors—poverty, societal problems, and inadequate resources—is a major constraint on education reform. Their effect in combination can be overwhelming. Some countries—China, Russia, South Africa, and Turkey, for example—have attempted to initiate complex school reforms while meeting the challenges arising from extensive child poverty and scarce resources for education. Often these challenges are exacerbated by large inequalities in resource distribution and extensive, competing societal needs.

Even in countries with a high GDP that invest heavily in education, there are large differences in the distribution of educational resources, in the income and wealth differential between rich and poor families, and in poverty rates. In comparison with many other industrialized countries, the U.S. has a high rate of "relative poverty"—defined as a low income compared with the country's average.[10] And the U.S. also has a highly unequal distribution of resources because most education funding comes from states and localities.[11] These gaps in family income and educational resources are exacerbated by the lack of social support systems that are often found in other industrialized countries, but they are mitigated by a wide range of options for higher education, along with second and third chances for students, which provide increased opportunities for low-income and minority students. The basic problem remains, however: the combined effects of poverty and inadequate resources in many of the schools serving low-income communities have led to a substantial gap in educational achievement.

Sweden provides a useful contrast with the United States because it has a much flatter distribution of income, wealth, and educational resources, along with a significant social support system. Sweden also has a smaller achievement gap between affluent students and poor students.[12] Although causation cannot be established with certainty, Sweden's public policies appear to have made a difference. However, they have not eliminated the gap: SES remains the strongest predictor of academic achievement in Sweden.

Values and political structure. In every country, traditional values and political structures play a major role in determining whether education reforms can be implemented successfully. In some cases, these traditions serve as facilitators; in others, they limit or prevent the implementation of reform initiatives.

Some countries have been able to make rapid change, as demonstrated most vividly in South Africa, when dramatic transformations in political leadership and values have been supported by legislation and regulation:

> The system is attempting a set of reforms that is much larger in scope than what was attempted in, say, the desegregation of school systems in the United States, in that it is starting from a much greater level of inequality, where the poor and disadvantaged are the majority rather than the minority, where there is a simultaneous modernization and quality agenda at the same time as an equity and justice agenda,

and while attempting to prevent, for the country as a whole, the sort of white-flight privatization of education common in American cities.[13]

Thus a nation that is still struggling with widespread poverty is also attempting to reform its education system to redress the past injustices suffered by a large majority of the population. At the same time, it must maintain the participation and support of all South Africans.

Major changes in educational practices have also occurred in China within an exceptionally short period. The rapid adoption of innovative teaching and examination practices has been attributed to the fact that the Chinese reforms have built on elements of traditional culture, among them the belief of Chinese teachers that there is a "best method"; the Chinese tradition of launching mass movements; and the high level of societal organization, which enables classroom changes to be supported by teacher training and development, curriculum changes, and far-reaching and consistent school inspections. Although the changes have not always gone smoothly, China appears to have been unusually successful in implementing change by building on traditional culture—or "holding new wine with the old bottle."[14]

England, too, has been able to make rapid change, although the reasons are quite different from those in China. England's highly centralized government is based on a system in which seats in Parliament go to the candidates who receive the most votes in their constituencies, even if those votes might represent only a minority of the total. Thus a single party tends to receive large majorities in Parliament, party members often vote as a bloc, and governments can quickly mandate radical changes based on the ideological principles of the party in power. In short, "a British government has been able to pass whatever laws it likes, provided the members of its own party will accept them."[15]

England's political structure is in sharp contrast to that of the United States, where change is much slower as a result of the "checks and balances" intrinsic to the three branches of the federal government and the fact that education is primarily a state and local responsibility. Moreover, unlike China, the U.S. does not easily translate a reform idea into practice because the system is not designed to encourage alignment between the reform and the support systems required to implement it. Indeed, the multiplicity of attempted reforms in the United States often results in

reforms that conflict with one another. The outcome is that large-scale implementation of a new educational practice has proved to be a slow process, despite the fact that innovation is considered basic to the American system. Innovation in the U.S., more often than not, is local, at least initially. It is not easy to transfer a "best practice" across the country in the short term, although some reforms have been implemented nationally over a period of many years.

Moreover, even when the federal government attempts to centralize control (e.g., by increasing testing requirements as has recently been done), the requirements are implemented in very different ways across the country. The curricula and tests differ, the definitions of a passing score differ, and the decisions about which students do and do not take the test differ. One commentator predicted the eventual outcome of No Child Left Behind this way:

> As the reforms of the past two decades pile up on the schools, as pressure from civil rights groups is brought to bear on what they regard as tests and standards that discriminate against minority children, as education funding is rolled back, and as terrorism, recession, oil shortages, and other issues overwhelm education in the nation's political debates and in the public mind, fatigue is likely to combine with backlash to produce, if not another swing of the pendulum, a rollback in the demands and standards.… None of this is likely to involve much conscious, systematic reexamination of the overall reform policies of the past generation, but it will produce a gradual attrition toward a more pragmatic, less utopian mean. That, too, has always been the American way.[16]

The challenge of balancing education reform with long-standing traditions, exemplified in South Africa, China, England, and the United States, is faced by all countries that seek to change existing policies and practices.

Some countries that have experienced major political and ideological transitions continue their former education policies. Others struggle to reform their education systems but are constrained by conflicting values. Chile made a transition from an authoritarian to a democratic government but maintained the education policies—decentralization, vouchers, and testing—begun under the military regime. After initial attempts to reverse these policies with the establishment of democratic gov-

ernment in 1990, the teachers now generally accept them, perhaps in part because of the generous benefits they have received in recent years under a policy of *reivindicación* (reclaiming the right to be repaid) for human rights abuses they suffered during the military regime.

After reunification, Germany faced a conflict between two education systems that had grown out of different ideologies. The East German system, based on Communism, was centrally controlled, and students attended comprehensive schools. West Germany, on the other hand, was a pluralistic society with a decentralized education system, and schools were stratified by student achievement levels. The conflict between the two traditions was resolved by transferring the West German system to schools in the east. Russia, on the other hand, still copes with a conflict, rooted in practices from the Soviet era, between a highly intellectual academic tradition and a tradition that emphasizes rote learning and narrow vocational training. That conflict continues to constrain attempts to implement Russia's centers of academic excellence and innovation on a large scale.

Even countries that have not experienced major political and ideological change find that proposed reform initiatives sometimes conflict with the public's values and expectations. France currently attempts to balance the public's strong support for the "national character" of education with attempts to move toward decentralization in a system that for centuries has concentrated power in Paris. The decentralization process proceeds slowly: "It exists on paper; all the rules and regulations to implement it have been published. Yet in practice less has happened than was aimed for."[17] In Canada, the province of Quebec gives priority to maintaining the French language and culture—a position that, in practice, often conflicts with attempts to encourage large-scale immigration and to create a school environment that supports a multicultural student body.

Each of the countries I have discussed here has experienced similar types of tradeoffs. Although in most cases change is occurring, the translation of a reform proposal from theory into practice typically proceeds at a slower pace than was initially envisioned. But despite constraints, uncertainty about the efficacy of some reforms, and unintended consequences, there are positive developments. Countries are increasingly focusing on issues of equity, access, and the necessity of providing a broad-based education for diverse populations. Educators know that achievement measures inevitably reflect factors that are far more powerful than any education reforms and that they will be held accountable for results over which they have only uncertain influence. They know too that schools, directly or indirectly, will be held accountable for societal and economic problems that are outside their control. Despite these challenges, however, educators throughout the world initiate reforms, consider tradeoffs, and make difficult choices—all in an effort to ensure equity, access, and a decent education for children.

Notes

1. Iris C. Rotberg, ed., *Balancing Change and Tradition in Global Education Reform* (Lanham, Md.: ScarecrowEducation, 2004).

2. *Learning for Tomorrow's World—First Results From PISA 2003* (Paris: Organisation for Economic Co-operation and Development, 2004).

3. Mary Canning and Stephen T. Kerr, "Russia: Struggling with the Aftermath," in Rotberg, p. 46.

4. Kai-ming Cheng, "China: Turning the Bad Master into a Good Servant," in Rotberg, pp. 3–19.

5. Batia P. Horsky and Phyllis Ghim-Lian Chew, "Singapore: Schools in the Service of Society," in Rotberg, p. 258.

6. Ryo Watanabe, "Japan: Encouraging Individualism, Maintaining Community Values," in Rotberg, p. 237.

7. See, for example, Alison Wolf, *Does Education Matter? Myths About Education and Economic Growth* (London: Penguin Books, 2003).

8. David W. Grissmer et al., *Student Achievement and the Changing American Family* (Washington, D.C.: RAND Institute on Education and Training, 1994).

9. Canning and Kerr, p. 37.

10. McKinley L. Blackburn, *Comparing Poverty: The United States and Other Industrial Nations* (Washington, D.C.: AEI Studies on Understanding Economic Inequality, American Enterprise Institute, 1997).

11. Stephen M. Barro, "How Countries Pay for Schools: An International Comparison of Systems for Financing Primary and Secondary Education," paper prepared for the Finance Center of the Consortium for Policy Research in Education, Washington, D.C., 1996.

12. *Learning for Tomorrow's World.*

13. Luis Crouch, "South Africa: Overcoming Past Injustice," in Rotberg, p. 54.

14. Cheng, pp. 15–16.

15. Alison Wolf, "England: New Governments, New Policies," in Rotberg, p. 319.

16. Peter Schrag, "United States: America's Orgy of Reform," in Rotberg, p. 380.

17. Gérard Bonnet, "France: Diverse Populations, Centralized Administration," in Rotberg, p. 132.

IRIS C. ROTBERG *is Research Professor of Education Policy in the Department of Educational Leadership, Graduate School of Education and Human Development, George Washington University, Washington, D.C. This article is adapted from her concluding chapter in* Balancing Change and Tradition in Global Education Reform *(Scarecrow Education, 2004), for which she served as editor.*

Teaching Against Idiocy

Contemplating the root of the word "idiocy" leads Mr. Parker to explore the challenge that democratic societies face of developing public-minded citizens. The schools, he argues, are the most likely institutions to succeed in that task.

WALTER C. PARKER

IDIOCY IS the scourge of our time and place. Idiocy was a problem for the ancient Greeks, too, for they coined the term. "Idiocy" in its original sense is not what it means to us today—stupid or mentally deficient. The recent meaning is deservedly and entirely out of usage by educators, but the original meaning needs to be revived as a conceptual tool for clarifying a pivotal social problem and for understanding the central goal of education.

Idiocy shares with idiom and idiosyncratic the root *idios*, which means private, separate, self-centered—selfish. "Idiotic" was in the Greek context a term of reproach. When a person's behavior became idiotic—concerned myopically with private things and unmindful of common things—then the person was believed to be like a rudderless ship, without consequence save for the danger it posed to others. This meaning of idiocy achieves its force when contrasted with *politēs* (citizen) or public. Here we have a powerful opposition: the private individual versus the public citizen.

Schools in societies that are trying in various ways to be democracies, such as the United States, Mexico, and Canada, are obliged to develop public citizens. I argue here that schools are well positioned for the task, and I suggest how they can improve their efforts and achieve greater success.

DODGING PUBERTY

An idiot is one whose self-centeredness undermines his or her citizen identity, causing it to wither or never to take root in the first place. Private gain is the goal, and the community had better not get in the way. An idiot is suicidal in a certain way, definitely self-defeating, for the idiot does not know that privacy and individual autonomy are entirely dependent on the community. As Aristotle wrote, "Individuals are so many parts all equally depending on the whole which alone can bring self-sufficiency."[1] Idiots do not take

part in public life; they do not *have* a public life. In this sense, idiots are immature in the most fundamental way. Their lives are out of balance, disoriented, untethered, and unrealized. Tragically, idiots have not yet met the challenge of "puberty," which is the transition to public life.

The former mayor of Missoula, Montana, Daniel Kemmis, writes of the idiocy/citizenship opposition, though he uses a different term, in his delightful meditation on democratic politics, *The Good City and the Good Life*:

> People who customarily refer to themselves as *taxpayers* are not even remotely related to democratic citizens. Yet this is precisely the word that now regularly holds the place which in a true democracy would be occupied by "citizens." Taxpayers bear a dual relationship to government, neither half of which has anything at all to do with democracy. Tax payers pay tribute to the government, and they receive services from it. So does every subject of a totalitarian regime. What taxpayers do not do, and what people who call themselves taxpayers have long since stopped even imagining themselves doing, is *governing*. In a democracy, by the very meaning of the word, the people govern.[2]

Alexis de Tocqueville, writing 150 years before Mayor Kemmis, also described idiocy. All democratic peoples face a "dangerous passage" in their history, he wrote, when they "are carried away and lose all self-restraint at the sight of the new possessions they are about to obtain."[3] De Tocqueville's principal concern was that getting "carried away" causes citizens to lose the very freedom they are wanting so much to enjoy. "These people think they are following the principle of self-interest," he continues, "but the idea they entertain of that principle is a very crude one; and the more they look after what they call their own business, they neglect their chief business, which is to remain their own masters."

Just how do people remain their own masters? By maintaining the kind of community that secures their liberty. De Tocqueville's singular contribution to our understanding of idiocy and citizenship is the notion that *idiots are idiotic precisely because they are indifferent to the conditions and contexts of their own freedom.* They fail to grasp the interdependence of liberty and community, privacy and puberty.

Similarly, Jane Addams argued in 1909 that, if a woman was planning to "keep on with her old business of caring for her house and rearing her children," then it was necessary that she expand her consciousness to include "public affairs lying quite outside her immediate household." The individualistic consciousness was "no longer effective":

> Women who live in the country sweep their own dooryards and may either feed the refuse of the table to a flock of chickens or allow it innocently to decay in the open air and sunshine. In a crowded city quarter, however, if the street is not cleaned by the city authorities, no amount of private sweeping will keep the tenement free from grime; if the garbage is not properly collected and destroyed a tenement house mother may see her children sicken and die of diseases from which she alone is powerless to shield them, although her tenderness and devotion are unbounded.[4]

Addams concluded that for women to tend only to their "own" households was "idiotic," for to do only that would prevent women, ironically, from doing just that at all. One cannot maintain the familial nest without maintaining the public, shared space in which the familial nest is itself nested. "As society grows more complicated," she continued, "it is necessary that woman shall extend her sense of responsibility to many things outside of her own home if she would continue to preserve the home in its entirety."

Leaving aside individuals, families can be idiotic, too. The paradigm case is the Mafia—a family that looks inward intensely and solely. A thick moral code glues the insiders together, but in dealing with outsiders who are beyond the galaxy of one's obligations and duties, anything goes. There is no organized cooperation across families to tackle shared problems (health, education, welfare), no shared games, not even communication save the occasional "treaty." There are no bridging associations. Edward Banfield called this *amoral familism* and articulated its ethos as "maximize the material, short-run advantage of the nuclear family; assume that all others will do likewise."[5]

Amoral familism is certainly not restricted to the Mafia. Social scientists who examine popular culture find no shortage of it today. Perhaps the best contemporary example in the U.S., because it is both so mundane and so pervasive, is the SUV craze. Here, the suburban family provides for its own safety and self-esteem during such mobile tasks as commuting to work and running household errands, but it does so at others' expense. When criticized for putting other drivers and passengers at risk, for widening the ozone hole, and

for squandering nonrenewable resources, SUV drivers often justify their behavior by speaking of their "rights" or the advantage of "sitting up higher than others." But they focus especially on "family safety."[6] It is my right to do whatever I choose, goes the argument, with the added and supposedly selfless rationalization of protecting "my" family from dangers real and imagined. To draw the line of obligation so close to the nuclear family is idiotic because it undermines, as Addams and De Tocqueville argued, that family's *own* safety along with everyone else's.

We could continue this survey of idiocy from its individual and familial forms to its large-scale enactments in ethnocentrism, racism, or the nationalistic variety, wherein a nation secures its own needs and wants in such a way that the world environment—every human's nest—is fouled, whether by conquest or by dumping poisons into the air and water. But let me instead conclude this section with a puzzle: How did idiocy grow from an exception in the Greek *polis* to a commonplace in contemporary, economically developed societies? Numerous social scientists have asked just this question. Karl Marx saw idiocy ("alienation," he called it) as the inevitable by-product of capitalism, wherein accumulating profit becomes an end in itself and nearly everything—from labor to love—is commodified toward that end. Robert Bellah and his colleagues located idiocy in a deeply pervasive culture of rugged individualism. John Kenneth Galbraith focused on the mass affluence of contemporary North American society, in which, for example, beef cattle are consumed at such a rate as to flood the environment with their waste, while farmland is misdirected to their feed. As Galbraith wrote, "Few people at the beginning of the nineteenth century needed an adman to tell them what they wanted."[7]

How did idiocy grow from an exception in the Greek polis to a commonplace in contemporary, economically developed societies?

SCHOOLS AND IDIOCY

Capitalism, individualism, and affluence are a powerful brew. But what about the education sector of society? Do schools marshal their human and material resources to produce idiots or citizens? Does the school curriculum cultivate private vices or public virtues? Can schools tame the rugged individualism and amoral familism that undermine puberty and foul the common nest?

Actually, schools already educate for citizenship to some extent, and therein lies our hope. By identifying how schools accomplish at least some of this work now, educators can direct and fine-tune the effort. The wheel doesn't need to be reinvented; it is at hand and only needs to be rolled more intentionally, explicitly, and directly toward citizenship. There are three assumptions that propel this work and three keys to its success.

The first assumption is that democracy (rule by the people) is morally superior to autocracy (rule by one person), theocracy (rule by clerics), aristocracy (rule by a permanent upper class), plutocracy (rule by the rich), and the other alternatives, mainly because it better secures liberty, justice, and equality than the others do. Among actually attainable ways of living together and making decisions about common problems and projects, democracy (that is, a republic, a constitutional democracy) is, as Winston Churchill said, the worst form of government except for all the others.[8] Democracy is better than the alternatives because it aspires to and, to varying degrees, is held accountable for securing civil liberties, equality before the law, limited government, competitive elections, and solidarity around a common project (a civic *unum*) that exists alongside individual and cultural manyness (*pluribus*).

That democracies fall short of achieving these aspirations is obvious, and it is the chief impetus of social movements that seek to close the gap between the actual and the ideal. Thus Martin Luther King, Jr., demanded in his 1963 March on Washington address not an alternative to democracy but its fulfillment:

We have come to our nation's capital to cash a check. When the architects of our republic wrote the magnificent words of the Constitution and the Declaration of Independence, they were signing a promissory note to which every American was to fall heir.... We have come to cash this check, a check that will give us upon demand the riches of freedom and the security of justice.[9]

The purpose of the civil rights movement was not to alter the American Dream but to realize it. When a democracy excludes its own members for whatever reason (slavery, patriarchy, Jim Crow, etc.), it is "actively and purposefully false to its own vaunted principles," wrote Judith Shklar.[10] Here is democracy's built-in progressive impulse: to live up to itself.

The second assumption required if schools are to educate for citizenship is that there can be no democracy without democrats. Democratic ways of living together, with the people's differences intact and recognized, are not given by nature; they are created. And much of the creative work must be undertaken by engaged citizens who share some understanding of what it is they are trying to build together. Often, it is the unjustly treated members of a community who are democracy's vanguard, pushing it toward its principles. "We know through painful experience that freedom is never voluntarily given by the oppressor; it must be demanded by the oppressed," King wrote in the "Letter from Birmingham Jail."[11] The Framers of the U.S. Constitution may have been the birth parents of democracy, American style, but those who were excluded, then and now, became the adoptive, nurturing parents.

The third assumption is that engaged citizens do not materialize out of thin air. They do not naturally grasp such knotty principles as tolerance, impartial justice, the separation of church and state, the need for limits on majority power, or the difference between liberty and license. They are not born already capable of deliberating about public policy issues with other citizens whose beliefs and cultures they may abhor. These things are not, as the historical record makes all too clear, hard-wired into our genes. (Just ask any school principal!) Rather, they are social, moral, and intellectual achievements, and they are hard won. This third assumption makes clear the enormous importance of educating children for democracy.

On the foundation of these three assumptions, taken together, educators are justified in shaping curriculum and instruction toward the development of democratic citizens. In poll after poll, the American public makes clear its expectation that schools do precisely this.[12]

SCHOOLS ARE PUBLIC PLACES

As it turns out, schools are ideal sites for democratic citizenship education. The main reason is that a school is not a private place, like our homes, but a public, civic place with a congregation of diverse students. Some schools are more diverse than others, of course, but all schools are diverse to some meaningful extent. Former kindergarten teacher Vivian Gussin Paley put it plainly: "The children I teach are just emerging from life's deep wells of private perspective: babyhood and family. Then, along comes school. It is the first real exposure to the public arena."[13] Boys and girls are both there. Jews, Protestants, Catholics, Muslims, Buddhists, and atheists are there together. There are African Americans, European Americans, Mexican Americans, Asian Americans, and many more. Immigrants from the world over are there in school.

This buzzing variety does not exist at home, or in churches, temples, or mosques either. It exists in public places where diverse people are thrown together, places where people who come from numerous private worlds and social positions congregate on common ground. These are places where multiple social perspectives and personal values are brought into face-to-face contact around matters that "are relevant to the problems of living together," as John Dewey put it.[14] Such matters are mutual, collective concerns, not mine or yours, but *ours*.

Compared to home life, schools are like village squares, cities, crossroads, meeting places, community centers, marketplaces. When aimed at democratic ends and supported by the proper democratic conditions, the interaction in schools can help children enter the social consciousness of puberty and develop the habits of thinking and caring necessary for public life. They can learn the tolerance, the respect, the sense of justice, and the knack for forging public policy with others *whether one likes them or not*. If the right social and psychological conditions are present and are mobilized, students might even give birth to critical consciousness. This is the kind of thinking that enables them to cut through conventional wisdom and see a better way.

This, then, is the great democratic potential of the public places we call schools. As Dewey observed, "The notion that the essentials of elementary education are the three R's mechanically treated, is based upon ignorance of the essentials needed for realization of democratic ideals."[15] Used well, schools can nurture these "essentials," which are the very qualities needed for the hard work of living together freely but cooperatively and with justice, equality, and dignity. Schools can do this because of the collective problems and the diversity contained within them. Problems and diversity are the essential assets for cultivating democratic citizens.

THREE KEYS

But how actually to accomplish this? Three actions are key.

First, increase the variety and frequency of interaction among students who are culturally, linguistically, and racially different from one another. Classrooms sometimes do this naturally. But if the school itself is homogeneous or if the school is diverse but curriculum tracks keep groups of students apart, then this first key will be all the more difficult to turn. It is not helping that resegregation has intensified in recent years, despite an increasingly diverse society. White students today are the most segregated from all other races in their schools.[16] (On this criterion, they may be at the greatest risk of idiocy.) Still, race is not the only source of diversity among students. School leaders must capitalize on whatever diversity is present among students—be it race, religion, language, gender, or social class—and increase the variety and frequency of opportunities for interaction.

Second, orchestrate these contacts so as to foster competent public talk—deliberation about common problems. In schools, this is talk about two kinds of problems: social and academic. Social problems arise inevitably from the friction of interaction itself (Dewey's "problems of living together"). Academic problems are at the core of each subject area.

The interaction in schools can help children enter the social consciousness of puberty and develop the habits of thinking and caring necessary for public life.

Third, clarify the distinction between deliberation and blather and between open (i.e., inclusive) and closed (i.e., exclusive) deliberation. In other words, expect, teach, and model competent, inclusive deliberation.

I lay out the pedagogical details of teaching deliberation in elementary and secondary schools in *Teaching Democracy* (Teachers College Press, 2003). In it, I feature numerous successful programs already under way. Here are some highlights.

Deliberation exploits the assets afforded by schools: problems and a diverse student body. Deliberation is discussion aimed at making a decision across these differences about a problem that the participants face in common. The main action during a deliberation is weighing alternatives with others in order to decide on the best course of action. In schools, deliberation is not only a means of instruction (teaching *with*

deliberation) but also a curricular goal (teaching *for* deliberation), because it generates a particular kind of social good: a democratic community, a public culture. The norms of this culture include, first, engagement in cooperative problem solving. This is in contrast to avoiding engagement either by being idiotically consumed by private affairs or by electing others to do the deliberation and then relapsing into idiocy for the four years between elections. Other norms include listening as well as talking, perspective taking, arguing with evidence, sharing resources, and forging a decision together rather than merely advocating positions taken before the deliberation begins.

Deliberation is ideally done with persons who are more or less different from one another; for pedagogical purposes, therefore, deliberative groups—schools and classrooms—should be as diverse as possible. Teachers and administrators can expand the opportunities for interaction by increasing the number and kind of mixed student groups. These groups should be temporary, because separating students permanently, for whatever reason, undermines both individual and civic health. What the participants have in common in these mixed groups is not culture, race, or opinion but the problems they face together and must work out together in ways that strike everyone as fair.[17]

THE SOCIAL CURRICULUM

Probably the best-known example of young children deliberating their shared social problems comes from the kindergarten classroom of Vivian Gussin Paley. In a number of books, Paley has captured the look and feel of actual classroom-based deliberation, and she shows how entirely possible it is to do such work in everyday classroom settings, even with the youngest children. In *You Can't Say You Can't Play*, she tells how she facilitated a lengthy deliberation about whether to establish the classroom rule of the book's title. She engages the kindergartners in an ongoing discussion about the desirability and practicability of having such a rule. She tells them, "I just can't get the question out of my mind. Is it fair for children *in school* to keep another child out of play? After all, this classroom belongs to all of us. It is not a private place, like our homes."[18] The children find this a compelling question, and they have lots to say. Paley brings them to the discussion circle again and again to weigh the alternatives. "Will the rule work? Is it fair?" she asks. Memories and opinions flow. "If you cry, people should let you in," Ben says. "But then what's the whole point of playing?" Lisa complains.

Paley sometimes interviews older children to ascertain their views and brings them back to her kindergartners. Trading classes with a second-grade teacher, Paley tells those children: "I've come to ask your opinions about a new rule we're considering in the kindergarten.... We call it, 'You can't say you can't play.'" These older children know the issue well. Vivid accounts of rejection are shared. Some children believe the rule is fair but just won't work: "It would be impossible to have any fun," offers one boy. In a fourth-grade class, students conclude that it is "too late" to give them such a rule. "If you want a rule like that to work, start at a very early age," declares one 9-year-old.[19]

Paley takes these views back to the discussion circle in her own classroom. Her children are enthralled as she shares the older children's views. The deliberation is enlarged; the alternatives become more complex. In the Socratic spirit, she gently encourages them to support their views with reasons, to listen carefully, and to respond to the reasoning of other children, both classmates and older children.

High school deliberative projects exist, too. Perhaps the most widely documented are the Just Community schools conducted by Lawrence Kohlberg and his associates.[20] In these projects, democratic governance becomes a way of life in high schools. These projects aim to transform the school culture—its hidden or implicit curriculum—and in this way to systematically cultivate democratic citizenship. Even if the values of justice, liberty, and equality are well explored in the academic curriculum, the students are quick to perceive whether the school itself runs on a different set of values. They will learn the latter as the real rules of the game.

Students in Just Community schools participate in the basic governance of the school. They deliberate on everything from attendance policy to the consequences for stealing and cheating. Today, students might consider whether, as a move against resegregation, cafeteria seating should be assigned randomly.

The Just Community high schools and the kindergarten deliberations of Vivian Paley together suggest five conditions of ideal deliberation.

- Students are engaged in integrated decision-making discussions that involve genuine value conflicts that arise in the course of relating to one another at school. These value conflicts may concern play and name-calling in an elementary school, cliques and taunting in a middle school, and cheating, attendance, and segregation in a high school.
- The discussion group is diverse enough that students have the benefit of exposure to reasoning and social perspectives different from their own.
- The discussion group is free of domination—gross or subtle—by participants who were born into privileged social positions or by those who mature physically before others.
- The discussion leader is skilled at comprehending and presenting reasoning and perspectives that are missing, countering conventional ideas with critical thinking, and advocating positions that are inarticulate or being drummed out of consideration.
- Discussions are dialogic. Discussants engage in conversation about their viewpoints, claims, and arguments, not in alternating monologues.

THE ACADEMIC CURRICULUM

Citizens need disciplinary knowledge just as much as they need deliberative experience and skill. The suggestion to engage students in dialogues on the shared problems of school life is not an argument for "process" without "content." It is not an argument for lessening emphasis on subject-matter learning. To the contrary, making decisions without knowledge—whether immediate knowledge of the alternatives under consideration or background knowledge—is no cause for celebration. Action without understanding is not wise action except by accident. The Klan acted; the Nazis acted; bullies act every day.

Consequently, a rigorous liberal arts curriculum that deals in powerful ideas, important issues, and core values is essential alongside deliberations of controversial public issues. Moreover, if deliberation is left to the school's social curriculum only—that is, to the nonacademic areas of student relations and school governance—then students are likely to develop the misconception that the academic disciplines are settled and devoid of controversy. Nothing could be further from the truth. The disciplines are loaded with arguments and debates, and expertise in a discipline is measured by one's involvement in these discussions. A good teacher, on this view, is able to engage students, in developmentally appropriate ways, in the core problems of the subject matter.

Historians, for example, argue about everything they study: about why Rome fell, why slavery lasted so long in the U.S., and what forces contributed to the fall of the Soviet Union. What historians do is develop theses—warranted assertions—about such matters. They defend their claims with their interpretations of the evidentiary record. Political scientists likewise don't know with certainty why in the past few years the U.S. has abandoned the UN Charter and embarked on rugged unilateralism, nor do they "know" a host of other things: whether nation states will survive their contest with globalization or why the current cohort of 18- to 25-year-olds has proven so unengaged in politics.

Engaging students in deliberations of academic controversies is arguably the most rigorous approach to disciplinary education available. Its advantage over drill-and-cover curricula, whether of the middle-track pedestrian variety or the Advanced Placement version, is that it involves students in both the substantive (facts and theories) and syntactical (methods of inquiry) dimensions of the disciplines.[21] At the same time, such engagement prepares them for the reasoned argumentation of democratic living.

Fortunately, some resources are readily available that help teachers and curriculum leaders decide which issues are appropriate for study and then lay out several alternatives for students to consider. Two of the best low-cost resources for the high school social studies classroom, especially history and government courses, are published by the National Issues Forum and by Choices for the 21st Century.[22] Each organization produces a series of booklets containing background information on a pressing problem (contemporary or historical) and three to four policy alternatives. Both engage students in the kind of deliberation that develops their understanding of one another, of the array of alternatives, of the problem itself, and of its historical context.[23]

The authors of these materials have developed the policy alternatives. Consequently, students are given (and don't have to generate) grist for the analytic mill. Students can evaluate the authors' diagnosis of the problem and judge their representation of stakeholders on the issue. Then they can deliberate about the options presented. The provision of alternatives by the authors scaffolds the task in a helpful way, modeling for students what an array of alternatives looks like and allowing them to work at understanding these and at listening to one another. After such experience, students are ready to have the scaffold removed and to investigate an issue of their own choosing and create their own briefing booklet.

THE THREE R'S?

I would like to see a national campaign against idiocy, and I believe schools are ideal sites for it. Put differently, schools are fitting places to lead young people through puberty and into citizenship. Schools are the sites of choice because they have, to some extent, the two most important resources for this work: diversity and problems.

I realize that this view is apt to be too optimistic for some readers. After all, schools are products of society and are embedded in it. They are not autonomous places where massive social forces can be stopped with a lesson plan. Still, schools are not insignificant sources of social progress. At some level, everyone seems to believe this. It is the reason that curriculum debates are often the most impassioned to be found anywhere in society. My view is that the three R's—mechanically treated and, now, tested with Puritanical fervor—are not the only essentials needed for the realization of democratic ideals. A proper curriculum for democracy requires both the study and the practice of democracy.

Notes

1. Aristotle, *The Politics of Aristotle*, trans. Ernest Barker (New York: Oxford University Press, 1958), p. 6. See also Christopher Berry, *The Idea of a Democratic Community* (New York: St. Martin's Press, 1989).

2. Daniel Kemmis, *The Good City and the Good Life* (Boston: Houghton Mifflin, 1995), p. 9.

3. Alexis de Tocqueville, *Democracy in America*, trans. George Lawrence, ed. J. P. Mayer (Garden City, N.J.: Doubleday, 1969), p. 540.

4. Jane Addams, "Why Women Should Vote," in Aileen S. Kraditor, ed., *The Ideas of the Woman Suffrage Movement, 1880–1920* (1909; reprint, New York: Norton, 1981), p. 69.

5. Edward C. Banfield, *The Moral Basis of a Backward Society* (New York: Free Press, 1958); see also Robert D. Putnam, *Making Democracy Work: Civic Traditions in Modern Italy* (Princeton, N.J.: Princeton University Press, 1994).

6. Sarah Jain, "Urban Errands: The Means of Mobility," *Journal of Consumer Culture*, vol. 2, 2002, pp. 419–38; and Keith Bradsher, *High and Mighty: SUVs* (New York: Public Affairs, 2002).

7. Karl Marx, *Capital*, trans. Ben Fowkes, 3 vols. (1867; reprint, New York: Penguin Classics, 1990), vol. 1; Robert N. Bellah et al., *Habits of the Heart: Individualism and Commitment in American Life* (Berkeley: University of California Press, 1985); and John

Kenneth Galbraith, *The Affluent Society*, 40th anniversary ed. (Boston: Houghton Mifflin, 1998).

8. See Amy Gutmann's treatment of Churchill's statement in "Democracy, Philosophy, and Justification," in Seyla Benhabib, ed., *Democracy and Difference* (Princeton, N.J.: Princeton University Press, 1996), pp. 340–47.

9. Martin Luther King, Jr., "I Have a Dream," in Clayborne Carson and Kris Shepard, eds., *A Call to Conscience* (New York: Warner Books, 2001), pp. 81–82.

10. Judith N. Shklar, *American Citizenship: The Quest for Inclusion* (Cambridge, Mass.: Harvard University Press, 1991), p. 12.

11. Martin Luther King, Jr., *Why We Can't Wait* (New York: Mentor, 1963), chap. 5, p. 80; see also Gary Y. Okihiro, *Margins and Mainstream: Asians in American History and Culture* (Seattle: University of Washington Press, 1994).

12. Jennifer L. Hochschild and Nathan Scovronick, "Democratic Education and the American Dream: One, Some, and All," in Walter C. Parker, ed., *Education for Democracy: Contexts, Curricula, and Assessments* (Greenwich, Conn.: Information Age, 2002), pp. 3–26.

13. Vivian Gussin Paley, *You Can't Say You Can't Play* (Cambridge, Mass.: Harvard University Press, 1992), p. 21.

14. John Dewey, *Democracy and Education*, in Jo Ann Boydston, ed., *The Middle Works of John Dewey, 1899–1924*, vol. 9 (1916; reprint, Carbondale: Southern Illinois University Press, 1985), p. 200.

15. Ibid.

16. Gary Orfield, "Schools More Separate: Consequences of a Decade of Resegregation," Harvard Civil Rights Project, 2001, available on the website of the Harvard Civil Rights Project. For access, simply Google the title. Orfield found, "Whites on average attend schools where less than 20% of the students are from all of the other racial and ethnic groups combined. On average, Blacks and Latinos attend schools with 53% to 55% students of their own group. Latinos attend schools with far higher average Black populations than Whites do, and Blacks attend schools with much higher average Latino enrollments. American Indian students attend schools in which about a third (31%) of the students are from Indian backgrounds."

17. See Thomas F. Pettigrew, "Intergroup Contact: Theory, Research, and New Perspectives," in James A. Banks and Cherry A. McGee Banks, eds., *Handbook of Research on Multicultural Education* (San Francisco: Jossey Bass, 2004), pp. 770–81; see also Elliot Aronson et al., *The Jigsaw Classroom* (Beverly Hills, Calif.: Sage, 1978).

18. Paley, p. 16.

19. Ibid., p. 63.

20. F. Clark Power, Ann Higgins, and Lawrence Kohlberg, *Lawrence Kohlberg's Approach to Moral Education* (New York: Columbia University Press, 1989); and Ralph Mosher, Robert A. Kenny, Jr., and Andrew Garrod, *Preparing for Citizenship: Teaching Youth to Live Democratically* (Westport, Conn.: Praeger, 1994).

21. Joseph J. Schwab, "Structure of the Disciplines: Meanings and Significances," in G. W. Ford and Lawrence Pugno, eds., *The Structure of Knowledge and the Curriculum* (Chicago: Rand McNally, 1964), pp. 6–30.

22. Information about the National Issues Forum is available at www.nifi.org; information about Choices for the 21st Century is available at www.choices.edu.

23. John Doble, *The Story of NIF: The Effects of Deliberation* (Dayton, Ohio: Kettering Foundation, 1996).

WALTER C. PARKER *is a professor of education and an adjunct professor of political science at the University of Washington, Seattle. His most recent book is* Teaching Democracy: Unity and Diversity in Public Life *(Teachers College Press, 2003), from which the arguments in this article have been drawn.*

From *Phi Delta Kappan*, January 2005, pp. 344–351. Copyright © 2005 by Phi Delta Kappa International. Reprinted by permission of the publisher and author.

SCHOOL ACCOUNTABILITY
AN ALTERNATIVE TO TESTING

Ken Jones

*F*or some time now, it has been apparent to many in the education community that state and federal policies intended to develop greater school accountability for the learning of all students have been terribly counterproductive. The use of high-stakes testing of students has been fraught with flawed assumptions, oversimplified understandings of school realities, undemocratic concentration of power, undermining of the teaching profession, and predictably disastrous consequences for our most vulnerable students. Far from the noble ideal of leaving no child behind, current policies, if continued, are bound to increase existing inequities, trivialize schooling, and mislead the public about the quality and promise of public education.

What is needed is a better means for evaluating schools, an alternative to the present system of using high-stakes testing for school accountability. A new model, based on a different set of assumptions and understandings about school realities and approaches to power, is required. It must be focused on the needs of learners and on the goals of having high expectations for all rather than on the prerequisites of a bureaucratic measurement system.

PREMISES

In the realm of student learning, the question of outcomes has often been considered primary: what do we want students to know and be able to do as a result of schooling? Once the desired outcomes have been specified, school reform efforts have proceeded to address the thorny questions of how to attain them. Starting from desired outcomes is an important shift in how to think about what does or does not make sense in classroom instruction.

In the realm of school accountability, however, little attention has been paid to corresponding outcome-related questions. It has simply been assumed that schools should be accountable for improved student learning, as measured by external test scores. It has been largely assumed by policy makers that external tests do, in fact, adequately measure student learning. These and other assumptions about school accountability must be questioned if we are to develop a more successful accountability model. It would

be well to start from basic questions about the purposes and audiences of schools. For what, to whom, and by what means should schools be held accountable? The following answers to these questions provide a set of premises on which a new school accountability system can be based.

FOR WHAT SHOULD SCHOOLS BE ACCOUNTABLE?

Schools should be held accountable for at least the following:

- *The physical and emotional well-being of students*. The caring aspect of school is essential to high-quality education. Parents expect that their children will be safe in schools and that adults in schools will tend to their affective as well as cognitive needs. In addition, we know that learning depends on a caring school climate that nurtures positive relationships.

- *Student learning*. Student learning is complex and multifaceted. It includes acquiring not only knowledge of disciplinary subject matter but also the thinking skills and dispositions needed in a modern democratic society.

- *Teacher learning*. Having a knowledgeable and skilled teacher is the most significant factor in student learning and should be fostered in multiple ways, compatible with the principles of adult learning. Schools must have sufficient time and funding to enable teachers to improve their own performance, according to professional teaching standards.

- *Equity and access*. Given the history of inequity with respect to minority and underserved student populations, schools must be accountable for placing a special emphasis on improving equity and access, providing fair opportunities for all to learn to high standards. Our press for excellence must include a press for fairness.

- *Improvement*. Schools should be expected to function as learning organizations, continuously engaged in self-assessment and adjustment in an effort to meet the needs of their students. The capacity to do so must be ensured and nurtured.

TO WHOM SHOULD SCHOOLS BE ACCOUNTABLE?

Schools should be held accountable to their primary clients: students, parents, and the local community. Current accountability systems make the state and federal governments the locus of power and decision making. But the primary clients of schools should be empowered to make decisions about the ends of education, not just the means, provided there are checks to ensure equity and access and adherence to professional standards for teaching.

BY WHAT MEANS SHOULD SCHOOLS BE HELD ACCOUNTABLE?

To determine how well schools are fulfilling their responsibilities, multiple measures should be used. Measures of school accountability should include both qualitative and quantitative approaches, taking into account local contexts, responsiveness to student and community needs, and professional practices and standards. Because schools are complex and unique institutions that address multiple societal needs, there should also be allowances for local measures, customized to meet local needs and concerns. A standardized approach toward school accountability cannot work in a nation as diverse as the U.S.

Given these premises, what are the proper roles of a government-developed and publicly funded school accountability system?

- It should serve to improve student learning and school practices and to ensure equity and access, not to reward or punish schools.
- It should provide guidance and information for local decision making, not classify schools as successes or failures.
- It should reflect a democratic approach, including a balance of responsibility and power among different levels of government.

A BALANCED MODEL

An accountability framework called the "balanced scorecard" is currently employed in the business world and provides a useful perspective for schools. This framework consists of four areas that must be evaluated to give a comprehensive view of the health of an organization. The premise is that both outcomes and operations must be measured if the feedback system is to be used to improve the organization, not just monitor it. In the business context, the four components of the framework are: 1) financial, 2) internal business, 3) customer, and 4) innovation and learning.

THE MODEL

Applying this four-part approach to education, we can use the following aspects of school performance as the components of a balanced school accountability model: 1) student learning; 2) opportunity to learn; 3) responsiveness to students, parents, and community; and 4) organizational capacity for improvement.

Each of these aspects must be attended to and fostered by an evaluation system that has a sufficiently high resolution to take into account the full complexity and scope of modern-day schools.

1. Student learning. Principles of high-quality assessment have been well articulated by various organizations and should be followed. What is needed is a system that

- is primarily intended to improve student learning;
- aligns with local curricula;
- emphasizes applied learning and thinking skills, not just declarative knowledge and basic skills;
- embodies the principle of multiple measures, including a variety of formats such as writing, open-response questions, and performance-based tasks; and
- is accessible to students with diverse learning styles, intelligence profiles, exceptionalities, and cultural backgrounds.

Currently, there is a mismatch between what cognitive science and brain research have shown about human learning and how schools and educational bureaucracies continue to measure learning. We now know that human intellectual abilities are malleable and that people learn through a social and cultural process of constructing knowledge and understandings in given contexts. And yet we continue to conduct schooling and assessment guided by the outdated beliefs that intelligence is fixed, that knowledge exists apart from culture and context, and that learning is best induced through the behaviorist model of stimulus/response.

Scientific measurement cannot truly "objectify" learning and rate it hierarchically. Accurate decisions about the quality and depth of an individual's learning must be based on human judgment. While test scores and other assessment data are useful and necessary sources of information, a fair assessment of a person's learning can be made only by other people, preferably by those who know the person best in his or her own context. A reasonable process for determining the measure of student learning could involve local panels of teachers, parents, and community members, who review data about student performance and make decisions about promotion, placement, graduation, and so on.

What is missing in most current accountability systems is not just a human adjudication system, but also a local assessment component that addresses local curricula, contexts, and cultures. A large-scale external test is not sufficient to determine a student's achievement. District, school, and classroom assessments must also be developed as part of a comprehensive means of collecting data on student learning. The states of Maine and Nebraska are currently developing just such systems.

ASSESSMENT LITERACY

Most important, locally developed assessments depend on the knowledge and "assessment literacy" of teachers. Most teachers have not been adequately trained in assessment and need substantial and ongoing professional development to create valid and reliable tasks and build effective classroom assessment repertoires. This means that an investment must be made in teacher learning about assessment. The value of such an investment is not only in the promise of improved classroom instruction and measurement. Research also shows that improved classroom assessment results in improved student achievement on external tests.

Last, the need to determine the effectiveness of the larger state school system can either support or undermine such local efforts. If state or federal agencies require data to be aggregated from local to state levels, local decision making is necessarily weakened, and an undue emphasis is placed on standardized methods. If, however, the state and federal agencies do not rely on local assessment systems to gauge the health of the larger system, much may be gained. In New Zealand, for example, a system of educational monitoring is in place that uses matrix sampling on tasks that include one-to-one videotaped interviews, team tasks, and independent tasks. No stakes are entailed for schools or students. The data are profiled and shared with schools for the purpose of teacher professional development and as a means of developing model tasks for local assessments. Such a system supports rather than undermines local assessment efforts.

2. Opportunity to learn. How can students be expected to meet high standards if they are not given a fair opportunity to learn? This question has yet to be answered with respect to school accountability. Schools should be accountable for providing equitable opportunities for all students to learn, and we must develop ways to determine how well they do so.

At the heart of the matter is that the responsibility for opportunity to learn must be shared by the district and state. The inequitable funding of public schools, particularly the disparity between the schools of the haves and those of the have-nots, places the schools of disadvantaged students in unjust and often horrifying circumstances. Over the past decade, there have been lawsuits in various states attempting to redress this imbalance, which is largely a result of dependence on property taxes for school funding. Yet not a great deal of progress has been made.

How should we define and put into practice our understanding of opportunity to learn? How will we measure it? How can an accountability system foster it?

At a minimum, one might expect that schools and school systems will provide qualified teachers, adequate instructional materials, and sound facilities. This is the contention in a recent lawsuit, *Williams v. State of California*, in which the plaintiffs argued for an accountability system that is reciprocal—that is, while schools are held accountable for performance, the state is held accountable for ensuring adequate resources.

But there is more to this issue than just funding. Jeannie Oakes describes a framework that includes opportunity-to-learn indicators for access to knowledge, professional teaching conditions, and "press for achievement." Linda Darling-Hammond stresses the "fair and humane treatment" of students in a set of standards for professional practice.

As such standards for opportunity to learn are articulated, the question arises as to how to monitor and report on them. Clearly, the degree of adherence to these standards cannot be determined through the proxy of testing. It is necessary to conduct observations in schools and classrooms and to evaluate the quality both of individual teachers and of the school as a whole.

TEACHER EVALUATION

Teacher evaluation has received a great deal of criticism for being ineffective. The hit-and-run observations that principals typically conduct do little to determine whether teachers are meeting established professional teaching standards. Unions have been described as more interested in protecting their membership than in ensuring high-quality teaching. A promising development that has potential for breaking through this impasse is the recent initiation of peer-review processes by a number of teacher unions. Adam Urbanski, president of the Rochester Teachers Association and director of the Teacher Union Reform Network (TURN), has been a leader in advocating for and implementing such teacher evaluation processes. In a recent unpublished manuscript, he describes how the process should work:

- Some classroom observation by peers and supervisors, structured by a narrative instrument (not a checklist) based on professional standards such as those of the National Board for Professional Teaching Standards (NBPTS) and framed by the teacher's goals for the lesson/unit;
- Information from previous evaluations and feedback, such as structured references from colleagues and other supervisors;
- Portfolios that might include examples of teaching syllabi, assignments made, feedback given to students and samples of student work, feedback received from parents and students as well as colleagues, data on student progress, teaching exhibitions such as videotaped teaching samples, professional development initiatives taken, and structured self-evaluation. All summative evaluation decisions about promotions or continued employment should be made by a specially established committee of teachers and administrators.

Urbanski goes on to describe safeguards for due process and for preventing malpractice. He also describes how such a process could be used in conjunction with professional development for improving teaching and school practice.

SCHOOL REVIEW

In order to evaluate the performance of a school as a whole, a school review process will be necessary. Variations of inspectorates and school-quality reviews have been developed in New York, Rhode Island, Maine, and other states, as well as in Britain, New Zealand, Australia, and other countries. In order for such reviews to serve the purpose of school improvement, the data should be collected in a "critical friend" manner, through a combination of school self-assessment and collegial visitations. Findings from such a process should not be employed in a bureaucratic and judgmental way but rather should be given as descriptions to local councils charged with evaluating school accountability. As with all aspects of any school renewal initiative, the quality and effectiveness of a review system will depend on the time, resources, and institutional support given to it.

Who will ensure that adequate opportunities to learn are present in schools? As described below, a system of reciprocal accountability must be set up so that both local accountability councils and the state itself serve to "mind the store" for all students. The issue of equitable funding will undoubtedly be resolved through the courts.

3. Responsiveness to students, parents, and community. Current accountability systems move power and decision making away from the primary clients of the education system and more and more toward state and federal agencies. As high-stakes testing dictates the curriculum, less and less choice is available for students. Parent or community concerns about what is happening in the classroom and to the students have become less important to schools than meeting state mandates.

As the primary stakeholders in the schools, parents and communities must be made part of the effort to hold schools accountable. There are many examples of local community organizations, especially in urban areas, that have taken on the task of insisting that schools are responsive to the needs of children.

To demonstrate responsiveness to students, parents, and the community, schools must go beyond sponsoring parent/teacher organizations or encouraging parent involvement as a means to gain support for existing school practices. They must also do more than gather survey information about stakeholders' satisfaction. True accountability to the primary clients for schools entails shifting power relationships.

COUNCILS

Local school-based councils must be created that have real power to effect school change. These councils would review accountability information from state and local assessments as well as from school-quality review processes and make recommendations to school boards about school policies and priorities. They would hold school boards accountable for the development and implementation of school improvement plans. Phillip Schlechty discusses how such councils might work:

> Community leaders who are concerned about the futures of their communities and their schools should join together to create a nonprofit corporation intended to support efforts of school leaders to focus on the future and to ensure that lasting values as well as immediate interests are included in the education decision-making process. It would also be the function of this group to establish a small subgroup of the community's most trusted leaders who would annually evaluate the performance of the school board as stewards of the common good and would make these evaluations known to the community....
>
> In a sense, the relationship between the school district and the monitoring function of the new corporation should be something akin to the relationship between the quality assurance division of a corporation and the operating units in the corporation....
>
> When the data indicate that goals are not being met, the president of the corporation, working with the superintendent and the board of education, would seek to discover why this was the case, and would seek as well to create new approaches that might enhance the prospect of achieving the stated goals and the intended ends. It is not intended that the new corporation simply

identify problems and weaknesses, it is intended that the leaders of this organization also participate in the creation of solutions and participate in creating support for solutions once they have been identified or created.

Communities must determine how to sustain such councils and ensure that they do not pursue narrow agendas. The composition of councils in urban settings will probably be different from those in rural or suburban settings. Standards and acceptable variations for councils will be important topics for public discussion.

4. Organizational capacity. If schools are going to be held accountable to high levels of performance, the question arises: Do schools have the internal capacity to rise to those levels? To what degree are the resources of schools "organized into a collective enterprise, with shared commitment and collaboration among staff to achieve a clear purpose for student learning"?

The issue of meaningful and ongoing teacher professional development is especially pertinent to whether or not schools are capable of enabling all students to meet higher standards of performance. A great deal of research has shed light on what kind of professional development is most effective in promoting school improvement.

Schools must also attend to the issue of teacher empowerment. Teachers are increasingly controlled and disempowered in various ways. This leads to a declining sense of efficacy and professionalism and a heightened sense of job dissatisfaction and has become a factor in the attrition that is contributing to the growing teaching shortage. Principals must share leadership with teachers and others as a means of sustaining capacity.

To be an effective collective enterprise, a school must develop an internal accountability system. That is, it must take responsibility for developing goals and priorities based on the ongoing collection and analysis of data, it must monitor its performance, and it must report its findings and actions to its public. Many schools have not moved past the stage of accepting individual teacher responsibility rather than collective responsibility as the norm. States and districts must cooperate with schools to nurture and insist upon the development of such collective internal norms.

THE NEW ROLE OF THE STATE

For a balanced model of school accountability to succeed, there must be a system in which states and districts are jointly responsible with schools and communities for student learning. Reciprocal accountability is needed: one level of the system is responsible to the others, and all are responsible to the public.

The role of state and federal agencies with respect to school accountability is much in need of redefinition. Agencies at these levels should not serve primarily in an enforcement role. Rather, their roles should be to establish standards for local accountability systems, to provide resources and guidance, and to set in place processes for quality review of such systems. Certainly there should be no high-stakes testing from the state and federal levels, no mandatory curricula, and no manipulation through funding. Where there are clear cases of faulty local accountability systems—those lacking any of the four elements discussed above (appropriate assessment systems; adequate opportunities to learn; responsiveness to students, parents, and community; or organizational capacity)—supportive efforts from the state and federal levels should be undertaken.

Are there any circumstances in which a state should intervene forcibly in a school or district? If an accountability system is to work toward school improvement for all schools, does that system not need such "teeth"? This question must be addressed in a way that acknowledges the multi-level nature of this school accountability model. One might envision at least three cases in which the state would take on a more assertive role: 1) to investigate claims or appeals from students, parents, or the community that the local accountability system is not meeting the standards set for such systems; 2) to require local schools and districts to respond to findings in the data that show significant student learning deficiencies, inequity in the opportunities to learn for all students, or lack of responsiveness to students, par-

ents, or communities; and 3) to provide additional resources and guidance to improve the organizational capacity of the local school or district. Is it conceivable that a state might take over a local school or district in this model? Yes, but only after the most comprehensive evaluation of the local accountability system has shown that there is no alternative—and then only on a temporary basis.

It is of great importance to the health of our public schools that we begin as soon as possible to define a new model for school accountability, one that is balanced and comprehensive. Schools can and should be held accountable to their primary clients for much more than test scores, in a way that supports improvement rather than punishes deficiencies. The current model of using high-stakes testing is a recipe for public school failure, putting our democratic nation at risk.

Mr. Jones is the director of teacher education at the University of Southern Maine, Gorham. From "A Balanced School Accountablity Model," by Ken Jones, Phi Delta Kappan, *April 2004, pages 584–590*

Distance Education in High Schools

Benefits, Challenges, and Suggestions

DAVISON M. MUPINGA

Over the years, instruction has shifted from the traditional face-to-face delivery to instruction that is done from a distance. *Distance education* is instruction that occurs when the instructor and student are separated by distance, time, or both (WCET 2004). Some common technologies used in distance education are videotape, broadcast television, ITFS (instructional television fixed service), satellite, interactive video, audio tapes, audio conferencing, CD-ROM, and computer (WCET 2004). More recently, the computer and Internet have played a large role in distance education through computer-based instruction (CBI) and Web-based (online) courses. These innovations have changed the face of distance education and revolutionized the concepts of teaching and training. In CBI, the computer is the primary medium for instruction and learning; in online instruction, the learning is delivered via the Web and often through a Learning Management System (LMS; Wise 2004).

Distance education, specifically online courses, now is commonly judged by the number of schools and colleges advertising for diplomas or degrees without leaving one's home (see Florida's Virtual High School or the University of Phoenix). Fast becoming a reality are "virtual high schools" (VHS) in which the entire school has access to online courses (Emeagwali 2004; Winograd 2002). It is estimated that 25 percent of public schools have distance learning programs, while nineteen states have officially recognized VHS (Emeagwali 2004).

Although online education has increased, it has not been without challenges. Teaching distance education is not the same as teaching in a face-to-face environment; administration of distance education programs requires different experience; and for students, learning in face-to-face environments is unlike learning online. Because of the growing demand for distance education and the unique experience it creates, it is important for high schools to know the benefits, pitfalls, and challenges of

distance education and VHS. This article looks at particular formats of distance education in high schools and the benefits and challenges of each. It also provides suggestions for teaching online courses.

Distance Education Formats

A number of distance education formats are in use, each with its own advantages and disadvantages. Common formats include cable and public broadcast television, correspondence, interactive television (ITV), and online (Web-based) courses.

1. *Cable television*. The cable television format (for example, the Learning Channel) allows for the broadcasting of courses live through a cable network. Students watch classes at home, interact with the instructor by telephone, and submit and receive assignments through e-mail (WCET 2004).
2. *Correspondence courses*. In contrast, the correspondence or "course-in-a-box" format provides students with a box of videotapes or compact disks (CDs) containing the course material. Students complete the assignments and send them back to the instructor. Lately, the more portable and easily accessible CDs have become popular. They save paper and allow students to access a large volume of material, including extremely detailed images and video clips, without the download speed concerns associated with Internet images (Michener Institute 2004).
3. *Interactive television (ITV)*. The ITV format is for synchronous classes held over an interactive network (for example, the Indiana Higher Education Telecommunication Service [IHETS]). In this format, the instructor and students are in different classrooms or locations, but the class is totally "live" and "interactive": The instructor can see and hear the students at the remote site and vice versa. The result is that

students at a remote site can join a class that is being taught on campus.

4. *Online courses.* The online (Web-based) format allows students to pursue their studies entirely on the Internet without attending classes in person (Maeroff 2003). This format uses a course management platform such as Blackboard or WebCT, which is entirely Web-based and does not require lengthy downloads or installation (Michener Institute 2004). Students can access course information and assignments, email the instructor and classmates, submit and receive assignments online, participate in online discussions, and link to other online resources through the course management platforms (Berner 2004; Maeroff 2003). Many courses combine technologies to enhance the students' learning experiences.

5. *Hybrid model.* Although satellite and correspondence were once the primary means of distance learning, they have been replaced by videoconferencing and completely online educational experiences (Schrum 2002). The most widespread approach to using the Internet for coursework is the course supplement, Web-assisted, or hybrid model (Tinker 2001). This is a face-to-face course augmented with assignments, readings, discussion groups, and tests that are completed online. The hybrid approach is considered a solution to high dropout rates for online classes (Oblender 2002) because students attend normal schools and get to see the teacher while incorporating an online component of the course, which helps prevent students from getting lost in cyberspace from lack of direct contact with the instructor.

Some of the high school courses offered online include career and technical education (for example, business computer information systems, food marketing, principles of marketing, and retailing), English language arts, fine arts, health and physical education, mathematics, science, social studies, and Spanish. A number of states have VHS; however, among the best known are the Florida Virtual High School, a pioneer of online education and a model for other online ventures in the United States (Doherty 2002; Vail 2001); Kentucky Virtual High School; The Concord Consortium; and Visions High School Academy (Winograd 2002).

Benefits of Distance Education

Distance learners come from a variety of backgrounds and range in age (WCET 2004). The students select distance education to suit their social and work commitments (Richards and Ridley 1999) and generally are people who, because of time, geography, financial considerations, family obligations, work requirements, or other constraints, choose not to attend a traditional classroom (WCET 2004). Distance education students also en-

joy the flexibility of time and space. "Regardless of where they live, students have equal access to quality courses through the web. [At times] students have flexibility in when and where they take needed courses, and schools can expand their offerings" (Thomas 2000, 4). Other groups of students that prefer distance education are rural students, sick or hospitalized children, gifted children, traveling families, and students who have problems in regular classrooms (WCET 2004). With this amount of flexibility, it is unsurprising that a greater percentage of students with special needs enroll in distance education programs.

Distance education programs are an option in financially tight times. Julie Young, the director of the Florida Virtual High School, observes, "With deepening budget cuts, brick-and-mortar schools will have to make every effort to find creative and cost-effective solutions to continue providing the same quality of educational opportunities for their students. Distance learning is one of these solutions" (Winograd 2002).

Online Advanced Placement (AP) courses are another reason for online courses in high schools. The online AP courses are said to have an advantage in that students who take them do better on the final tests than students who take the in-class versions (Carnevale 2002). Other advantages of online classes are the ability to add multimedia activities making the subjects come alive and the course management platform, which provides self-help and incorporates self-assessment tools that help students work on their own to improve their skills (University of Texas 2004). To an extent, the multimedia activities motivate the students, and the self assessments reduce remedial work for teachers.

Challenges Facing Distance Education

Despite the popularity of distance education courses in high school, critics worry that schools will use online classes to rid themselves of troublesome students or that opportunities for socialization and personal interaction will disappear (Vail 2001). Even when such opportunities are provided through other means, a number of issues need to be addressed before providing distance education. Among these are formulating workload policies, changing the existing bias toward face-to-face learning, and training teachers and students for the online environment.

A policy on workload for online instructors needs to be developed. With teacher time being a scarce resource and the dominant cost in most schools being instructional time, educational administrators often seek to decrease this cost by increasing the number of students that each teacher reaches (Tinker 2001). Distance education courses, on the other hand, offer a solution to dealing with large school enrollments. Administrators have to come up with a formula for defining the workload of online teachers (for example, how many students in an online class equal the load in a face-to-face class?). Even colleges that have had distance education programs for some time use different formulas for determining workload for online instructors.

Changing biases toward face-to-face learning is another challenge. Raymond Rose, vice president for The Concord Consortium, a nonprofit educational research organization, says, "The current model of education is based on a standard of measuring learning based on seat-time. Virtual high school programs are currently restricted by having to fit into the brick-and-mortar model for schools" (Winograd 2002).

Training online teachers and students in times of budget cuts is another challenge. Online programs are sometimes "thought of as a degree-in-a-box, or a piece of cake, but this is not … [I]t [online education] is not for the person who procrastinates, or can't find it on their own to get motivated," according to Debbie Drewien (Cavanagh 2004, 20). Given the challenges of technology, the need for student self-direction and motivation, and the inexperience of many faculty members with the demands of Web-based instruction, adequate student and faculty preparation is essential. The preparation of online faculty only is fighting half the battle (CITE 2002).

Suggestions for Teaching Online Courses

Although decisions on who teaches an online course rest with administrators, Berner (2004) suggests, "Not just any instructor should be asked to design and teach an online course." By the same token, not all students do well in online environments. Online students need solid technical skills; otherwise, they may have difficulty succeeding in Web-based learning environments (Osika and Sharp 2003). Therefore, to increase success in online classes, both instructors and students need to acquire necessary skills for the environment. One suggestion for teaching online courses is that faculty should attend related workshops and conferences on online teaching before designing such courses and, if possible, also should take an online course themselves (Berner 2004). Berner also adds that instructors should not just transfer residence courses to online courses; instead, they need to transform them to fit the format.

Another suggestion is to determine the "online instruction readiness" of virtual high school students. Several instruments, such as "Is Distance Education Right for Me?,"[1] are available on the Web. Alternatively, the Educational Success Prediction Instrument (ESPI),[2] a more reliable instrument to determine whether students are suited for online courses, can be used. This tool identifies students that need counseling and support to make them more effective online learners (Roblyer and Marshall 2003).

Communicating with online students is one area that needs to be properly managed by online instructors and students. To reduce possible communication challenges, Boettcher (1999) suggests instructors manage communication expectations from the very beginning by setting up a framework for turnaround time for responding to students' e-mails and phone calls and also announcing when the response time is suspended. Another effective communication technique is to create a list of "Frequently Asked Questions" (FAQs) and a "Cyber Café," "Orientation," or "Parking Lot" forum where students post questions about the class so that other students who know the answer can respond. This reduces the large volume of e-mails that online instructors often get, thus eliminating a source of frustration. Using the e-mails and phone messages from students to make course revisions also is an excellent idea.

In addition to attending professional development workshops and conferences and participating in discussion forums on distance education, several other resources are available for preparing and developing online courses. The Public Broadcasting Service (PBS) has an interactive videotape, "Surviving and Thriving in Your First Online Course,"[3] featuring three instructors discussing online courses. This is an excellent reference for both novices and experienced online instructors. For other helpful articles and texts, see Shimabukuro (2002), White and Weight (2000), and this article's reference list.

Conclusion

Distance learning, particularly online education, is becoming a norm in education as funding and geographies affect the delivery of educational lessons (Trivette and Kinsey 2002). In support, an analyst for a consulting group in education businesses says, "The virtual-school market is definitely expanding" (Arnone 2001, 32). The current teacher shortages and overcrowded facilities are driving secondary schools to handle their burgeoning student populations any way they can, including through online programs. Therefore, high schools contemplating distance education programs are headed in the right direction but will need to make adequate preparation before embarking on online learning.

Notes

1. "Is Distance Education Right for Me?" is available at http://www.distancelearning.ufl.edu/students/selfassessment.asp or http://www.ccsn.nevada.edu/distanceed/DEforYOU/isdeforyou.htm.
2. For more about the Educational Success Predition Instrument (ESPI), please consult http://www.iste.org/jrte/35/2/abstracts/espri.cfm.
3. A complete description of the PBS video "Surviving and Thriving in Your First Online Course" is available at http://www.pbs.org/als/programs/itsk0101.htm.

REFERENCES

Arnone, M. 2001. U. of Washington creates online high-school courses. *Chronicle of Higher Education* November 30, 2001, A32.

Berner, R. T. 2004. *Less is more: Designing an online course.* DEOSNEWS 13, no. 4 (April). http://www.ed.psu.edu/acsde/deos/deosnews/deosnews.asp (accessed August 25, 2004).

Boettcher, J. V. 1999. The dangers and pitfalls of communicating with students or what not to do when communicating with students on the Internet. http://www.cren.net/~jboettch/comm.htm (accessed July 25, 2004).

Carnevale, D. 2002. Kentucky adds online tools for high-school students preparing for college. *Chronicle of Higher Education.* January 11, 2002, A44.

Cavanagh, S. 2004. Online teacher-training classes win converts. *Education Week* 23, no. 23 (February 18): 20.

Center for Internet Technology in Education (CITE). 2002. Annual conference, http://citereg.ecollege.com/regProposal.learn.

Doherty, K. M. 2002. Students speak out. *Education Week* 21, no. 35 (May 9): 19–23.

Emeagwali, N. S. 2004. High school students increasingly learn from a distance. *Techniques* 79, no. 5 (May): 14–16.

Maeroff, G. I. 2003. Classroom of one. *American School Board Journal* 190, no. 2 (February): 22–28.

McVay-Lynch, M. 2001. Effective student preparation for online learning. *The Technology Source* (November/December), http://ts.mivu.org/default.asp?show=article&id=901 (accessed July 25, 2004).

Michener Institute. 2004. *Distance education.* http://www.michener.on.ca/de/distance_education.php (accessed July 20, 2004).

Oblender, T. E. 2002. A hybrid course model: One solution to the high online drop-out rate. *Learning and Leading with Technology* 29, no. 6 (March): 42–46.

Osika, R., and D. Sharp. 2003. Minimum technical competencies for distance learning students. *Journal of Research on Technology in Education* 34 (3): 318–25.

Richards, C. N., and D. F. Ridley. 1999. Factors affecting college student's persistence in online computer managed instruction. *College Student Journal* 31, no. 4 (December): 490–95.

Roblyer, M. D., and J. C. Marshall. 2003. Predicting success of virtual high school students: Preliminary results from an educational success prediction instrument. *Journal of Research on Technology in Education* 35, no. 2 (Winter): 241–255.

Schrum, L. 2002. Oh, what wonders you will see: Distance education past, present, and future. *Learning and Leading with Technology* 30, no. 3 (November): 7–9.

Shimabukuro, J. 2002. How to survive in an online class: Guidelines for students. http://leahi.kcc.hawaii.edu/org/tcon99/papers/shimabukuro.html (accessed August 10, 2004).

Thomas, W. R. 2000. *Web courses for high school students: Potential and issues.* ERIC ED441398.

Tinker, R. 2001. E-learning quality: The Concord model for learning from a distance. *NASSP Bulletin* 85, no. 628 (November): 36–47.

Trivette, N. J., and S. Kinsey. 2002. Emerging trends: Distance learning. *Agricultural Education Magazine* 75, no. 3 (November/December): 16–18.

University of Texas. 2004. *Distance education center: High school courses.* http://www.utexas.edu/cee/dec/uths/ (accessed August, 30, 2004).

Vail, K. 2001. Online learning grows up. *American School Board Journal* 188, no. 9 (September): 12.

Western Cooperative for Educational Telecommunications (WCET). 2004. *Distance education: A consumer's guide.* http://www.wcet.info/Resources/publications/conguide/ (accessed August 20, 2004).

White, K. W., and B. H. Weight. 2000. *The online teaching guide: A handbook of attitudes, strategies, and techniques for the virtual classroom.* Boston: Allyn and Bacon.

Winograd, K. 2002. ABC's of the virtual high school. *The Technology Source* (March/April), http://ts.mivu.org/default.asp?show=article&id=98 (accessed November 19, 2004).

Wise, L. 2004. *Distance education via the World Wide Web.* http://www.mdhsonline.unimelb.edu.au/presentations/distance_ed.html (accessed November 19, 2004).

Davison M. Mupinga is an assistant professor of industrial technology education at Indiana State University in Terre Haute. He also teaches online courses in career and technical education and human resource development.

From *The Clearing House*, January/February 2005, pp. 105-108. Reprinted by permission of the Helen Dwight Reid Educational Foundation. Published by Heldref Publications, 1319, Eighteenth St., NW, Washington, DC 20036-1802. Copyright © 2005. www.heldref.org

UNIT 3

Striving for Excellence: The Drive for Quality

Unit Selections

Key Points to Consider

- Identify some of the different points of view on achieving excellence in education. What value conflicts can be defined?

- What are some assumptions about achieving excellence in student achievement that you would challenge? Why?

- What can educators do to improve the quality of student learning?

- Have there been flaws in American school reform efforts in the past 20 years? If so, what are they?

- Has the Internet affected the critical thinking skills of students? Defend your answer.

Student Website

www.mhcls.com/online

Internet References

Further information regarding these websites may be found in this book's preface or online.

Awesome Library for Teachers
   http://www.awesomelibrary.org

Education World
   http://www.education-world.com

EdWeb/Andy Carvin
   http://edwebproject.org

Kathy Schrock's Guide for Educators
   http://www.discoveryschool.com/schrockguide/

Teacher's Guide to the U.S. Department of Education
   http://www.ed.gov/pubs/TeachersGuide/

The debate continues over which academic standards are most appropriate for elementary and secondary school students. Discussion regarding the impact on students and teachers of state proficiency examinations goes on in those states or provinces where such examinations are mandated. We are still dealing with how best to assess student academic performance. Some very interesting proposals on how to do this have emerged.

There are several incisive analyses of why American educators' efforts to achieve excellence in schooling have frequently failed. Today, some interesting proposals are being offered as to how we might improve the academic achievement of students. The current debate regarding excellence in education clearly reflects parents' concerns for more choices in how they school their children.

Many authors of recent essays and reports believe that excellence can be achieved best by creating new models of schooling that give both parents and students more control over the types of school environments available to them. Many believe that more money is not a guarantor of quality in schooling. Imaginative academic programming and greater citizen choice can guarantee at least a greater variety of options open to parents who are concerned about their children's academic progress in school.

We each wish the best quality of life that we can attain, and we each desire the opportunity for an education that will optimize our chances to achieve our objectives. The rhetoric on excellence and quality in schooling has been heated, and numerous opposing concepts of how schools can reach these goals have been presented for public consideration in recent years. Some progress has been realized on the part of students as well as some major changes in how teacher education programs are structured.

In the decades of the 1980s and 1990s, those reforms instituted to encourage qualitative growth in the conduct of schooling tended to be what education historian David Tyack once referred to as "structural" reforms. Structural reforms consist of demands for standardized testing of students and teaching, reorganization of teacher education programs, legalized actions to provide alternative routes into the teaching profession, efforts to recruit more people into teaching, and laws to enable greater parental choice as to where their children may attend school. These structural reforms cannot, however, in and of themselves produce higher levels of student achievement. We need to explore a broader range of the essential purposes of schooling, which will require our redefining what it means to be a literate person. We need also to reconsider what we mean by the "quality" of education and to reassess the essential purposes of schooling.

When we speak of quality and excellence as aims of education, we must remember that these terms encompass aesthetic and affective as well as cognitive processes. Young people cannot achieve the full range of intellectual capacity to solve problems on their own simply by being obedient and by memorizing data. How students encounter their teachers in classrooms and how teachers interact with their students are concerns that encompass both aesthetic and cognitive dimensions.

There is a real need to enforce intellectual standards and yet also to make schools more creative places in which to learn, places where students will yearn to explore, to imagine, and to hope.

Compared to those in the United States, students in European nations appear to score higher in assessments of skills in mathematics and the sciences, in written essay examinations in the humanities and social sciences, and in the routine oral examinations given by committees of teachers to students as they exit secondary schools.

What forms of teacher education and in-service reeducation are needed? Who pays for these programmatic options? Where and how will funds be raised or redirected from other priorities to pay for this? Will the "streaming and tracking" model of secondary school student placement that exists in Europe be adopted? How can we best assess academic performance? Can we commit to a more heterogeneous grouping of students and to full inclusion of handicapped students in our schools? Many individual, private, and governmental reform efforts did not address these questions.

Other industrialized nations champion the need for alternative secondary schools to prepare their young people for varied life goals and civic work. The American dream of the common school translated into what has become the comprehensive high school of the twentieth century. But does it provide all the people with alternative diploma options? If not, what is the next step? What must be changed? For one, concepts related to our educational goals must be clarified and political motivation must be separated from the realities of student performance.

Policy development for schooling needs to be tempered by even more "bottom-up," grassroots efforts to improve the quality of schools that are now under way in many communities in North America. New and imaginative inquiry and assessment strategies need to be developed by teachers working in their classrooms, and they must nurture the support of professional colleagues and parents.

Excellence is the goal: the means to achieve it is what is in dispute. There is a new dimension to the debate over assessment of academic achievement of elementary and secondary school students. In addition, the struggle continues of conflicting academic (as well as political) interests in the quest to improve the quality of preparation of our future teachers, and we also need to sort these issues out.

No conscientious educator would oppose the idea of excellence in education. The problem in gaining consensus over how to attain it is that the assessment of excellence of both teacher and student performance is always based on some preset standards. Which standards of assessment should prevail?

How Schools Sustain Success

Showing improvement in student achievement is one thing.
The challenge is sustaining it year after year.

Valerie Chrisman

Under the microscope of increased accountability, a growing number of U.S. schools have been identified as underperforming on the basis of their low test scores. No Child Left Behind (NCLB) legislation demands that low-performing schools improve their students' academic achievement annually. Yet sustained increases in student achievement are problematic for underperforming schools. A case in point: Only 83 of the 430 schools that participated in California's Immediate Intervention Underperforming Schools Program met their students' test score growth targets for two consecutive years (Just & Boese, 2002).

To better understand the differences and similarities between the 83 low-performing schools that sustained improved student test scores and the schools that were unable to sustain this improvement, I conducted a study of California's primary and secondary reform program schools. I compared the 83 schools that sustained growth on California's academic program index for two consecutive improvement program years with the 273 schools that showed growth for only one of the two years. (The remaining 74 schools in the program showed no growth in either year and were not included in the study.)

I compared the successful and unsuccessful schools according to three criteria: analyses of test scores and school characteristics: interview responses from four teachers and the principal at each of eight representa-

tive sample schools, four from each group; and questionnaire responses from the 356 principals whose schools experienced growth in at least one of the two years of the reform program.

Analysis of sample school characteristics revealed that the successful schools actually had higher levels of student mobility and a smaller percentage of fully credentialed teachers than the unsuccessful schools. Larger schools were also more successful than smaller schools at sustaining improved student test scores.

This is not to suggest that schools should advocate for increased student mobility, uncredentialed teachers, or larger enrollments to improve student achievement. Neither specific characteristics of schools nor qualities of students seemed to account for the striking differences between successful and unsuccessful schools in this study. Rather, improved student achievement seems to be the product of how well a school operates and depends on the quality of leadership and the effectiveness of instructional programs and practices.

Teacher Leadership

Strong teacher leadership was apparent in each of the four successful sample schools. Teacher leadership appeared to develop when three conditions were present. First, the teachers had ample opportunities to make decisions about teaching and learning. Successful schools provided teachers

with time to meet as grade-level or subject-matter teams. Moreover, teachers at successful schools reported that they regularly used this collaborative time to review student work and to discuss how to strengthen their classroom instruction.

Second, teachers engaged in various forms of informal action research. They used the results of their students' assessments to compare different instructional strategies and different classroom environments to see which strategies and environments encouraged student learning. Working together in this way enabled them to create a continual improvement cycle for their instruction.

Third, teachers developed their own internal leadership structures—such as team teaching, mentoring new teachers, and collaborating to share lesson designs—to support one another's resolve to improve student achievement.

Teacher leaders at the successful schools also made policy decisions. These decisions included the design of student intervention programs, the creation of student learning groups based on the individual student's skill weaknesses, the implementation of new standards-based grading systems, and a new focus on instructional strategies, such as reciprocal teaching. The teachers implemented these new programs themselves. To ensure consistency of implementation, they met informally to monitor teacher usage of the programs. When asked which changes contributed to sustained increases in student achievement, teachers at the successful schools cited these kinds of teacher-initiated changes in teaching and learning.

Teacher leadership was strengthened in the successful schools when teachers made decisions regarding professional development. To select appropriate professional development, teachers analyzed student data and determined where students needed academic support. For example, in one middle school, students tested poorly on reading comprehension. Teachers arranged for professional development for all staff members—including mathematics, science, and social studies teachers—in how to teach reading using informational text. After receiving the professional development and implementing specific instructional strategies in the classroom, teachers reassessed the students to see whether their test scores had improved.

In three of the four successful sample schools, teachers sought professional development that focused on improved pedagogy. Their selection of professional development for staff members focused on learning how to use Marzano's nine effective teaching strategies (Marzano, Pickering, & Pollock, 2001) and on increasing the rigor of their instruction by asking questions that required students to analyze, synthesize, and evaluate new concepts. The teachers believed that their focus on pedagogy strengthened their collaborative teams.

Teachers at successful schools spent between one and four hours weekly in collaborative lesson planning. This took place informally, during lunch or after school, as well as in formal weekly planning meetings. Informal conversations focused on successful lessons or problems in teaching specific concepts. In the formal weekly planning meetings, teachers shared student assessment data, analyzed student work, and monitored their own progress toward teaching the standards. Most of the successful schools hired substitutes to provide teachers with regular collaboration time. Teachers from unsuccessful schools reported that they collaborated "when the principal scheduled it in place of a staff meeting." These meetings generally focused on planning for field trips, special events, and state testing.

Increased teacher leadership also created challenges. Teacher leaders cited personality conflicts with colleagues and perceived resentment from those teachers who were not in leadership positions. All teachers were subsequently offered professional development to improve their leadership skills. Staff development included video models of effective teacher-team meetings that foster collegial and professional relationships. Professional development included training in creating an effective agenda and conducting productive meetings. Teachers experienced in meeting management and creating consensus coached and mentored teachers who were new to leadership positions.

Principal Leadership

The successful schools in the study, as opposed to the unsuccessful ones, more often had the same principal for the last three years. Principals from successful schools believed that their previous experience in high-performing schools helped them hold higher expectations for students in their state improvement program schools. Principals stated that few colleagues, however, voluntarily sought principal positions at such schools. One experienced principal recently assigned to a state improvement program school said that when his colleagues learned of his new assignment, they asked, "Who did you tick off?"

> **Previous experience in high-performing schools helped principals hold higher expectations for students in their state improvement program schools.**

Principals at the successful schools were more likely to create time for teachers to collaborate and to provide them with structured support. This included the principal's frequent attendance at grade-level or department meetings and the expec-tation that teachers provide feedback on the meetings and let the principal know what he or she could do to help them. As a result, teachers at these schools said that they regularly reviewed student work, created rubrics and assessments, modeled lessons, and monitored how they used the professional development in the classroom.

When asked what they did to improve student achievement at their schools, principals from successful schools produced lists of programs, interventions, and professional development opportunities that contributed to this goal. These principals were comfortable using data and making changes when the data demonstrated that student achievement had not risen. "You can't feel sorry that something doesn't work; you just have to try something different," explained one principal after determining that the school would have to abandon an unsuccessful after-school program.

The principals from the unsuccessful schools were far less comfortable with data. One principal from an unsuccessful school described his attempts to use data to improve his school's effectiveness in raising student achievement as "shooting at moving targets." He claimed that the school could not achieve its state growth targets because "the failing group just keeps changing."

District Office Leadership

When asked to list three factors that were most likely to improve test scores, surveyed principals from both successful and unsuccessful schools included district leadership. All the unsuccessful sample schools demonstrated a lack of strong district leadership.

District leaders in successful schools provided more services than their counterparts in unsuccessful schools did. The successful schools benefited from focused districtwide professorial development on pedagogy. Moreover, each summer the district office delivered follow-up professional development for new hires so that all teachers would have the opportunity to learn the same teaching strategies.

At the start of each school term, successful schools more often received assessment data desegregated by teacher and by individual student than did unsuccessful schools. Teachers and principals also received training on how to use these data to improve instruction and academic achievement. In successful schools, teachers were more likely to find value in the district-provided benchmark assessments designed to track a student's learning. Teachers talked about how they used the assessment results to modify their instruction, such as creating student intervention and enrichment groups. The teachers sometimes agreed to alter their pacing calendars when they learned that the students were grasping new concepts either more quickly or more slowly than they had anticipated.

Principals from both successful and unsuccessful schools discussed their districts' practice of assigning experienced principals to schools with the greatest parent involvement and the greatest potential for parent conflicts. These schools tended to be in the highest socioeconomic areas of the district. New principals were placed in schools in which parent demands and conflicts were expected to be fewer. These schools tended to be in the lowest socioeconomic areas of the district. This practice contributed to a belief that ultimately became part of the culture—that assignment to low socioeconomic schools was either an entry-level position for new principals or a way of penalizing them for being unable to effectively handle parent conflicts. Transferring from lower to higher socioeconomic areas naturally represented a promotion.

A few districts changed this negative perception by placing principals alternately at high-achieving schools and at state improvement program schools. Experience at both types of schools helped principals develop high expectations for their students' academic achievement and increased the number of principals who had firsthand knowledge of both types of schools. The practice also fostered a new belief that both kinds of schools offer opportunities for professional growth.

Each of the eight principals interviewed for the study stated that the workload and pressure was greater for principals at low-performing schools. Principals from the successful schools said that their districts scheduled monthly cohort meetings with all the district s state improvement program schools. The principals so valued these meetings that they have continued to meet two years after leaving the state improvement program. Said one principal.

> For the first time, I went to a meeting where I felt safe to share all the problems I was having. I say things in our cohort meeting that I would never say when all the district principals get together.

Some districts implemented a policy for state improvement program schools to receive additional district services. These services included additional professional development, additional visitations and support in curriculum and instruction from district personnel, district-provided grant writers, more comprehensive data analysis, and greater on-site visibility of the district superintendent. Unsuccessful schools did not receive these services.

Programs and Practices

Students who are learning English as a second language and students who are academically below grade level attending the successful schools had quite different experiences from those of comparable students who attended unsuccessful schools.

At the successful schools, teachers presented instruction that directly reinforced the students' understanding of how the English language works instead of teaching students conversational English. For example, rather than use curriculum that focused on teaching situational vocabulary—such as how to order a meal in a restaurant—teachers at successful schools used curriculum that focused on academic English and taught students how to use root words, suffixes, prefixes, and verb endings. Teachers believed that their focus on academic English gave all their students—both native and non-

native speakers of English—an advantage on the state test.

Teachers from the successful schools reported that students were grouped by their English language levels. The students received at least 40 minutes of instruction daily in how to read, write, and speak English. In contrast, teachers at the unsuccessful schools did not always group students by language levels and said they taught English language development "when they had time." At successful schools, students not making adequate progress in English language acquisition received personal intervention and additional instruction in a pullout program.

In the successful schools, principals and district office personnel were instrumental in supporting all newly adopted district programs. At one successful elementary school, a new English language development program received far greater district support than the unsuccessful schools received. In this particular school, the district office paid for teacher training in the first year of program implementation and repeated the training yearly for all teachers new to the district. Administrators also made frequent classroom visits to verify consistent implementation and provide additional materials or training if needed.

Students who performed below grade level in language arts and mathematics at successful schools were far more likely to receive intervention in addition to their regular instruction than were students attending unsuccessful schools. This additional instruction occurred during the school day with credentialed teachers. One teacher in a successful school stated, "We used to have paraeducators running the intervention groups until we realized that we needed our strongest teachers with our most at-risk students." When students showed proficiency in the targeted skills, they either exited the intervention programs or received additional instruction in other weak skill areas.

Encouraging News

The results of this study support the research studies of Mintrop (2003).

Darling-Hammond (1997), and Barth (1990), which suggest that the solutions to improving education lie inside the schoolhouse. Schools and districts can replicate the successful strategies discussed here if they are willing to change in crucial ways.

One of the study's sample schools did just that. The overcrowded urban elementary school, with a student population of 1,119, is on a year-round multitrack and has a staggered schedule for 1st and 2nd grade. This schedule requires two teachers and 40 students to share a classroom for nearly two hours daily. Each 3rd through 6th grade class has 40 students enrolled. Eighty percent of students are English language learners, and 95 percent receive free or reduced price lunch. In the last four years, the school has had three principals and a 40 percent turnover in teaching staff. In 2003, the school moved to a temporary school site to allow for the construction of new classrooms. The school is scheduled to return to the original site sometime this year.

Despite the challenges, the school made its growth targets for four consecutive years.

When asked how they transformed their school from one that had the lowest test scores in the state to one noted for sustained improvement in student achievement, teachers credited changes in the district office's support of the school and changes in the schools instructional practices and programs. "We became very focused," said one teacher Another teacher cited evidence that these efforts are working. "Now the teachers *want* to be here," she said. "Last year we only lost two teachers." A telling comment made by a teacher revealed the staff's optimistic view of the school's future:

> When we return to the original school site in 2000, we won't be overcrowded and sharing classrooms. We're going to make even bigger jumps in student learning.

Schools and districts can bring about student achievement and sustain that achievement if they are willing to examine their practices and embrace change. All schools can replicate these strategies and make improved education available to everyone.

References

Barth, R. S. (1990). *Improving schools from within*. San Francisco: Jossey-Bass.

Darling-Hammond, L. (1997). *The right to learn*. San Francisco: Jossey-Bass.

Just, A. E., & Boese, L. E. (2002). *Immediate intervention/underperforming schools program: How California's low-performing schools are continuing their efforts to improve student achievement* (Research Summary). Sacramento. CA: California Department of Education Policy and Evaluation Unit.

Marzano, R. J., Pickering, D. J., & Pollock, J. E. (2001). *Classroom instruction that works*. Alexandria. VA: ASCD.

Mintrop, H. (2003). The limits of sanctions in low-performing schools: A study of Maryland and Kentucky schools on probation. *Education Policy Analysis Archives, 11*(3), 32.

Valerie Chrisman is Director of District and School Support Services at the Ventura County Superintendent of Schools Office, Ventura, California; vchrisman@vcss.k12.ca.us.

A CASE FOR SCHOOL CONNECTEDNESS

Students are more likely to succeed when they feel connected to school.

Robert W. Blum

School bonding, school climate, teacher support, student engagement: Researchers have used these terms over the years to address the concept of school connectedness. School connectedness refers to an academic environment in which students believe that adults in the school care about their learning and about them as individuals.

Klem and Connell (2004) provide a frightening statistic in this regard, noting that

> By high school, as many as 40 to 60 percent of all students—urban, suburban, and rural—are chronically disengaged from school, (p. 262)

Is it possible that half of our high school students may *not* believe that adults in school care about their learning and about them as individuals? More to the point, what can educators do to reconnect these large numbers of chronically disconnected students?

Although connecting students to school is important at all grade levels, it's especially crucial during the adolescent years. In the last decade, educators and school health professionals have increasingly pointed to school connectedness as an important factor in reducing the likelihood that adolescents will engage in health-compromising behaviors. A connected school environment also increases the likelihood of academic success.

A great deal of research looks at school connectedness. But because this research spans so many

fields—medicine, education, psychology, and sociology—and because it tackles so many related concepts, such as student engagement and school climate, the concept of school connectedness does not offer a clearly defined empirical base. In this era of accountability and standards, school connectedness can seem like a soft approach to school improvement. It can, however, have a substantial impact on the measures of student achievement for which schools are currently being held accountable.

In response to the weight of evidence that supports school connectedness, my colleagues and I convened an invitational conference at the Wingspread Conference Center in Racine, Wisconsin. Our goal was to bring together key researchers as well as representatives from the government, education, and health sectors to identify the current state of research-based knowledge related to school connectedness. Using this information, we synthesized a set of core principles about school connectedness to guide schools across the United States.[1] We titled this synthesis the *Wingspread Declaration on School Connections*.

DISTILLING THE RESEARCH

When one looks at the research literature across the different fields of inquiry, three school characteristics stand out as helping young people feel connected to school while simultaneously encouraging student achievement: (1) high academic standards coupled with strong teacher

support; (2) an environment in which adult and student relationships are positive and respectful; and (3) a physically and emotionally safe school environment. Students who feel connected to school (independent of how these students are faring academically) are less likely to use substances, exhibit emotional distress, demonstrate violent or deviant behavior, experience suicidal thoughts or attempt suicide, and become pregnant (Lonczak, Abbott, Hawkins, Kosterman, & Catalano, 2002; Samdal, Nutbeam, Wold, & Kannas, 1998). In addition, when young people feel connected to school, they are less likely to skip school or be involved in fighting, bullying, and vandalism (Schapps, 2005; Wilson & Elliott, 2003). These students are more likely to succeed academically and graduate (Connell, Halpern-Felsher, Clifford, Crichlow, & Usinger, 1995; Wentzel, 1998).

> **IS IT POSSIBLE THAT HALF OF OUR HIGH SCHOOL STUDENTS MAY NOT BELIEVE THAT ADULTS IN SCHOOL CARE ABOUT THEIR LEARNING AND ABOUT THEM AS INDIVIDUALS?**

What are the factors that influence school connectedness? Students who experience school connectedness like school, feel that they belong, believe teachers care about them and their learning, believe that education matters, have friends at school, believe that discipline is fair, and have opportunities to participate in extracurricular activities.

Major threats to school connectedness include social isolation, lack of safety in school, and poor classroom management. Social isolation, which is especially risky for adolescents, can result from students being ignored, bullied, or teased (Bishop et al., 2004) and tends to flourish in environments predominated by social cliques. Unsafe or chaotic schools and schools with poorly managed classrooms simply cannot provide a stable environment for respectful and meaningful student learning.

HOW SCHOOLS CAN HELP

How can schools encourage school connectedness? It does not come about purely as the result of rules, regulations, and zero-tolerance policies, which can actually mold harsh school environments. Connections spring instead from individual action on the part of both teachers and administrators as well as from more elusive factors, such as school environment.

Teachers are obviously central to the equation. Although school connectedness might suggest smaller class sizes, the classroom s culture seems to matter more than its size does. Effective teachers can create connectedness in the classroom in a number of ways. When teachers make learning meaningful and relevant to their students' lives, students develop a stake in their own education. When teachers create a clear classroom structure with consistent expectations for behavior and performance, they provide a healthy setting in which students can exercise autonomy and practice decision-making skills. Teachers build connectedness in the classroom when they encourage team learning exercises. Cooperative learning tends to break down social isolation by integrating student teams across gender, academic ability, and ethnicity. Rewarding a variety of student achievements and recognizing student progress—not only top performance—are also important components.

But teachers cannot create school connectedness on their own. Without a supportive administration, teachers

> **SCHOOL CONNECTEDNESS CAN HAVE A SUBSTANTIAL IMPACT ON THE MEASURES OF STUDENT ACHIEVEMENT FOR WHICH SCHOOLS ARE CURRENTLY BEING HELD ACCOUNTABLE.**

will not be able to effectively support their students. For example, when a school allows a young person to fail—when it doesn't do everything in its power to retain that student—students get the message, "In this school, there are winners and there are losers." This assumption sets up a dysfunctional dichotomy: Those less likely to do well academically will strive to create an antiacademic climate because they know they can't win at the game. The perceived winners—those who are academically proficient—are seen as "nerds," as "dorks," and, ironically enough, as "losers." But when a principal calls home, when he or she follows up every time a student misses school, students get a different message entirely: in this school, all students are expected to succeed."

A study panel from the National Research Council and the Institute of Medicine (2004) identified a series of factors associated with school engagement. Educators can substantially increase school connectedness in their students when they

- Avoid separating students onto vocational and college tracks.
- Set high academic standards for all students and provide all students with the same core curriculum.
- Limit the size of the school to create small learning environments.
- Form multidisciplinary education teams in which groups of teachers work with students.
- Ensure that every student has an advisor.
- Provide mentorship programs.
- Ensure that course content is relevant to the lives of students.
- Provide service learning and community service projects.
- Provide experiential, hands-on learning opportunities.
- Use a wide variety of instructional methods and technologies.
- Extend the class period, school day, and/or school year.

- Provide opportunities for students who are falling behind to catch up.

THE WINGSPREAD DECLARATION ON SCHOOL CONNECTIONS

A generation of exciting research has reviewed strategies that have proven effective in creating engaging school climates in which young people feel connected. The Wingspread Declaration on School Connections is based on a detailed review of this research as well as on in-depth discussions among leaders in the health and education fields. The declaration's insights can form the foundation for school environments in which all students, regardless of their academic capacity, are engaged and feel part of the education endeavor.

> **WE NEED TO USE WHAT RESEARCH AND EXPERIENCE HAVE TAUGHT US TO CREATE SCHOOLS WHERE STUDENTS FEEL CONNECTED.**

We are responsible for our schools. We need to use what research and experience have taught us to create schools where students feel connected. We want high schoolers who are convinced that the adults with whom they interact care about them as individuals and care about their learning these schools must establish high standards, challenge all students to reach their potential, and provide the support students need to succeed.

NOTE

1. This work was supported by the Centers for Disease Control and Prevention's Division of Adolescent and School Health (DASH). The proceedings from the invitational conference and the *Wingspread Declaration on School Connections* are available at www.allaboutkids.umn.edu/WingfortheWeb/schooldeclaration.pdf. ASCD was a conference participant.

Wingspread Declaration on School Connections

Students are more likely to succeed when they feel connected to school. School connection is the belief by students that adults in the school care about their learning as well as about them as individuals. The critical requirements for feeling connected include students' experiencing

- High academic expectations and rigor coupled with support for learning.
- Positive adult/student relationships.
- Physical and emotional safety. Increasing the number of students connected to school is likely to influence critical accountability measures, such as
- Academic performance.
- Incidents of fighting, bullying, or vandalism.
- Absenteeism.
- School completion rates.

Strong scientific evidence demonstrates that increased student connection to school promotes

- Motivation.
- Classroom engagement.
- Improved school attendance.

These three factors in turn increase academic achievement. These findings apply across racial, ethnic, and income groups.

Likewise, there is strong evidence that a student who feels connected to school is less likely to exhibit

- Disruptive behavior.
- School violence.
- Substance and tobacco use.
- Emotional distress.
- Early age of first sex.

The most effective strategies for increasing the likelihood that students will be connected to school include

- Implementing high standards and expectations and providing academic support to all students.
- Applying fair and consistent disciplinary policies that are collectively agreed upon and fairly enforced.
- Creating trusting relationships among students, teachers, staff, administrators, and families.
- Hiring and supporting capable teachers skilled in content, teaching techniques, and classroom management to meet each learner's needs.

- Fostering high parent/family expectations for school performance and school completion.
- Ensuring that every student feels close to at least one supportive adult at school.

Best Bets Warranting Further Research

- Programs and approaches that create positive and purposeful peer support and peer norms.
- Strategies that work to promote connection to school among disenfranchised groups.
- Analysis of the costs and effectiveness of different programs for fostering school connectedness.
- Evaluation of new and existing curricular approaches, staff and administrator training, and various institutional structures.
- Effects of school connectedness in students on teacher morale, effectiveness, and turnover.

REFERENCES

Bishop, J. H., Bishop, M., Bishop, M., Gelbwasser, L., Green, S., Peterson, E., et al. (2004). *Journal of School Health, 74*(7), 235–251.

Connell, J. P., Halpern-Felsher, B., Clifford, E., Crichlow, W., & Usinger, P. (1995). Hanging in there: Behavioral, physiological, and contextual factors affecting whether African-American adolescents stay in school. *Journal of Adolescent Research, 10*(1), 41–63.

Klem, A. M., & Connell, J. P. (2004). Relationships matter: Linking teacher support to student engagement and achievement. *Journal of School Health, 74*(7), 262-273.

Lonczak, H. S., Abbott, R. O., Hawkins, J. D., Kosterman, R., & Catalano, R. (2002). "The effects of the Seattle Social Development Project: Behavior, pregnancy, birth, and sexually transmitted disease outcomes by age 21. *Archives of Pediatric Adolescent Health, 156*, 438–447.

National Research Council and Institute of Medicine. (2004). *Engaging schools: Fostering high school students' motivation to learn.* Washington, DC: The National Academies Press. Available: www.nap.edu/books/0309084350/html/

Samdal, O., Nutbeam, D., Wold, B., & Kannas, L. (1998). Achieving health and educational goals through schools. *Health Education Research, 13*, 383–397.

Schapps, E. (2003, April). *The role of supportive school environments in promoting academic success.* Sacramento, CA: California Department of Education Press.

Wentzel, K. R. (1998). Social relationships and motivation in middle school. *Journal of Educational Psychology, 90*(2), 202–209.

Wilson, D., & Elliott, D. (2003. June). *We interface of school climate and school connectedness: An exploratory review and study.* Paper presented at the Wingspread Conference on School Connectedness: Strengthening Health and Educational Outcomes for Teens, Racine, Wisconsin.

Robert W. Blum is Professor and William H. Gates Sr. Chair, Department of Population and Family Health Sciences, Johns Hopkins Bloomberg School of Public Health, Baltimore, Maryland.

From *Educational Leadership,* April 2005, pp. 16-20. Reprinted by permission of the Association for Supervision and Curriculum Development. Copyright © 2005 by ASCD. All rights reserved. The Association for Supervision and Curriculum Development is a worldwide community of educators advocating sound policies and sharing best practices to achieve the success of each learner. To learn more, visit ASCD at www.ascd.org

NO CHILD LEFT BEHIND

The Illusion of School Choice

Lisa Snell

Like every junior high school student in Camden, New Jersey, 12-year-old Ashley Fernandez attends a school that has been designated as failing under state and federal standards for more than three years. But low expectations were the least of this seventh-grader's problems. In 2004 Ashley's gym teacher became irritated by his unruly class and punished all the girls by putting them in the boys' locker room. Two boys dragged Ashley into the shower room. One held her arms and the other held her legs while they fondled her for more than 10 minutes. The teacher was not present, and no one helped Ashley.

Ashley's principal, who has refused to acknowledge the assault, denied her a transfer out of Morgan Village Middle School. Since the gym incident, Ashley has received numerous threats, including repeated confrontations with male students who grab her and then run away. When Ashley's mother began keeping her home from school, she got a court summons for allowing truancy.

Ashley is not alone. Last year Carmen Santana's grandson Abraham was afraid to go to his classes at Camden High School after two boys hit him in the face, broke his nose, and chipped his teeth. Santana was also charged with allowing truancy while she sought permission for Abraham to complete his senior year studies at home.

In 2004 Samet Kieng was almost killed at Camden's Woodrow Wilson High School after refusing to give up his chemistry class stool to a latecomer. According to a *Philadelphia Inquirer* story based on Samet's account, "his assailant, who outweighs him by about 60 pounds, typically arrived late for chemistry class and demanded Kieng's seat. Kieng was studying for the state's high school proficiency exam and refused to move. Kieng said he was surprised when the student confronted him later in the locker room." He was beaten by at least four students. Samet could transfer to the other public high school in Camden, but it is officially designated as "persistently dangerous."

In all, more than 100 parents have removed their children from Camden schools because of safety concerns. The school district's response: a truancy crackdown.

BETRAYAL OF ADULT RESPONSIBILITY

This situation is exactly the sort of problem that George W. Bush's much-ballyhooed No Child Left Behind Act (NCLB) was supposed to address. As the president said in a January 2001 press conference introducing the law, "American children must not be left in persistently dangerous or failing schools. When schools do not teach and will not change, parents and students must have other meaningful options. And when children or teenagers go to school afraid of being threatened or attacked or worse, our society must make it clear it's the ultimate betrayal of adult responsibility."

NCLB was supposed to rescue kids like Ashley, Abraham, and Samet. The legislation was passed in December 2001 by a bipartisan coalition led by President Bush and Sen. Ted Kennedy (D-Mass.). Its central components include annual math and reading tests for students in grades 3 to 8 based on state standards; parent-friendly report cards with assessment results broken out by poverty, race, ethnicity, disability, and English-language proficiency; and the promise to offer parents a choice of a better public school when their child's school is designated as dangerous or has failed to meet its state's academic standards for two years in a row.

As Bush explained in a January 8, 2002, speech at the University of New Hampshire, "If a school can't change, if a school can't show the parents and community leaders that they can teach the basics, something else has to take place. In order for there to be accountability, there has [sic] to be consequences. And the consequence in this bill is that after a period of time, if a parent is tired of their child being trapped into [sic] a failed school, that parent will have different options, public school choice, charter, and private tutoring."

Similarly, Kennedy—who has since charged that NCLB has been inadequately funded and implemented—initially declared that the bill's "message to every parent" is "help is on the way." In one of many press releases celebrating the act, U.S. Rep. John Boehner (R-Ohio), chairman of the House Education Committee, promised that "these changes represent a significant departure from the status quo and will empower low-income parents with new options and new choices."

Three years later, Camden's families across the United States are still trapped in failing and dangerous schools. There are many adjectives that describe their relationship with the public school system, but *empowered* is not one of them.

Since the No Child Left Behind Act was passed, less than 2 percent of parents nationwide have transferred their children to other public schools. Teachers unions, school administrators, and journalists have argued that the low transfer rates prove parents do not want more choices and that they prefer their local schools. But while parents have more information than ever about the quality of their children's schools, in most cases they still have no way out of a failing institution.

Districts have not made a good-faith effort to implement public school choice. Sometimes parents are not notified of their option to change schools at all; other times they're told only after the school year is well under way. Some districts send parents letters discouraging them from transferring their kids. The choices themselves are limited to marginally better schools, with superior institutions often refusing to accept low-performing students.

ONE BAD SCHOOL TO ANOTHER

A February 2004 report by the Civil Rights Project at Harvard found that in 10 urban school districts with large concentrations of children eligible to exercise school choice under NCLB, less than 3 percent of eligible students requested a transfer. Even with the small number of requests, no district in the study was able to approve all or even most of the transfer requests.

Many parents of students in failing schools are not even aware of the right to transfer. A federally funded survey of Buffalo parents by the Brighter Choice Public School Project found that 75 percent of the parents surveyed did not realize their children attended a school designated as in need of improvement, which means it did not make adequate yearly progress in reading or math for two consecutive years. A full 92 percent said they would like to switch schools. A comparable percentage of parents in Albany also were unaware of the transfer option.

Similarly, a survey by the Boston-based Pioneer Institute found that only 29 percent of parents with children in underperforming schools knew the status of their children's schools, compared to 59 percent of parents whose children attended satisfactorily performing schools. Few Massachusetts parents knew they could transfer their children from underperforming schools to more successful schools. Out of about 100,000 Massachusetts students eligible to transfer out of underperforming schools, fewer than 300 have opted to do so.

In the end, though, the problem is not the parents but the law itself. Under NCLB, Title I federal funding—money used to provide extra educational services to disadvantaged students in high-poverty schools—does not follow children to better-performing, non-Title I schools. The result is that better-performing schools have no financial incentive to admit low-performing children.

In practice, children are offered transfers only to other Title I schools. Since most Title I schools are mediocre performers at best, parents have a choice of schools that are only marginally better. Furthermore, the school districts decide which schools parents will be allowed to "choose"; often they offer only one or two alternatives.

FALSE CHOICE

Many parents are offered "choice" schools that are just as low-performing as the failing school they are trying to break away from. In the words of school choice advocate Angel Cordero of the New Jersey-based Education Excellence for Everyone, "Camden children are transferred from one bad school to another bad school."

In Chicago students in only 50 of the 179 federally identified failing elementary schools would be allowed to move into higher-performing schools. Parents could choose from a list of 90 schools and could not pick a school more than three miles away from home. In 70 of the 90 schools open to transfers, most pupils failed state tests last year.

In San Bernardino, California, the designated school of choice for high school students was Arroyo Valley High School, which had lower test scores than the schools that were officially designated as failing. How could that happen? Federal standards did not designate Arroyo as underperforming only because until 2003-04 it was not considered "fully functional." (That was the first year it served all four grade levels.) District officials acknowledge that Arroyo isn't necessarily any better than the rest, but it is the only high school option available, since four out of the five high schools are underperforming and considered in "program improvement," an NCLB euphemism for schools that have failed for more than three years in a row.

In October 2003 Connecticut's *Hartford Courant* described how for months Stacy May fought to transfer her son Taren out of Kinsella Elementary. Hartford school officials confirmed to the newspaper that May was welcome to transfer her son because Kinsella was now labeled a "school in need of improvement." But the district limited May's choices to three other schools, all of which had low scores on the state's standardized test and all of which are now also designated "in need of improvement."

In Palm Beach County, Florida, district officials are projecting that as many as 50,000 students at 64 of the poorest schools could choose another school this fall. But here again, many high-performing schools will be off-limits—and parents will have only two weeks to decide whether they want their children to move.

Even when parents make direct requests for transfers, districts frequently refuse to grant them. In New York

City in 2002-03, more than 278,000 students were eligible for school choice transfers, 6,400 students requested transfers, and the district granted only 1,500 requests. That same year Richmond, Virginia, had just 120 requests for transfer out of 8,000 eligible children, and the district honored only 30.

Transfers are refused because the better schools are at capacity. The federal law ignores the grim reality that many urban districts have few high-performing schools with open slots. As the chief executive of Chicago Public Schools, Arne Duncan, told *Time* magazine in September 2003, "It's not like we have a lot of high-performing schools at 50% capacity."

CHICAGO SOLUTION

The lack of slots might be less of a problem if Title I dollars could follow children to higher-performing schools. But a better solution is to break up the education dollars to increase capacity, allow more competition, and increase high-quality choices. In June 2004, for example, Chicago Mayor Richard Daley, who is in the unique position of legally controlling Chicago schools, introduced a plan to open 100 of the city's worst-performing schools to competition. By 2010 Daley intends to recreate more than 10 percent of the city's schools—one-third as charter schools, one-third as independently operated contract schools, and the remainder as small schools run by the district. Unfortunately, the governance structures of most school districts make it politically difficult to replicate Daley's plan: They would require approval by a school board or state legislation.

When parents are provided with real choice, demand increases dramatically. Since 1999, the privately funded Children's Scholarship Fund (CSF) has provided more than 62,000 low-income children across the nation with scholarships to attend private schools. The first year, more than 1.25 million children applied in 20,000 communities; since it was launched, the average income of participating families has been $22,000. The children's new schools may be parochial, denominational, independent, or a home school. They do not have to belong to any organization or meet any other requirement. The choice is left up to each family.

This year more than 24,000 kids are using CSF tuition assistance to attend a wide variety of private schools. In Los Angeles in 2003, only 229 children managed to transfer to a different public school under No Child Left Behind. Yet the Southern California Children's Scholarship Fund placed 1,600 children and has a waiting list of more than 5,000 names. Los Angeles charter schools such as Fenton Avenue Charter School, Camino Nuevo, and Accelerated Learning also have long waiting lists.

Around the country, the few bona fide school choice and tax credit programs continue to add children every year and often have long waiting lists as well. For example, Florida's Corporate Tax Credit Scholarship program, which provides scholarships to low-income children to attend public or private schools, serves 13,000 children, with another 20,000 waiting to get in. Parents may not be getting much choice, but they are getting a big tax bill. In a July study, the Cato Institute's Neal McCluskey notes that federal spending at the more than 36 departments and organizations that run major education programs ballooned from about $25 billion in 1965 (adjusted for inflation) to more than $108 billion in 2002. This year funding for the U.S. Department of Education is at an all-time high: $56 billion, an increase of $2.9 billion over last year and $13.8 billion since Bush took office.

The president's 2005 budget would raise education spending still further, to $57.3 billion. Under No Child Left Behind, Title I aid has risen to $12.4 billion. Title I spending has increased more during the first two years of the Bush administration than it did during all eight years of Bill Clinton's administration.

UNENFORCEABLE CHOICE

Despite state education leaders' cries that schools cannot afford the choices that NCLB was supposed to enshrine in law, districts are sitting on $5.8 billion in unspent federal funding from previous years, including nearly $2 billion in Title I aid. New York ranks first with $689 million in unspent funds; California is second with $671 million. Such money could provide many scholarships to better-performing private or public schools. Local districts claim that the unused funding is already obligated to existing programs and that federal funding rules are responsible for the delays.

Extra dollars do not necessarily equal better performance. More than 26,000 schools have been designated as failing under NCLB. The 2003 National Assessment of Educational Progress (NAEP) found that more than two-thirds of fourth- and eighth-graders were not proficient in math and reading. The NAEP also provides troubling news for students in Title I schools. In math, for example, 7 percent of black eighth-graders and 11 percent of Hispanics are proficient, while 61 percent and 53 percent, respectively, are "below basic."

Camden schools show that more money is not the answer. Camden is one of New Jersey's 30 *Abbott* districts—districts with low property-tax bases that receive supplemental funding from the state. As a result, Camden's per-pupil funding is higher than the New Jersey state average of $10,000 and the national average of $8,000; the Camden district has revenues of approximately $15,000 per pupil and receives large portions of federal Title I dollars. Camden schools had more than 1,200 incidents of serious violence in 2001-02, an increase of 300 percent from the previous year. The district has refused to release updated school violence numbers since then, but this year saw several highly publicized incidents, including a foiled Columbine-style plot to shoot students and an increase in the number of schools labeled persistently dangerous.

NOT ENFORCED

In the beginning, supporters of No Child Left Behind argued that its problems were just a matter of districts' adjusting to the new law. But as we begin the third school year in which kids are supposed to be able to escape failing schools, a lack of meaningful choice appears to be the norm.

The paucity of choice reflects another failure of the law: It has no real sanctions for schools that fail to comply. Parents can't even sue the government to compel federal officials to enforce the law. When parents in New York City and Albany sued their districts for denying children their rights to transfer and to receive tutoring services, a federal judge dismissed the suit, ruling that the law did not confer "choice" rights that could be enforced in court.

To judge from education activists' reports, going directly to the U.S. Department of Education doesn't seem to be an effective course of action either. New Jersey activist Angel Cordera repeatedly has tried in vain to get the Department of Education to enforce the law's school choice provision. In the meantime, he has worked tirelessly to find private scholarships for the most victimized children. Cordera recently found a place for Ashley Fernandez in a local Catholic school.

In the last two years, the Camden City Council (whose current members have never enrolled their own children in Camden's public schools) has twice passed resolutions calling for immediate school vouchers for the city's trapped children. Last fall the council voted 5-1 to ask the state of New Jersey to allow public funds to be used for scholarships. Such scholarships would enable children who are eligible to attend a school outside the Camden district, or even a private school. A 2003 survey by Rutgers University's Eagleton Institute found that 72 percent of residents in *Abbott* districts such as Camden support vouchers.

But for the time being, such options aren't available for students such as Ashley—and Abraham Santana and Samet Kieng. They don't have 15 years to wait for the No Child Left Behind Act to increase reading and math proficiency. They don't need Washington rhetoric about accountability, empowerment, or the imminent arrival of help. They need real choices now—while they're still in school and while they still have a chance to learn.

Lisa Snell is director of the Education and Child Welfare Program at the Reason Foundation. From "No Way Out," by Lisa Snell, Reason, October 2004, pages 35-39.

Charters "Yes!" Vouchers "No!"

Joe Nathan

We now have enough evidence that the charter school movement works if it's done right, as it has been here [in Minnesota].

—President Bill Clinton, May 2000

Charter schools are a marvelous Minnesota innovation that is spreading throughout the country.

—U.S. Senator Paul Wellstone, February 1997

More than forty years after Rosa Parks refused to give up her seat to a white passenger on a bus, the opening salvo in what became the Montgomery, Alabama, bus boycott, she is trying to set up one of the first charter schools in Detroit.

—Halimah Abdullah, June 1997

Why did our former president and the late progressive U.S. Senator Paul Wellstone support the charter public school approach, while rejecting public funds for private or parochial schools? Why has civil rights legend Rosa Parks been a strong charter supporter? Why has the number of states with some form of charter law grown from one in 1992 to forty-one today, and the number of charter schools from one to more than 3,000? This essay attempts to help answer those questions.

In order to understand the answers, one must understand how charters differ from vouchers. In the anchor essay of this issue of *Educational Horizons*, Charles Glenn lays the foundation for that discussion with his listing of the thirteen key points upon which he and I agree and the key points upon which we do not, which include "publicly funding religious schools, either directly or with vouchers…and allowing schools to set admissions requirements related to their educational mission." Although I have deep respect for the commitment and insights of Dr. Glenn, I consider those two points of disagreement to be of the utmost importance. They share a common denominator—vouchers—so it is in contrasting charters and vouchers that I can best address the topics of distinctive schools and parental choice.

This essay includes two sections. The first offers a brief explanation of the charter idea and shows how it is different from the voucher idea. The second describes some of the experience and research that help define the charter movement, including some that the American Federation of Teachers has attempted to promote in furtherance of its goal of blocking or blunting the movement.

What is the charter idea? How does it differ from the voucher approach?

The charter idea builds on four fundamental American principles:

1. People should have an opportunity to carry out their dreams and use their best ideas, including the opportunity to create schools that make sense.
2. This is a country of responsibilities, not just rights. Schools should have responsibilities, including the responsibility to improve student achievement, measured in various ways.
3. We believe in extensive, but not unlimited freedom; for example, the classic limitation on the freedom of speech is that Americans may not yell "Fire!" in a crowded theater. Educational freedom— within limits—is important.
4. We are skeptical of monopoly and support choice. Our system of public education should not be monolithic: it should offer choices to parents and students.

What is the charter idea? As adopted in 1991 by the Minnesota legislature, the charter idea has the following key features:

- The state will give more than one publicly accountable organization the power to authorize or sponsor new kinds of public schools. That could include the State Board of Education, local school boards, cities, universities, foundations, major non-profit organizations, etc.
- Those sponsors will develop a "charter" or contract with a group of people who want to create a new kind of public school, or want to convert an existing public school to something new.
- The contract will specify improvements in student achievement that the school will have to produce in order to have its contract renewed.
- The school will be public. It will be nonsectarian. It will not charge tuition. It will not have

admissions tests of any kind. It will follow health and safety regulations.

- Existing public schools may convert to charter status. That should happen if a majority of the teachers in the school vote to convert.

- The state will offer an up-front waiver of rules about curriculum, management, and teaching. The state may specify student outcomes, but determining how the school operates should be up to the people who establish and operate it. The charter school concept trades bureaucracy for accountability, regulation for results.

- The charter school will be a school of choice. Faculty, students, and families actively choose it. No one is assigned to be there.

- The school will become a discrete entity: The law may let the founders choose any organization available under general state law or may specify an organization, such as non-profit. As a legal entity, the school will have its board. There is real site management. Teachers, if employees, have full rights to organize and bargain collectively; however, their bargaining unit is separate from any district bargaining unit.

- The full per-pupil allocation will move with the student. That amount should be roughly the average state allocation per pupil or the average in the district from which the student comes. If the state provides extra funds for students from low-income families or with disabilities, those funds also should follow the students.

- Participating teachers should be protected and given new opportunities. To teach in charter schools, teachers may take leaves from public school systems, and while on leave will retain their seniority. They may continue to participate in the local or state retirement programs. New teachers may join state retirement programs. They may choose to be employees, or to organize a professional group under which they collectively own and operate the school.

How does the charter idea differ from the voucher approach? The key differences are two: First, with the charter idea schools must be nonsectarian, whereas with the voucher approach schools may be faith-based. Second, with the charter idea schools may not use admissions tests, whereas with the voucher approach schools may use admissions tests that do not violate antidiscrimination laws.

Let's talk about those issues, one by one.

Faith-based Schools: Within the last year, courts in Florida and Colorado have ruled that their state constitutions prohibit funding religious schools at the K-12 level. While the "separation of church and state" argument can be argued in several ways at the federal level, states appear to

be deciding that public funds should not go to religious K-12 schools. That makes great sense to me.

In this issue's anchor essay, Charles Glenn wrote that he and I both would "bar from participation schools which teach hatred or disrespect for any racial, religious, ethnic, or sexual group." True, but just try enforcing that. Faith-based schools are established to, among other things, promote a religion. One of the ways they do that is to show how their religion, whether it is Lutheran, Jewish, Catholic, Muslim, Hindu, or whatever, is superior to any and all others. Elsewhere in this issue, Steven Vryhof writes eloquently on the other side of the debate, but as I see it, while a school might also try to teach tolerance, the bottom line for most religious schools is the promotion of one religion over all others.

America already is an enormously diverse country and is becoming more so all the time. By and large we have avoided the centuries-long religious battles that we see in places like Ireland, the Middle East, and the Balkans. No one knows for certain how much religious schools have contributed to those conflicts, but materials from religious schools in those areas have been examined, and some are quite inflammatory.

Dr. Glenn has been, for decades, a passionate, articulate spokesperson and activist for educational equity. His characterization of the two of us as "allies" in that cause is accurate, so this statement clearly is not intended in any way to diminish respect for him or Steven Vryhof. However, it does not appear to me that they have given sufficient weight to the risk that schools might promote further religious divisions in this country.

Admissions tests: Glenn would allow for admissions tests except when they are used to exclude someone of a particular race or religion.

A major federal study found that thousands of magnet public schools use admissions tests, including the majority of magnet schools at the secondary level (Steel and Levine 1994). However, that has resulted in huge frustration in many communities. In fact, one of the nation's first voucher laws was sponsored by a Wisconsin African-American Democrat, Representative Polly Williams, who was frustrated with the fact that her relatives could not get into a magnet school in her Milwaukee neighborhood. Magnet schools have created a two-tier system in many communities, with the magnets able to screen out all but those they want. So low-achieving, troubled, or angry, alienated students have been screened out.

One of the reasons the charter movement was started was that its founders were deeply disturbed by the injustice of allowing some schools receiving public funds to screen students while insisting that other schools take all comers. Our center is working closely with high schools in a metropolitan area where there is a handful of elite "public" high schools that use admissions testing. That results in the elite schools having less than 5 percent students with disabilities and the neighborhood schools having more than 30 percent students with disabilities. The use of admissions tests is deeply unfair.

Why does the charter idea merit support?

Success stories: One reason the charter idea merits support is that the movement has helped generate ideas and approaches that clearly help students who traditionally have not done well in public education. Individual success stories abound, for example:

- Lawrence Hernandez, a young man from Pueblo, Colorado, was the first in his family to attend college. Hernandez taught at the Harvard Graduate School of Education, then he decided to return to his hometown to found Cesar Chavez Academy. The school mixes intensive instruction in the arts with a deep belief that students from low-income, limited-English-speaking families can do as well as students from middle-class communities where English is the first language and therefore is spoken at home. The Cesar Chavez Academy currently is rated among Colorado's top-achieving schools, and Hernandez is now working to start a high school (*Pueblo Chieftain* 2003).

- Codman Academy, an inner-city high school using many progressive education ideas,was featured in a recent *New York Times* article because its inner-city students are doing as well as most suburban students on the state's standardized tests (Rimer 2003).

- The Academy for the Pacific Rim, working with secondary students in urban Boston, has consistently been one of the city's top-ranked public schools among those that do not use admissions tests. The school starts each day with a "pep rally" for academics and gives some students a "gambatte" award recognizing academic persistence. ("Gambatte" is a Japanese term that translates roughly as "persist, keep going.") The school also mixes high expectations with active learning; for example, students attend a model Constitutional Convention in which they play the parts of people who attended the original convention (Nathan and Febey 2001).

- The Bill and Melinda Gates Foundation gave Minnesota New Country School about $7 million to replicate itself, based on the success of this rural charter. MNCS developed the idea of teacher owned schools run as cooperatives. That is a new option in the profession, giving educators the chance to act more like some doctors and attorneys who select their office administrators and run institutions as they think appropriate. MNCS also operates a secondary school that uses a project-based learning approach in which few classes are offered. Instead,

its 120 grade 7-12 students work with their families and an adviser to develop an individual plan that helps them meet their own needs and interests, and that also satisfies performance-based graduation requirements. Students are expected to make public presentations three times a year. There are no bells and virtually no classes, and students may move freely around the school, operating much like adults. Students work on projects for a time and then, on their own schedule, get up and go to the restroom or spend a few minutes as they wish, then return to work (Dirkswager 2002).

- Charter schools using the KIPP (Knowledge Is Power Program) approach developed by three young teachers have consistently outperformed other public schools serving similar low-income students. The founder of the Gap clothing store chain has given the KIPP founders $25 million to help create similar programs around the country (Wingert and Kantrowitz 2003).

A growing body of research: Another reason that the charter idea deserves support is that in addition to the individual success stories, scholarly research is demonstrating that in certain circumstances charter schools as a group perform better than traditional schools; for example:

- A report released in January 2004 by California's non-partisan Legislative Analyst's Office praised that state's charter movement and urged that it be expanded. Among the conclusions were that "charter schools are a viable reform strategy, expanding families' choices, encouraging parental involvement, increasing teacher satisfaction, enhancing principals' control over school-site decision-making, and broadening the curriculum without sacrificing time spent on core subjects." The report recommended, among other things, eliminating the state's cap on charter schools, consolidating fourteen categorical programs into block grants to make it easier for charter schools to apply for those funds, and allowing multiple authorizers of charter schools (Legislative Analyst's Office 2004).

- A study of charter schools serving a general education population (as opposed to charters established to serve students with whom traditional schools have failed) found that "charter schools serving the general student population outperformed nearby regular public schools on math tests by 0.08 standard deviations, equivalent to a benefit of 3 percentile points for a student starting at the 50th percentile, and outperformed regular public schools on reading tests by 0.04 standard deviations, or about two points for a student starting at the 50th percentile" (Greene et al. 2003).

- A study of California charter schools that converted from district to charter status finds "many conversion charters are producing average test scores with populations of children historically associated with low test scores" (Loveless 2003, 33).

- A Center for School Change study of charters in Minneapolis found that over a one-year period a higher percentage of students at six of the nine charters sponsored by the district made a year's worth of progress in reading, math, or both than the district average; over the previous two years, students at five of the seven district-sponsored charter schools had made more progress than the district average. That, despite the fact that Minneapolis charters enroll a higher percentage of students who do not speak English at home, a higher percentage of students of color (minorities), and a higher percentage of students from low-income families (Brandt 2003).

- A Wisconsin study found that fourth-graders in charter schools "are significantly less likely to perform at minimal or basic levels of achievement than their traditional counterparts (i.e., the charter school students performed higher). We found similar results, though not as strong, for 8th graders.... Charter schools may not be for all students—that is why they are a choice—but they serve some extremely well." That report is especially noteworthy because it was written by Professor John Witte, who had published earlier, critical questions about the impact of vouchers in Milwaukee (Witte 2004).

What about a report from the American Federation of Teachers analyzing federal data, which received extensive coverage in August 2004 (Nelson et al. 2004)?

Let's be clear: the AFT is far from a neutral group. The AFT and its state affiliates have battled the charter idea for years, strongly opposing the creation of laws allowing new schools that would not be controlled by unions and school boards. In 1993, AFT President Albert Shanker wrote that "vouchers, charters, and for-profit management schemes are all quick fixes that won't fix anything" (Shanker 1993). (Ironically, in the same column Shanker praised President Bill Clinton's initiatives in education, despite the fact that Clinton was a strong supporter of the charter movement.)

The National Assessment of Educational Progress Web site cited by the AFT represented less than 1 percent of all charter school students in the United States. The National Assessment did not, as other studies cited earlier in this essay have done, examine what *progress* students in charters have made relative to students in district schools.

After examining the AFT report and other reports on charter schools, newspapers around the United States concluded that the charter movement remained, as the liberal-leaning (Minneapolis) *Star Tribune* wrote, "[a]n option [the] U.S. still needs" (*Star Tribune* 2004).

- The *Wisconsin State Journal* in Madison wrote, "Educators and policymakers should embrace the spread of charter schools, which improve prospects for students who are low achievers in traditional classrooms" (*Wisconsin State Journal* 2004).

- A *Denver Post* editorial concluded, "Charters aren't a silver bullet, but they can offer an alternative that suits some students" (*Denver Post* 2004).

- And the St. Paul, Minnesota *Pioneer Press* wrote, "Charter schools provide [a] needed choice.... Many charter schools perform well academically." The editors urged that communities should be "replicating their success while eliminating schools that fail to deliver academic progress over time..." (*St. Paul Pioneer Press* 2004).

As the *Wisconsin State Journal* editorial pointed out,

> This analysis by the American Federation of Teachers is just another salvo in a campaign against innovation by defenders of the status quo. The study explores the wrong question and ignores some basic facts about the makeup of charter schools. The real question is: "Do charter schools improve student achievement?"

Stimulating broader system improvement. A third reason the charter idea is worth supporting is that in some places it has helped stimulate broader improvement. Research by Eric Rofes found that in states with strong laws that provided for multiple sponsorship the existence of a charter public school sector encouraged improvement in existing schools: "District personnel on at least five occasions in that study acknowledged, sometimes begrudgingly (sic), that charters had served to jump-start their efforts at reforms. While they initially opposed charters and the chartering had been accomplished outside their authority, they felt that district schools ultimately had benefited from the dynamics introduced by the charter school." Rofes noted, "States which had policies that provided for the chartering of new schools only through the local district showed significantly less evidence of reform efforts from the development of charter schools than did states which allowed for multiple sponsors" (Rofes, n.d., 19).

A few anecdotes help illustrate how competition can, in some circumstances, help stimulate improvement. About a year ago, a front-page article in Minnesota's largest daily paper noted that one district was modifying an existing elementary school to include studies of the Hmong culture. "School officials acknowledge that they are trying to keep Hmong parents from fleeing to nearby

Hope Academy Charter School, a Hmong-centered program" (Walsh 2003). Urban Coalition President Lee Pao Xiong is quoted as saying, "In the back of their mind, the school district knows they're losing students to charter schools. This is a way for them to keep those children."

Another example comes from Dr. Kent Matheson, the former Washington State superintendent of the year and president of the Washington State Superintendent's Association. In 1998, I was invited to debate Dr. Matheson in front of several hundred Idaho public school administrators. Matheson stunned the audience by noting that originally he had opposed the charter idea when he moved to Flagstaff, Arizona, to serve as superintendent. He said he initially regarded charters as "cutworms that would hurt the whole field of education," but had changed his mind. As he put it, "When planting a field, if you see cutworms, you use pesticide; that's what I wanted to do: stop the charter movement. But gradually I became a convert to the charter idea. Our state's charter law was a very strong motivating force making us want to compete" (Matheson 1998).

Matheson listed several reforms that were motivated, in part, by competition from local charter schools. One in particular stands out: he described a former state teacher of the year in his district who had been proposing a high school in cooperation with a local museum that would require all students to make presentations judged by local community and business people before graduating. The district principals resisted those ideas and he did not overrule them. When the charter law passed, that outstanding teacher made one last attempt to convince the district that her ideas made sense. When she was again rejected, she set up the proposed program as a charter school. After that, Matheson noted, when he and his high school principals went to local meetings, business and community leaders began to ask why the district was not requiring presentations from its own students. After some discussion, the high schools implemented the same practices.

Another example of response to competition comes from Boston. There, in the early 1990s, the local teachers union proposed creation of new small-school options within the district that would have been similar to those that have been created as part of the New Visions program in New York City. However, the local school board (called the School Committee) rejected that idea. Then the Massachusetts legislature passed a charter law allowing educators and community groups to apply directly to the state for permission to create charter schools. Eighteen of the first sixty-four charter proposals came from Boston. Faced with the potential loss of thousands of students, some of the district's most innovative teachers, and millions of dollars, the School Committee reversed itself and created the Boston Pilot School program. (See Nathan 1999 for more details.) [*For additional insight into the Boston Pilot School program, see also Deborah Meier's essay in* **educational HORIZONS** *82:4—Editor.*]

The growth of the charter idea

The charter idea has found support across the political spectrum. In a nationally televised campaign debate in 1992, both the Democratic candidate Bill Clinton and incumbent Republican President George H. W. Bush endorsed the idea. Liberal Democrat U.S. Senator Paul Wellstone praised the charter idea in a speech to a joint session of the Minnesota legislature, calling charter schools "that marvelous Minnesota innovation which is spreading throughout the country" (Wellstone 1997).

In 1992, only one state (Minnesota) had a charter law and only one charter school was operating. As of fall 2004, forty-one states have some form of charter law and approximately 3,000 charter schools are operating, serving between 600,000 and 700,000 students (Center for Education Reform 2004).

Will the charter movement by itself solve all of American education's problems? To this writer's knowledge after reviewing hundreds of documents on that subject, no one has suggested that the charter movement will be a panacea. The examples cited above suggest that the charter idea and individual charter schools sometimes helped stimulate improvements in traditional schools, but have the charter movement and individual charter schools produced dramatic improvements in every public school in America? Of course not. As Ted Kolderie notes:

> The prevailing notion is that existing schools will be transformed, like caterpillars into butterflies, as people who mean well and get resources try hard and act decisively after experts train them in how to "do better." The suggestion implicit in chartering is that the schools we want will be developed faster by creating them new. Neither theory need work perfectly: evaluation should simply compare the two; tell us whether chartering does some things that cannot be done as well in "regular" schools, or does them more quickly. (Kolderie 2003)

Wise states will use both strategies: trying to help improve existing schools and giving people opportunities to create new schools. And part of the opening of new schools and the improving of existing ones should be learning from success.

Almost twenty years ago, *New York Times* education editor Fred Hechinger wrote:

> Unfortunately, educators often pay no attention to success stories in newspapers or on television unless they are about their own schools. And when they do pay attention, they often complain that the reporter has been hoodwinked by a teacher or a principal seeking publicity. Or they cite particular circumstances that make it impossible for them to do the same thing. So successful experiments and outstanding performance are often left in isolation.… To those who lean on the established way of doing things, the successful rebel is not a model but a threat. For those

who want to find them, there are plenty of models of excellence.... Since American schools, in contrast to those of other countries, are not reformed by national edicts, emulation of these models is the only hope for education reform. It remains a dim hope as long as many educators, deliberately or not, fail to visit those islands of excellence and try to learn from them. Since the Deborah Meiers cannot be cloned, they might at least be studied. (Hechinger 1987)

Initially critics (such as the Minnesota Education Association) feared that charter schools would become "elite academies" (Furrer 1991). In fact, Minnesota's charter schools serve a higher percentage of students representing low-income, minority, and limited-English-speaking groups, and a higher percentage of students with disabilities. U.S. Department of Education figures show that nationally, charter schools enroll a higher percentage of minorities and a higher percentage of low-income students than do district schools.

These data are drawn from the U.S. Department of Education, National Center on Education Statistics figures in the School and Staffing Survey, 1999-2000. They are for charter public schools open as of the 1998-1999 school year and still operating in the 1999-2000 school year. (Percentages may not add up to 100 because of rounding.)

Combining the two highest categories (50-74 and 75-100) we find that at the elementary level there is a slightly higher percentage of charters serving predominantly low-income students and at the secondary level, a significantly higher percentage (43.6 percent compared to 28.4 percent). Those figures show charters serving a significantly higher percentage of low-income students and young people representing communities of color; however, it is vital to recognize that charters vary widely. A Rand Corporation researcher made this point, as part of his review of California charter schools:

Charter schools differ markedly from each other and consequently there is no single charter-school effect on student achievement. From campus to campus, charter schools are so diverse it is impossible to paint a single picture of them. To precisely evaluate performance, you really need to consider the type of charter school and the characteristics of the specific charter. (Zimmer and Gill 2003)

A teacher/researcher made a similar point, writing in *The Nation*:

It would probably be a mistake at any point to try to draw broad performance conclusions about "the charter movement." By design, that "movement" is a collection of unique schools ranging from international baccalaureate academies to intensive last resorts for juvenile lawbreakers; taking their average temperature probably won't be very enlightening. (Schorr 2000)

Race/Ethnicity of Students				
	Elementary		Secondary	
	Traditional public	Charter public	Traditional public	Charter public
White	61.4	44.7	66.6	48.9
Black	18.1	31.0	15.0	21.8
Hispanic	15.7	19.5	13.3	22.7
Asian/Pac Islander	3.6	3.3	3.9	3.1
American Indian	1.2	1.5	1.2	3.5

Percent of Students Eligible for Free/Reduced Lunch				
	Elementary		Secondary	
	Traditional public	Charter public	Traditional public	Charter public
Less than 15	21.1	3.9	31.3	29.8
15-29	18.6	11.0	20.0	9.8
30-49	21.8	16.6	20.3	16.8
50-74	19.9	14.1	14.7	19.9
75-100	18.7	27.4	13.7	23.7

The importance of accountability

Accountability is at the heart of the charter idea because charter schools differ in more than just focus and philosophy: they also differ in effectiveness. Putting it simply, some charter schools are more effective than others.

President Bill Clinton discussed the issue of accountability in a Minnesota speech given at the nation's first charter school:

One problem we have had is that not every state has had the right kind of accountability for the charter schools. Some states have laws that are so loose that no matter whether the charter schools are doing their jobs or not, they just get to stay open, and they become like another bureaucracy. Unfortunately, I think even worse, some states have laws that are so restrictive it's almost impossible to open a charter school in the first place. Minnesota's law is right. You basically have struck the right balance. You have encouraged the growth of charter schools, but you do hold charter schools responsible for results. That's what every state in the country [needs] to do. (Clinton 2000)

The unfortunate fact is that some people will abuse opportunities. That seems to be true for a small percentage of people in every profession, from teacher union presidents (such as the ones who were indicted in Miami-Dade and Washington, D.C.) to superintendents, principals, and directors of charter schools. So although the vast majority of people in each job seem to follow the rules, some people do not, or aren't sure of the rules they should be following. That makes monitoring necessary.

One of the challenges states face in developing the charter idea and offering relief from many (though not all) rules and regulations is how to balance flexibility, opportunity, and regulation. Wise states will periodically look at what problems are developing in the charter process on both sides. What rules and regulations frustrate educators, and should be reexamined? And what mistakes are some schools making that might be prevented if there were a better combination of training, monitoring, and regulation?

And charter schools must be ultimately accountable. As the *St. Paul Pioneer Press* encouraged, rather than merely chartering schools willy-nilly, communities should be replicating schools that *do* improve student achievement, and closing schools that, after several years, fail to achieve the level of performance achieved by traditional schools. With strong monitoring and accountability in place, a state encourages the development of effective charter schools and makes possible the continuous culling and improvement of the genre.

The charter idea is an idea whose time has come

Many years ago, Victor Hugo wrote that "Stronger than all the armies of the world is an idea whose time has come" (Hugo 649). The rapid growth of charter schools throughout the nation shows how much momentum has developed behind the charter idea. Despite intense, ongoing opposition from powerful groups, the number of schools and the number of students participating in the charter movement continue to grow. Though some critics and opponents downplay or deny the contributions of individual schools and those of the charter movement on the whole, more and more families are saying, "We want this!"

References

Abdullah, Halimah, "Rights Hero Seeks to Open School in Detroit," *The New York Times*, June 30, 1997.

Brandt, Steve, "New Test Data Analysis Favors Charter Schools," *Star Tribune*, December 22, 2003.

Center for Education Reform, *National Charter School Directory*, Eighth Edition, 2004, Washington, D.C.: author.

Clinton, William Jefferson, remarks by the President to the St. Paul Community, May 4, 2000 (available at www.centerforschoolchange.org).

Denver Post, "The Reality of Charter Schools," August 24, 2004.

Dirkswager, Edward J., editor, *Teachers as Owners*, 2002, Lanham, Maryland: Scarecrow Press.

Furrer, Cheryl, *Why MEA Opposes Chartered Schools*, duplicated material accompanying letter addressed to State Senator Ember Reichgott, April 11, 1991.

Greene, Jay, Forster, Greg, and Winters, Marcus A., 2003, *Apples to Apples: An Evaluation of Charter Schools Serving General Populations*, New York City: Manhattan Institute.

Hechinger, Fred, "The Short Life of the Success Story," *The New York Times*, July 7, 1987, p. 16.

Hugo, Victor, *Histoirie d'un Crime*, Conclusion.

Kolderie, Ted, "Chartering: How Are We to Evaluate It?" *Education Week*, October 8, 2003.

Legislative Analyst's Office, *Assessing California's Charter Schools*, Sacramento 2004.

Loveless, Tom, *How Well Are American Students Learning?* Washington, D.C.: Brookings Institution, October 2003.

Matheson, Ken D., speech at the Idaho School Administrators Conference, February 2, 1998 (summary available from Center for School Change).

Nathan, Joe, *Charter Schools: Creating Hope and Opportunity in American Education*, San Francisco, Jossey Bass, 1999.

Nathan, Joe, and Febey, Karen, *Smaller, Safer, Saner Successful Schools*, 2001, Washington, D.C., National Clearinghouse for Educational Facilities.

Nelson, F. Howard, Rosenberg, Bella, and Van Meter, Nancy, *Charter School Achievement on the 2003 National Assessment of Educational Progress*, Washington, D.C., American Federation of Teachers, August 2004.

Pueblo Chieftain, "An Attractive Alternative," December 29, 2003.

Rimer, Sara, "A Small-Scale Attack on Urban Despair," *The New York Times*, December 17, 2003.

Rofes, Eric, n.d., *How Are School Districts Responding to Charter Laws and Charter Schools?* Berkeley: Graduate School of Education Policy Analysis for California Education.

St. Paul Pioneer Press, "Charter Schools Provide Needed Choice," August 19, 2004, p. 14A.

Schorr, Jonathan, "Giving Charter Schools a Chance," *The Nation*, June 5, 2000, pp. 19-22.

Shanker, Albert, "Goals, Not Gimmicks" (paid advertisement), *The New York Times*, November 7, 1993.

Star Tribune (Minneapolis), "Charter Schools," August 21, 2004.

Steel, L., and Levine, R., *Educational Innovation in Multiracial Contexts: The Growth of Magnet Schools in American Education*, prepared for the U.S. Department of Education, contract #LC 90043001 (Palo Alto, California, American Institutes for Research, 1994).

Walsh, James, "Phalen Lake Plans Pioneering Move," *Star Tribune* (Minneapolis), p. 1A, 6A, January 20, 2003.

Wellstone, Paul, "Putting Our Children First: Closing the Gap by Forging a New Partnership," remarks by the Honorable Paul Wellstone delivered at the Minnesota State Legislature, Monday, February 17, 1997.

Wingert, Pat, and Kantrowitz, Barbara, "At the Top of the Class," *Newsweek*, March 24, 2003.

Wisconsin State Journal, "One Style Doesn't Fit All Students," Madison, Wisconsin, August 19, 2004.

Witte, John F., *Wisconsin Charter Schools Study*, Madison: LaFollette School of Public Affairs, University of Wisconsin, 2004.

Zimmer, Ron, and Gill, Brian, *Charter School Operations and Performance: Evidence from California*, 2003, Santa Monica, California: Rand Corporation.

Joe Nathan is director of the Center for School Change at the University of Minnesota's Humphrey Institute of Public Affairs. He was one of the founders of the charter movement in Minnesota, which is widely recognized as not only one of the first charter movements in the nation, but also one of the most successful.

Intuitive Test Theory

Many of us have an intuitive understanding of physics that works surprisingly well to guide everyday action, but we would not attempt to send a rocket to the moon with it. Unfortunately, Mr. Braun and Mr. Mislevy argue, our policy makers are not as cautious when it comes to basing our school accountability system on intuitive test theory.

HENRY I. BRAUN AND ROBERT MISLEVY

ALONG WITH making sure that our bodily needs are met, one of our first tasks upon entering this world is to try to make sense of it. We do so by continuous observation and generalization, as well as by absorbing the norms of the culture in which we find ourselves. Our understandings typically take the form of stories—narratives, as the psychologist Jerome Bruner has called them. These stories are attempts to identify why people do what they do—their beliefs, motives, and plans.

This mode of developing and retaining understanding carries over to the physical world, whether natural or human-made. We hear thunder and see lightning, see objects being thrown and falling to the ground, observe cars and computers working (or not), and we construct stories about causes, patterns, and linkages. Now, we make up these stories whether or not we truly understand what is going on. Adults are driven, in exactly the same way as 5-year-olds are, to express their understanding of what is happening around them in terms of narratives.

As Howard Gardner has pointed out, stories can differ, often substantially.

> In most domains of knowledge, we develop very powerful theories when we are very young. ... No one has to tell a kid that heavy objects fall more quickly than light objects. It's totally intuitive. It happens to be wrong. Galileo showed that it was wrong. Newton explained why it was wrong. But, like others with a robust 5-year-old mind, I still believe heavier objects fall more quickly than lighter objects.
>
> The only people on whom these engravings change are experts. Experts are people who actually think about the world in more sophisticated and different kinds of ways. ... In your area of expertise, you don't think about what you do as you would when you were five years of age. But

I venture to say that if I get to questioning you about something that you are not an expert in, the answers you give will be the answers you would have given before you had gone to school.[1]

Richard Feynman's story for what happens when we throw a rock might be based on the principle of the path of least action and admit to a rigorous rendering in differential calculus, whereas little Jimmy's story is that the rock wanted to get back down to the ground where it belongs. The point is that people construct plausible stories for actions and events based on what they've experienced themselves and on what they've picked up, however loosely or informally, from the culture around them.

The Gardner quote highlights two other aspects of these narratives. The first is their tendency to persist, even in the face of evidence to the contrary or confrontation with methods of analysis that are much more powerful. Bruner makes the same point with respect to what he calls "folk psychology." He defines folk psychology as a system by which people organize their experience in, knowledge about, and transactions with the social world. We learn our culture's folk psychology along with its language and norms of social behavior. Bruner asserts, "Folk psychology changes but is not displaced by scientific psychology."[2] It is the persistence of these narratives (say, in physics) that can be so frustrating for teachers.

The second aspect of these stories is that expertise is often very narrowly focused. That is, outside one's area of specialized training, it is uncommon to do much better than a 5-year-old. Indeed, the situation may be even more dire. In a now classic study, the psychologists Amos Tversky and Daniel Kahneman questioned a large number of research psychologists on various aspects of probability and statistics (the design of experiments and the interpretation of the results) that would ordinarily be relevant to their work. Surprisingly, a majority of the respondents harbored naive (and incorrect) beliefs that, presumably, influenced how they conducted their research.[3]

What is true of psychology or physics is true of just about every discipline you can think of. It is also true, we will argue, in educational assessment. Before we begin to explore this, our own field, we will examine briefly how people who are not experts in physics think about physical phenomena. This "intuitive physics" is a set of basic premises about how the world works. It consists of story elements or subplots, as it were, called phenomenological primitives (or p-prims, for short), a term coined by psychologist Andrea diSessa. These p-prims are primitive notions in the sense that they "stand without significant explanatory substructure or explanation."[4] And just as the idea of p-prims can help explain most people's understanding of the physical world, so too can p-prims help us explain the "intuitive test theory" that nonexperts use to explain the world of assessment.

Perhaps it is not surprising that such p-prims—and the narratives in which they are embedded—work well enough for most situations in our everyday lives. After all, they are grounded in the experiences of many people over many, many years. They can lead to trouble, though, when employed in situations that lie outside their range, in which case expert models are indispensable. Unfortunately, unlike prescription drugs, p-prims (in physics or other disciplines) are usually not accompanied by warning labels with contraindications for use. In a fast-changing world, it is increasingly likely that we will find ourselves relying on p-prims that are not up to the task.

INTUITIVE PHYSICS

One consequence of the "cognitive revolution" in psychology that began in the 1960s was a closer look at how people develop expertise in real-life activities as varied as radiology, writing, chess, and volleyball. A significant finding across domains is that experts don't simply know more facts than novices—although they usually do—but that they also organize what they know around deeper principles and relationships. The knowledge novices have is more fragmented and is related to particular situations or organized around surface features of problems.

For example, Micki Chi, Paul Feltovich, and Robert Glaser asked expert physicists and novices to sort a number of problems into groups. The novices produced piles of spring problems, pulley problems, and inclined-plane problems. The experts produced piles associated with equilibrium, Newton's third law, and the conservation of energy, each containing some spring problems, some pulley problems, and some inclined-plane problems. The experts' categorization leads directly to solution strategies for the problems.[5]

When diSessa introduced the term "p-prims" in 1983, it was expressly to explain nonexperts' ways of reasoning about physics. Familiar examples of such p-prims are

"Heavy objects fall faster than light objects," "Things bounce because they are 'springy,'" and "Continuing force is needed for continuing motion." These physical p-prims are based on our everyday experience. A box moves when we push it, and it stops moving when we stop pushing. Cannon balls really do fall faster than feathers. Physicists know this, of course, but, when necessary, they can appeal to a deeper level of explanation, to the more sophisticated primitives of scientific physics. The distinguishing feature of intuitive physics (or intuitive reasoning in any field) is that the p-prims are the bottom line. For nonexperts, they are the final explanation. In other words, sometimes we just have to say, "Well, that's just the way it is."

Some of the p-prims of intuitive physics use such words as force, energy, and momentum, a legacy of the general culture or of a physics class taken long ago. But the terms are not employed in the same way that experts use them. Nonexperts don't sort concepts in the same ways as experts or embed them in the same web of qualitative and quantitative relationships. A set of p-prims is not a coherent system, and a person's set of p-prims can easily contain some that contradict others. They are employed to reason about physical situations, and a model of sorts is assembled to address a given situation. The surface features of a situation tend to elicit some p-prims but not others, so a person's intuitive models can be quite different for two situations that are formally equivalent.

The surprising thing is how well they work for guiding everyday action. You can think you are imparting a substance called "impetus" to the tennis ball when you throw it for your dog. The ball flies until the impetus wears off. You estimate how much of this substance you want to impart to the ball and gauge your throw accordingly—and, by golly, the ball goes where you want it to. Your impetus theory is wrong, but neither you, nor the dog, nor the ball knows this, and the job gets done just fine.

Intuitive physics works well enough for playing catch with your dog or for building a birdhouse. But it doesn't work for constructing a bridge or shooting a rocket to the moon. One aspect of becoming an expert in physics is learning more sophisticated ways of thinking, but another is knowing when you need to use them, and yet another is recognizing when they fail. (Science is also about telling stories, but they are stories that submit to reality checks.) In scientific physics, concepts and relationships that may be nonintuitive, or even counterintuitive, can be brought to bear on familiar and unfamiliar situations alike. Individuals facing challenges that lie outside everyday experience ignore scientific physics at their peril.

SCIENTIFIC TEST THEORY

To Americans who go to school or hold jobs in the 21st century, taking tests is an experience nearly as familiar as pushing boxes or watching things fall. So we need to tell stories about tests—their purposes, their construction, our performances on them—and we need concepts to do so. Below, we will briefly sketch how experts in assessment think about these aspects of tests. But unless you are an expert in assessment, it is probably not the way you think about them. Indeed, some of the ideas may be quite foreign to you.

A scientific approach to assessment recognizes that, fundamentally, assessment isn't about items and scores. These are more like the springs and pulleys of testing. Rather, assessment is a special kind of evidentiary argument. Assessment is about reasoning from a handful of particular things students say, do, or make, to more broadly cast inferences about what they know, have accomplished, or are apt to do in the future.[6]

The starting point for an application of scientific test theory is a clear understanding of the purpose of the assessment and a perspective on the nature of the knowledge or skills that are the focus of attention. Next is the link between this view of knowledge and skills, which you can't see, to things that you can see—right and wrong answers, problem-solving steps, justifications for building designs, or comparisons of characters in two novels in terms of transaction theory, to cite just a few examples. This analysis resolves into making a case, in light of the purpose of the assessment, for what is meaningful in a student's performance and why. A rationale is also required for the kinds of assignments or challenges that will elicit the evidence to support the intended inferences about students. Conceptual links connect tasks to student performances to judgments about what they know and can do. These are the testing counterparts of Newton's laws.

Now, Newton's laws of motion are deterministic. That is, given a complete description of an object (e.g., its mass, current position, and velocity), we can calculate exactly the effect on its motion of an application of a particular force. In test theory, we can formulate a student model that describes one or more aspects of a student's knowledge or skills. Since the components of the student model cannot be observed directly, we have to use probability theory to express our beliefs about the likely values of these components. As we accumulate more data about the student, we can employ the calculus of probabilities to update our beliefs.

The use of probability-based models to describe what we know, and what we don't know, about a student is a key tool in scientific assessment. It provides a quantitative basis for planning test configurations, calculating the accuracy and reliability of the measurement process, figuring out how many tasks or raters we need to be sufficiently sure about the appropriateness of decisions based on test scores, or monitoring the quality of large-scale assessment systems. We can also apply the tools of probability to new kinds of testing processes, such as ones that select discrete tasks to present to individual students in light of how well they are doing or their instructional backgrounds, or computer-based tests of problem solving in which the problem itself evolves in response to the student's actions. These probability models and their essential role in reasoning are all but unknown to the nonexpert.

It is worth pointing out that the use of probability models to manage information doesn't restrict the kinds of knowledge and skills we can model. While psychometrics arose around 1900 with the goal of measuring traits such as intelligence, the same modeling approach can be applied with all kinds of psychological perspectives and all kinds of data. The variables in the student model can be many or few; they can be measures or categories; they can concern knowledge, procedures, strategies, or attunement to social situations; they can be as coarse as "verbal reasoning" or as fine-grained as "being able to describe playground situations in terms of Newton's laws."

What is observed and how it is modeled and evaluated will depend partly on a psychological perspective and partly on the job at hand. Designing an assessment is like building a bridge. The evidentiary arguments and the probability models are like Newton's laws in that you have to get them right or the entire structure will collapse. But they aren't sufficient to determine the project. In architecture and engineering, decisions about location, materials, and various features of the design are strongly influenced by the resources available, by the situational constraints, and by the needs of the clients. Similar processes are at work in measurement.[7]

The typical classroom teacher brings to bear little if any of this machinery in constructing, analyzing, and drawing inferences from Friday's math quiz. Usually, this is perfectly fine and appropriate to the purpose and the context. Assessment practices have evolved into familiar forms of testing that often work well enough in common situations. The principles that account for why they work in the situations for which they evolved are there—invisible but built into the pieces that we can see. Popular conceptions of how and why familiar tests work hold the same ontological status as impetus theory—dead wrong in the main, but close enough to guide everyday work in familiar settings. It is when we move beyond the familiar that these notions can betray us.

P-PRIMS UNDER SCRUTINY

Let us now consider a number of p-prims of test theory. Just as in intuitive physics, these are the underpinnings of the view of testing held by many nonexperts. Our goal is to use the insights of scientific test theory to begin to understand how these beliefs might have arisen and in which situations they can break down. In what follows, we sometimes use the phrase "drop-from-the-sky" to describe a test—by which we mean a test that is developed outside the school context. The term is meant to connote the remoteness of the test from the day-to-day experiences of the students.

A test measures what it says at the top of the page. It is natural to assume that a name carries meaning. Thus we expect that a test called a history test will measure a student's accomplishments or proficiency in history. However, a student's score on such a test can be determined less by how well a student can analyze or interpret historical materials than by a host of other factors that also influence performance and on which individuals can differ substantially. Such factors include, for example, a student's familiarity with the testing situation, the kind of test and mode of administration, and even what the grader of the test is looking for.

A common manifestation of this p-prim is making inferences from test scores that extend well beyond what can be reasonably supported. Perhaps the most notorious example is the overinterpretation of the results of standardized intelligence tests. Performance on a particular drop-from-the-sky intelligence test does typically indicate a capability to do productive reasoning in certain circumstances. But there are many kinds of intelligent behavior, some of which are predicted pretty well by scores on intelligence tests and others that are not.[8] For example, people are good chess players not because they are intelligent in a general sense but because—through study, practice, and reflection on their performance in many, many games—they have learned a great deal about the patterns and successful strategies in the domain of chess.[9]

A test is a test is a test. This p-prim is a corollary of the preceding one. Some tests that are called fourth-grade mathematics tests, for example, focus more on concepts, others focus on computations, and still others focus on using math in real-world situations. They reflect different aspects of what students know about and can do with math. Furthermore, a classroom teacher can build her quiz assuming that students are familiar with her notation, item types, and evaluation standards. This is more difficult for a drop-from-the-sky test. Moreover, assessments in the form of projects requiring extended work in math can be done over time as part of a program of instruction, but they aren't well suited for a drop-from-the-sky test that occurs on a single day.

Each assessment can be described in terms of the skills and knowledge it can tell you about, how much information it provides, its implications for learning, how closely it corresponds to students' background and instruction, and its demands on such resources as equipment, money, and student and teacher time. The trick is to match a test—with all its many characteristics—with the purpose of the testing and the context in which it will be used. Getting the proper match can be a delicate balancing act. For any number of reasons, the same test can be exactly right for one purpose and situation but quite useless for another. Good test developers know this, and they design different assessments for different purposes in light of the characteristics of the students, the available resources, and the constraints of the setting.

A particularly dangerous fallacy follows from this p-prim: you can take a drop-from-the-sky test constructed to gauge knowledge in a broad content area, give it to students about whom you know little else, and, by coming up with a different way of scoring it, obtain diagnostic information that will be useful for individual, small-scale instructional decisions. This generally doesn't work, and the problem isn't with the items or the scoring rules. It is that effective information about what to do next requires assessment that takes into account what a teacher already knows about a student and provides information in terms of instructional options—not necessarily better items or more items, just the right items for the right student at the right time. Good diagnostic information results from good match-ups, not from good one-size-fits-all tests.

A score is a score is a score. With all the criticism that testing attracts, it is remarkable how much credence is typically attached to a single test score. After all, the reasoning goes, how could there be a "truer" score than the score a student actually gets? This p-prim is reinforced by the familiar practice of making decisions on the basis of a single test score without considering what the scores might have been in hypothetical administrations of alternative measures. Measurement experts recognize that different data could have arisen from testing on other occasions; from using more, fewer, or different test items; or from employing more, fewer, or different raters. (Perhaps the best way to bring home the concept of "noise" in test scores is to administer multiple tests and let people see for themselves the surprisingly large differences that result.)

Once we decide what we want to make inferences about from the data available, we can use scientific test theory to gauge how much evidence we have and compare it with what might have occurred in a variety of hypothetical alternative situations. This concept, roughly that of measurement error, is not a natural part of everyday reasoning about test scores (with the major exception that occurs when someone's score is lower than he or she expected). Assessment data are not perfect. Relying on a single score without regard to the uncertainty attached to it may be good enough for typical, low-stakes applications, but it is problematic for more consequential ones. Without scientific test theory, we could neither quantify that uncertainty nor evaluate the validity of the use of a particular test score in a particular setting.

Any two tests that measure the same thing can be made interchangeable with a little "equating" magic. This is intuitive test theory's equivalent of the perpetual motion machine. Why do people believe it? First, it seems to happen all the time. Almost everyone knows that large-scale testing programs like the SAT I and the Iowa Tests of Basic Skills (ITBS) regularly generate new test forms and that psychometricians routinely equate scores on the new forms to scores on the old ones. Second, it seems to make sense, because it follows from the preceding p-prims. If you think that tests measure what they say they measure and that all tests that measure it are essentially the same, and if you don't concern yourself with measurement error, then there is no apparent reason not to treat evidence from different tests as more or less equivalent.

But the strength of the correspondence between the evidence from one test and that from another, superficially similar, test is determined by the different aspects of knowledge and skills that the two tests tap, by the amount and quality of the information they provide, and by how well they each match the students' instructional experiences. The SAT I and ITBS testing programs can do this not so much because of the equating procedures they use but because they expend considerable effort in creating test forms with very similar combinations of questions (item types, content areas, mix of difficulties), in order to tap the same sets of skills in the same ways. When tests are not designed to be "parallel" in this way, quantifying in what ways information from one test can be used as if it came from another requires expert-level (scientific) test theory. Some inferences across tests will work well, and others will fail.

With legislation mandating the measurement of student progress and the establishment of common standards for achievement, policy makers have expressed considerable interest in linking tests from different states or different test publishers to the National Assessment of Educational Progress (NAEP). There is a long and definitive line of scientific publications pointing out the very real limitations of linking and equating different tests with the same name.[10] Unfortunately, the notion that disparate tests can somehow be made equivalent by applying equating magic will not die, because life would be much easier if it were true. And by the reasoning of intuitive test theory, there is no reason why it can't be done.

You score a test by adding up scores for items. Almost all classroom quizzes and tests are graded in this way, and it works just fine for their purposes. Consequently, one can hardly be blamed for holding this p-prim. But it presumes that the target of inference is a student's overall proficiency in some domain and that the tasks on the test are relatively independent positive indicators of that proficiency. Indeed, this is the simplest (and most familiar) case of a relationship between targets of inference and bits of evidence about them. When interest focuses on dependencies among more complex forms of evidence and multifaceted models of knowledge and skill, however, this "natural" approach to scoring is severely deficient.

This approach fails for large integrated performances such as the videotaped lesson plans and teaching sessions of the National Board for Professional Teaching Standards, because multiple, interconnected judgments across many parts of the work are required. It fails for interactive problem-solving simulations (e.g., troubleshooting or patient management), because each action taken changes the situation and constrains or facilitates the next action. It fails for collections of tasks that tap a

variety of skills and knowledge in different mixes, such as language tests that assess not only vocabulary and grammar but also how to conduct meaningful conversations, use cultural information, and accomplish real-world aims such as bargaining. Patterns of what is done well and where performance is inadequate are required, with the added complication that people trade off their strengths against their weaknesses when they use language in real life.

This approach also fails for assessments that aim to distinguish conceptions and misconceptions (as opposed to correctness). That is, it fails when the goal isn't to count how many problems a student can solve, but rather to develop a useful description of her thinking—so that we can better decide what she might work on next to improve her understanding.

In all of these cases, simple scoring rules don't make the "grade" because they extract only a part of the evidence contained in students' responses—sometimes completely missing the patterns that are most important—and therefore can't support the nuanced inferences that are desired. Scientific test theory, extended and elaborated as needed to deal with new kinds of data and new kinds of inferences about students, is the best foundation for both effectively designing these more complex assessments and for making sense of the data they produce.

An A is 93%, a B is 85%, a C is 78%, and 70% is passing. This p-prim follows from the previous one, with the additional assumption that the tasks that make up a test have been written so that these percentages line up nicely with the traditional percent-correct metric of satisfaction for how well students have done on tests of materials that were specifically matched to their instruction. It presumes that somehow, for all tests and all uses and all students, the same percentage of correct answers corresponds to the same level of performance.

A colleague who works on certification and licensing tests tells the story of a state legislature that passed a law mandating that "the passing score on the plumber's licensing exam will be 70." Following good test-design practices, our colleague worked with plumbers to determine the kinds of knowledge and skills needed to be a competent plumber, one who is able to ply the craft ably and with due regard to safety. The committee then created a collection of tasks to probe the targeted knowledge and skills and pilot-tested them with groups of competent plumbers and with apprentices who were judged to be not yet ready to practice on their own. A passing score was selected that best differentiated the two groups. This is a sound foundation for creating a valid licensing assessment and setting a defensible level of performance for a high-stakes decision. When they got that number, it shouldn't have mattered what its numerical value was. Within the constraints of the testing program, it had been constructed to be a valid cut point for the purpose of obtaining a license. As a final step, however, the test developers had to add (or subtract) a "fudge factor" to make the passing score exactly 70.

This p-prim is plausible because for many of the tests we took in school, this grading scheme is not a bad choice. But this didn't happen by accident. Good teachers who wanted to use this grading scheme thought carefully about what they wanted students to learn and about the conditions under which students could exhibit that learning. They set up tasks and evaluated them to get data. Then they looked hard at the numbers. If the scores they saw from their students didn't jibe with their expectations, they went back to the drawing board to figure out why. Were the items unreasonable or unclear? If so, then revise or replace them. We r e the students just not learning what was intended? If so, then check whether the students have the background they need, verify that they are really working, improve the pedagogy, and so on.

The difficulties encountered in applying this p-prim and the previous one in more complex settings have led to advances in measurement theory. Indeed, it is possible to construct both easy and hard tests from the same collection of items, and the same level of knowledge will produce a higher score on the easy test than on the hard one. Psychometric models based on item response theory originated in the 1960s to characterize items in terms of their difficulty and other features, so that students can be given different sets of items and still be compared on the same scale—harder ones for fifth-graders and easier ones for third-graders, for example, or computer-administered tests that are customized to each examinee on the basis of his or her performance as it unfolds.[11] So what now is an A, a B, or a C? You can't decide just by calculating the percentage of correct answers; you should decide on the basis of the pattern of correct and incorrect answers, taking into account the relative difficulty of the items presented.

Under some circumstances, the results may be reasonably well approximated by a simple sum. But the underlying principles provide a deeper understanding of why the standard procedures work in familiar situations, as well as the machinery for creating new procedures for novel situations—very different arrangements of springs and pulleys, but undergirded by the same Newtonian laws.

Multiple-choice questions measure only recall. This p-prim is often stated as an epithet, as part of a comparison to open-ended questions. Certainly most of the multiple-choice questions that people encounter in school test only recall, and it is surely true for multiple-choice questions written by someone who believes the p-prim. But while factual recall items may be the easiest kinds of multiple-choice items to write, other types are certainly possible. For example, a multiple-choice test of subtraction can be written so that patterns of right answers and wrong answers will reflect particular misconceptions and tell us more about a student's understanding than would overall performance on a test made up of only open-ended items.

Similarly, research in physics education sparked by work like diSessa's has led to the development of multiple-choice tests that reveal which p-prims students are using. Rather than the usual open-ended computation and modeling items, the items on the Force and Motion Conceptual Evaluation present descriptions of everyday situations and ask students to choose explanations of what is happening or predict what will happen next.[12] Some alternatives reflect Newton's laws , but others reflect p-prims that are more consistent with Galileo's thinking, medieval impetus theory, Aristotle's beliefs, or wholly nonscientific reasoning. The situations vary in ways that research suggests will bring particular p-prims to light.

For example, Newton's third law says that for every action (or force) there is an equal and opposite reaction. If object number 1 exerts a force on object number 2, then object number 2 exerts an equal and opposite force on object number 1. When a car and a small truck of the same weight moving at the same speed collide head-on, most students chose the response that says, "The truck exerts the same amount of force on the car as the car exerts on the truck." That's okay so far, but this is a canonical example for the third law—easy to give the answer Newton would without understanding the underlying principle. When the small pickup truck is replaced with a huge semi traveling only half as fast, more students choose "The truck exerts a larger force on the car" because the truck is larger. Or they choose "The car exerts a larger force on the truck" because the car is going faster. These responses reflect alternative—and in this case, conflicting—p-prims.

In and of itself, the format of a task—be it multiple-choice, open-ended, simulation-based, or hands-on performance—doesn't fully determine the kind of thinking it will elicit from a student. What's more, the same task can give rise to different kinds of thinking in different students, depending on how it fits with their background and experiences. To a high school algebra student, figuring out the sum of the numbers from 1 to 100 is a simple application of a familiar formula. But rather different cognitive processes were at play when the 7-year-old Karl Friedrich Gauss derived the formula as an original insight.

Multiple-choice items can be used to test recall of facts, and most of them are used in this way. But if one has clearly in mind the concepts and relationships one wants to probe, as well as the kinds of discriminations that an understanding of them entails, then it is possible to write multiple-choice items that go far beyond recall. The principles for creating such items aren't obvious and, unfortunately, aren't a part of most people's theory of tests.

You can tell if an item is good by looking at it. Like most of the others, this p-prim rests on the assumption that items and tests are really simple objects whose essence can be grasped by their surface characteristics. However, for an item to serve a given purpose, there has to be a reasonable coherence between its particular purpose, what the item provides and what it requires, the student's understanding of the context of the item and the scoring rules, and what else the assessor knows about what the student knows. A bad mismatch at any point, and the item may fail to generate the evidence needed, no matter how "good" it looks.

For example, consider an open-ended item devised by a teacher for her Advanced Placement calculus class that uses her notation, will be scored with the rubric her students have become used to, and calls for applying what they've been studying for the last month to a real-world situation that is similar to one discussed in class. This is an ideal probe to elicit their understanding of an important learning objective. However, it would be a poor item to include in the grade-12 NAEP, which presents tasks to a random sample of students across the country—many of whom would not be familiar with the notation or the grading rubric. Ten minutes of valuable testing time would be wasted for almost everyone who confronted the question. (The converse of this p-prim is more nearly true: You can often tell an item is bad just by looking at it. Logical flaws and confusing instructions, for example, will keep an item from providing useful information for almost any purpose.)

That the appropriateness of an item depends on "more than meets the eye" implies that writing good items is more difficult than most people would imagine. In addition to having a coherent conceptual framework and a strong evidentiary perspective, item writers must also work under constraints of time and money as they build tasks and assemble tests. It is not a vocation for the faint of heart or the novice, as recent missteps in many high-stakes state tests attest. Ironically, the more one knows about writing test items, the more challenging it is to write good ones.

Multiple-choice tests equal standardized tests equal high-stakes tests. Many of the highly visible tests used today for college admissions, for licensure and certification, and for state accountability for public schools are alike in three important ways: they have meaningful consequences for students or schools, they are presented under standard conditions, and they use multiple-choice items. This configuration occurs often enough that these three distinct properties are conflated in the public eye so that the adjectives "multiple-choice," "standardized," and "high-stakes" are thought to be synonymous—all ways of describing the same familiar package.

But high-stakes tests can be less standardized and require performances, as is the case with doctoral dissertations and solo flights for pilot certification. Multiple-choice items are found as often in low-stakes classroom quizzes as they are in high-stakes assessments. Finally, standardization is not an all-or-nothing quality. For each aspect of an assessment, there are options about how similar to make the experience for different examinees. And, as always, seeking to standardize involves tradeoffs. Greater similarity across examinees in some facets tends to support comparisons and facilitate communication of results across time and distance. More individualization allows the tests to be better targeted to individuals' circumstances, although the interpretation of results is more tightly bound to those circumstances.

DISCUSSION

While intuitive test theory is sufficient for classroom testing and for the quizzes in *Seventeen* magazine, it gets you into trouble when you want to evaluate performance on simulation-based activities, run a high-stakes testing program, or measure change in populations using an achievement survey like NAEP. There is a strong similarity—and an important difference—between intuitive physics and intuitive test theory that has implications for assessment use and policy. As one's understanding and expertise in physics become more profound, the concepts and tools depart from everyday physics. The same is true with assessment design and analysis at the frontiers.

It is generally accepted that this is the case in physics and, moreover, that the complexity must be confronted if one is embarking on a serious undertaking. Consider the paradigmatic example of launching a rocket to the moon. In fact, in 1961, when President Kennedy made his famous promise that by the end of that decade the U.S. would send a man to the moon and return him safely back to Earth, his staff had already consulted with experts about the feasibility of such an endeavor. Two points are noteworthy. First, everyone expected that all the options that would be considered would be in accord with Newton's laws of motion, not Aristotle's. Second, President Kennedy did not assert that, on its flight to the moon, the rocket would have to meet specific milestones that he and his advisors deemed appropriate.

In most issues that involve technical considerations, experts are consulted, and their perspectives become part of the policy debate. They don't make the decisions, and they shouldn't. In any social setting, there are more considerations than purely technical ones. But policy options should be restricted to those that are in accord with basic principles and broadly held standards of practice—the analogs of Newton's laws of motion.

Unfortunately, this is often not the case in assessment, as a review of the testing policies in many states and the legislative history of the No Child Left Behind Act demonstrate. As assessment-based accountability becomes a more prominent feature of education policy, those standing on the technical side of assessment must confront the reality that critical decisions are made and regulations are drafted on the basis of intuitive test theory, with untoward consequences a likely result. The advent of technology-based assessment may, in many ways, exacerbate the problem. No doubt voluminous data will be produced, but insight will still be in short supply. In fact, a disciplined application of the principles of evidentiary reasoning to design, development, and analysis will be all the more necessary if the investment in technology is to yield meaningful returns.

We remain, then, with the problem that p-prims are both widely held and persistent. What, then, should those of us in educational measurement do? There are at least three lines of attack, one negative and two positive. First, we should not shy away from critiquing policies and programs that are based on intuitive test theory. This involves telling lots of people (some of them very important) that what they want to do won't work and that doing something right is harder or takes longer than they might like.

A second approach is to use scientific test theory, in conjunction with developments in psychology and technology, to achieve goals that could not have been accomplished otherwise—certainly not by relying on intuitive test theory. These existence proofs are the most compelling argument for test theory as a scientific discipline and for its utility in the setting of education policy.

Finally, we need to do a much better job of communicating to a variety of audiences the basics of testing and the dangers we court when we ignore the principles and methods of educational measurement. Communication is a form of teaching, and we should take the challenge of this kind of teaching more seriously than ever before. Perhaps we should consider using narratives as a framework for this effort. We have an obligation to be as creative in this effort as we pride ourselves on being in our technical research.

Notes

1. Howard Gardner, *Educating the Unschooled Mind* (Washington, D. C . : Federation of Behavioral, Psychological, and Cognitive Sciences, 1993), p. 5.

2. Jerome Bruner, *Acts of Meaning* (Cambridge, Mass.: Harvard University Press, 1990), p. 14.

3. Amos Tversky and Daniel Kahneman, "Belief in the Law of Small Numbers," *Psychological Bulletin,* vol. 76, 1971, pp. 105-10.

4. Andrea diSessa, "Phenomenology and the Evolution of Intuition," in Dedre Gentner and Albert L. Stevens, eds., *Mental Models* (Hillsdale, N.J.: Erlbaum, 1983), p. 15.

5. Micki T. H. Chi, Paul Feltovich, and Robert Glaser, "Categorization and Representation of Physics Problems by Experts and Novices," *Cognitive Science,* vol. 5, 1981, pp. 121-52.

6. Robert J. Mislevy, "Substance and Structure in Assessment Arguments," *Law, Probability, and Risk,* December 2003, pp. 237-58.

7. Henry I. Braun, "A Postmodern View of the Problem of Language Assessment," in Antony J. Kunnan, ed., *Studies in Language 9: Fairness and Validation in Language Assessment: Selected Papers from the 19th Language Testing Research Colloquium* (Cambridge: Cambridge University Press, 2000), pp. 263-72.

8. Howard Gardner, *Frames of Mind: The Theory of Multiple Intelligences* (New York: Basic Books, 1983); and Robert J. Sternberg, *The Triarchic Mind: A New Theory of Human Intelligence* (New York: Viking-Penguin, 1988).

9. Adrianus de Groot, *Thought and Choice in Chess* (The Hague: Mouton, 1965).

10. See, for example, Michael J. Feuer et al., eds., *Uncommon Measures: Equivalence and Linkage Among Educational Tests* (Washington, D.C.: National Academies Press, 1999).

11. Howard Wainer et al., *Computerized Adaptive Testing: A Primer,* 2nd ed. (Hillsdale, N.J.: Erlbaum, 2000).

12. Ronald K. Thornton and David R. Sokoloff, "Assessing Student Learning of Newton's Laws: The Force and Motion Conceptual Evaluation," *American Journal of Physics,* vol. 66, 1998, pp. 228-351.

HENRY I. BRAUN is Distinguished Presidential Appointee at the Educational Testing Service (ETS), Princeton, N.J. **ROBERT MISLEVY** is a professor in the Department of Measurement, Statistics, and Evaluation, University of Maryland, College Park. They wish to acknowledge Neal Dorans, Paul Holland, and Howard Wainer for stimulating conversations on the topic of this article during its preparation. The research reported here was underwritten by ETS and grants from the Office of Educational Research and Improvement, U.S. Department of Education (No. R305B60002), and from the National Center for Research on Evaluation, Standards, and Student Testing, UCLA. However, the opinions expressed are solely those of the authors.

No Flower Shall Wither;
or,
Horticulture in the Kingdom of the Frogs

by Gary K. Clabaugh

In olden times, when hope still mattered, a little boy named Horace was in love with flowers. When they bloomed, Horace was very, very happy; and when they withered, he was very, very sad.

Now Horace was a small frog, living in the Kingdom of the Frogs. In this realm, Bullfrogs reigned supreme because of their ability to croak very loudly and remain hidden for long periods in the muck at the bottom of ponds.

Happily for Horace, Bullfrogs professed a great love of flowers. In fact, the Kingdom's residents were compelled to pay tribute to support community greenhouses where small frogs sent their seedlings. Bullfrogs preferred private greenhouses for their own seedlings.

One fine day the Bullfrogs began harrumphing that the state-run greenhouses were in an awful mess. In *A Kingdom at Risk*, a blue-ribbon Bullfrog panel even proclaimed, "If an enemy dominion were in charge of our greenhouses, their condition would be a cause for war." Bullfrogs were fond of finding causes for wars.

Few stopped to consider that public greenhouses operated under Bullfrog rules and that Bullfrogs determined their resources. Fewer still seemed to notice that public greenhouse conditions mirrored public conditions in the Kingdom (bad neighborhoods, bad greenhouses; better neighborhoods, better greenhouses).

When Horace came of age and it was time to make his way in the world, he thought and thought about what to do. "I know!" exclaimed Horace with a smile, "I shall become a licensed horticulturalist"—certification being necessary for state greenhouse employment—"and bring flowers to bloom."

In the Kingdom of the Frogs, learning vital things—such as how to remove Bullfrog bunions or assist Bullfrog tax avoidance—required lengthy and focused schooling. Horticultural training was far easier. Colleges, largely controlled by Bullfrog trustees, saw horticultural programs as a source of ready revenue and little more. Bullfrogs even set up easier "alternative routes" to certification—"Grow for the Kingdom," for example—just in case traditional routes were too tough. "Such alternatives," Bullfrogs earnestly croaked, "open careers in horticulture to bright people who are enthusiastic about plant growth."

Horace wondered, "Why is it so easy to become a horticulturalist when other important things are hard?" Nonetheless, he took the standard training and learned as much as he could. Meanwhile, the Bullfrogs continued to stoke dissatisfaction regarding public greenhouses.

When Horace graduated he found a position in a public greenhouse in one of the poorer neighborhoods of the Kingdom. There were many such neighborhoods. Horace quickly discovered that he and his fellow horticulturalists had little say about how the communal greenhouse was run. Horace was not permitted to whitewash the greenhouse glass, so his sun-sensitive plants soon were scalded. He had no control over the greenhouse heat; so his cool-weather plants soon were cooked. Greenhouse managers even decided what type of fertilizer he should use.

If leggy seedlings needed pinching back, Horace wasn't permitted to do it. Seedling owners had to be consulted, and then greenhouse management made the final decision. Horace was not even permitted to apply insecticide or pull a weed. Only administrators, who in turn were controlled by a greenhouse board operating under strict Bullfrog rules, could make such decisions.

Horace would fill in the requisite pink slips requesting spraying or weeding, but nothing came of them. In consequence, Horace's plants soon were sucked dry by white flies, mealy bugs, and aphids, while weeds stole their nourishment.

It wasn't clear to Horace why the greenhouse was run that way. Some said Bullfrog mandates left the manager little choice. Others blamed it on the manager's desire to be a Bullfrog. Still others thought it was because greenhouse board members had no horticultural training and knew little about growing flowers.

In this Kingdom it was customary for agronomical ignoramuses to control horticultural affairs. Even the Bullfrog Secretary of Horticulture had no knowledge of plant husbandry—though he was well connected at the pond. In lieu of knowledge he substituted croaky solemnity. He regularly admonished greenhouse managers, for instance, to "demand higher expectations at all levels." In self-defense, greenhouse managers afterward declared that when plants didn't thrive, it was some horticulturalist's fault.

Meanwhile Horace was realizing how important it was that he had no control over how plants were sprouted and first raised as seedlings. By the time plant owners brought them to the greenhouse, their all-important early growth period was over. Horace would get seedlings that were leggy from insufficient sun, stunted from inadequate fertilizer, or wilted from too little water, and often it was too late for him to undo the damage.

Old-timers told Horace that there was a time when struggling seedlings were put into a smaller greenhouse and given special care. But Bullfrogs declared that as many plants as possible should be put in the main greenhouse. Thus Horace received seedlings requiring more care than he could give.

Horace and his co-workers also controlled their seedlings only part of the day, five days a week, 180 days of the year. The rest of the time, and that was a great deal of time indeed, seedlings were "cared for" by their owners. That gave them ample opportunity to undo whatever Horace did.

It wasn't that the seedling owners were all indifferent. Many cared about their plants, but they were too besieged or uninformed to care properly. You see, small frogs were underpaid, often out of work, and sometimes homeless. Many were sick, and without health care. All that was because only Bullfrogs mattered in the Kingdom of the Frogs.

No matter what shape seedlings were in when he got them, Horace tried his best to make them thrive. In the end, though, the damaged condition of many new seedlings, inane greenhouse rules, incessant hectoring of Bullfrog officials, and seeing his work undone by plant owners combined to grind Horace down.

About this time the Frog King emerged from the muck on the bottom of his pond, swam to the surface, stuck his thick Bullfrog head out of the water, and croaked a royal decree. "Henceforth," he thrummed mightily," no flower shall wither!" And with that he dove back into the muck.

Little additional money followed for public greenhouses, but new mandates did. Bullfrog officials declared, for instance, that all public greenhouses must measure and report plant development. "Henceforth," the Bullfrogs croaked, "public greenhouse plant growth must be assessed, the results proclaimed, and horticulturalists held accountable." (There was no mention of measuring plant growth in the private greenhouses that served the Bullfrog's seedlings.)

Accountable Horace struggled mightily, but the neglected seedlings given him proved his undoing. He just couldn't get them all to measure up. Soon Horace was under the greenhouse manager's baleful stare. Sternly he said to Horace, "Too many of your plants are not meeting standards." Horace started to explain, "But there is so much I don't contro—" "Ah, ah, ah!" the manager interrupted. "I had hoped you wouldn't offer excuses! Truly professional growers just admit they must do a better job."

Horace wasn't the only horticulturalist whose damaged plants often failed to thrive. So many plants were stunted that the Bullfrogs threatened to label the greenhouse "dangerously substandard." "If that happens," the greenhouse administrator warned, "I'm not going down alone!" Then he began drawing up the Bullfrog-mandated Seedling Safety Plan.

Plant owners began thinking about transferring their seedlings to other greenhouses. Bullfrogs assured them it was every plant owner's right. Practically, though, their choices were limited to the same poor neighborhood. Oddly, the Bullfrogs knew that would happen, though they never said so.

Soon Bullfrog corporations began taking over communal greenhouses, operating them for profit. Just as many seedlings withered as before, but the Bullfrogs were much more contented.

The greenhouse season came to an end and there was sadness in Horace's eyes that had never been there before. He was unsure into what realm he was withdrawing. He also wondered what made him weary before his life had truly begun. Yes, Horace still loved flowers. Only now, when he saw a blossom, he found it difficult not to think of all the seedlings that had no real chance to bloom.

It was then that Horace's "miracle plant" came into flower. When Horace had received this seedling, it was in sad, sad shape. But it evidenced an uncanny resilience, responding eagerly to Horace's tender care. Yes, every time the plant went home, it came back worse for wear. But Horace would nurse it back to health, and the plant gained even more vigor.

When Horace's "miracle plant" finally came into bloom, it was a wonderful thing! Covered with fleshy pink blossoms that had blood-red interiors, it revealed a beauty that took Horace's breath away. "I've never seen anything so magnificent!" Horace said, as his weariness fled and the sadness left his eyes.

Horace spent the vacation recovering and considering his future. Eventually, because of that one glorious plant, he decided to return to the greenhouse for a second year. When he did, Horace found that things were worse than ever. Thanks largely to Bullfrog mandates, love of flowers was either an afterthought, or not thought of at all. The focus was on growth charts and standards instead.

Horace still was determined to once again do his very best. "Few worthwhile things are easy," he thought. But beneath that surface hopefulness, his sadness and weariness already were reemerging.

THE END

Gary K. Clabaugh, Ed.D., is a professor in the Department of Education at La Salle University in Philadelphia.

Why Students Think They Understand— When They Don't

How does the mind work—and especially how does it learn? Teachers make assumptions all day long about how students best comprehend, remember, and create. These assumptions—and the teaching decisions that result—are based on a mix of theories learned in teacher education, trial and error, craft knowledge, and gut instinct. Such gut knowledge often serves us well, but is there anything sturdier to rely on?

Cognitive science is an interdisciplinary field of researchers from psychology, neuroscience, linguistics, philosophy, computer science, and anthropology who seek to understand the mind. In this regular American Educator column, we will consider findings from this field that are strong and clear enough to merit classroom application.

By Daniel T. Willingham

Question: Very often, students will think they understand a body of material. Believing that they know it, they stop trying to learn more. But, come test time, it turns out they really don't know the material. Can cognitive science tell us anything about why students are commonly mistaken about what they know and don't know? Are there any strategies teachers can use to help students better estimate what they know?

Answer: There are multiple cues by which each of us assess what we know and don't know. But these cues are fallible, which explains why students sometimes think that they know material better than their classroom performance indicates.

* * *

How do we know that we know something? If I said to you, "Could you name the first President of the United States?" you would say, "Yes, I could tell you that." On the other hand, if I said, "Could you tell me the names of the two series of novels written by Anthony Trollope?" you might say, "No." What processes go into your judgment of what you know? The answer may at first seem obvious: You look in your memory and see what's there. For the first question, you determine that your memory contains the fact that George Washington was the first U.S. President, so you answer "yes." For the second question, if you determine that your memory contains little information

about Trollope (and doesn't include the novel series named *Barchester* and *Palliser*), you would answer "no."

But, if the mechanism were really so simple, we would seldom—if ever—make mistakes about what we know. In fact, we do make such mistakes. For example, we have all confidently thought that we knew how to get to a destination, but then when put to the test by actually having to drive there, we realize that we don't know. The route may seem familiar, but that's a far cry from recalling every turn and street name.

The feeling of knowing has an important role in school settings because it is a key determinant of student studying (e.g., Mazzoni & Cornoldi, 1993). Suppose a third-grader has been studying the Vikings with the goal of understanding where they were from and what they did. At what point does the third-grader say to him or herself: "I understand this. If the teacher asks me, 'Who were the Vikings?' I could give a good answer."

Every teacher has seen that students' assessments of their own knowledge are not always accurate. Indeed, this inaccuracy can be a source of significant frustration for students on examinations. The student is certain that he or she has mastered some material, yet performs poorly on a test, and may, therefore, conclude that the test was not fair. The student has assessed his or her knowledge and concluded that it is solid, yet the examination indicates that it is not. What happened? What cues do students use to decide that they *know* something?

Cognitive science research has shown that two cues are especially important in guiding our judgments of what we know: (1) our "familiarity" with a given body of information and (2) our "partial access" to that information. In this column, I'll discuss how these two cues can lead students to believe that they know material when they don't. And, in the box, I suggest ways that teachers can help students develop more realistic self-assessments of their knowledge.

"Familiarity" Fools Our Mind into Thinking We Know More than We Do

The idea of familiarity is, well, familiar to all of us. We have all had the experience of seeing someone and sensing that her face is familiar but being unable to remember who that person is or how we know her.

Psychologists distinguish between *familiarity* and *recollection*. Familiarity is the knowledge of having seen or otherwise experienced some stimulus before, but having little information associated with it in your memory. Recollection, on the other hand, is characterized by richer associations. For example, a young student might be familiar with George Washington (he knows he was a President and maybe that there's a holiday named after him), whereas an older student could probably recollect a substantial narrative about him. (See Yonelinas, 2002, for an extended review of the differences between recollection and familiarity.)

Although familiarity and recollection are different, an insidious effect of familiarity is that it can give you the feeling that you know something when you really don't. For example, it has been shown that if some key words of a question are familiar, you are more likely to think that you know the answer to the question. In one experiment demonstrating this effect (Reder, 1987), subjects were exposed to a variety of word pairs (e.g., "golf" and "par") and then asked to complete a short task that required them to think at least for a moment about the words. Next, subjects saw a set of trivia questions, some of which used words that the subjects had just been exposed to in the previous task. Subjects were asked to make a rapid judgment as to whether or not they knew the answer to the question—and then they were to provide the answer.

If the trivia question contained key words from the previous task (e.g., "What term in golf refers to a score of one under par on a particular hole?"), those words should have seemed familiar, and may have led to a feeling of knowing. Indeed, Reder found that subjects were likely to say that they knew the answer to a question containing familiar words, irrespective of whether they could actually answer the question. For questions in which words had not been rendered familiar, subjects were fairly accurate in rapidly assessing their knowledge.

A similar effect was observed in an experiment using arithmetic problems (Reder & Ritter, 1992). On each trial of this experiment, subjects saw an addition or multiplication problem (e.g., 81 + 35) and they had to rapidly decide whether they would calculate the answer or answer from memory. If they chose to calculate, they had 20 seconds to do so; if they chose

to answer from memory, they had just 1.4 seconds. Sometimes problems repeated, so subjects might have had the answer to a complex problem in memory. Subjects were paid depending on their speed and accuracy, so the decision about whether or not to calculate was important. As in the trivia question experiment, subjects were accurate in knowing when they could retrieve an answer from memory and when they needed to calculate it—except in one situation, when the experimenters repeated a two-digit problem but changed the operation (e.g., addition to multiplication). In that case, subjects were just as likely to try to retrieve an answer from memory for a problem they had actually just seen (e.g., 81 + 35) as they were for a problem they had *not* just seen but which used familiar operands (e.g., 81−35). The experimenters argued that subjects made their judgment about whether to calculate based on the familiarity of the problem components, not on the whether the answer was in memory.

"Partial Access": Our Mind Is Fooled When We Know Part of the Material or Related Material

A second basis for the feeling of knowing is "partial access," which refers to the knowledge that an individual has of either a component of the target material or information closely related to the target material. Suppose I ask you a question and the answer doesn't immediately come to mind, but some related information does. For example, when I ask for the names of the two series of Trollope novels, you readily recall *Barchester* and you know I mentioned the other series earlier; you even remember that it started with the letter P, and you believe it had two or three syllables. Your quick retrieval of this partial information will lead to a feeling of knowing the relevant information— even if *Palliser* is not actually in your memory.

The effect of partial access was demonstrated in an experiment (Koriat & Levy-Sadot, 2001) in which subjects were asked difficult trivia questions. If subjects couldn't answer a particular question, they were asked to judge whether they would recognize the answer if they saw it (i.e., to make a feeling-of-knowing judgment). The interesting twist: Some of the questions used categories for which lots of examples came to mind for their subjects (e.g., composers) and matching questions used categories for which few examples came to mind (e.g., choreographers)—that is, these subjects could easily think of at least a few famous composers, but couldn't think of more than one or two choreographers, if any.

The results showed that whether or not they could actually recognize the right answer, people gave higher feeling-of-knowing judgments to questions using many-example categories (e.g., "Who composed the music for the ballet *Swan Lake*?") than to questions using few-example categories (e.g., "Who choreographed the ballet *Swan Lake*?"). The experimenters argued that when people see the composer question, the answer doesn't come to mind, but the names of several composers do. This related information leads to a feeling of knowing. Informally, we could say that subjects conclude (consciously or unconsciously), "I can't retrieve the *Swan Lake* composer right now, but I certainly seem to know a lot about composers. With a little more time, the answer to the question could probably be found." On the other hand, the choreographer question brings little information to mind and, therefore, no feeling of knowing.*

These studies, and dozens of others like them, confirm two general principles of how people gauge their memories. First, people do not assess their knowledge directly by inspecting the contents of memory. Rather, they use cues such as familiarity and partial access. Second, most of the time these cues provide a reasonable assessment of knowledge, but they are fallible.

If a student believes that he knows material, he will likely divert attention elsewhere; he will stop listening, reading, working, or participating.

How Students End Up with "Familiarity" and "Partial Access" to Material

If a student believes that he knows material, he will likely divert attention elsewhere; he will stop listening, reading, working, or participating. Mentally "checking out" is never a good choice for students, but all the more so when they disengage because they *think* they know material that, in fact, they do not know. The feeling of knowing becomes a problem if you have the feeling without the knowing. There are some very obvious ways in which students can reach this unfortunate situation in a school setting. Here are several common ones:

1. Rereading. To prepare for an examination, a student re-reads her classnotes and textbook. Along the way, she encounters familiar terms ("familiar" as in she knows she's heard these terms before), and indeed they become even more familiar to her as she rereads. She thinks, "Yes, I've seen this, I know this, I understand this." But feeling that you understand material as it is presented to you is not the same as being able to recount it yourself.

---

* Another important aspect of this phenomenon is that the accuracy of partially retrieved information is irrelevant to the feeling of knowing. In an experiment illustrating this phenomenon, Asher Koriat (1993) asked subjects to learn strings of letters. Later, subjects were asked to recall as many letters as possible and then judge whether they would sucessfully recognize the entire letter string from among several choices. Subjects' confidence that they would recognize the letter string increased with the number of letters that they had recalled, regardless of whether or not those letters were correct. The more they thought they were pulling out of memory, the more confident they were that they really knew the whole string and would recognize it when they saw it.

As teachers know, this gap between feeling that you know and genuine recollection can cause great frustration. I have frequently had exchanges in which one of my students protests that despite a low test grade, he or she really knew the material. When I ask a general question or two, the student struggles to answer and ends up sputtering, "I can't exactly explain it, but I know it!" Invariably, a student with this problem has spent a great deal of time reading over the course material, yielding a lot of familiarity, but not the necessary and richer recollective knowledge.

2. Shallow Processing. A teacher may prepare an excellent lesson containing a good deal of deep meaning. But this deep meaning will only reside in a student's memory if the student has actively thought about that deep meaning (see "Students Remember...What They Think About," *American Educator,* Summer 2003, www.aft.org/american_educator/summer2003/cogsci.html). Let's say, for example, that a teacher has prepared a lesson on the European settlement of Australia and on the meaningful issue of whether that settlement should be viewed as a colonization or invasion. But, let's say that a given student did not process and retain the deep meaning intended by the lesson. He did absorb key terms like "Captain Cook" and "Aborigines." His familiarity with these key terms could mislead him into believing he was ready for a test on the subject.

3. Recollecting Related Information. Sometimes students know a lot of information *related* to the target topic, and that makes them feel as though they know the target information. (This is analogous to the subjects in the experiment who knew the names of many composers and so felt that they knew who composed *Swan Lake*.) Suppose that a fifth-grade class spent three weeks studying weather systems, including studying weather maps, collecting local data, keeping a weather journal, learning about catastrophic weather events like hurricanes, and so on. In preparation for a test, the teacher says that there will be a question on how meteorologists use weather maps to predict hurricanes. When the student hears "weather map," she might recall such superficial information as that they are color coded, that they include temperature information, and so on; she feels she knows about weather maps and doesn't study further. In fact, she hasn't yet come to understand the core issue—how weather maps are used to predict weather. But her general familiarity with the maps has tricked her into believing she had the necessary knowledge when she didn't. (Ironically, the problem of recollecting related information is most likely to occur when a student has mastered a good deal of material on the general topic; that is, he's mastered related material, but not the target material. It's the knowledge of the related material that creates the feeling of knowing.)

Cognitive science research confirms teachers' impressions that students do not always know what they think they know. It also shows where this false sense of knowledge comes from and helps us imagine the kinds of teaching and learning activities that could minimize this problem. In particular, teachers can help students test their own knowledge in ways that provide

How To Help Students See When Their Knowledge is Superficial or Incomplete

What can be done to combat spurious feelings of knowing in students? Remedies center on jostling students away from a reliance on familiarity and partial access as indices of their knowledge, and encouraging (or requiring) them to test just how much knowledge they recall and understand.

- *Make it clear to students that the standard of "knowing" is the "ability to explain to others," not "understanding when explained by others."* I have found the following analogy helpful in explaining the difference in the two types of knowing: You and a friend are watching a movie that only you have seen before. As the plot unfolds, each event, even those meant to be surprising, seems predictable and familiar. Yet if your friend asks you, "How does it end?" you can't quite remember. To truly know about a movie (or a mathematical concept or historical event), you must be able to discuss it in your own words.

- *Require students to articulate what they know in writing or orally, thereby making what they know and don't know explicit, and therefore easier to evaluate, and easier to build on or revise.* Suppose that you've just gone over a rather tricky point in class. You want to be sure that they've understood the lesson. As we all know, asking "Does everyone understand the main point here?" yields only silence. Calling on one student makes it clear to that student whether or not he or she understands the main point, but brings little benefit to other students. An alternative is to have students pair off and then take turns explaining the main idea to each other. (This will work best if the teacher provides clear criteria by which students can judge each other's answers; otherwise it can be a case of the blind leading the blind.) The process of having to explain aloud to someone else makes it clear to students whether or not they understand what they are meant to understand. The process breaks the ice of silence, and if the teacher afterwards asks if there are questions, students are usually more willing to ask for help. Indeed, observing the pairs will usually make the extent of students' understanding clear to the teacher.

- *Begin each day (or selected days) with a written self test.* The teacher may pose a few questions reviewing the material from the previous lesson. The success of this strategy depends on students writing their answers rather than having the class shout out answers or calling on students who raise their hands. Again, the question you pose will likely lead to a feeling of knowing in most students because it is material they were recently taught. If, moments after hearing the question, they hear the answer provided by another student, they will likely think, "Sure, right, I knew that" because of this feeling of knowing. To get an accurate assessment of memory, each student must see whether he or she can recollect it.

- *Ask students to do self tests at home or in preparing for examinations.* For students who are a bit older, teachers can facilitate this process by organizing "study buddies" who agree to meet at least once before an examination, or at regular intervals, to test one another. Study buddies ask one another questions to ensure that they understand the material, and then go over whatever they don't understand. This procedure brings several benefits. It's another way to force students to actually recall information, rather than to simply recognize what is in the book. The process of generating questions for a partner is also an excellent way to encourage students to think deeply about the material; it is tantamount to asking oneself, "What is really important here? What must I know about this material?" That students pose questions for each other means that students will share their perspectives on the material—a point that one student missed or understood dimly will be supported by the other student's knowledge.

- *Help students prepare for examinations with study guides.* All students, but especially younger students, need help identifying the core information to be tested. Teacher-developed study guides are an excellent way to be sure that students are aware of the critical questions and key elements of the answers. Whether they study alone or with a buddy, the guide assures that all students will tackle the most difficult concepts or materials being tested.

—DW

more accurate assessments of what they really know—which enables students to better judge when they have mastered material and when (and where) more work is required.

References

Koriat, A. (1993). How do we know that we know? *Psychological Review, 100,* 600-639.

Koriat, A. & Levy-Sadot, R. (2001). The combined contribution of the cue-familiarity and accessibility heuristics to feelings of knowing. *Journal of Experimental Psychology: Learning, Memory, and Cognition, 27,* 34-53.

Mazzoni, G. & Cornoldi, C. (1993). Strategies in study time allocation: Why is study time sometimes not effective? *Journal of Experimental Psychology: General, 122,* 47-60.

Reder, L. M. (1987). Strategy selection in question answering. *Cognitive Psychology, 19,* 90-138.

Reder, L. M. & Ritter, F. (1992). What determines initial feeling of knowing? Familiarity with question terms, not with the answer. *Journal of Experimental Psychology: Learning, Memory, and Cognition, 18,* 435-451.

Yonelinas, A. P. (2002). The nature of recollection and familiarity: A review 30 years of research. *Journal of Memory and Language, 46,* 441-517.

Daniel T. Willingham is associate professor of cognitive psychology and neuroscience at the University of Virginia and author of Cognition: The Thinking Animal. *His research focuses on the role of consciousness in learning.*

From *American Educator,* Winter 2003/2004, pp. 38-41, 48. Copyright © 2003 by American Educator, the quarterly journal of the American Federation of Teachers, AFL-CIO. Reprinted by permission of the AFT and the author.

UNIT 4

Morality and Values in Education

Unit Selections

Key Points to Consider

- What is character education? Why do so many people wish to see a form of character education in schools?

- Are there certain values about which most of us can agree? Should they be taught in schools? Why, or why not?

- What can teachers do to help students become caring, morally responsible persons?

- Do you agree with Aristotle that virtue can and should be taught in schools? Explain.

Student Website

www.mhcls.com/online

Internet References

Further information regarding these websites may be found in this book's preface or online.

Association for Moral Education
http://www.amenetwork.org/

Child Welfare League of America
http://www.cwla.org

Ethics Updates/Lawrence Hinman
http://ethics.acusd.edu

The National Academy for Child Development
http://www.nacd.org

Morality has always been a concern of educators. It is possible that there has not been a more appropriate time to focus attention on ethics and standards of principled conduct in our schools. The many changes in American family structures in past years make this an important public concern, especially in the United States. We are told that all nations share concern. In addition to discerning how best to deal with moral and ethical educational issues, there are also substantive value controversies regarding curriculum content, such as the dialogue over how to infuse multicultural values into school curricula. On the one hand, educators need to help students learn how to reason and how to determine what principles should guide them in making decisions in situations where their own well-being and/or the well-being of another is at stake. On the other hand, educators need to develop reasoned and fair standards for resolving the substantive value issues to be faced in dealing with questions about what should or should not be taught.

There is frustration and anger among some American youth, and we must address how educators can teach moral standards and ethical decision-making skills. This is no longer simply something desirable that we might do; it has become something that we *must* do. How it is to be done is the subject of a national dialogue that is now occurring.

Students need to develop a sense of genuine caring both for themselves and others. They need to learn alternatives to vio-

lence and human exploitation. Teachers need to be examples of responsible and caring persons who use reason and compassion in solving problems in school.

Some teachers voice their concerns that students need to develop a stronger sense of character that is rooted in a more defensible system of values. Other teachers express concerns that they cannot do everything and are hesitant to instruct on morality and values. Most believe that they must do something to help students become reasoning and ethical decision makers.

What teachers perceive to be worthwhile and defensible behavior informs our reflections on what we as educators should teach. We are conscious immediately of some of the values that affect our behavior, but we may not be as aware of what informs our preferences. Values that we hold without being conscious of them are referred to as tacit values—values derived indirectly after reasoned reflection on our thoughts about teaching and learning. Much of our knowledge about teaching is tacit knowledge, which we need to bring into conscious cognition by analyzing the concepts that drive our practice. We need to acknowledge how all our values inform and influence our thoughts about teaching.

Teachers need to help students develop within themselves a sense of critical social consciousness and a genuine concern for social justice. Insight into the nature of moral decision making should be taught in the context of real current and past social problems and should lead students to develop their own skills in social analysis relating to the ethical dilemmas of human beings.

The controversy over teaching morality deals with more than the tensions between secular and religious interests in society. We argue that the construction of educational processes and the decisions about the substantive content of school curricula involve moral issues as well.

One of the most compelling responsibilities of schools is that of preparing young people for their moral duties as free citizens of free nations. Governments have always wanted schools to teach the principles of civic morality based on their respective constitutional traditions. Indeed when the public school movement began in the 1830s and 1840s, the concept of universal public schooling as a mechanism for instilling a sense of national identity and civic morality was supported. In every nation, school curricula have certain value preferences embedded in them.

For whom do the schools exist? Is a teacher's primary responsibility to his or her client, the student, or to the student's parents? Do secondary school students have the right to study and to inquire into subjects not in officially sanctioned curricula? What are the moral issues surrounding censorship of student reading material? What ethical questions are raised by arbitrarily withholding information regarding alternative viewpoints on controversial topics?

Teachers cannot hide all of their moral preferences. They can, however, learn to conduct just and open discussions of moral topics without succumbing to the temptation to indoctrinate students with their own views.

Teaching students to respect all people, to revere the sanctity of life, to uphold the right of every citizen to dissent, to believe in the equality of all people before the law, to cherish freedom to learn, and to respect the right of all people to their own convictions—these are principles of democracy and ideals worthy of being cherished. An understanding of the processes of ethical decision making is needed by the citizens of any free nation; thus, this process should be taught in a free nation's schools.

What part ought the schooling experience play in the formation of such things as character, informed compassion, conscience, honor, and respect for self and others? The issue of public morality and the question of how best to educate to achieve responsible social behavior, individually and collectively, are matters of great significance today.

Seven Worlds of Moral Education

Character education is often regarded as synonymous with moral education. But, Ms. Joseph and Ms. Efron point out, it is only one of many possible approaches, each based on different assumptions about best practice, about learners, and about morality itself.

PAMELA BOLOTIN JOSEPH AND SARA EFRON

IN HIS striking critique of character education, Alfie Kohn suggests that educators might want to "define our efforts to promote children's social and moral development as an *alternative*" to character education.[1] In this article, we address Kohn's question "What does the alternative look like?" by describing the aims, practices, advantages, and difficulties of seven worlds of moral education—of which character education is only one. Lastly, we consider why character education should be the dominant approach to moral education in the United States when there are inspiring alternatives.

Viewing moral education as comprising various "moral worlds" helps us to imagine classrooms and schools that consistently support the beliefs, values, and visions that will shape students into adults and determine the world they will make. In such environments, moral education is a coherent endeavor created with purpose and deliberation. Educators in moral worlds believe that they must create a process through which young people can learn to recognize values that represent prosocial behaviors, engage in actions that bring about a better life for others, and appreciate ethical and compassionate conduct.

We describe below the moral worlds of character education, cultural heritage, caring community, peace education, social action, just community, and ethical inquiry. These worlds do not exist in isolation, nor are their purposes diametrically opposed; they may, in fact, share several characteristics. Classrooms and schools can also create coherent hybrid approaches that combine aspects of several moral worlds. Nonetheless, to clarify and foster conversations about moral education, we explore these approaches to social and ethical development as distinct moral worlds.

CHARACTER EDUCATION

The moral world of character education rests on the conviction that schooling can shape the behavior of young people by inculcating in them the proper virtues. Proponents of this world argue that children need clear directions and good role models and, implicitly, that schools should shape character when families are deficient in this task. Advocates also recommend giving students numerous opportunities to do good deeds, such as taking part in service learning, which they believe will eventually lead to moral habits. Moreover, character educators believe in establishing strong incentives for good behavior.[2]

To no small extent, *The Book of Virtues*, by William Bennett, influences many character education programs. The virtues Bennett describes are "self-discipline, compassion, responsibility, friendship, work, courage, perseverance, honesty, loyalty, and faith." Another strong influence is Character Counts, a coalition that posits "six pillars of character": 1) be honest; 2) treat others with respect; 3) do what you are supposed to do; 4) play by the rules; 5) be kind; and 6) do your share to make your school and community better. Communities have also developed their own sets of traits or rules that guide character education programs.[3]

How do schools create a moral world using character traits as starting points? First, modeling virtuous behavior is a key component of character education programs—teachers, administrators, and students are instructed to be role models. Many schools call attention to character traits in public forums and displays such as assemblies, daily announcements, bulletin boards, and banners, as well as in the study of history and literature. School 18 in Albany, New York, uses "positive reinforcement of good character traits" through a Kids for Character program. "Students who are 'caught' doing something that shows good character have their names posted where the entire school community can see. Then, each Friday, those students are called to the office to receive a reward."[4]

Schools may emphasize a different character trait each month in curricular content and assemblies. In the Kent City Schools in Ohio, November is "compassion" month. In social studies classes, students "study those who immigrated to this country at great personal sacrifice, develop a school or community service project, and research the Underground Railroad and consider how people extended help to those escaping slavery." Self-control is the trait for December. In physical education classes, students "devise an exercise chart to help monitor personal fitness." In language arts, they "keep a personal journal of times self-control was used." And in math classes, they "graph the number of times students hand in assignments on time." Teachers may also infuse their classroom management strategies and lessons with respect for aspects of character.[5]

A strength of the character education moral world is educators' belief that it is their responsibility to form character rather than remain indifferent to their students' moral development. Another positive aspect of this approach is the goal of proponents to infuse character education throughout the curriculum and school environment in order for students to experience the consistency of a moral world both academically and socially.

However, character education raises a number of critical questions that its advocates have not satisfactorily addressed. Are behavioral traits in fact the same as moral character? Do displays of virtues or desired traits truly encourage moral behavior? Does the posting of character traits on banners and bulletin boards result in a "marquee mentality" and therefore not reach the hearts and minds of young people? Is character education merely indoctrination of dominant cultural standards that may not represent the values of diverse communities? And finally, do the values chosen by character educators reflect the status quo and encourage compliance with it?[6]

CULTURAL HERITAGE

Like character education, the moral world of cultural heritage emphasizes values. These values, however, are not those of the mainstream but, instead, are drawn from the traditions of non-dominant cultures. Unlike character education, there are no underlying assumptions that schools may have better values than those of communities and families or that schools need to instill character traits in children that may run counter to students' own cultural values. In the cultural heritage moral world, the spheres of school, home, and community are interconnected. Parents, elders, and cultural leaders educate children within and outside the walls of the school. Moreover, students learn cultural traditions and values not through direct instruction but by deep understanding of and participation in the culture's arts and ceremonies.

One embodiment of the cultural heritage world is the values instruction offered in Afrocentric schools. For example, the mission statement of the African American Academy for Acceler-

ated Learning in Minneapolis affirms the importance of "reconnecting African American families to their cultural heritage, spirituality and history." The mission of the African American Academy, a public school in Seattle, is to instruct students in a way that "embraces the history, culture and heritage of African and African American people by studying and putting into practice the seven principles of Nguzo Saba: Umoja (Unity), Kujichagulia (Self-Determination), Ujima (Collective Work and Responsibility), Ujamaa (Cooperative Economics), Nia (Purpose), Kuumba (Creativity), and Imani (Faith)." Afrocentric schools emphasize parent involvement. In a report to the Kansas City Missouri Board of Education, the African Centered Education Task Force affirmed the African proverb "It takes an entire village to raise just one child" by giving parents an essential role in African-centered schools as "partners of the village."[7]

Native American schools that teach language, customs, and history also create the moral world of cultural heritage. In Native American education, cherished values include "respect [for] people and their feelings, especially respecting elders, and living in harmony with nature." Schools are imbued with a "sense of empathy and kinship with other forms of life" and a belief that "there should be no division between school climate and culture and family and community climate and culture." Parents and elders are present throughout the school, and students and teachers are expected to be in the community and the natural environment as well as in the classroom. The Tulalip Heritage School in Washington State (jointly sponsored by the public school district, the Boys and Girls Club, and the Tulalip Tribe) transmits its ethos to the students by having them learn the stories of ancestors, cultivating respect for Native American culture and "respect for one another," and recognizing the importance of community. The NAWAYEE Center School, an alternative high school in Minneapolis, offers cultural classes that "include art, spirituality, family, community, and oral traditions" but also strives to ensure that "American Indian cultural values and beliefs are modeled and integrated throughout the entire curriculum."[8]

The cultural heritage moral world has a number of advantages. Cultural heritage schools demonstrate respect for the cultures of their students by not just paying lip service to cultural diversity but being seriously committed to the sustenance of cultures. Partnerships with communities and meaningful parent involvement create active stakeholders in these schools and foster greater commitment to education. Continuity between the culture of the home and that of the school allows for moral instruction to use familiar patterns of communication, both verbal and nonverbal. As they learn through culturally congruent education, students do not experience a disjunction between their families' and schools' moral instruction. Furthermore, students have opportunities to learn more about their communities' moral values through the study of their history and culture, so moral learning is embedded within academic scholarship.[9]

A difficulty in implementing this model of moral education is its dependence on educators who come from the students' cultures or who themselves have deep knowledge of the culture. Districts clearly must do all that is possible to attract such educators and to sponsor community members in teacher preparation programs. Also, although all schools benefit from parents' and elders' participation, a fully realized moral world of cultural heritage would be most desired in certain schools or districts in which a significant percentage of the students are from one ethnic culture. It is crucial, however, to be sensitive to the concerns of the community. This model of moral education cannot be imposed upon a community, but it should be provided if the community so desires. Moreover, a focus on the cultural heritage of a community in no way precludes the need to learn the skills required for success in the dominant culture. Indeed, all the schools mentioned here also have a strong academic focus.

CARING COMMUNITY

The caring community emphasizes the ethic of care—nurturing, closeness, emotional attachment, and respectful, mutually supportive relationships. This moral world also focuses on the social and emotional health of all its community members. As the individuals in the classroom and the school begin to feel like a family, the school's institutional image is replaced by that of a home. Educators' moral influence stems from their caring relationships with students, parents, and one another. In the caring community, students are not rewarded for individual empathic actions; instead, these behaviors are considered the norm of the classroom culture.[10]

Accounts of schools as caring communities describe how teachers, administrators, parents, and students feel that they are members of a community. In these schools, class size is small, teachers are mentored, and all staff members feel and demonstrate genuine concern for students. In the classroom, nurturing peer relationships develop as students care for one another through informal and planned activities and structures such as buddy systems.[11]

In academics, the theme of caring is introduced through service learning projects and the study of literature that accentuates interpersonal and intercultural understanding. The classroom environment features discussions and cooperative learning activities and is defined not by rules but by how students feel about being in the class and being with one another. For example, at the Russ School in California, children developed a list of "Ways We Want to Be in Room Eight" as their classroom rules rather than a list of prohibitions.[12]

Inclusiveness is another theme in the caring community, as schools welcome and nurture diverse populations, including special education students. For instance, when the Lincoln Center Middle School in Milwaukee chose to become a caring community, it expressed caring by selecting students by means of a lottery for all who were interested in its arts-based curriculum rather than by holding auditions or having specific admissions requirements. This moral world also features schoolwide activities that involve parents and community members. Moreover, families and school personnel communicate with one another about students' academic progress, social development, and emotional health.[13]

The caring community has numerous benefits for students. Researchers from the Developmental Studies Center Child Development Project report that children educated in such schools perceive their classrooms as fair, safe, caring places that are conducive to learning. Once more, students "with a strong sense of community [are] more likely to act ethically and altruistically, develop social and emotional competencies, avoid drug use and violent behavior, and [be] academically motivated." Emotional well-being is the catalyst for moral development in the caring community. As students feel respected and cared for in loving classroom and school environments, they are less likely to act out "from feelings of inferiority, cynicism, or egocentrism that blind them to others' feelings." Furthermore, students who are nurtured are more likely to expand their sphere of caring from friends, teachers, and families to others in their communities.[14]

Difficulties for educators who wish to create a caring community occur when school culture—large class size, disruptive pullout programs, and a history of not welcoming families—thwarts the building of caring relationships. Although educators may strive to create a caring classroom, students and teachers may feel "uncared for" when the school environment is hostile. Unfortunately, the students most in need of caring often have schools whose resources cannot support this moral world.[15]

PEACE EDUCATION

The moral world of peace education stems from an ethic of care that extends beyond the classroom. Moral commitments underpinning peace education include valuing and befriending the Earth, living in harmony with the natural world, recognizing the interrelatedness of all human and natural life, preventing violence toward the Earth and all its peoples, and learning how to create and live in a culture of peace. Peace education promotes "awareness of the interdependence of all things and a profound sense of responsibility for the fate of the planet and for the well-being of humanity."[16]

The components of peace education include:

- conflict resolution—developing skills and appreciation for nonviolent problem solving;
- peace studies—examining the causes of war and its prevention and participating in activities that focus on the meaning of peace and raise peace awareness;
- environmental education—developing an appreciation of and the desire to inquire into the interrelationships of humans, their cultures, their surroundings, and all forms of life;
- global education—recognizing the interdependent nature of the world and studying problems and issues that cut across national boundaries; and
- human rights education—learning about the universal rights of human beings and strengthening respect for fundamental freedoms.[17]

Although many U.S. schools teach violence-reduction skills, few create a holistic moral world that makes a connection between peaceful personal behaviors and promoting peace throughout the world. Maria Montessori's belief that education can contribute to world peace has been a profound influence on some schools that emphasize her vision. One World Montessori School in California is an example of a school devoted to peace as an ultimate moral goal. In its K–8 peace curriculum, "teachers assist the children in developing a common language of peace and work on their own communication, peace making, and peace keeping skills."[18]

Peace educators teach that all lives and actions matter and that students are connected to all of life through a vision of peace, harmony, and Earth stewardship.

Another school that teaches for peace and interconnectedness is the Global Village School in California, which develops materials for home-schoolers. Its "Peacemakers" course "presents role models who work to enact nonviolent social change and concrete examples of such successfully enacted change." And the peace awareness curriculum of the New School at South Shore, a public primary school in Seattle, is inspired by the school's mission to "view each child as a bright spirit on a magnificent journey in our quest to contribute powerfully to the healing of humanity and Mother Earth." The goal of the Environmental and Adventure School, a public school in Washington State, is to develop responsible citizens who are stewards of the Earth. This school's mission is based on the belief that "when students are out in their environment and learn to respect and care for their surroundings, they also learn to respect and care for their classmates and teachers." The theme of "interdependent relationships—people and environments" is woven into the junior high school curriculum both in the classroom and in the many natural settings nearby.[19]

Peace educators teach that all lives and actions matter and that students are connected to all of life through a vision of peace, harmony, and Earth stewardship. Peace educators aim to create "moral sensitivity to others in the immediate classroom [and] concern for local communities and for all life on the planet." Thus the greatest advantage of this moral world is that it nourishes students' desire for personal meaning in increasingly violent times. An academic benefit is that peace education can be integrated into a stimulating curriculum that covers all disciplines, including science, language, and history.[20]

Creating an integrated peace education curriculum is difficult within traditional education systems in which content is taught in discrete disciplines. The greatest hurdle to creating this moral world, however, is the potential for conflict with community values. Undoubtedly, teaching about justice, sustainability, and peace challenges the prevailing world view in the U.S. by promoting values that confront uncontrolled economic development, consumerism, and militarism.

SOCIAL ACTION

In the moral world of social action, the values of justice and compassion guide a curriculum focused on the political nature of society. Educators believe that students are both empathic human beings and social agents who are capable of effecting change by critically examining unjust situations and participating in political processes. Teachers encourage students to ask, "What should I be paying attention to in my world?" The social action approach taps students' idealism for bringing about a better world—to "heal, repair and transform the world."[21]

Students are encouraged to generate ideas, negotiate subject matter, and find learning resources outside of the school setting. They venture into the community to gather documents, conduct interviews, and make observations. Teachers believe that their role is to confront students' ignorance or prejudices by helping the students to understand both privilege and oppression and by cultivating a "critical consciousness" of the perspectives of others.[22]

An example of this moral world occurred at Nova Alternative High School, a public school in Seattle. A junior who works with a human rights group told her classmates and teachers about the difficult situation in East Timor. In response, students began meeting once a week to study East Timor's history, politics, and culture and to raise money for Kay Rala, a small high school in Manatuto that "was burned to the ground by Indonesian soldiers in the late 1990s." Rather than donating money to a charity, the Seattle students established direct contact with Kay Rala and developed a fund-raising system with the students in East Timor. The Seattle students raised thousands of dollars for the school. The student whose concerns sparked the project reported that her "world [had] opened up"—helping her "not only to see people who are less fortunate but instead of accepting dreary situations, to change them."[23]

Another account of the social action moral world is from a fifth-grade class in Aurora, Colorado. When her students were studying the Civil War, teacher Barbara Vogel explained to her pupils that slavery was not merely a defunct system from a bygone era in American history but that people in Sudan and elsewhere were enslaved in the present day. Although the children were horrified and distraught, Vogel did not try to comfort them or to rationalize such horrors. Instead, she sought to channel their feelings of concern and outrage into social action by helping her students start a letter-writing campaign to bring this dire situation to the public's attention. When their letters did not change the fate of Sudanese slaves, the children raised money to buy freedom for a few slaves. As newspapers publicized the children's efforts, donations came in from around the world, and the class eventually purchased the freedom of more than 1,000 people. The class even developed a website to encourage others to stop slavery in Sudan.[24]

A highlight of the social action world is its integrated curriculum—rich in academic, social, and political knowledge—which reflects the moral concerns of children and adolescents. Educators report that students learn to view themselves as social and political beings with the right to access the systems of influence in communities and the larger world. Through involvement in social action, students come to believe in themselves as moral agents.[25]

Creating this moral world is not without challenges. Teachers are responsible for creating an atmosphere in which students feel comfortable voicing their moral concerns and ensuring that students' ideas are not dismissed. Also, it requires a contemporary, integrated curriculum not constrained by rigid disciplinary boundaries. Moreover, despite the opportunities to make a difference, the social action moral world requires students to encounter misery and critically analyze the reasons for unjust acts and conditions. Accordingly, can students resist pessimism when they cannot easily change the world?

JUST COMMUNITY

In the just community moral world, classrooms and schools become democratic settings that provide students with opportunities to deliberate about moral dilemmas and to participate in cooperative decision making. Students, teachers, and administrators openly discuss and address matters of mutual concern, construct the school community's policies and rules through procedures that are viewed as fair and just, and resolve moral conflicts. In the process of building community, students gain perspectives on the principles of justice and fairness by experiencing moral deliberations and by applying the principles to real and specific problems in the school community.[26]

The just community model, based on the ideas of Lawrence Kohlberg, holds that the goal of moral education is the enhancement of students' development from lower to higher stages of moral reasoning. Advocates for the just community assert that students influence their own moral development by deliberating about and seeking to resolve moral conflicts. Social interactions—i.e., lived moral dilemmas—advance learners' moral judgment as students clarify and refine their thoughts while listening and responding to other points of view. In such environments, "teachers and students engage in philosophical deliberation about the good of the community." Teachers can prepare even young students to participate in a just community by encouraging them to think about rules not as "immutable laws" but as constructed moral guidelines necessary for living in a community.[27]

Two examples of just community schools are in New York State: the Pablo Neruda Academy for Architecture and World Studies in the Bronx and the Scarsdale Alternative School. Both public high schools emphasize students' deliberation about moral dilemmas within real-world situations—freedom combined with responsibility, cooperation over competition, and "how to balance the needs of individuals with those of the community." Features of these schools include community meetings, in which decisions are made about essential school policy; fairness committees, in which conflicts among students or students and teachers are resolved; and advisories, in which students discuss their own problems and plan the agendas for community meetings.[28]

An advantage of the just community is its unequivocal naming of justice as a safeguard of individuals' rights and the community's well-being. The ideal of democracy is both a moral standard and a guiding light, raising awareness of good citizenship within a moral context. Finally, students learn that their views and actions make a difference because their moral inquiries do not seek to resolve hypothetical situations or to prepare them for life outside of school but are focused on the school itself.[29]

One problem with the just community approach is that it takes a great deal of time for students to develop real trust among themselves and to deliberate about and resolve issues. Another difficulty is that most teachers have not been trained to facilitate "an apprenticeship in democracy." Finally, truly democratic school cultures with shared authority have been exceedingly rare, and this moral world cannot exist without students' uninhibited conversations and real decision-making authority.[30]

ETHICAL INQUIRY

In the world of ethical inquiry, moral education is a process by which students engage in "moral conversation" centered on dilemmas. Also influenced by Lawrence Kohlberg's theories, this ethical inquiry approach to moral education is grounded on the premise that deliberation promotes students' moral development. Within respectful, egalitarian, and carefully facilitated discussions, teachers invite students to investigate values or actions and to imagine alternatives. In this world, students consider "how human beings should act," "life's meaning and the human place in the world," "the sources of evil and suffering," and "universal existential concerns and ways of knowing such as the meaning of friendship, love, and beauty."[31]

Teachers guide discussions on the moral dilemmas embedded within subjects across the curriculum. Springboards for ethical inquiry include literature, history, drama, economics, science, and philosophy. In particular, students learn about the consequences of making moral decisions and how fictional characters and real people make choices when aware that a moral question is at stake. Through this process of inquiry, students ponder the effects that moral, immoral, and amoral actions have on themselves and others, empathize with and appreciate the perspectives of others (their classmates as well as fictional characters or historical figures), and construct their understanding of what it means to be a moral human being.[32]

There are numerous accounts of how teachers integrate moral inquiry into their literature, social studies, and science classrooms—illustrating that most topics have ethical dimensions. Teachers also use published curricula, such as Philosophy for Children, that provide stories and other media for ethical deliberation. Facing History and Ourselves, a curriculum about 20th-century genocide, focuses on teaching middle and high school students "the meaning of human dignity, morality, law, citizenship, and behavior." This curriculum aims to help students learn to reason morally as they think about their individual decisions and behavior toward others.[33]

A value of the ethical inquiry world is that it is not an "add-on" program but rather a way to integrate genuine moral deliberation into all academic areas—becoming a norm of the classroom culture. Ethical inquiry provides opportunities for students to appreciate others' viewpoints and to bring different perspectives into their own deliberations—important skills for democratic citizenship. This moral world also capitalizes on the process of identity development, making the search for moral identity an explicit goal.[34]

Because it is a process of inquiry and negotiation, a criticism of ethical inquiry is that it does not explicitly teach values. Teachers act as important intellectual role models who care about their students' ideas and their construction of personal ethics, but they do not overtly advocate particular moral standards. Another concern is ethical inquiry's cognitive approach to moral education. Educators do not guide students to help others or to bring about a better society but instead trust that students who think ethically will actively participate in the world beyond the classroom.

CHOOSING A MORAL WORLD

Our description of seven worlds of moral education reveals that there is "no perfect world." All moral worlds have their limitations, and educators face challenges no matter which approach they take to moral education. How then do we select a moral world for classrooms and schools?

Educators face hard choices, but choose they must, as these seven worlds hold dissimilar assumptions about what constitutes best practice for moral education. These worlds also reveal different conceptions of learners. They posit that moral educators can think about students as material to be shaped, as feelers with emotional needs, as thinkers whose judgments can be stimulated, or as villagers who learn from elders. Indeed, these moral worlds hold different understandings of *morality* itself. Does morality mean having good character, nurturing peers, caring for those who suffer (those both near and far), or being stewards of the Earth?

Serious ethical deliberation about the aims and practices of moral education cannot be avoided. It would be a mistake to try to create an approach to moral education that represents the "best of all worlds," because forming an amalgam of many approaches is more likely to result in a haphazard environment in which students receive conflicting messages. Moral educators need to decide on one approach or to create a thoughtfully considered hybrid that has clear aims and coherent practices. Too often, consideration of moral education (as well as any aspect of education) focuses only on the inadequate question of what works rather than on what we define as our utmost hopes for our students and the society in which they will live. When we ask the moral question, not merely the operational one, we allow ourselves to imagine our students having lives of meaning, taking part in genuine and peaceful relationships, and living without violence, cynicism, and despair.

The most popular world of moral education at present is character education. Numerous politicians, organizations, and boards of education advocate its implementation. Yet, as we explore these seven moral worlds, we see that character education has the most limited vision of morality and moral education—despite its advocates' good intentions.

How do we compare naming "the trait of the month" to teaching children to have a deep appreciation for peace and for sustaining the Earth? Why should we select stories in the hope that students will assimilate certain values or emulate heroes when we can teach literature as a springboard for pondering moral dilemmas and developing moral identities? Why should we settle for posting the names of "good" children on a bulletin board when we can aim to create loving, familial classrooms or a village of moral educators? How do we equate mandated service learning with a thoughtfully conceived student-led effort of social action, not only to alleviate suffering but also to stop cycles of poverty and injustice?

We question why the dominant approach to moral education consists of the practice of giving rewards to students just for following rules and for occasional acts of kindness. Instead, should we not help students to engage in profound ethical deliberation, revere peace, be cared for and be caring, and develop as moral agents who can repair the world? Why are these not among the endorsed goals of moral education?

In conclusion, the other six moral worlds hold more humane, imaginative, and profound visions of morality and moral education than those of character education. These compelling alternatives deserve serious consideration on the part of educators.

Notes

1. Alfie Kohn, "How Not to Teach Values: A Critical Look at Character Education," *Phi Delta Kappan*, February 1997, p. 436.

2. Thomas Lickona, *Educating for Character: How Our Schools Can Teach Respect and Responsibility* (New York: Bantam, 1991); Kevin Ryan and Karen E. Bohlin, *Building Character in Schools: Practical Ways to Bring Moral Instruction to Life* (San Francisco: Jossey-Bass, 1999), p. 11; and Edward A. Wynne and Kevin Ryan, *Reclaiming Our Schools: A Handbook on Teaching Character, Academics, and Discipline* (New York: Macmillan, 1993).

3. William J. Bennett, *The Book of Virtues: A Treasury of Great Moral Stories* (New York: Simon & Schuster, 1993). The six ethical values of the Character Counts Youth Ethics Initiative can be found at www.charactercounts.org/defsix.htm. The Kent City Schools in Ohio developed a list of character virtues: cooperation, self-control, trustworthiness, tolerance, compassion, commitment and dedication, work ethic and responsibility, respect for self and others, fairness and justice, and respect for our community and environment, which is available at http://kent.k12.oh.us/kcs/cep/traits.php.

4. For information on the School 18 program, see www.albanyschools.org/Schools/school18/school18program.htm.

5. For information on these and other character activities, see http://kent.k12.oh.us/kcs/cep/activities.php.

6. See J. Wesley Null and Andrew J. Milson, "Beyond Marquee Morality: Virtue in the Social Studies," *Social Studies*, May/June 2003, pp. 119–22; Don Jacobs, "The Case for the Inclusion of an Indigenous Perspective in Character Education," paper presented at the annual meeting of the American Educational Research Association, New Orleans, April 2002; and David Purpel, "The Politics of Character Education," in idem, ed., *Moral Outrage in Education* (New York: Peter Lang, 1999), pp. 83–97.

7. For more information on these examples, visit www.aaalmn.org/index.htm; www.seattle-schools.org/schools/aaa/nguzo_s.htm; www.afrocentric.info/AfricanCentered; and www.duboislc.org/EducationWatch/faqs.html.

8. In this article, we focus on examples from Indian schools that are not strictly tribal schools. For example, see Sandra M. Stokes, "Curriculum for Native American Students: Using Native American Values," *Reading Teacher*, vol. 50, 1997, pp. 576–84; Angayuqaq Oscar Kawagley and Ray Barnhardt, "Education Indigenous to Place: Western Science Meets Native Reality," in Gregory A. Smith and Dilafruz R. Williams, eds., *Ecological Education in Action: On Weaving Education, Culture, and the Environment* (Albany: State University of New York Press, 1998), pp. 117–40; G. Mike Charleston, "Toward True Native Education: A Treaty of 1992: Final Report of the Indian Nations at Risk Task Force," *Journal of American Indian Education*, Winter 1994, pp. 1–23; and Washington Education Association, "Tulalip Heritage School: Linking Cultures and Generations," 9 November 2000, available at http://www.wa.nea.org/articles/2000-4/Choice3.htm. For information on the Center School, see www.centerschool.org.

9. For discussions on culturally relevant moral education, see Cynthia Ballenger, "Because You Like Us: The Language of Control," *Harvard Educational Review*, vol. 62, 1992, pp. 199–208; Peter Murrell, "Afrocentric Immersion: Academic and Personal Development of African American Males in Public Schools," in Theresa Perry and James W. Frazer, eds., *Freedom's Plow: Teaching in the Multicultural Classroom* (New York: Routledge, 1993), pp. 231–59.

10. Nel Noddings, *The Challenge to Care in Schools* (New York: Teachers College Press, 1992); and Jane Roland Martin, *The Schoolhome: Rethinking Schools for Changing Families* (Cambridge: Harvard University Press, 1992).

11. Victor Battistich et al., "Students and Teachers in Caring Classroom and School Communities," paper presented at the annual meeting of the American Educational Research Association, New Orleans, April 1994; and Rick Weissbourd, "Moral Teachers, Moral Students," *Educational Leadership*, March 2003, pp. 6–11.

12. Lynn H. Doyle and Patrick M. Doyle, "Building Schools as Caring Communities: Why, What, and How?," *The Clearing House*, May/June 2003, pp. 259–61; and Jean Tepperman, "Schooling as a Caring Community," *Children's Advocate*, September/October 1997, available at www.4children.org/news/9-97cdp.htm.

13. Doyle and Doyle, op. cit.

14. Eric Schaps, "Creating a School Community," *Educational Leadership*, March 2003, pp. 31–33.

15. Ibid.; and Weissbourd, op. cit.

16. Ian M. Harris, Mary Lee Morrison, and Timothy Reagan, *Peace Education*, 2nd ed. (Jefferson, N.C.: McFarland & Company, 2002); "What Is Peace Education?," in *A Teachers' Guide to Peace Education* (New Delhi, India: United Nations Educational, Scientific, and Cultural Organization, 2001), available at www.ncte-in.org/pub/unesco/ch1.htm; Frans C. Verhagen, "The Earth Community School: A Back-to-Basics Model of Secondary Education," *Green Teacher*, Fall 1999, pp. 28–31; William Scott and Chris Oulton, "Environmental Values Education: An Exploration of Its Role in the School Curriculum," *Journal of Moral Education*, vol. 27, 1998, pp. 209-24; and American Montessori Society, "AMS Position Paper: Holistic Peace Education," available at www.amshq.org/positions/documents/peace.pdf.

17. Mary Lee Morrison, "Peace Education in Theory and Practice," *Delta Kappa Gamma Bulletin*, Fall 2002, pp. 10–14.

18. For information on the One World Montessori School, see www.oneworldmontessori.org.

19. For more information on these examples, see www.globalvillageschool.org; www.seattleschools.org/schools/southshore; www.lkwash.wednet.edu/lwsd/pdf/environmental0203.pdf; and www.pps.k12.or.us/schools-c/pages/environmental.

20. Morrison, op.cit.

21. Peter McLaren, *Life in Schools: An Introduction to Critical Pedagogy in the Foundations of Education* (New York: Longman, 1989); and Henry Giroux, *Border Crossings: Cultural Works and the Politics of Education* (New York: Routledge, 1993), p. 104.

22. Pamela Bolotin Joseph and Mark Windschitl, "Fostering a Critical and Caring Classroom Culture," *Social Education, Middle Level Learning Supplement*, May/June 1999, pp. 14–15.

23. Regine Labossiere, "Nova Sister-School Class Aids East Timor Students," *Seattle Times*, 13 October 2003, p. B-3.

24. See David Field, "Freedom Writers," *Teacher Magazine on the Web*, February 1999; Nat Hentoff, "Fifth-Grade Freedom Fighters," *Washington Post*, 1 August 1998, p. A-15; Mindy Sink, "School children Set Out to Buy Freedom for Slaves," *New York Times*, 2 December 1998, p. B-14; and Richard Woodbury, "The Children's Crusade," *Time*, 21 December 1998, p. 44.

25. Joseph and Windschitl, op. cit.

26. Lawrence Kohlberg, *The Psychology of Moral Development: Moral Stages and the Life Cycle*, vol. 2 (San Francisco: Harper & Row, 1984).

27. Clark Power, "Building Democratic Community: A Radical Approach to Moral Education," in William Damon, ed., *Bringing in a New Era in Character Education* (Palo Alto, Calif.: Hoover Institution, 2002), pp.1–32; and Elsa K. Weber, "Rules, Right and Wrong, and Children," *Early Childhood Education Journal*, Winter 2000, pp. 107–11.

28. For more information on these examples, see www.pablonerudaacademy.org/justcom.htm; and www.scarsdaleschools.k12.ny.us/hs/Aschool.

29. Sara Efron, "Beyond Character Education: Democracy as a Moral Goal," *Critical Issues in Teacher Education*, vol. 8, 2000, pp. 20–28.

30. Barbara J. Thayer-Bacon, "Democratic Classroom Communities," *Studies in Philosophy and Education*, vol. 15, 1996, pp. 333–51; F. Clark Power, "Building Democratic Community: A Radical Approach to Moral Education," in Damon, pp. 129–48; and Edward R. Mikel, "Deliberating Democracy," in Pamela Bolotin Joseph et al., eds., *Cultures of Curriculum* (Mahwah, N.J.: Lawrence Erlbaum, 2000), pp. 115–35.

31. Robert J. Nash, *Answering the "Virtuecrats": A Moral Conversation on Character Education* (New York: Teachers College Press, 1997); and Katherine G. Simon, *Moral Questions in the Classroom: How to Get Kids to Think Deeply About Real Life and Their Schoolwork* (New Haven, Conn.: Yale University Press, 2001), pp. 37–38.

32. Joe Winston, "Theorising Drama as Moral Education," *Journal of Moral Education*, December 1999, pp. 459–71; Vaille Dawson, "Addressing Controversial Issues in Secondary School Science," *Australian Science Teachers Journal*, November 2001, pp. 38–44; and Larry R. Johannessen, "Strategies for Initiating Authentic Discussion," *English Journal*, September 2003, pp. 73–79.

33. Linda Leonard Lamme, "Digging Deeply: Morals and Ethics in Children's Literature," *Journal for a Just and Caring Education*, October 1996, pp. 411–20; Steven Wolk, "Teaching for Critical Literacy in Social Studies," *Social Studies*, May/June 2003, pp. 101–6; Lena Green, "Philosophy for Children: One Way of Developing Children's Thinking," *Thinking*, vol. 13, no. 2, 1997, pp. 20–22; www.chss.montclair.edu/iapc/homepage.html; Margot Stern Strom, Martin Sleeper, and Mary Johnson, "Facing History and Ourselves: A Synthesis of History and Ethics in Effective History Education," in Andrew Garrod, ed., *Learning for Life: Moral Education Theory and Practice* (Westport, Conn.: Praeger, 1992), pp. 131–53; and Melinda Fine, "Facing History and Ourselves: Portrait of a Classroom," *Educational Leadership*, December 1991, pp. 44–49.

34. Constance M. Perry, "How Do We Teach What Is Right?: Research and Issues in Ethical and Moral Development," *Journal for a Just and Caring Education*, October 1996, pp. 400-10; and Ruth W. Grant, "The Ethics of Talk: Classroom Conversation and Democratic Politics," *Teachers College Record*, Spring 1996, pp. 470–82.

PAMELA BOLOTIN JOSEPH *is core faculty member in the Center for Programs in Education at Antioch University, Seattle, Wash.* **SARA EFRON** *is an associate professor in the Educational Foundations Department of National-Louis University, Evanston, Ill.* ©2005, *Pamela B. Joseph.*

Pathways to Reform:
Start With Values

*Educators' deeply held philosophical beliefs point
to many diverse pathways, all leading to school excellence.*

David J. Ferrero

The Northtown Academy campus of Chicago International Charter School (CICS) combines a commitment to classical learning with innovative citizenship education grounded in public debate. KIPP Academies rely on academic pressure and tough love to help students meet state standards. At Withrow University High School in Cincinnati, Ohio, students wear uniforms and boys and girls attend separate classes. The Francis Parker Charter School in Harvard, Massachusetts, boasts a democratic-communitarian ethic in which students take an active role in school governance and pursue learning through thematic group projects. Students at The Met in Providence, Rhode Island, pursue a curriculum composed entirely of self-designed projects and internships. At the Oakland School for Social Justice and Community Development in Oakland, California, students learn community organizing and critical theory. And at High Tech High in San Diego, California, students pursue project-based courses of study keyed to careers in technology industries.

These are just seven of the many great small high schools that I have had the privilege of getting to know through my work at the Bill & Melinda Gates Foundation. These schools differ profoundly in their curriculum, instruction, and culture. An individual teacher or student might feel at home in one or a few of these schools, but certainly not in all of them. Yet these small schools have important things in common. They all have high percentages of minority and low-income students. They all strive to offer students a supportive, rigorous, and coherent learning environment in compliance with state standards. They all aim to prepare students for higher education, work, and citizenship.

Common ends, diverse pathways. School reformers have embraced this vision, but we still face the question of how to achieve it. We know most of the structural conditions necessary to make such a vision a reality: site-based autonomy, family and faculty choice, performance-based accountability, data-driven decision making, and research-based practice. But these structural features only get us so far. They explain what these schools have in common, but they don't account for what makes them distinctive.

Belief Systems and Practice

One crucial but often overlooked source of the distinctiveness among high-performing schools is *philosophy*—the beliefs and values that create our sense of what makes life worth living, and therefore what is worth teaching and how we should teach it. In our drive to be "research-based," we tend to forget that between the science of learning and the practice of teaching the important value judgments that color our reading of the research and the implications for practice we derive from it. These value judgments reflect deeply held philosophical worldviews.

Few of us went into education out of a burning desire to raise students' test scores. We went into it out of a deep sense of what's good for kids and society, what's worth knowing and thinking about, what it means to he a good citizen and person—indeed, what it means to lead a good life. Philosophy matters.

In fact, education's fiercest and most intractable conflicts have stemmed from differences in philosophy. Take the 100 years War between "progressives" and "traditionalists."[1] To oversimplify an already oversimplified dichotomy, progressives incline toward pedagogical approaches that start with student interests and emphasize hands-on engagement with the physical and social environments, whereas traditionalists tend to start with pre-existing canons of inquiry and knowledge and emphasize ideas and concepts mediated through words and symbols.

The evolution of these differences is not grounded in science, but in history, philosophy, and ideology. So-called progressivism evolved over the 19th and 20th centuries out of a complex interaction of romanticism, socialism, pragmatism, and progressive politics. So-called traditionalism has Aristotelian origins refracted through Renaissance humanism and later through romanticism, as well as pre-libertarian forms of conservatism. The former could be described as populist, small-*d* democratic, and attuned to the flux of modern life; the latter could be characterized as aristocratic, small-*r* republican, and attentive to the continuities that underlie and influence modern change.

Common ends, diverse pathways. School reformers have embraced this vision, but we still face the question of how to achieve this vision.

Notice that romanticism appears as a source for both philosophies. This is not the only point of overlap. Education progressives and traditionalists from the 19th century to the present have shared certain overarching perspectives. For example, all espouse liberal democratic values inherited from the Enlightenment, such as rights, liberty, and popular government.

All subscribe to a developmental theory of childhood and learning. All strive to produce young adults who are good citizens, caring people, critical thinkers, and productive contributors to the economy. All believe that learning should be relevant to students. They simply disagree about the exact meaning of these ideals and their curricular and pedagogical implications. Does a relevant education start with student interests and backgrounds, current needs of the job market, and current events? Or should we teach students to recognize the relevance of ancient Greek thought, the Copernican revolution, and Shakespeare's soliloquies?

How can we devise a study to adjudicate these different views empirically? We can't. Normative questions are not easily settled by empirical means because our normative points of view color how we understand empirical evidence.

Not that empirical research is meaningless. On the contrary research has produced many insights that help us distinguish between good teaching and bad. We know, for example, that the mind constructs knowledge—that people learn by connecting new information to existing understandings and conceptual frameworks. We know that teaching needs to attend to both basic and higher-order skills, and to both cognitive and noncognitive development. We know that students learn best in safe, challenging, personally supportive, and authoritative communities.

These findings, however, must be interpreted and translated into practice. I or some educators, constructivist learning theory justifies discovery learning driven by student interests; for others, it merely describes what happens whenever a learner's brain takes in information, even "passively" through a lecture. Which interpretation is correct? On this question and many others, even the most rigorous and credible research provides little guidance.

Within the bounds of shared values and research-based principles lie a range of legitimate practices, and between science and practice lie a number of judgments that are irreducibly values-based. This idea was once cause for concern, because it belied the quest for the single code of best practices" that would certify teachers as true professionals. But we need not view the influence of philosophical values as an embarrassment anymore. As reformers and education professionals have moved away from large, tracked, one-size-fits-all comprehensive schools and toward small, focused schools of choice that offer multiple pathways to postsecondary opportunity, we have begun to recognize what should have been obvious all along: There are many ways for a school to be good" (see Cuban, 2000).

Reflecting on Key Questions

From time to time we remind ourselves about the importance of values, beliefs, and culture to education. But we are not conditioned to take them seriously in our deliberations about what schools should be. We need help, because enabling educators, parents, and other constituents to be more articulate about their convictions and the philosophical judgments behind them is a crucial step in forming effective learning communities. This step involves answering key questions both individually and collectively.

The following questions can help educators and their constituencies organize into philosophically and pedagogically coherent learning communities. The process of reflecting on these questions is especially useful for groups of educators who are creating new, small high school learning communities, such as schools-within-schools, but it applies to any school community striving to transform practice around shared goals.

What motivated me to go into teaching? We all know that teaching is a vocation. We don't do it for money or glory but for some intrinsic reward. Was it a passion for a particular subject? A social service mission? A desire to help young people realize individual talents? This gut check will tease out your deep motivation and basic orientation toward practice.

What do I think students should know and be able to do? We need to answer this question as concretely as possible; otherwise everyone's answers will sound the same. We all believe in developing students' literacy, mathematical facility, critical thinking, citizenship, workforce competence, and commitment to lifelong learning. This level of collective affirmation is important; it reminds us that whatever our differences, we are ultimately on the same side. But these broad values need to be unpacked with more pointed questions.

To become literate, what kinds of books should students read, and why? What should be the ratio of printed text to other media? Who should choose the medium—student or teacher? Which comes first in teaching literacy—decoding skills or comprehension? What should take priority in teaching mathematics—numeric manipulations or mathematical reasoning? Regarding science, is it OK if students graduate from high school without knowing what gravity is as long as they have mastered the scientific method? When it comes to citizenship, does living in a North Atlantic democracy like the United States mean that a student should leave school with a deep knowledge of the history and traditions that made North Atlantic democracies possible, or do immigration and globalization necessitate a more multicultural curriculum?

Notice that many of the foregoing are questions of priority rather than forced choices. Most sober educators would argue "both" in many instances—at least in the abstract. But priorities imply choices and different ways to organize learning. Our broad affirmations of consensus values usually degenerate into unproductive bickering when the hard work of constructing an instructional program begins.

Who are the influences on my education philosophy. Because our deep motivations and priorities tend to form without conscious reflection, they often remain inchoate. One good way to become articulate fast is to read. I would start with books that survey thought and debate about education in a schematized way. My favorites, because of their clarity and evenhandedness are Gerald Gutek's textbookish but readable *Philosophical and Ideological Voices in Education* (Allyn and Bacon, 2004) and Herbert Kliebard's *The Struggle for the American Curriculum. 1893–1958* (Routledge, 1995). Such books will furnish your group members with a common vocabulary and framework for situating themselves in the landscape of modern education thought.

Most participants will identify quickly with certain philosophies. They can then choose from a menu of books that represent and develop those points of view. (See "Readings on Vision," p. 14. for a selection.) Browse around for the book that gets you most excited, and pay close attention to its vision of the ideal school. Chances are that the kind of school the book describes or suggests is the kind of school in which you would feel most fulfilled.

Which colleagues share my vision? Once people have made their initial self-identifications, they might want to do their vision readings together with likeminded colleagues. Teachers in a school probably know some colleagues well and have already gravitated toward those who share certain core beliefs about their work. Forming reading groups on the basis of these affinities can extend and deepen those networks, help members develop a shared normative vocabulary, and form the basis of design groups for small schools or school-within-a-school learning communities.

What do parents, students, and local citizens want, need, and believe? Ideally, other constituents would engage in the same exploration that teachers and administrators do. If that proves unrealistic, the school should conduct some kind of outreach to ascertain the degree to which parents and students share the points of view that emerge among educators. Reaching out to the community early helps create broad ownership and ensures that there will be demand for the learning communities that are likely to grow out of this exercise.

Initially these reflective and deliberative exercises will be self-initiated and self-guided—hence the heavy dose of reading. School change consultants, coaches, and workshop leaders are no more proficient at disentangling the empirical from the normative than the typical faculty. In fact, like most of us, education consultants are so habituated to reading research through the lens of their own normative value systems that they are more likely to steer school communities in a preferred direction than to help them identify their own direction. After the nascent learning communities have organized themselves, they can choose consultants

with more care and begin the usual planning efforts.

Grappling with Dilemmas

The shift to a true system of distinct pathways for students will likely heighten anxiety over certain issues. When we introduce candid talk about values and pluralism, the following questions are likely to arise almost immediately.

Won't this lead to segregation? It certainly can. Suppose that after deliberation, educators and parents at a comprehensive high school agree to create the following four small learning communities: a women's leadership school, an International Baccalaureate (IB) school, a high-tech school, and a school of African American and Latin American Studies. Each small school reflects a significant group of constituents within the existing school, among whom it enjoys strong support. But the women's leadership school will draw more girls, the IB school more affluent Asian American and white students, the high-tech school (probably) more boys, and the African American and Latin American Studies school more black and Hispanic students.

It is possible to mitigate this problem, but not to eliminate it. Educators and other constituents must address upfront how much separation by race, gender, and aptitude they are willing to tolerate. If the tolerance is low, then schools that explicitly target gender, cultural, or racial groups will prove too divisive; the planners must rule out women's leadership and African American and Latin American Studies schools and recognize that authentically integrating IB and high-tech schools will require aggressive outreach. If constituents are willing to accept less-than-perfectly-integrated schools in the interest of better serving different constituencies and drawing on teacher strengths, it will be crucial to monitor those schools for resource equity and academic quality and to provide students with frequent opportunities to interact meaningfully with students from the other learning communities.

What about the common school? Underneath the anxiety over segregation lies the ideal of the common school as a crucible where children of diverse backgrounds come together to forge a common citizenry. If we allow schools to reflect our pluralism, what institution will bind us together as a people?

This question, although important, underestimates the degree to which both research and consensus values can enforce certain common goals and common learning for all students, regardless of school type. We should prohibit all schools from teaching antiliberal values, such as ethnic hatred or the rejection of secular government; we should require all schools to teach the principles of the U.S. Constitution and to provide civic education that goes beyond the minimal expectations of tolerance and cooperation. But schools need latitude with regard to how they accomplish these goals. Some will emphasize service learning, others critical theory, and still others immersion in the traditions of Western political thought. All of these approaches reflect credible ways of thinking about democratic citizenship.

Those who still recoil at the thought of schools designed to teach different things in different ways to different kids might ask themselves this: Do I want a national curriculum? Not *my* national curriculum, but the one we'd likely get if one were developed? The United States has rejected a national curriculum for good reasons, and these include the pedagogical pluralism we've been exploring (see Gardner, 2001), pp. 222–228).

If we base pedagogical choices on value judgments, won't we undermine teacher professionalism? For a century now, educators have sought recognition as a profession on par with medicine—self-governing, restrictive with respect to who can practice, and scientifically based. This aspiration has abetted the suppression of philosophical differences in education decision making by derogating these differences as "ideology" and "politics." If only we could eliminate such distractions, say the professionalizers, we could enact evidence-based policy and practice. But as we have seen, the research isn't enough.

Acknowledging that teaching isn't a science in no way implies that it isn't a profession that requires considerable apprenticeship and skill to perform

well. There remains a body of empirical evidence that teachers must internalize, and centuries of accumulated craft knowledge that they must master. Between the ideal of the teacher-as-physician and the notion that anyone with a bachelor s degree, a high SAT verbal score, and a clean arrest record can teach lies a craft model of professionalism that upholds rigorous quality standards while honoring diverse approaches. A more philosophically informed self-understanding can help the profession flourish within this zone.

Between science and practice lie a number of judgments that are irreducibly values-based.

Recognizing the value judgments that both guide research and color the multiple legitimate inferences that we draw from it could generate several favorable outcomes for the education profession. First, such recognition would defuse a lot of the internecine bickering—the Reading Wars, Math Wars, Culture Wars—that make us look silly and faddish to outsiders. Second, it would facilitate the formation of communities of practice capable of developing coherent courses of study in settings where parents, students, and teachers share a common understanding of the enterprise—all qualities associated with teacher satisfaction, parent approval, and high student achievement. Third, the resulting system would require certain policies that educators have long championed—such as site-based autonomy, streamlined performance standards, and flexible approaches to state assessment—because multiple pathways depend on an accountability system supple enough to support all of them.

If we allow educators to organize schools around coherent philosophies, won't those educators be imposing adult values on students. We like to tell ourselves that schooling is about the kids, not the adults, and that the needs of the former must trump those of the latter. Hence we

naively strive for a pose of dispassionate diagnosis and treatment in our work and advocacy. But whether we like it or not, schooling is an extension of childrearing. We're not aiming to produce high test scores; we're striving to create good people. This aspiration is by definition normative.

Take the goal of helping students become autonomous, self-governing persons—the same goal that makes us uncomfortable "imposing" adult values on them. The importance we assign to personal autonomy itself reflects a philosophical point of view stemming from our liberal democratic worldview. In many cultures, past and present, qualities such as deference to elders and loyalty to tribe or nation have held higher priority. So the expectation that children grow up to be autonomous and critical is itself an imposition of values. We're fooling ourselves if we think we can meet our highest aspirations for students without seeking to shape them according to a normative ideal.

Isn't conflict educative? If we permit students to self-segregate on the basis of education philosophy—to attend schools where everyone else shares their values—won't we deprive students of exposure to differing points of view? This would be a serious drawback. But it overstates the case I've been arguing.

First, there's a practical limit to how far we can take this. If our goal were to form learning communities where everyone agreed on *all* normative questions, we would end up with universal homeschooling—and even that would work only until children were old enough to start questioning their parents' worldviews. But there's a more principled reply: The point here is *not* to create homogeneous communities of value, but rather to create homogeneity with respect to certain core beliefs concerning curriculum, instruction, norms of comportment, and civic virtue This arrangement leaves plenty of room for students to encounter diverse points of view on substantive matters. Every philosophy of education, every approach to every curriculum, generates disagreements and provides a shared framework for deliberations about them.

Diversity as Opportunity

I recognize how strange all this talk about philosophy and pluralism must sound. We have become so accustomed to thinking of our work as a service commodity, in which adult professionals provide student-clients with diagnoses and treatments, that we sometimes forget that schooling is always and inevitably about cultivating persons. Not that the standards movement is misguided, or that we don't need research to guide practice. Both common standards and research, along with certain broadly shared societal ideals, help us define good schooling and provide necessary limits to diversity. But these boundaries still admit a rich variety of approaches.

The move to small, distinctive schools of choice provides an opportunity to exploit that richness. Such schools will not make a difference if their goal is merely diversity for diversity's sake. Rather, we should treat the creation of these schools as a means to enhance the reflectiveness of educators, develop authoritative communities of practice, provide meaningful options for families, and improve academic, civic, and personal outcomes for young people.

Note

1. I dislike the terms "progressive" and "traditionalist" because they paper over a lot of diversity and disagreement that exist *within* the two philosophies. Of the seven schools mentioned in my introduction, three are traditional and four are progressive, but all are philosophically and pedagogically distinct—in many cases, profoundly.

References

Cuban, L. (2000). Why is it so hard to get "good" schools? In D. Shipps & L. Cuban (Eds.). *Reconstructing the common good in education* (pp. 148–172). Palo Alto CA: Stanford University Press.

Gardner, H. (2000). *The disciplined mind: Beyond facts and standardized tests, the K–12 education that every child deserves.* New York: Penguin Books.

David J. Ferrero, *a former high school teacher, is Director of Education Research and Evaluation at the Bill & Melinda Gates Foundation, 1551 Eastlake Ave., Seattle, WA 98115; 206-709-3454; david@gatesfoundation.org.*

The Employment of Ethical Decision-Making Frameworks in Educational Change

Abstract

In this article, the author provides a prefacing narrative that examines the work of Simpson et al. (2004, this issue), situating the reader as the importance of a framework for curriculum design. Importantly, the author illuminates a set a democratic values that animate the framework, and which work to instruct a democratic ethic of curriculum design.

Raymond A. Horn, Jr.,
Pennsylvania State University, Harrisburg

Introduction

In the original call for this themed issue of the *Scholar-Practitioner Quarterly*, two questions were raised that are addressed by the article, "Toward a Democratic Ethic of Curricular Decision-Making—A Guide for Educational Practitioners." What is the relationship of social justice and democracy? And, what is meant by "Taking a Stand" on social justice and democracy? In their proposal, Simpson et al. (2004) indirectly define democracy through the social justice concepts and processes that are inherent in their framework. In relation to both questions, those educational practitioners who would utilize this framework are participating in a process that not only promotes social justice but also defines democracy as a socially just enterprise. In essence, by their participation, they are taking an ethical stance on the design of curriculum, the development of their students as critically aware and participatory citizens, and on the promotion of a socially just and caring democratic society.

On one level, this framework proposes decision-making considerations that are included in most, if not all, curriculum design initiatives. However, one way in which it differs is in its explicit promotion of democratic values. Many individuals have argued that all curriculum is value-laden, and therefore, designed to reproduce a specific value system. When curriculum design is a locally controlled process, the result is a curriculum that closely aligns with the values of the local community. Likewise, standardized curriculum that is imposed by a governmental body, such as a state or nation, or curriculum that is promoted by a professional organization also is grounded in the values of the external agency or special interest group. In both local or centralized curriculum design and implementation, there is no guarantee that democratic principles guide this process, or are embedded within the process to facilitate the re-production of a democratic society. This raises the question of what is the purpose of public education?

Historically, education has been used to achieve many different purposes. For instance, many individuals ranging from Herbert Kliebard (1995) to Joel Spring (2001) have documented attempts by various interests to use public education as a means to promote various visions of American democracy, or to use public education to promote a specific political, cultural, economic, or social goal. Often, these values and their consequences are not extensively debated, or even critically recognized by the practitioners who implement this curriculum or by the stakeholders who are affected by the reform. On an instrumental level, practitioners do engage these curriculum initiatives with an evaluation of their impact on the: local educational context that relates to the aims of the local school and community, curriculum, instruction, assessment, and the students. However, the comprehensive and ethically grounded inquiry framework proposed by Simpson et al. (2004) transforms the evaluation process to a critically pragmatic level that is tightly focused on the promotion of a democratic society.

Their proposal is important for a number of reasons. First, large-scale curricular initiatives are often not subjected to a degree of public debate that facilitates a significant and critical awareness of the values that ground the initiative. For instance, only within the last year has significant public debate begun about the No Child Left Behind Act (NCLB). As the states move forward with their compliance programs, individuals are becoming increasingly critically aware of the effects of this reform. What motivates their participation in this debate is the conflict between the foundational values of specific aspects of NCLB and their own values as reflected in certain educational practices and outcomes. In addition, the concern of the public about the degree of national, state, and local control of education is an issue that has significant implications for the promotion of social justice and the definition of a democratic society. Prior to the passage of NCLB, the debate that occurred between government officials and other individuals interested in educational policy was couched in generalizations that were acceptable to a wide range of the citizenry. Much of the criticism of the specific and technical aspects of this reform approach and plan occurred within the scholarly community, and was mostly inaccessible to not only the general public but also to many educational practitioners. If a participatory democracy requires participation by the public in policy decisions, than frameworks such as Simpson et al.'s (2004) inherently require the participation of educational practitioners, and can be extended to include other educational stakeholders such as students, parents, and other community members. The importance of this type of framework lies in its requirement that the participants confront the competing perspectives and the foundational values of these perspectives in relation to all of the components of an educational system.

Secondly, the use of frameworks such as this ensures the inclusion of a critical component in the design of educational systems. Even though the design of curricular initiatives may involve a systemic design process to improve the chances of implementation, stakeholder participation is often limited, and both the local values and any externally imposed values are not critically interrogated. A systems design process can be used by a relatively select and small group of decision makers to increase the possibility of a successful implementation. In cases like this, the role of the other stakeholders is to often merely to implement reform without any participation in the design process. Another design process, idealized systems design (Banathy, 1991, 1996), requires stakeholder participation in all levels of the change process starting with the identification of the fundamental and hence guiding principles and values. In this sort of change process, values clarification unfolds with the construction of the vision and continues throughout the design process. The framework proposed by Simpson et al. (2004) is, on a smaller scale, conceptually aligned with the participatory and value awareness of an idealized systems design process.

Finally, decision making frameworks that are ethically oriented require educators, and whoever else that may participate, to engage educational change with an informed concern for the development of reflective, caring, and participatory democratic citizens. The motivation to engage the change process with informed concern is located within the enumerated points of this framework. To consider all of these points requires the participants to extend their knowledge and critically interrogate all of the values that arise from their comprehensive inquiry into the purpose and nature of the change situation. In other words, a comprehensive, informed, and disciplined inquiry of this kind is precisely the kind of process utilized by scholar-practitioners.

References

Banathy, B. H. (1991). *Systems design of education: A journey to create the future*. Englewood Cliffs, NJ: Educational Technology Publications.

Banathy, B. H. 1996. *A systems view of education: Concepts and principles for effective practice*. Englewood Cliffs, NJ: Educational Technology Publications.

Kliebard, H. M. (1995). *The struggle for the American curriculum: 1893–1958* (2nd Ed). New York: Routledge.

Simpson, D. J., Jackson, M. J. B., Bunuan, R. L., Chan, Y., Collins, B, R., King, E. L., & Mosley, L. K. (2004). Toward a democratic ethic of curricular decision-making: A guide for educational practitioners. *Scholar-Practitioner Quarterly, 2*(2), 79–.

Spring, J. (2001). *Deculturalization and the struggle for equality: A brief history of the education of dominated cultures in the United States (3rd ed.)*. New York: McGraw-Hill.

About the Author

Dr. Raymond A. Horn, Jr., is an Assistant Professor in the School of Behavioral Sciences and Education at Pennsylvania State University at Harrisburg. His research interests include post-formal thinking, educational change, educational leadership, and teacher education. He has published articles, books, and chapters. Dr. Horn's most recent book is Standards Primer, published in the Peter Lang Primer series.

THE MISSING VIRTUE

Lessons from dodge ball & Aristotle

Gordon Marino

Americans are inclined to ring the moral alarm and then hit the snooze button. After the latest moral crisis on Wall Street (I won't go into the sexual-abuse crisis), there were loud cries for more ethics classes. Not a bad idea, but if you are going to talk with students about ethics, which is something I do for a living, it helps to know where they are calling from. In the mid-sixties, Philip Rieff (*The Triumph of the Therapeutic*) apprized us of the fact that therapy had become the organizing motif in much of Western culture and, as a result, our understanding of moral character was shifting. Rieff was right. In the early eighties, the moral philosopher Alastair Macintyre (*After Virtue*) observed that for postmodern men and women, candor, rather than moral accountability, had become a cardinal virtue. Over the years, I have taken some soundings in my ethics classes and have been surprised to find that a cardinal virtue that everyone used to salute now evokes a shrug.

In *Nichomachean Ethics*, Aristotle invites us to think about the connection between moral character and happiness. He asks, Can you be happy and a cad? Definitely not. If that is the case, which moral virtues are essential to happiness? Before unveiling Aristotle's recipe, I press my students, "Which moral virtues do you believe are indispensable to the good life?" A hand shoots up; respect gets the first vote, then compassion, and this year, a sense of humor comes in the third. After a while, some of the more traditional virtues such as wisdom and justice are invited in. Honesty eventually makes it onto the blackboard without my prompts. Raising my voice and making a vee with my eyebrows, I nudge them, "Is there something missing?" Students look around puzzled, as if to say, OK, what's the trick?

"What about courage?" "Oh yeah, I guess so," is invariably the grudging response. Save for the two years that I taught at the Virginia Military Institute, I have never seen courage hit the top of the list. I hector my captive audience, "How can you be honest without courage? Truth telling, for example, only becomes difficult when there are unpleasant consequences for being honest." The

sermonette continues, "And if you can't bear the consequences, you will be unwilling to tell the truth."

I close with an object lesson. Suppose it is the end of the spring semester and you did not hand your paper in for your ethics class. The professor believes that, in the interest of fairness, all students ought to have the same amount of time to work on their term papers and so has promised to dish out an F to anyone who does not hand the essay in on time. The deadline is fast approaching. You planned to write your term paper when you were on break in Cancún, but you never got around to it. You are a junior, planning to apply to medical school in the fall. No paper, and you are sure to get a D in the course and torpedo your chances for admission. Still, there is hope. While the professor may be a martinet, he is also a trusting soul. You could easily get a few extra days if you told him you were suffering from mononucleosis or that your grandmother died. What will it be? Truth and consequences or a white, maybe gray, lie?

My students at Saint Olaf College are as morally earnest as any I have ever taught, but there can be no denying that the death rates of grandparents rise here at semester's end as much as they do at other campuses. Unless he is even more afraid of getting caught in a lie, the student who cannot control his fears will start working up a short story on deadline day. Again, trying to give a boost to the ancient virtue, I pace dramatically and repeat, "You can't be an honest coward." Usually delivered in midsemester, this is one of my better half-time speeches. Students seem to walk out of class thinking (if only for a few hours) that courage is essential to the life they aspire to, and I shuffle out speculating on how courage could ever have become an afterthought.

Courage was touted as a keystone virtue in the post–World War II era in which I grew up. It was then common to hear stories about boys who would not be allowed back into their homes until they faced down some bully. Television, movies, and popular literature emphasized the signal importance of grace under pressure. The president was famous for having penned a Pulitzer Prize–winner called *Profiles in Courage*. A quick study of the "self help" literature of the nineteenth century also hints that our ancestors thought of courage as the bedrock of moral character. Again, what prompted the demotion of courage?

Prior to the war in Vietnam, the values of the military were widely respected and well represented in the larger culture. The qualities that were imagined necessary for good soldiering were incorporated into our notions of an ideal moral life. But as many Americans came to see the military as misguided and worse, a pall was cast over traditionally martial virtues, such as honor and courage. At best, the teaching elite now thinks of the military as a necessary evil and the virtues associated with the guardian class have become déclassé. (It will be interesting see how the military's reputation fares after the second Gulf War.) As the subconscious reasoning goes, courage is good for people intent upon combat but useless for less primitive, more pacific people.

Aristotle, however, taught that we acquire virtuous dispositions by practicing the actions that we want to be disposed toward. In accord with Aristotle, our moralists today rightly recommend diversity workshops as a means to develop a tolerant disposition. Yet in most of our lives there is very little opportunity for getting practice in coping with physical fear. Indeed, last year after much dispute, dodge ball was bounced out of many public schools. Those who defended the game argued that it helped develope mettle. Those who argued against it noted that some students found big red balls being hurled at their skulls traumatic. Guess who won the debate? And yet, the ramifications of regarding courage as a moral elective are potentially catastrophic, not only for our ability to tell the truth, but for our foreign policy as well. A nation of people who cannot tolerate feeling afraid might be unduly inclined to send their subcontracted military into actions that will quiet the sources of their fears. Courage by proxy is no courage at all.

Gordon Marino *is a philosophy professor and the director of the Hong Kierkegaard Library at Saint Olaf College in Northfield, Minnesota.*

From *Commonweal*, April 25, 2003, pp. 12-13. © 2003 by Commonweal Foundation. Reprinted by permission.

UNIT 5
Managing Life in Classrooms

Unit Selections

Key Points to Consider

- Describe some of the myths associated with bullying behavior. How do you see the reality of bullying? What do you think school policy and teachers in particular can do to control bullying?

- Prepare your own roadmap of how you would create positive and productive approaches to the classroom instruction of middle-school-age children. Summarize your ideas about what features would lead to effective classroom management in a given school system.

Student Website

www.mhcls.com/online

Internet References

Further information regarding these websites may be found in this book's preface or online.

Classroom Connect
http://www.classroom.com

Global SchoolNet Foundation
http://www.gsn.org

Teacher Talk Forum
http://education.indiana.edu/cas/tt/tthmpg.html

All teachers have concerns regarding the "quality of life" in classroom settings. All teachers and students want to feel safe and accepted when they are in school. There exists today a reliable, effective knowledge base on classroom management and the prevention of disorder in schools. This knowledge base has been developed from hundreds of studies of teacher/student interaction and student/student interaction that have been conducted in schools in North America and Europe. We speak of managing life in classrooms because we now know that there are many factors that go into building effective teacher/student and student/student relationships. The traditional term *discipline* is too narrow and refers primarily to teachers' reactions to undesired student behavior. We can better understand methods of managing student behavior when we look at the totality of what goes on in classrooms, with teachers' responses to student behavior as a part of that totality. Teachers have tremendous responsibility for the emotional climate that is set in a classroom, whether students feel secure and safe and whether they want to learn to depend—to an enormous extent—on the psychological frame of mind of the teacher. Teachers must be able to manage their own selves first in order to effectively manage the development of a humane and caring classroom environment.

Teachers bear moral and ethical responsibilities for being witnesses to and examples of responsible social behavior in the classroom. There are many models of observing life in classrooms. Arranging the total physical environment of the room is a very important part of the teacher's planning for learning activities. Teachers need to expect from students the best work and behavior that they are capable of achieving. Respect and caring are attitudes that a teacher must communicate to receive them in return. Open lines of communication between teachers and students enhance the possibility for congenial, fair dialogical resolution of problems as they occur.

Developing a high level of task orientation among students and encouraging cooperative learning and shared task achievement will foster camaraderie and self-confidence among students. Shared decision making will build an *esprit de corps*, a sense of pride and confidence, which will feed on itself and blossom into high-quality performance. Good class morale, well managed, never hurts academic achievement. The importance of emphasizing quality, helping students to achieve levels of performance that they can feel proud of having attained, and encouraging positive dialogue among them leads them to take ownership in their individual educative efforts. When that happens, they literally empower themselves to do their best.

When teachers (and prospective teachers) discuss what concerns them about their roles (and prospective roles) in the classroom, the issue of discipline—how to manage student behavior—will usually rank near or at the top of their lists. A teacher needs a clear understanding of what kinds of learning environments are most appropriate for the subject matter and ages of the students. Any person who wants to teach must also want his or her students to learn well, to acquire basic values of respect for others, and to become more effective citizens.

There is considerable debate among educators regarding certain approaches used in schools to achieve a form of order in classrooms that also develops respect for self and others. The dialogue about this point is spirited and informative. The bottom line for any effective and humane approach to discipline in the classroom, the necessary starting point, is the teacher's emotional balance and capacity for self-control. This precondition creates a further one—that the teacher wants to be in the classroom with his or her students in the first place. Unmotivated teachers cannot motivate students.

Helping young people learn the skills of self-control and motivation to become productive, contributing, and knowledgeable adult participants in society is one of the most important tasks that good teachers undertake. These are teachable and learnable skills; they do not relate to heredity or social conditions. They can be learned by any human being who wants to learn them and who is cognitively able to learn them. There is a large knowledge base on how teachers can help students learn self-control. All that is required is the willingness of teachers to learn these skills themselves and to teach them to their students. There are many sound techniques that new teachers can use to achieve success in managing students' classroom behavior, and they should not be afraid to ask colleagues questions and to develop peer support groups with whom they can work with confidence and trust.

Teachers' core ethical principles come into play when deciding what constitutes defensible and desirable standards of student conduct. Teachers need to realize that before they can control behavior, they must identify what student behaviors are desired in their classrooms. They need to reflect, as well, on the emotional tone and ethical principles implied by their own behaviors. To optimize their chances of achieving the classroom atmosphere that they wish, teachers must strive for emotional balance within themselves; they must learn to be accurate observers; and they must develop just, fair strategies of intervention to aid students in learning self-control and good behavior. A teacher should be a good model of courtesy, respect, tact, and discretion. Children learn by observing how other persons behave and not just by being told how they are to behave. There is no substitute for positive, assertive teacher interaction with students in class.

This unit addresses many of the topics covered in basic foundations courses. The selections shed light on classroom management issues, teacher leadership skills, and the rights and responsibilities of teachers and students. In addition, the articles can be discussed in foundations courses involving curricula and instruction. This unit falls between the units on moral education and equal opportunity because it can be directly related to either or both of them.

The Key to Classroom Management

*By using research-based strategies combining appropriate levels of
dominance and cooperation and an awareness of student needs, teachers
can build positive classroom dynamics.*

Robert J. Marzano and Jana S. Marzano

Today, we know more about teaching than we ever have before. Research has shown us that teachers' actions in their classrooms have twice the impact on student achievement as do school policies regarding curriculum, assessment, staff collegiality, and community involvement (Marzano, 2003a). We also know that one of the classroom teacher's most important jobs is managing the classroom effectively.

A comprehensive literature review by Wang, Haertel, and Walberg (1993) amply demonstrates the importance of effective classroom management. These researchers analyzed 86 chapters from annual research reviews, 44 handbook chapters, 20 government and commissioned reports, and 11 journal articles to produce a list of 228 variables affecting student achievement. They combined the results of these analyses with the findings from 134 separate meta-analyses. Of all the variables, classroom management had the largest effect on student achievement. This makes intuitive sense—students cannot learn in a chaotic, poorly managed classroom.

Research not only supports the importance of classroom management, but it also sheds light on the dynamics of classroom management. Stage and Quiroz's meta-analysis (1997) shows the importance of there being a balance between teacher actions that provide clear consequences for unacceptable behavior and teacher actions that recognize and reward acceptable behavior. Other researchers (Emmer, Evertson, & Worsham, 2003; Evertson, Emmer, & Worsham, 2003) have identified important components of classroom management, including beginning the school year with a positive emphasis on management; arranging the room in a way conducive to effective management; and

identifying and implementing rules and operating procedures.

In a recent meta-analysis of more than 100 studies (Marzano, 2003b), we found that the quality of teacher-student relationships is the keystone for all other aspects of classroom management. In fact, our meta-analysis indicates that on average, teachers who had high-quality relationships with their students had 31 percent fewer discipline problems, rule violations, and related problems over a year's time than did teachers who did not have high-quality relationships with their students.

The quality of teacher-student
relationships is the keystone for all
other aspects of classroom
management.

What are the characteristics of effective teacher-student relationships? Let's first consider what they are not. Effective teacher-student relationships have nothing to do with the teacher's personality or even with whether the students view the teacher as a friend. Rather, the most effective teacher-student relationships are characterized by specific teacher behaviors: exhibiting appropriate levels of dominance; exhibiting appropriate levels of cooperation; and being aware of high-needs students.

Appropriate Levels of Dominance

Wubbels and his colleagues (Wubbels, Brekelmans, van Tartwijk, & Admiral,

1999; Wubbels & Levy, 1993) identify appropriate dominance as an important characteristic of effective teacher-student relationships. In contrast to the more negative connotation of the term *dominance* as forceful control or command over others, they define dominance as the teacher's ability to provide clear purpose and strong guidance regarding both academics and student behavior. Studies indicate that when asked about their preferences for teacher behavior, students typically express a desire for this type of teacher-student interaction. For example, in a study that involved interviews with more than 700 students in grades 4–7, students articulated a clear preference for strong teacher guidance and control rather than more permissive types of teacher behavior (Chiu & Tulley, 1997). Teachers can exhibit appropriate dominance by establishing clear behavior expectations and learning goals and by exhibiting assertive behavior.

Establish Clear Expectations and Consequences

Teachers can establish clear expectations for behavior in two ways: by establishing clear rules and procedures, and by providing consequences for student behavior.

The seminal research of the 1980s (Emmer, 1984; Emmer, Sanford, Evertson, Clements, & Martin, 1981; Evertson & Emmer, 1982) points to the importance of establishing rules and procedures for general classroom behavior, group work, seat work, transitions and interruptions, use of materials and equipment, and beginning and ending the period or the day. Ideally, the class should establish these rules and procedures through discussion and mutual consent by teacher and students (Glasser, 1969, 1990).

Along with well-designed and clearly communicated rules and procedures, the teacher must acknowledge students' behavior, reinforcing acceptable behavior and providing negative consequences for unacceptable behavior. Stage and Quiroz's research (1997) is instructive. They found that teachers build effective relationships through such strategies as the following:

- Using a wide variety of verbal and physical reactions to students' misbehavior, such as moving closer to offending students and using a physical cue, such as a finger to the lips, to point out inappropriate behavior.
- Cuing the class about expected behaviors through prearranged signals, such as raising a hand to indicate that all students should take their seats.
- Providing tangible recognition of appropriate behavior—with tokens or chits, for example.
- Employing group contingency policies that hold the entire group responsible for behavioral expectations.
- Employing home contingency techniques that involve rewards and sanctions at home.

Establish Clear Learning Goals

Teachers can also exhibit appropriate levels of dominance by providing clarity about the content and expectations of an upcoming instructional unit. Important teacher actions to achieve this end include

- Establishing and communicating learning goals at the beginning of a unit of instruction.
- Providing feedback on those goals.
- Continually and systematically revisiting the goals.
- Providing summative feedback regarding the goals.

The use of rubrics can help teachers establish clear goals. To illustrate, assume that a teacher has identified the learning goal "understanding and using fractions" as important for a given unit. That teacher might present students with the following rubric:

4 points. You understand the characteristics of fractions along with the different types. You can accurately describe how fractions are related to decimals and

percentages. You can convert fractions to decimals and can explain how and why the process works. You can use fractions to understand and solve different types of problems.

3 points. You understand the basic characteristics of fractions. You know how fractions are related to decimals and percentages. You can convert fractions to decimals.

2 points. You have a basic understanding of the following, but have some small misunderstandings about one or more: the characteristics of fractions; the relationships among fractions, decimals, and percentages; how to convert fractions to decimals.

1 point. You have some major problems or misunderstandings with one or more of the following: the characteristics of fractions; the relationships among fractions, decimals, and percentages; how to convert fractions to decimals.

0 points. You may have heard of the following before, but you do not understand what they mean: the characteristics of fractions; the relationships among fractions, decimals, and percentages; how to convert fractions to decimals.

The clarity of purpose provided by this rubric communicates to students that their teacher can provide proper guidance and direction in academic content.

Exhibit Assertive Behavior

Teachers can also communicate appropriate levels of dominance by exhibiting assertive behavior. According to Emmer and colleagues, assertive behavior is

the ability to stand up for one's legitimate rights in ways that make it less likely that others will ignore or circumvent them. (2003, p. 146)

Assertive behavior differs significantly from both passive behavior and aggressive behavior. These researchers explain that teachers display assertive behavior in the classroom when they

- Use assertive body language by maintaining an erect posture; facing the offending student but keeping enough distance so as not to appear threatening and matching the facial expression with the content of the message being presented to students.
- Use an appropriate tone of voice, speaking clearly and deliberately in a

pitch that is slightly but not greatly elevated from normal classroom speech, avoiding any display of emotions in the voice.

- Persist until students respond with the appropriate behavior. Do not ignore an inappropriate behavior; do not be diverted by a student denying, arguing, or blaming, but listen to legitimate explanations.

Appropriate Levels of Cooperation

Cooperation is characterized by a concern for the needs and opinions of others. Although not the antithesis of dominance, cooperation certainly occupies a different realm. Whereas dominance focuses on the teacher as the driving force in the classroom, cooperation focuses on the students and teacher functioning as a team. The interaction of these two dynamics—dominance and cooperation—is a central force in effective teacher-student relationships. Several strategies can foster appropriate levels of cooperation.

Provide Flexible Learning Goals

Just as teachers can communicate appropriate levels of dominance by providing clear learning goals, they can also convey appropriate levels of cooperation by providing flexible learning goals. Giving students the opportunity to set their own objectives at the beginning of a unit or asking students what they would like to learn conveys a sense of cooperation. Assume, for example, that a teacher has identified the topic of fractions as the focus of a unit of instruction and has provided students with a rubric. The teacher could then ask students to identify some aspect of fractions or a related topic that they would particularly like to study. Giving students this kind of choice, in addition to increasing their understanding of the topic, conveys the message that the teacher cares about and tries to accommodate students' interests.

Teachers with effective classroom management skills are aware of high-needs students and have a repertoire of specific techniques for meeting some of their needs.

Take a Personal Interest in Students

Probably the most obvious way to communicate appropriate levels of cooperation is to take a personal interest in each student in the class. As McCombs and Whisler (1997) note, all students appreciate personal attention from the teacher. Although busy teachers—particularly those at the secondary level—do not have the time for extensive interaction with all students, some teacher actions can communicate personal interest and concern without taking up much time. Teachers can

- Talk informally with students before, during, and after class about their interests.
- Greet students outside of school—for instance, at extracurricular events or at the store.
- Single out a few students each day in the lunchroom and talk with them.
- Be aware of and comment on important events in students' lives, such as participation in sports, drama, or other extracurricular activities.
- Compliment students on important achievements in and outside of school.
- Meet students at the door as they come into class; greet each one by name.

Use Equitable and Positive Classroom Behaviors

Programs like Teacher Expectations and Student Achievement emphasize the importance of the subtle ways in which teachers can communicate their interest in students (Kerman, Kimball, & Martin, 1980). This program recommends many practical strategies that emphasize equitable and positive classroom interactions with all students. Teachers should, for example,

- Make eye contact with each student. Teachers can make eye contact by scanning the entire room as they speak and by freely moving about all sections of the room.
- Deliberately move toward and stand close to each student during the class period. Make sure that the seating arrangement allows the teacher and students clear and easy ways to move around the room.
- Attribute the ownership of ideas to the students who initiated them. For instance, in a discussion a teacher might say, "Cecilia just added to Aida's idea by saying that...."

- Allow and encourage all students to participate in class discussions and interactions. Make sure to call on students who do not commonly participate, not just those who respond most frequently.
- Provide appropriate wait time for all students to respond to questions, regardless of their past performance or your perception of their abilities.

Awareness of High-Needs Students

Classroom teachers meet daily with a broad cross-section of students. In general, 12–22 percent of all students in school suffer from mental, emotional, or behavioral disorders, and relatively few receive mental health services (Adelman & Taylor, 2002). The Association of School Counselors notes that 18 percent of students have special needs and require extraordinary interventions and treatments that go beyond the typical resources available to the classroom (Dunn & Baker, 2002).

Although the classroom teacher is certainly not in a position to directly address such severe problems, teachers with effective classroom management skills are aware of high-needs students and have a repertoire of specific techniques for meeting some of their needs (Marzano, 2003b). Figure 1 summarizes five categories of high-needs students and suggests classroom strategies for each category and subcategory.

- *Passive* students fall into two subcategories: those who fear *relationships* and those who fear *failure*. Teachers can build strong relationships with these students by refraining from criticism, rewarding small successes, and creating a classroom climate in which students feel safe from aggressive people.
- The category of *aggressive* students comprises three subcategories: *hostile, oppositional,* and *covert*. Hostile students often have poor anger control, low capacity for empathy, and an inability to see the consequences of their actions. Oppositional students exhibit milder forms of behavior problems, but they consistently resist following rules, argue with adults, use harsh language, and tend to annoy others. Students in the covert sub-category may be quite pleasant at times,

but they are often nearby when trouble starts and they never quite do what authority figures ask of them. Strategies for helping aggressive students include creating behavior contracts and providing immediate rewards and consequences. Most of all, teachers must keep in mind that aggressive students, although they may appear highly resistant to behavior change, are still children who are experiencing a significant amount of fear and pain.

- Students with *attention* problems fall into two categories: *hyperactive* and *inattentive*. These students may respond well when teachers contract with them to manage behaviors; teach them basic concentration, study, and thinking skills; help them divide tasks into manageable parts; reward their successes; and assign them a peer tutor.
- Students in the *perfectionist* category are driven to succeed at unattainable levels. They are self-critical, have low self-esteem, and feel inferior. Teachers can often help these students by encouraging them to develop more realistic standards, helping them to accept mistakes, and giving them opportunities to tutor other students.
- *Socially inept* students have difficulty making and keeping friends. They may stand too close and touch others in annoying ways, talk too much, and misread others' comments. Teachers can help these students by counseling them about social behaviors.

The most effective classroom managers did not treat all students the same; they tended to employ different strategies with different types of students.

School may be the only place where many students who face extreme challenges can get their needs addressed. The reality of today's schools often demands that classroom teachers address these severe issues, even though this task is not always considered a part of their regular job.

In a study of classroom strategies (see Brophy, 1996; Brophy & McCaslin, 1992), researchers examined how effective classroom teachers interacted with specific types of students. The study found that the most effective classroom managers did not

FIGURE 1 Categories of High-Needs Students

Category	Definitions & Source	Characteristics	Suggestions
Passive	Behavior that avoids the domination of others or the pain of negative experiences. The child attempts to protect self from criticism, ridicule, or rejection, possibly reacting to abuse and neglect. Can have a biochemical basis, such as anxiety.	**Fear of relationships:** Avoids connection with others, is shy, doesn't initiate conversations, attempts to be invisible. **Fear of failure:** Gives up easily, is convinced he or she can't succeed, is easily frustrated, uses negative self-talk.	Provide safe adult and peer interactions and protections from aggressive people. Provide assertiveness and positive self-talk training. Reward small successes quickly. Withhold criticism.
Aggressive	Behavior that overpowers, dominates, harms, or controls others without regard for their well-being. The child has often taken aggressive people as role models. Has had minimal or ineffective limits set on behavior. Is possibly reacting to abuse and neglect. Condition may have a biochemical basis, such as depression.	**Hostile:** Rages, threatens, or intimidates others. Can be verbally or physically abusive to people, animals, or objects. **Oppositional:** Does opposite of what is asked. Demands that others agree or give in. Resists verbally or nonverbally. **Covert:** Appears to agree but then does the opposite of what is asked. Often acts innocent while setting up problems for others.	Describe the student's behavior clearly. Contract with the student to reward corrected behavior and set up consequences for uncorrected behavior. Be consistent and provide immediate rewards and consequences. Encourage and acknowledge extracurricular activities in and out of school. Give student responsibilities to help teacher or other students to foster successful experiences.
Attention problems	Behavior that demonstrates either motor or attentional difficulties resulting from a neurological disorder. The child's symptoms may be exacerbated by family or social stressors or biochemical conditions, such as anxiety, depression, or bipolar disorders.	**Hyperactive:** Has difficulty with motor control, both physically and verbally. Fidgets, leaves seat frequently, interrupts, talks excessively. **Inattentive:** Has difficulty staying focused and following through on projects. Has difficulty with listening, remembering, and organizing.	Contract with the student to manage behaviors. Teach basic concentration, study, and thinking skills. Separate student in a quiet work area. Help the student list each step of a task. Reward successes; assign a peer tutor.
Perfectionist	Behavior that is geared toward avoiding the embarrassment and assumed shame of making mistakes. The child fears what will happen if errors are discovered. Has unrealistically high expectations of self. Has possibly received criticism or lack of acceptance while making mistakes during the process of learning.	Tends to focus too much on the small details of projects. Will avoid projects if unsure of outcome. Focuses on results and not relationships. Is self-critical.	Ask the student to make mistakes on purpose, then show acceptance. Have the student tutor other students.
Socially inept	Behavior that is based on the misinterpretation of nonverbal signals of others. The child misunderstands facial expressions and body language. Hasn't received adequate training in these areas and has poor role modeling.	Attempts to make friends but is inept and unsuccessful. Is forced to be alone. Is often teased for unusual behavior, appearance, or lack of social skills.	Teach the student to keep the appropriate physical distance from others. Teach the meaning of facial expressions, such as anger and hurt. Make suggestions regarding hygiene, dress, mannerisms, and posture.

Source: Marzano, R. J. (2003). *What works in schools: Translating research into action* (pp. 104–105). Alexandria, VA: ASCD.

treat all students the same; they tended to employ different strategies with different types of students. In contrast, ineffective classroom managers did not appear sensitive to the diverse needs of students. Although Brophy did not couch his findings in terms of teacher-student relationships, the link is clear. An awareness of the five general categories of high-needs students and appropriate actions for each can help teachers build strong relationships with diverse students.

Don't Leave Relationships to Chance

Teacher-student relationships provide an essential foundation for effective classroom management—and classroom management is a key to high student achievement. Teacher-student relationships should not be left to chance or dictated by the personalities of those involved. Instead, by using strategies supported by research, teachers can influence the dynamics of their classrooms and build strong teacher-student relationships that will support student learning.

References

Adelman, H. S., & Taylor, L. (2002). School counselors and school reform: New directions. *Professional School Counseling, 5*(4), 235–248.

Brophy, J. E. (1996). *Teaching problem students.* New York: Guilford.

Brophy, J. E., & McCaslin, N. (1992). Teachers' reports of how they perceive and cope with problem students. *Elementary School Journal, 93,* 3–68.

Chiu, L. H., & Tulley, M. (1997). Student preferences of teacher discipline styles.

Journal of Instructional Psychology, 24(3), 168–175.

Dunn, N. A., & Baker, S. B. (2002). Readiness to serve students with disabilities: A survey of elementary school counselors. *Professional School Counselors, 5*(4), 277–284.

Emmer, E. T. (1984). *Classroom management: Research and implications.* (R & D Report No. 6178). Austin, TX: Research and Development Center for Teacher Education, University of Texas. (ERIC Document Reproduction Service No. ED251448)

Emmer, E. T., Evertson, C. M., & Worsham, M. E. (2003). *Classroom management for secondary teachers* (6th ed.). Boston: Allyn and Bacon.

Emmer, E. T., Sanford, J. P., Evertson, C. M., Clements, B. S., & Martin, J. (1981). *The classroom management improvement study: An experiment in elementary school classrooms.* (R & D Report No. 6050). Austin, TX: Research and Development Center for Teacher Education, University of Texas. (ERIC Document Reproduction Service No. ED226452)

Evertson, C. M., & Emmer, E. T. (1982). Preventive classroom management. In D. Duke (Ed.), *Helping teachers manage classrooms* (pp. 2–31). Alexandria, VA: ASCD.

Evertson, C. M., Emmer, E. T., & Worsham, M. E. (2003). *Classroom management for elementary teachers* (6th ed.). Boston: Allyn and Bacon.

Glasser, W. (1969). *Schools without failure.* New York: Harper and Row.

Glasser, W. (1990). *The quality school: Managing students without coercion.* New York: Harper and Row.

Kerman, S., Kimball, T., & Martin, M. (1980). *Teacher expectations and student achievement.* Bloomington, IN: Phi Delta Kappan.

Marzano, R. J. (2003a). *What works in schools.* Alexandria, VA: ASCD.

Marzano, R. J. (with Marzano, J. S., & Pickering, D. J.). (2003b). *Classroom management that works.* Alexandria, VA: ASCD.

McCombs, B. L., & Whisler, J. S. (1997). *The learner-centered classroom and school.* San Francisco: Jossey-Bass.

Stage, S. A., & Quiroz, D. R. (1997). A meta-analysis of interventions to decrease disruptive classroom behavior in public education settings. *School Psychology Review, 26*(3), 333–368.

Wang, M. C., Haertel, G. D., & Walberg, H. J. (1993). Toward a knowledge base for school learning. *Review of Educational Research, 63*(3), 249–294.

Wubbels, T., Brekelmans, M., van Tartwijk, J., & Admiral, W. (1999). Interpersonal relationships between teachers and students in the classroom. In H. C. Waxman & H. J. Walberg (Eds.), *New directions for teaching practice and research* (pp. 151–170). Berkeley, CA: McCutchan.

Wubbels, T., & Levy, J. (1993). *Do you know what you look like? Interpersonal relationships in education.* London: Falmer Press.

Robert J. Marzano is a senior scholar at Mid-continent Research for Education and Learning in Aurora, Colorado, and an associate professor at Cardinal Stritch University in Milwaukee, Wisconsin; (303) 796–7683; robertjmarzano@aol.com. His newest book written with Jana S. Marzano and Debra J. Pickering is *Classroom Management That Works* (ASCD, 2003). **Jana S. Marzano** is a licensed professional counselor in private practice in Centennial, Colorado; (303) 220–1151; janamarzan@aol.com.

Reach Them to Teach Them

Four high school teachers show that teaching adolescents is about relevance and challenge, affection and respect.

Carol Ann Tomlinson and Kristina Doubet

Two observations from teachers of adolescents are so prevalent these days that they sound like theme music. The more recurrent refrain says that there's no time for covering anything in high school classes other than curriculum or standards: There's no time for discussion, for student interests, for products beyond mandatory quizzes and tests, or for activities. Teachers are under relentless pressure to prepare students for high-stakes tests and for advanced placement or International Baccalaureate exams. The amount of material to cover simply exceeds the time available for covering it.

The second refrain has to do with the impracticality—if not impossibility—of really knowing one's students in a high school setting. There are too many of them, and they are indifferent—or ill-behaved. Combined with the avalanche of pressure for high test scores, these factors make it unfeasible for teachers to know their students more than superficially.

Snapshots of four high school classrooms challenge these two pervasive beliefs. We profile four teachers who connect with their students and who persevere in making learning a process that engages the minds and imaginations of the adolescents they teach. These teachers' professional work centers on knowing their students well enough to make learning interesting and on knowing their content well enough to shape it to their students' needs. These snapshots serve as an antidote to the very real pressures that can make us forget what lies at the core of transformational high school classrooms.

Katie Carson's Classroom:

A Labor of Love

Katie Carson, a fifth-year teacher at Fauquier High School in Warrenton, Virginia, teaches English to 9th and 11th graders. She is a young teacher who spends some of her free time acting in and directing a comedy improvisation troupe in Washington, D.C. But teaching is her labor of love.

With the exception of a few overachievers in each class, says Carson, kids in high school "have zero desire to learn more about grammar, literature, and punctuation." The magic of early experiences with reading and writing is gone. So unless I create a class in which they discover one another's gifts and challenge one another, or unless they have a relationship with me," she adds, "students have no desire to learn those things."

Getting to Know One Another

Carson creates an environment in which students learn about one another and get to know their peers' strengths. She places students in groups in which they'll work for a quarter of the year. Once a week, on a randomly selected day, she gives the groups five-minute challenges, such as building the tallest tower in the class out of bits of paper and paper clips. You can hear students saying among themselves, "We need Steven for this job. He's the man!" This kind of focus is particularly important for students who are not initially seen as academic contributors.

The room is set up to welcome students who can sit in armchairs, on a couch, or at tables. Carson also studies learning preferences and gives students opportunities to learn in ways that meet their various needs. "It's part of showing respect," she says.

Attendance-taking begins with an "attendance question" as soon as the bell rings. As Carson calls their names, students respond to the day's question, providing a brief justification for their responses.

"OK, people, this is a big one today. Definitive answer. Coke or Pepsi?" On another day, she begins, "OK, folks, you've just been given a sampler box of Russell Stover candy, but the map is missing. You bite into a piece and much to your dismay, find you've chosen a_____." Students answer by filling in the blank. Before long, students bring her slips of paper, whispering, "Here's an attendance question. It's really good!"

Sharing Stories

Carson encourages students to tell their own stories. "I'll even delay a test for a few minutes for a good story," she says, "but it has to be a good one." On the first day of class, she puts on the board a story arc, which contains seven numbered lines:

1. Once upon a time …
2. And every day …
3. Until one day …
4. And then …
5. And then …
6. Until finally …
7. And ever since …

This is her way of teaching students about exposition, rising action, conflict, climax, and denouement. Teacher and students use the academic words in their conversations about stories, but the story arc serves as a barometer for assessing the stories that they share with one another. "You all have experiences that make good stories," she reminds the students. "But it's all in how you tell them."

Mastering the Content

Carson embeds the required content standards in her instruction, but the students feel that she's teaching them, not just "covering material." In a recent Utopia project, nearly all her juniors said that they would do away with state standards if they could. "What's the point?" they asked, and they lamented the number of times their teachers say, "Now you'll need to remember this because it's on the standards test."

Carson reminded those juniors that this was, in fact, a standards test year and that in three weeks, they would be taking the standards test in her class. "Yeah, but you don't bring it up all the time," they responded. "You prepare us without teaching to the test."

This is evident in a unit on 19th century American poetry. As the students compare various poems with artwork and photographs, Carson presents a quotation from a British author indicating that Americans have no literature. The students argue heatedly against the author's sentiment, using works that they have read as evidence to the contrary, and they ask whether they'll be able to "critique more artwork" after lunch.

Making Writing Relevant

When her class discusses a golden age of literature, Carson asks students to describe golden ages in their own lives and uses their descriptors as a segue into a serious discussion of literature. She notes,

> My job is to make sure the kids know that I care, that I appreciate their sharing the truth about their lives, and that I value their opinions. When we have that personal trust, it's not so horrifying for them to write and turn that writing in to me.

Too often, she says, writing in high school is an exercise of turning in a paper to get it back covered with red marks. We forget, she suggests, how important it is for students to know that they have stories to tell and that those stories are full of discoveries about human nature.

Ned, for example, was a low-achieving student who did not—would not—write. Then he made the junior varsity football team. Carson told him that she was impressed because she'd never understood football. "Gosh," he said, "you must be

dumb." For the rest of the year, he wrote about football in his journal, and she wrote back about football. In passing, she would mention in class that she had watched part of a game on TV or at school. "I understood why the flag was thrown. Thanks so much, Ned!" His stories had helped someone—and he was proud. ●

George Murphy's Classroom:

It's All About Inquiry

As Students enter George Murphy's 10th grade biology class, he chats with them individually about their reading and experiments. Murphy is science department chair at Fauquier High School in Warrenton, Virginia, and has taught for 24 years. When class begins, he proclaims, "Welcome to your favorite class of the day!" Students grin as he launches into the daily agenda posted on the board. There's a sense of urgency and excitement about the class: Important work is waiting, and there's no time to waste.

Demonstrating Understanding

The current science unit centers on energy and respiration. Murphy has embedded the key understandings in an exploration of diet and energy. He begins the unit with an Interactive demonstration that introduces the key concepts of energy, action, and reaction. Students observe a new piece of equipment—an empty fermentation apparatus—and they hypothesize about its possible use. Their ideas initiate a demonstration of a basic working fermentation setup. Once students are clear about what is required for fermentation, they launch into an inquiry process to determine what caused the reaction they witnessed in the demonstration. Murphy carefully guides the process to be sure that students "get it" before they design their own experiments, in which they will pose and test a hypothesis about the nature of energy. Murphy's students demonstrate their understandings about energy both by completing a lab report and by creating a product that they choose from a list of teacher-provided and student-designed options.

Students select one of three tasks to continue learning about energy: Some students finish their experiments; some work with a study guide on the topic; and others work on laptops to complete a diet planner, an exercise that helps them analyze energy consumed and energy expended in their own lives.

There is no class textbook. Instead, Murphy guides students in finding authentic and reputable information sources, in print or on the Web.

> **Very real pressures can make us forget what lies at the core of transformational high school classrooms.**

Making It Relevant

Inquiry is at the root of Murphy's instruction. "I think everything in biology should be relevant to what students experience in their own lives," he says. "It's the study of life, so a student should be able to connect biology with everything we do."

He tells his students that if they can't see how a given topic connects to their lives, they probably shouldn't be studying it—either because it's not biology or because he hasn't clearly communicated the essence of the topic. He realizes that he must sometimes reteach material in new ways to help students find that connection. "We can talk about the ATP cycle, photosynthesis, and respiration, but that doesn't grab kids," Murphy says. What *does* rouse their curiosity is analyzing the foods they're eating and burning and figuring out the caloric content.

Murphy teaches his students on a half-year block schedule. That constricts the time he has to get to know them, so he makes his curriculum and instruction compelling from the start.

He explains,

> It's not the standards that will make school relevant and vital for students. I want to get them interested in what they're doing. I'm not up front to dance for them. I want to present the students with a challenge, see them rise to the challenge, see them *want* to learn. I want to dare them to have a good time with science.

Probing Student Thinking

Murphy moves among the students as they work with absorption on their tasks. Two girls who are using computers and the Body Mass Index (BMI) instrument to work on their diet profiles commiserate with him about their results, declaring that switching from whole to low-fat milk is doable but that giving up cookies in exchange for fruit is asking too much. A sturdy football player tells Murphy, "That's two pieces of bad news today. I have to lower my carbs—and I love carbs. I also have to lower my fat, and that stinks." Another boy is searching on the Internet for a formula that he believes could call into question the figure generated by the BMI device. Two girls discuss the feasibility of "fooling" the instrument by combining their weights.

Two boys in the design phase of their experiment explain their hypothesis and how they arrived at it and then return to a discussion about what amount of glucose and water will work best in their experiment. A boy working with the study guide talks with Murphy about his topic, his research, and the Internet itself.

That Murphy engages both the interest and trust of his students is evident in the purposefulness of the classroom, in the respectful exchanges between Murphy and his students, and in the spirit of cooperation among the students themselves. As the students learn about biology, they discover its capacity to reveal life and to help them develop as thinkers. His instruction has nothing to do with coverage—it's about inquiry and community. •

Chad Prather's Classroom:

Making Connections

Chad Prather is a second-year teacher who teaches 9th graders world geography and world history at Charlottesville High School in Charlottesville, Virginia. Most of his world geography students read well below grade level, and they have little motivation to learn. Says Prather,

> These students haven't been celebrated throughout their education. They've gotten used to tracking and very used to worksheets. When teachers give them something challenging, the students rebel because they're so used to worksheets that [the new assignment] just seems too hard.

Prather finds this situation tragic and is determined to show the students their untapped potential.

He's discovered that success lies in making two kinds of connections: connecting students with important ideas and establishing his own connection with students as individuals.

Connecting With Ideas

Prather organizes curriculum around key concepts rather than memorization of facts. Too much of what goes on in school, he believes, is focused on knowledge rather than on understanding. Knowledge, he says, may get students to answer "who" and "what" questions on a state test, but it falls short of helping them answer the more meaningful "how" and "why" questions. He adds,

> Teachers have given these kids worksheets over the years in the hope that the worksheets would pound knowledge into their heads, that repetition would create memory. It doesn't. No one expects these students to understand. I tell them that I won't give them what they're used to. They need to step up to the challenge of understanding. Then the knowledge will take care of itself.

Prather's students work with units that raise important ideas in geography. The unit on space and interaction, for example, probes how humans adapt to and alter the environments in which they live. He explains,

> When I prepare a lesson, I try to imagine myself as one of my students, and I ask myself—as though I were that student—Is this an engaging use of my time? Then I ask myself—as the teacher now—Is this an effective way of demonstrating meaning?

Connecting With Students

Prather says that connecting with his students is even more important than his sustained work to connect his students with the curriculum. "I had the idea early on." he says, that if I were assertive and hard-core with the rules, then the students would work hard for me." That's not proven to be the case. What *does* work is connecting with students. Not only does it more successfully get them to work, but it also encourages them to accept living within the classroom rules. "The curriculum that I write has to come from a place that the kids are comfortable with," says Prather. "And that obviously starts with the teacher-student relationship."

The world geography class begins with a review that prepares students for a brief Jeopardy-like game. "I don't hear all of you reviewing," prompts Prather, "and that gives me great displeasure. My heart is breaking as though it were the Earth's crust during plate tectonics." Students grin and begin reviewing individually, in pairs, or in small groups. In the 10-minute Jeopardy game that follows, excitement builds to a pinnacle when an unlikely student selects and correctly answers a 1,000-point question. The class erupts in whoops of joy and praise.

Prather quickly transitions to a slide presentation designed to give his students images of the Earth's power. He understands that the process of a hurricane forming over an ocean means little to his students because most have never seen the ocean. He gives them cues about what matters most for them to understand, and he emphasizes the relationships, causes, and effects among the ideas depicted in the images.

Students move next to their "Thug Nasty Big Eartha" projects. For the unit's final product, students are asked to assume the role of lead producer of a new CD and select a project from a number of options that demonstrate that the Earth is a "thug nasty" place. Some students choose in write the lyrics for the hit single. "Big Eartha's House"; others may choose to design the CD cover. All product options focus on the Earth's power. "It's hard-core," says Prather, "It doesn't back down."

Students look at ways in which the Earth exerts its supremacy, especially in terms of extreme weather and climatic forces. Students use teacher-provided grids to take notes on "molten hot performers," such as Twisted Sister (tornado), Dry Bones (drought), and Grand Rapid (flood). Each product choice has a checklist for success, and all choices focus on the important information and ideas from the unit. Product options address varied student interests and learning modes.

In class, students work on their products as their teacher walks among them, coaching them. Because many of Prather's students have difficulty completing schoolwork at home, he said some colleagues provide a place in school in the afternoons for the many students who need time, space, and support for their work.

Prather knows he has much to learn about his students and about how best to connect them with ideas that they thought were out of their reach, but his students send him signals that he's working in the right direction: They talk with him about issues related to race and school, write him thank-you notes, and come by his classroom to share their successes. •

From *Educational Leadership,* April 2005, pp. 8-13. Reprinted by permission of the Association for Supervision and Curriculum Development. Copyright © 2005 by ASCD. All rights reserved. The Association for Supervision and Curriculum Development is a worldwide community of educators advocating sound policies and sharing best practices to achieve the success of each learner. To learn more, visit ASCD at www.ascd.org

Dealing with Rumors, Secrets, and Lies: Tools of Aggression for Middle School Girls

Betsy Lane

Getting Started

My own middle school years remain vivid in my memory. I was excluded, and I manipulated the exclusion of others. I could be mean, yet, in turn, I was deeply hurt by others. If my friends and I did speak to an adult about these problems, we heard such clichés as: "There are plenty of other girls who would love to be your friends" or "Can't you just try to be nice to each other" or my all time favorite, "Sticks and stones may break my bones, but words can never hurt me." Words break your heart and scar you for life instead.

The difference now, in addition to e-mail and instant messenger, is that young girls are more apt to seek an adult to help them problem solve, and I must confess before going any further that, as an assistant principal of a middle school, I hate to see them coming!

In complete frustration as a fledgling administrator, I assigned a group of sixth grade girls an office detention when I could not determine who was mad at whom, or why, or how it started, or why they could not just end it, and neither could they. My decision to assign detention, made in desperation, unsettled these girls, and certainly stopped them from coming to see me. Moreover, I have no doubt that the unrest and mean comments flourished insidiously.

A particular difficulty with girls' stories is that they can be long and involved, impossible to decipher, and excruciatingly boring. Minute details are provided with sincere emotion and expression while my mind swirls and screams, "Enough already!" However, it is important to remain focused on the primary goal: to get the girls talking and to develop a level of trust. In all likelihood, they only want someone to listen. Listening and reflecting provides an opportunity to help them figure out strategies for their problem (Wiseman, 2002).

Learning More

I decided it was my professional responsibility to learn more about the development of girls and constructive ways in which to help them work through these seemingly endless and painful struggles. My search for understanding or, more truthfully, for strategies to cope with the turbulence of young adolescent relationships, was the catalyst for this article. I weave together the following four themes: why and how girls bully, the applications and results of alternative aggressions, the phenomenon of popularity and cliques, and how adults might offer guidance and support.

Bullying in school, a form of social aggression, has recently become a hot topic nationally and has been referred to by some as an epidemic. The real surprise is not that bullying occurs in our schools, but that our bullies are not only boys. As early as fifth grade, girls can be extremely cruel, mean spirited and aggressive as they begin to form social hierarchies. According to Wiseman (2002), 99.99% of girls gossip and they will almost always blame their behavior on something or someone else. When a girl is accused of spreading a rumor, her initial response is to ask indignantly who told on her, as if that person is actually to blame.

The consensus that girls are less aggressive than boys began to change after Kaj Bjorkqvist, a Finnish professor, shared information from interviews with young adolescent girls. Bjorkqvist exposed the fact that girls are just as aggressive as boys, though the aggression manifests itself differently. Talbot (2002, February 24):

They are not as likely to engage in physical fights, for example, but their superior social intelligence enabled them to wage complicated battles with other girls aimed at damaging relationships or reputations ... leaving nasty messages by cell phone or spreading scurrilous rumors by e-mail, making friends with one girl as revenge against another, gossiping about someone just loudly enough to be overheard. Turning the notion of women's greater empathy on its head, Bjorkqvist focused on the destructive uses to which such emotional attunement could be put. "Girls can better understand how other girls feel," as he puts it; "so they better know how to harm them." (p. 4–5)

The anecdotes and information from each author are equally compelling. Simmons (2002) postulated that the roots of girls' bullying, which is not new, can be traced to society's expectations of females. Girls internalize a powerful and damaging message, reinforced while growing up, that they must be *good* above all else. It is difficult at best, not to mention tiresome, to be constantly *good*.

> Girls strive to be perfect, thinking that this is what adults want. The only way to preserve this image is to constantly judge others thus creating anxiety that divides and separates girls. The intensity with which girls gossip is connected to their own shame of not measuring up to a false, but pervasive, ideal of the perfect girl. (Nagel, 2002; p. 3–4)

Giannetti and Sagarese (2001) observed that young adolescent girls pour their hearts and souls into their relationships. Unfortunately, relationships erupt weekly, daily, even hourly in middle school and the psychological ramifications can be extremely harsh. Day to day, recess to recess, class period to class period, teachers hear the cruel comments and note the fearful expressions, as social status waxes and wanes. Simmons' (2002) research supports this:

> In friendship, girls share secrets to grow closer. Relational competitions corrupt this process, transforming secrets into social currency and, later, ammunition. These girls spread gossip: they tell other people's secrets. They spread rumors: they invent other people's secrets. They gain access to each other using intimate information. (p. 172)

It does not take long for girls to find power and satisfaction in such tactics as backstabbing, gossiping, belittling, and rumor spreading. The modern media of e-mail and instant messaging adds to the excitement and the fury of it all. The position of these girls as they reign over their cliques is temporarily tightened and secured by these tactics.

Middle level students' primary concerns are focused on their peers and what others think of them. It is a time of tremendous insecurity for both boys and girls, and most of them experience some kind of rejection or exclusion exactly when being included is of utmost importance. In particular, the deterioration of female relationships begins in middle school and tends to escalate as the girls mature. Friendship and belonging are key elements of adolescence, yet as Simmons (2002) reported, instead of being nurtured, they are abused and rejected:

> Girls' fierce attachment to their friends illustrates the powerful influence relationships exert over their lives. As they grow more socially sophisticated, the love between girls takes them into a new, enchanting territory. But for girls on the popularity treadmill, friendship is rarely just friendship: it's a ticket, a tool, an opportunity—or a deadweight. You can own anything Abercrombie ever made, but if you don't have the right friends, you're nobody. (p. 158–159)

Girls are passionate about their friends and share secrets as a means of bonding and securing the relationship. However, the relentless quest to be popular can destroy even the closest friendship. The powerful need to be included can outweigh any sense of loyalty or confidentiality.

Cliques are the unfortunate result of judgments made by the very few. Who is pretty enough, smart enough, athletic enough, or nice enough to belong to a particular group? As young adolescents divide themselves into groups, cliques are formed. Giannetti and Sagarese (2001) wrote:

> The term "clique" is used loosely to define a particular group of friends, but more often to define a group that revolves around more than camaraderie. Cliques deal in social power. Formed around a leader or two, the pack lets it be known that *not* everyone is welcome. Certain children are dubbed "worthy" while others are judged *not good enough*. "Excluding becomes a primary activity. The mentality is like a junior country club. The guest list to this invitation-only party is always changing."

Cliques are divisive and destructive to relationships as girls quickly abandon loyalty to close friends to be included in a group, if only briefly. The authority and power given temporarily to these *popular* girls gives them tremendous clout to include and exclude.

Unexpected exclusion or expulsion from a clique can happen to even the most popular girls. To be suddenly shut out is devastating and excruciatingly cruel. This abrupt and unexplainable change most likely happens because girls are unable to appropriately express feelings of anger. Remember, that they are taught to be nice above all else and have not learned how to deal with feelings of anger and jealousy. It is very difficult and confusing to be angry and nice simultaneously. Therefore, girls have learned to appear nice to bystanders, such as teachers, administrators, and parents, while cutting each other to shreds with vicious rumors, broken confidences, and harsh criticisms.

Researchers have contributed to understanding this phenomenon. They found that when threatened or presented with immediate danger, boys tend to choose "fight or flight" and girls are more apt to choose "tend and befriend," seeking group support which is more nurturing and less aggressive.

Relational aggression, one form of alternative aggression used frequently by girls, uses relationships as the swift sword to destroy friendships or exclude members of cliques or groups. Because girls crave close relationships and inclusion, relational aggression causes great emotional suffering for many girls. At one time or another, we have all witnessed this aggression that Simmons (2002) so clearly explains:

> Relationally aggressive behavior is ignoring someone to punish them or get one's way, excluding someone socially for revenge, using negative body language or facial expressions, sabotaging someone's relationships, or threatening to end a relationship unless the friend agrees to a request. In these acts, the bully uses her relationship with the victim as a weapon.

Stepping Forward

Honoring my relatively new determination to learn more and become involved and helpful with middle level girls and their social distress in grades five through eight, I welcomed into my office a small group of upset fifth graders. An instant message had circulated rapidly in cyberspace the night before in which one girl said that Amy was *stuck up*. One girl took it upon herself to print the message at home and bring it to the one accused of being *stuck up* because she did not have instant messenger at home. She did not really know why she delivered the message other than she thought that Amy should know. I took a deep breath, rallied my patience and compassion, and attempted to help them resolve the tangle of feelings and misunderstandings amid the tears and accusations. I asked them to keep a journal of their feelings and observations during the week following our discussion. My intent with this strategy was to return them to class (these sessions have the potential to absorb huge amounts of time and interfere with learning), yet honor the seriousness of the conflict by providing time and a place for them to vent and sort out their feelings. Following are a few interesting entries in their journals:

From Cathy:
I am very upset right after my counseling session with Mrs. Lane. Lisa started to get mad at me and I have no idea what to do. Everyone is telling me to give her the silent treatment until she forgives me, but I think to myself that I would hate it if someone did that to me so I stick to my instincts and don't do that. I asked Lisa why she was mad at me and she said that I already know and she already told me. Lisa is now forming a group of people to be mad at me. These people I have been in fights with before so they don't have a great impression of me and I don't have one of them. I went to see Mrs. Lane about Lisa and she called Lisa and me down to her office. Lisa and I worked everything out and Lisa said she was mad at me because I said I could not trust her because she told a secret that I told her not to tell.

From Lisa:
I want to punch Cathy in the face. She's been lying and crying every single second. I think that I could start hanging around Nancy (the author of the message that inflamed the initial argument) a little more at recess. She understands a little more of what she's been doing over the years. It's a lot funner to be friends again.

From Kate:
People are still crying and I don't think there is anything to cry about. Some people are talking in groups of 2s and 3s. Amy and Ellen are friends again and that made me feel good. I hate this fight and people are still mad and I hate it.

From Beth:
Tension at lunch. Cathy is still crying. I found out that Nancy is out of school today because she is troubled not because she is sick. Amy told me that she has no friends and she either wants to move to California or go to NYA. This is harsh! Everyone is trying to cheer Cathy up with songs, but it's not working. Amy says that everyone is ignoring her and she starts crying. Lisa said that she is mad at Cathy because she lied even if she did correct it.

And on and on the dialogue goes, written or spoken, swirling round and round losing its beginning as the drama and emotion ebb and flow. It is no wonder teachers and administrators often only shake their heads and wonder where to begin. These four sample journal entries are typical of girls' feelings as they twist and tangle through changes. Perhaps Lisa is the most honest of all in saying that she would just like to punch Cathy (direct aggression) and get on with things. Throughout the journals, there is strong evidence that girls criticize and judge while assuming nurturing and caring roles. This portrays the façade of kindness and caring while fully enjoying their involvement in the fight. Simmons (2002) affirmed my assumptions in her statement explaining the strong need girls have to belong:

> Girls have multiple incentives to become embroiled in others' conflicts. First alliance building offers a chance for girls to belong, even briefly, to an ad hoc clique. Jumping on another girl's bandwagon to show support in her time of conflict affords a rare moment of inclusion and comfort. One girl stated, "People don't know what we're fighting about, but they want to be in it. They want to be part of the gossip." (pp. 81–82)

I have learned through experience that the outcome to girls' fights can be unsettling because actually being *in* the fight, even if only briefly included, seems to be much more important than the fight itself. Asking girls to apologize with "sorry" does nothing more than get them to "act nice" to one another, while driving the hostility further underground. The spark that ignited the fight in the first place is left to smolder and will undoubtedly reignite. Apologizing temporarily reduces the heat and makes the involved adult feel somewhat helpful and, perhaps, a bit smug because the problem is *solved*, but it does nothing to discover the source of the flames and extinguish them.

Listening Carefully

As my interest in this social epidemic grew, I had the opportunity to interview a student who was once traumatized by alternative aggression. Kate vividly and painfully remembers sixth grade—a year in which her life as a middle school girl was "pure hell." As a college sophomore, the memories still prevent her from returning to the school and she avoids this small coastal town as much as possible. She continues to have trust issues with friends and does not like the middle school age group. Relocating in the middle of her sixth grade year, Kate found her new classmates to be reserved and tightly networked. A few of the girls in her class made Kate's life unbearable. In addition to snide comments, there were notes left in her locker ordering her to go back to New Jersey or threatening to burn her house down. Kate remains adamant that the students in this school system are not accepting of new students no matter at what age they join the system. "You're always seen as the new kid," she remembered.

At home in the safety of her family, Kate would cry and beg her family to return to New Jersey. Her parents went to the school and spoke with teachers, administrators, and the guidance counselor, yet the problem persisted. The teachers were oblivious because it was all underground. Suggestions such as "just ignore them"

and "try to be nice" and discussions with the guidance counselor proved useless.

"The cafeteria for a new kid is a war zone, a place of complete humiliation. It's a place of hell because there is no one to turn to," Kate painfully explained. When she would sit at a table, the girls would rise and move to the end of the table. If she joined a friendlier group, the girls gave those students a hard time. Kate described the middle school cafeteria as *intense*, a place where *who likes who* is determined. They continually haunted her, never relenting regardless of what was said or done. Kate's parents considered putting their house back on the market in sheer frustration and concern for their daughter, who was once a happy, confident student.

The girls involved in Kate's torment were not the so-called cool girls. Kate explained, "They were the *bottom dwellers* and that's why it didn't spread up through the popular chain." The popular chain had definite lines and seemed to be defined around a hierarchy of athletics. Kate's athletic ability proved to be a tremendous asset in helping her overcome the ridicule and humiliation from the few classmates.

Kate made new friends through soccer, basketball, and softball. She was accepted by her teammates and things began to improve with her new status. "Once I got the power of popular, they didn't mess with me because you don't cross the line."

Kate offered a few suggestions for me as an administrator to help students who find themselves in the same hostile situation. She fondly remembers two young teachers who really helped and "didn't try to intervene, they were my friends." In Kate's opinion, students who are being ostracized and isolated need a friend and not a psychiatrist. "They are lonely and need someone besides their mothers to talk with about school issues."

Kate's story is all too familiar. As stated by Giannetti and Sagarese (2001):

> Nearly every young adolescent gets victimized by a peer or group of peers at some time or other during the middle school years. That is a fact of life for our children. The push and pull of social gathering during early adolescence creates outcasts and crises by the dozen. (p. 90)

As the assistant principal of the school that Kate abhors, I am deeply concerned, yet fascinated with the social dynamics that develop between these young adolescent girls. They are fickle and unsure of themselves, willing to turn their backs on a good friend to gain acceptance by someone deemed more popular. Many friendships are tenuous and require frenetic energy to keep up with the unstable dynamics. The use of e-mail and instant messaging feeds and exacerbates rumors that are often at the heart of hurt feelings, exclusion, broken trusts, and friendships.

Reaching Out

My interest in this social phenomenon inspired me to design a survey for students in grades six through eight, which was administered to students in health science classes. The students were asked to list five words that describe popular and five words that describe unpopular. The 54 sixth graders who participated in the survey most often described popular as cool, athletic, good looking, nice, and included/well known. They described unpopular as unattractive, mean, not many friends, not athletic, and stupid/dumb.

The 40 seventh graders who took the survey described popular as: athletic, nice, cool, lots of friends, and funny. To them, unpopular is described as mean, not athletic, ugly/overweight, different/weird, and shy/quiet. The 57 eighth graders described popular as athletic, good looking, funny, nice, and cool. Unpopular was described as ugly/fat, weird/not cool, not athletic, nice, and quiet. Just as Kate claimed, the survey results support the idea that athletics play a highly prominent role in determining one's social status in today's middle schools. The literature supported this as well. Based on the work of Colorado sociologists Patricia and Peter Adler, Giannetti and Sagarese (2001) offered a summary of four basic social groups:

Popular Clique This is the cool group. The beautiful, the athletic, the charming, the affluent; these young adolescents combine to make up about 35% of the population.

The Fringe About 10% of children hover around the popular set. The fringers accept their part-time superiority because running with the "in crowd" some of the time is worth being left behind the rest of the time.

Middle Friendship Circle The majority of boys and girls, nearly half at 45%, form small groups of several friends apiece. They carry on with their daily lives with assorted measures of confidence and satisfaction.

The Loners These are the boys and girls who have no friends. Usually 10% of a class falls into this category. (p. 20 and 21)

I recently had lunch with two seventh grade girls who are most likely classified by themselves and others as unpopular. They talked about the cafeteria and how it is understood where certain students sit. The unpopular girls tend to sit near the stage and the more popular girls fill the tables on the opposite side. They proceeded to tell me that anywhere from 20 to 30 students join their group each day, which to me sounded like a very popular group. The difference in popular, to them, means hanging out with only certain people and making other students

feel invisible. "They have a way of looking right through you, they even turn their backs as if we don't exist," explained Susan.

Observing students in the cafeteria is both enlightening and heart wrenching. I know how the cafeteria *works*. The delineation and pattern is very clear and predictable, I know where to look for certain students at each grade level.

Making a Difference

Based on what is known about girls and their social development, it is no longer acceptable for me or other educators to shrug off alternative aggression between girls. "Girls need active guidance in how to stay clear and centered in their anger and disagreement, and they need to be encouraged to bring their strong feelings into public life in constructive ways," reported Nagle (2002, p. 4).

Simmons (2002) suggested that teachers, guidance counselors, and administrators, with very little training, offer the best chance of making significant change with this phenomenon. We have the ability to create cultures in our schools that do not tolerate alternative aggressive behaviors. Students must be held accountable and must come to understand the source of their anger or jealousy and the seriousness and painful results of their words and actions. School personnel must no longer look the other way and say, "That's just the way it is."

This will not be enough on its own. Adults need to model assertive, respectful relationships for all students. Girls, in particular, need to be taught how to manage their anger and resolve their conflicts constructively. It is imperative that we talk about alternative aggression with our students and teach them that it is indeed harmful and unacceptable.

In our genuine attempts to reduce the overall amount of aggression in our schools, we must accept the fact that exclusion does happen. It always has and always will in both childhood and adult relationships. It is as much a natural part of life as is the desire to be popular. Caring adults must try to be objective and distinguish between what is the natural social ordering of children and what is deliberately mean and hurtful. I offer several suggestions and interventions taken from the literature for your consideration:

- Make it a point to acknowledge students personally to let them know you care. Young adolescents crave our attention. Give students your full attention when they are talking to you and avoid' interjecting your own feelings.
- Encourage girls to write in journals. If students want to talk and are "stuck," ask them to write down words and phrases or draw pictures that describe how they feel.

- Emphasize a student's strengths and accomplishments to refocus identifiers away from social behaviors. Point out that he or she is an outstanding artist instead of shy or charming.

- When a student reports being humiliated by gossip, do not dismiss it with casual comments such as "I'm sure that no one even noticed." It is a very big deal, and students need to know that you understand and care.

- Insist that students apologize sincerely. Apologies are a public acknowledgement of the consequences of hurtful behavior and are, therefore, powerful.

- Avoid punishing or restricting privileges (as I did!). They may be appropriate and deserved, however, the most important thing is to get girls to accept responsibility for their harmful actions.

- "Don't say 'behavior' when you're talking about accountability, say 'actions' 'Behavior,' like, 'watch your tone of voice,' makes girls crazy."(Wiseman, 2002, p. 117)

- Assure students that you will not be offended or shocked by bad language if it is, a part of their story. Encourage them to talk freely and openly.

- Offer academic curricula or hold discussions that address the issues of social aggression and how to recognize and manage it.

- Get to know the girls who appear to be alone, and intervene with strategies and social skills to involve them more with others.

- Structure activities that allow girls opportunities to belong and gain confidence and a sense of competence. Girls may become bored and thus, turn to gossiping to spice up the approximate 2.5 hours a day they spend talking with friends.

- "The power of peers' immediately resisting negative evaluations of others suggests that intervention programs could teach girls strategies for quickly challenging malicious gossip, and perhaps also social exclusion. Because girls are prone to being agreeable, it would likely be important to teach them very specific statements and to practice these in role plays.... Although challenges, could be effective from high and low status youth (Eder and Enke, 1991) it might be especially effective to teach these skills to high status girls who' are already prone to assuming the defender role and likely to have the greatest impact on their peers." (Underwood, 2003, p. 227)

- "Helping [students] understand and deal with anger is perhaps one of the greatest lessons you can teach them. Anger is caused by hurt feelings and a loss of control. No age group feels less in control than young adolescents. They may get angry when ordered around by parents and teachers. And, they get angry when they cannot control their friendships. You cannot control their friendships either, but you can help them deal with anger that these liaisons may produce." (Giannetti & Sagarese, 2001, p. 55–56)

- "The best way to eliminate cliques and bullies is to encourage the silent majority to speak up. The kids, who stand on the sidelines, watching other children be humiliated, hold the key to reform in their hands. Standing by silently reaffirms the clique's power. Speaking up nullifies it."(Giannetti & Sagarese, 2001, p. 192)

Closing Thoughts

As I continue to work with middle school girls, I pledge to enforce antibullying strategies that alert girls to the dangers of their behavior. Earlier, I hated to see distraught and squabbling girls coming because I was unprepared and doubtful as to what to do. I clearly did not understand the dynamics behind girl fights and their perpetual scramble to be noticed and accepted. Now, I am better informed about alternative aggression and its negative impact on young adolescent girls. I look forward to working with them and helping middle level teachers and parents to have more understanding and compassion for the phenomenon. It seems that this is the least I can do since, mercifully, returning to my own middle school days and making better choices for my own behavior is not an option. I choose to be proactive and involved in an effort to make a difference for girls like Kate.

A special thank you to students:
Anne, Brenna, Caitlyn, Chaya, Emily, Kristin, Lizzie, Margaret, Maryann, and Suvanna

References

Brown, L., & Gilligan, C. (1992). *Meeting at the Crossroads: Women's psychology and girls' development*. New York: Ballantine Books.

Giannetti, C., & Sagarese, M. (2001). *Cliques: 8 steps to help your child survive the jungle*. New York: Broadway Books.

Nagle, M. (2002, Sept./Oct.). Fighting to be somebody: Research on girls' aggression shows the need for activism. *UMaine Today*, 2–4.

Simmons, R. (2002). *Odd girl out: The hidden culture of aggression in girls.* New York: Harcourt.

Talbot, M. (2002, February 24). *Girls just want to be mean.* The New York Times. Retrieved February 26, 2002, from `http://www.nytimes.com/2002/02/24/magazine/24GIRLS.html`

Underwood, M., (2003). *Social aggression among girls.* New York: The Guilford Press.

Wiseman, R., (2002). *Queen bees and wannabees.* New York: Three Rivers Press.

Betsy Lane *is an assistant principal at Frank H. Harrison Middle School in Yarmouth, Maine. E-mail: Betsy_Lane@yarmouth.k12.me.us*

Heading Off
Disruptive Behavior

*How Early Intervention Can Reduce Defiant Behavior—
and Win Back Teaching Time*

By Hill M. Walker, Elizabeth Ramsey, and Frank M. Gresham

More and more children from troubled, chaotic homes are bringing well-developed patterns of antisocial behavior to school. Especially as these students get older, they wreak havoc on schools. Their aggressive, disruptive, and defiant behavior wastes teaching time, disrupts the learning of all students, threatens safety, overwhelms teachers—and ruins their own chances for successful schooling and a successful life.

In a poll of AFT teachers, 17 percent said they lost four or more hours of teaching time per week thanks to disruptive student behavior; another 19 percent said they lost two or three hours. In urban areas, fully 21 percent said they lost four or more hours per week. And in urban secondary schools, the percentage is 24. It's hard to see how academic achievement can rise significantly in the face of so much lost teaching time, not to mention the anxiety that is produced by the constant disruption (and by the implied safety threat), which must also take a toll on learning.

But it need not be this way in the future. Most of the disruption is caused by no more than a few students per class*—students who are, clinically speaking, "antisocial." Provided intervention begins when these children are young, preferably before they reach age 8, the knowledge, tools, and programs exist that would enable schools to head off most of this bad behavior—or at least greatly reduce its frequency. Schools are not the source of children's

behavior problems, and they can't completely solve them on their own. But the research is becoming clear: Schools can do a lot to minimize bad behavior—and in so doing, they help not only the antisocial children, they greatly advance their central goal of educating children.

In recent decades, antisocial behavior has been the subject of intense study by researchers in various disciplines including biology, sociology, social work, psychiatry, corrections, education, and psychology. Great progress has been made in understanding and developing solutions for defiant, disruptive, and aggressive behavior (see Burns, 2002). The field of psychology, in particular, with its increasingly robust theories of "social learning" and "cognition," has developed a powerful empirical literature that can assist school personnel in coping with, and ultimately preventing, a good deal of problematic behavior. Longitudinal and retrospective studies conducted in the United States, Australia, New Zealand, Canada, and various western European countries have yielded knowledge on the long-term outcomes of children who adopt antisocial behavior, especially those who arrive at school with it well developed (see Reid et al., 2002). Most importantly, a strong knowledge base has been assembled on interventions that can head off this behavior or prevent it from hardening (Loeber and Farrington, 2001).

To date, however, this invaluable knowledge base has been infused into educational practice in an extremely limited fashion. A major goal of this article (and of our much larger book) is to communicate and adapt this knowledge base for effective use by educators in coping with the rising tide of antisocial students populating today's schools. In our book, you'll find fuller explanations

---

*In the AFT's poll, of the 43 percent of teachers who said they had students in their classes with discipline problems, more than half said the problems were caused by one to three students. Poll conducted by Peter D. Hart Research Associates, October 1995.

of the causes of antisocial behavior, of particular forms of antisocial behavior like bullying, and of effective—and ineffective—interventions for schools. And all of this draws on a combination of the latest research and the classic research studies that have stood the test of time.

In this article, we look first at the source of antisocial behavior itself and ask: Why is it so toxic when it arrives in school? Second, we look at the evidence suggesting that early intervention is rare in schools. Third, we look at a range of practices that research indicates should be incorporated into school and classroom practice. Fourth, in the accompanying sidebars we give examples of how these practices have been combined in different ways to create effective programs.

I. Where Does Antisocial Behavior Come from and What Does That Mean for Schools?

Much to the dismay of many classroom teachers who deal with antisocial students, behavior-management practices that work so well with typical students do not work in managing antisocial behavior. In fact, teachers find that their tried and true behavior-management practices often make the behavior of antisocial students much worse. As a general rule, educators do not have a thorough understanding of the origins and developmental course of such behavior and are not well trained to deal with moderate to severe levels of antisocial behavior. The older these students become and the further along the educational track they progress, the more serious their problems become and the more difficult they are to manage.

How can it be that behavior-management practices somehow work differently for students with antisocial behavior patterns? Why do they react differently? Do they learn differently? Do they require interventions based on a completely different set of learning principles? As we shall see, the principles by which they acquire and exercise their behavioral pattern are quite typical and predictable.

Frequent and excessive noncompliance in school (or home) is an important first indicator of future antisocial behavior.

One of the most powerful principles used to explain how behavior is learned is known as the Matching Law (Herrnstein, 1974). In his original formulation, Herrnstein (1961) stated that the rate of any given behavior matches the rate of reinforcement for that behavior. For example, if aggressive behavior is reinforced once every three times it occurs (e.g., by a parent giving in to a temper tantrum) and prosocial behavior is reinforced once every 15 times it occurs (e.g., by a parent praising a polite request), then the Matching Law would predict that,

on average, aggressive behavior will be chosen five times more frequently than prosocial behavior. Research has consistently shown that behavior does, in fact, closely follow the Matching Law (Snyder, 2002). Therefore, how parents (and later, teachers) react to aggressive, defiant, and other bad behavior is extremely important. The Matching Law applies to all children; it indicates that antisocial behavior is learned—and, at least at a young enough age, can be unlearned. (As we will see in the section that reviews effective intervention techniques, many interventions—like maintaining at least a 4 to 1 ratio of praising versus reprimanding—have grown out of the Matching Law.)

First Comes the Family...

Antisocial behavior is widely believed to result from a mix of constitutional (i.e., genetic and neurobiological) and environmental (i.e., family and community) factors (Reid et al., 2002). In the vast majority of cases, the environmental factors are the primary causes—but in a small percentage of cases, there is an underlying, primarily constitutional, cause (for example, autism, a difficult temperament, attention deficit/hyperactivity disorder [ADHD], or a learning disorder). Not surprisingly, constitutional and environmental causes often overlap and even exacerbate each other, such as when parents are pushed to their limits by a child with a difficult temperament or when a child with ADHD lives in a chaotic environment.

Patterson and his colleagues (Patterson et al., 1992) have described in detail the main environmental causes of antisocial behavior. Their model starts by noting the social and personal factors that put great stress on family life (e.g., poverty, divorce, drug and alcohol problems, and physical abuse). These stressors disrupt normal parenting practices, making family life chaotic, unpredictable, and hostile. These disrupted parenting practices, in turn, lead family members to interact with each other in negative, aggressive ways and to attempt to control each others' behavior through coercive means such as excessive yelling, threats, intimidation, and physical force. In this environment, children learn that the way to get what they want is through what psychologists term "coercive" behavior: For parents, coercion means threatening, yelling, intimidating, and even hitting to force children to behave. (Patterson [1982] conducted a sequential analysis showing that parental use of such coercive strategies to suppress hostile and aggressive behavior actually increased the likelihood of such behavior in the future by 50 percent.)

For children, coercive tactics include disobeying, whining, yelling, throwing tantrums, threatening parents, and even hitting—all in order to avoid doing what the parents want. In homes where such coercive behavior is common, children become well-acquainted with how hostile behavior escalates—and with which of their behaviors ultimately secure adult surrender. This is the fertile ground in which antisocial behavior is bred. The negative effects tend to flow across generations much like inherited traits.*

By the time they are old enough for school, children who have developed an antisocial profile (due to either constitutional or environmental factors) have a limited repertoire of cooperative behavior skills, a predilection to use coercive tactics to control and manipulate others, and a well-developed capacity for emotional outbursts and confrontation.

...Then Comes School

For many young children, making the transition from home to school is fraught with difficulty. Upon school entry, children must learn to share, negotiate disagreements, deal with conflicts, and participate in competitive activities. And, they must do so in a manner that builds friendships with some peers and, at a minimum, social acceptance from others (Snyder, 2002). Children with antisocial behavior patterns have enormous difficulty accomplishing these social tasks. In fact, antisocial children are more than twice as likely as regular children to initiate unprovoked verbal or physical aggression toward peers, to reciprocate peer aggression toward them, and to continue aggressive behavior once it has been initiated (Snyder, 2002).**

From preschool to mid-elementary school, antisocial students' behavior changes in form and increases in intensity. During the preschool years, these children often display aversive behaviors such as frequent whining and noncompliance. Later, during the elementary school years, these behaviors take the form of less frequent but higher intensity acts such as hitting, fighting, bullying, and stealing. And during adolescence, bullying and hit-

---

*It is important to note that the kind of coercive interaction described is very different from parents' need to establish authority in order to appropriately discipline their children. This is accomplished through the clear communication of behavioral expectations, setting limits, monitoring and supervising children's behavior carefully, and providing positive attention and rewards or privileges for conforming to those expectations. It also means using such strategies as ignoring, mildly reprimanding, redirecting, and/or removing privileges when they do not. These strategies allow parents to maintain authority without relying on the coercion described above and without becoming extremely hostile or giving in to children's attempts to use coercion.

**This unfortunate behavior pattern soon leads to peer rejection (Reid, Patterson and Snyder, 2002). When behaviorally at-risk youth are rejected and forsaken by normal, well-behaved peers, they often begin to form friendships amongst themselves. If, over several years (and particularly in adolescence), these friendships solidify in such a way that these youth identify with and feel like members of a deviant peer group, they have a 70 percent chance of a felony arrest within two years (Patterson et al., 1992).

ting may escalate into robbery, assault, lying, stealing, fraud, and burglary (Snyder and Stoolmiller, 2002).

Although the specific form of the behavior changes (e.g., from noncompliance to bullying to assault), its function remains the same: Coercion remains at the heart of the antisocial behavior. As children grow older, they learn that the more noxious and painful they can make their behavior to others, the more likely they are to accomplish their goals—whether that goal is to avoid taking out the trash or escape a set of difficult mathematics problems. An important key to preventing this escalation (and therefore avoiding years of difficult behavior) is for adults to limit the use of coercive tactics with children—and for these adults to avoid surrendering in the face of coercive tactics used by the child. This has clear implications for school and teacher practices (and, of course, for parent training, which is not the subject of this article).

Frequent and excessive noncompliance in school (or home) is an important first indicator of future antisocial behavior. A young child's noncompliance is often a "gate key" behavior that triggers a vicious cycle involving parents, peers, and teachers. Further, it serves as a port of entry into much more serious forms of antisocial behavior. By treating noncompliance effectively at the early elementary age (or preferably even earlier), it is possible to prevent the development of more destructive behavior.

II. Early Intervention Is Rare

How many children are antisocial? How many are getting help early? To study the national incidence of antisocial behavior among children, researchers focus on two psychiatric diagnoses: oppositional defiant disorder and conduct disorder. Oppositional defiant disorder, the less serious of the two, consists of an ongoing pattern of uncooperative, angry behavior including things like deliberately trying to bother others and refusing to accept responsibility for mistakes. Conduct disorder is characterized by severe verbal and physical aggression, property destruction, and deceitful behavior that persist over time (usually one or more years). Formal surveys have generally indicated that between two and six percent of the general population of U.S. children and youth has some form of conduct disorder (Kazdin, 1993). Without someone intervening early to teach these children how to behave better, half of them will maintain the disorder into adulthood and the other half will suffer significant adjustment problems (e.g., disproportionate levels of marital discord and difficulty keeping a job) during their adult lives (Kazdin, 1993). (It is worth noting that on the way to these unpleasant outcomes, most will disrupt many classrooms and overwhelm many teachers.) When we add in oppositional defiant disorder (which often precedes and co-occurs with conduct disorder), estimates have been as

Students with Emotional Disturbance Served by Age, Selected School Years

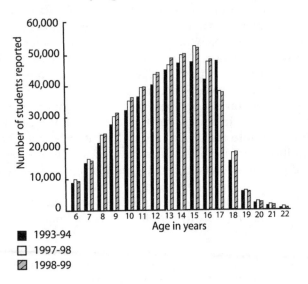

Legend:
- ■ 1993-94
- □ 1997-98
- ▨ 1998-99

high as 16 percent of the U.S. youth population (Eddy, Reid, and Curry, 2002).

In contrast, school systems typically identify (through the Individuals with Disabilities Education Act [IDEA]) slightly less than one percent of the public school population as having emotional and behavioral problems. Further, the great tendency of schools is to identify these behavioral problems quite late in a child's school career.

The figure above provides a stark example of this practice, which is more typical than not in today's public school systems. Walker, Nikiosha, Zeller, Severson, and Feil (2000) examined the number of K-12 students in the 1993-94, 1997-98, and 1998-99 school years who were certified as emotionally disturbed (the IDEA category that captures antisocial students). As the figure shows, the number of students certified as emotionally disturbed peaks around age 15 (approximately 50,000 cases) during the 1997-98 and 1998-99 school years. Similarly, the older data, from the 1993-94 school year, show the peak in referrals spread over the ages 14, 15, and 17. These results suggest that a large number of students, who were no doubt in need of supports and services for emotional disturbance in their elementary and middle school years, were not referred, evaluated, or served under special education.* Only in adolescence, when their behavior problems had become so intractable and difficult to accommodate, were many of these students finally identified and served. This practice

of delayed referral is the polar opposite of what research clearly shows is necessary.

Our society's social, cultural, and economic problems are spilling over into our schools. They are greatly complicating schools' central task of educating students safely and effectively. But the research is clear and growing: Even though many children and youth come from and return to chaotic, coercive home environments on a daily basis, they can still acquire sufficient behavioral control to succeed in school—and to allow classmates to learn in an orderly environment.

We have substantial knowledge about how to divert at-risk children, youth, and families from destructive outcomes.** We believe the problem is not one of knowing what to do, but of convincing schools to effectively use research-based intervention programs over the long term.

The remainder of this article is devoted to providing educators with guidelines and programs for early intervention that greatly reduce antisocial behavior. There are no magic bullets in the material presented herein. Dealing with the antisocial student population is difficult, frustrating, and, because schools tend to intervene too late, often without identifiable rewards. However, of all those who suffer from conditions and disorders that impair school performance, these students are among those with the greatest capacity for change—particularly when they first start school.

III. What Can Schools Do?

Schools are not the source of children's antisocial behavior, and they cannot completely eliminate it. But schools do have substantial power to prevent it in some children and greatly reduce it in others.

First, and in some ways most importantly, schools can help by being academically effective. The fact is, academic achievement and good behavior reinforce each other: Experiencing some success academically is related to decreases in acting out; conversely, learning positive behaviors is related to doing better academically. Kellam and his colleagues (1994), for example, showed experimentally that gains in first-grade academic achievement, as measured by standardized achievement tests, resulted in substantially reduced levels of aggression, according to behavior ratings by their teachers. And, confirming what common sense tells us, Caprara, Barbaranelli, Pastorelli, Bandura, and Zimbardo (2000) found that positive behaviors (like cooperating, sharing, and consoling) among very young children contributed to their later academic achievement.

---

*Kauffman (1999) suggests that the field of education actually "prevents prevention" of behavioral disorders through well-meaning efforts to "protect" difficult children from being labeled and stigmatized by the screening and identification process.

**Successful model programs have been reviewed and described extensively by Catalano, Loeber, and McKinney (1999), by Loeber and Farrington (2001), and by Reid and his colleagues (2002).

Second, schools can, to a large and surprising extent, affect the level of aggression in young boys just by the orderliness of their classrooms. An intriguing longitudinal study dramatically illustrates the role of this variable in the development or prevention of aggressive behavior from first grade to middle school (Kellam, Rebok, Ialongo, and Mayer, 1994). After randomly assigning students to first-grade classrooms, researchers found that nearly half of the classrooms were chaotic and the remainder were reasonably well-managed. Of the boys in the study who began schooling in the top quartile of aggressive behavior (as rated by their teachers), those assigned to orderly classrooms had odds of 3:1 in favor of being highly aggressive in middle school. However, those boys assigned to chaotic classrooms had odds of 59:1 for being highly aggressive in middle school. This seminal finding suggests that poor classroom management by teachers in grade one is a huge, but preventable, factor in the development of antisocial behavior—and, conversely, that effective classroom management can have an enormous long-term positive effect on behavior. Thus, working closely with first-grade teachers (and, presumably, other early-grade teachers) on their behavior management can yield substantial future benefits for students and their schools by offsetting destructive outcomes.

Aggressive first-grade boys assigned to orderly classrooms had odds of 3:1 in favor of being highly aggressive in middle school. Those assigned to chaotic classrooms had odds of 59:1 for being highly aggressive in middle school.

But to some extent, this just begs the larger question: How can schools and their teachers create and sustain orderly classrooms? We summarize here the key findings and conclusions from 40 years of research. First, we present a three-tiered intervention model that matches the extent of children's behavioral problems to the power (and, therefore, cost) of the programs implemented. Second, we offer tools that can accurately and effectively identify students as young as kindergarten (and, in daycare or preschool settings, even at-risk three-year-olds can be identified) who are likely to become school behavior problems (and, later in life, delinquents and even adult criminals). Third, we review five techniques that, in combination, are at the heart of preventing antisocial behavior. Fourth, we describe specific programs with substantial and growing records of effectiveness that successfully incorporate all of the above into entirely doable, economical, and feasible school interventions. These programs can be purchased by schools from a variety of

for-profit publishers and non-profit child and family services organizations. Some are inexpensive; the more expensive interventions tend to be individualized to meet the needs of highly aggressive children. All of the programs described in this article can be funded with either IDEA resources or school improvement funds. Programs for antisocial children, such as those described here, can also be funded in partnership with mental health agencies and/or through grants available through the Safe and Drug Free Schools division of the U.S. Department of Education. (See box, Funding Early Interventions.)

A. Three Levels of Intervention

Research has shown that the best way to prevent antisocial behavior is actually to start with an inexpensive school-wide intervention and then add on more intensive interventions for the most troubled kids. Building on work done by the U.S. Public Health Service, Hill Walker and his colleagues developed a model with three progressively more intensive levels of intervention to address challenging behavior within schools (Walker, Horner, Sugai, Bullis, Sprague, Bricker, and Kaufman, 1996). This model has proved to be very popular among educational researchers and has been broadly adopted by practitioners as a way to select and coordinate interventions. It is sometimes referred to in educational forums as "the Oregon Model." However, this approach is clearly a matter of public domain and is not owned by anyone. The three levels of intervention are known as "universal," "selected," and "indicated." Each is briefly described below.

"Universal" interventions are school or classroom practices that affect all students. Examples of universal interventions relevant to behavior are classwide social skills training and well-enforced school discipline codes. (Outside of education, the polio vaccination is an example of a "universal intervention.") It may seem odd to implement a program for all students when most teachers can easily identify children who have, or are developing, antisocial behavior. But schoolwide programs accomplish three things. First, they improve almost all students' behavior—and most students, even if they don't qualify as troublemakers, still need some practice being well-behaved. Second, universal interventions have their greatest impact among students who "are on the margins"—those students who are just beginning to be aggressive or defiant. Sometimes, systematic exposure to a universal intervention will be sufficient to tip them in the right direction. Third, the universal intervention offers a foundation that supports the antisocial students throughout the day by reinforcing what they are learning in their more intensive selected and indicated interventions; these latter interventions are more efficient and have a greater impact when they are applied in the context of a prior, well-implemented, universal intervention.

Approximately 80 to 90 percent of all students will respond successfully to a well-implemented universal intervention (Sugai et al., 2002). Once the school environment is orderly, the antisocial students pop up like corks in water. These students have "selected" themselves out as needing more powerful "selected" interventions that employ much more expensive and labor-intensive techniques. The goal with these students is to decrease the frequency of their problem behaviors, instill appropriate behaviors, and make the children more responsive to universal interventions (Sugai et al., 2002). While selected interventions typically are based in the school, to be their most effective they often require parental involvement. Nevertheless, even when parents refuse to participate, selected interventions still have positive effects and are well worth the effort.

The vast majority of antisocial students will start behaving better after being involved in universal and selected interventions, but schools can expect that a very small percentage of antisocial students (about one to five percent of the total youth population) will not. These are the most severe cases—the most troubled children from the most chaotic homes—and they require extremely intensive, individualized, and expensive interventions. These interventions, called "indicated," are typically family focused, with participation and support from mental health, juvenile justice, and social service agencies, as well as schools. Most non-specialized schools will find that running such an intervention is beyond their capacity. It's for such students that alternative education settings are necessary.

This three-tiered intervention model offers a structure that educators can use when they are reviewing and trying to coordinate programs. It ensures that all students' needs will be met efficiently—each child is exposed to the level of intervention that his behavior shows he needs. This is a very cost-effective model for schools because interventions become much more expensive as they become more specialized.

But it all begins with effective early screening.

B. Early Screening and Identification of Potentially Antisocial Students

Many fields have well-established practices to identify problems early and allow for more effective treatments. For instance, in medicine, routine screening procedures such as prostate-specific antigen (PSA) tests to detect prostate cancer, mammograms to detect breast cancer, and Papanicolaou (Pap) tests to detect the early states of cervical cancer have been routine for years. Unfortunately, similar proactive, early identification approaches are not commonly used to identify children with, or at risk of developing, antisocial behavior.

But research shows that early identification is absolutely critical: Children who have not learned appropriate, non-coercive ways to interact socially by around 8 years of age (the end of third grade) will likely continue displaying some degree of antisocial behavior throughout their lives (Loeber and Farrington, 1998). We also know that the longer such children go without access to

effective and early intervention services (particularly after the age of 8), the more resistant to change their behavior problems will be (Gresham, 1991) and the more expensive it will be to induce the change.

Yet, as discussed previously, schools offer special education services to just one percent of students, though two to 16 percent manifest some form of antisocial behavior—and virtually no special education services are provided before students become adolescents. The technology (usually simple normed checklists and observation instruments, as described below) for identifying such children is gradually becoming more accurate for children at younger and younger ages (Severson and Walker, 2002).

A particularly valuable approach to screening is known as "multiple gating" (Loeber, Dishion, and Patterson, 1984). Multiple gating is a process in which a series of progressively more precise (and expensive) assessments or "gates" are used to identify children who need help with their behavior. One such screening procedure is the Systematic Screening for Behavior Disorders (SSBD) (Walker and Severson, 1990).

This screening procedure offers a cost-effective, mass screening of all students in grades one to six in regular education classrooms. The SSBD is made up of a combination of teacher nominations (Gate 1), teacher rating scales (Gate 2), and observations of classroom and playground problem behavior (Gate 3). It was nationally standardized on 4,500 students for the Gate 2 measures and approximately 1,300 students for the Gate 3 measures. It represents a significant advance in enabling the systematic and comprehensive screening of behavioral problems among general education students (Gresham, Lane, and Lambros, 2002). The major advantage of the SSBD is first, its ease of use, and second, its common set of standards for teachers to use in evaluating students' behavior; these standards remove most of the subjectivity that is endemic to the referral process commonly used in schools (Severson and Walker, 2002). If all schools employed universal screening (and backed it up with effective early interventions), an enormous amount of defiant and destructive behavior could be prevented—and innumerable teaching hours could be preserved.

Researchers have found that teachers do tend to praise their regular students for good behavior, but they tend not to seize oportunities to praise antisocial students when they are behaving well.

C. Key Features of Effective Interventions

When dealing with well-established antisocial behavior, a combination of the following techniques is usually required in order to successfully bring about behavior change: (1) a consistently enforced schoolwide behavior code, (2) social-skills training, (3) appropriately-delivered adult praise for positive behavior, (4) reinforcement contingencies and response costs, and (5) time-out (see Wolf, 1978). Each of these techniques is briefly explained below.

Over the past three decades, an extensive body of research has developed on the effectiveness of these techniques for preventing and remediating problem behavior within the context of schools. Studies of the use of these techniques show that positive strategies (appropriate praise, social-skills training, providing free-time privileges or activities) are generally sufficient for developing and maintaining the appropriate behavior of most students. However, students with challenging behavior often also require sanctions of some type (e.g. time-out or loss of privileges) in order to successfully address their problems. Extensive research clearly shows that, to be most effective, intervention programs or regimens incorporating these techniques should be applied across multiple settings (classrooms, hallways, playgrounds, etc.), operate for a sufficient time period for them to work, and should involve teachers and parents in school-home partnerships whenever possible.

No single technique applied in isolation will have an enduring impact. Used together, however, they are effective—especially for antisocial students age 8 or younger. Assembling these techniques into feasible and effective daily routines can be done by individual teachers in well-run schools. But it is difficult, time-consuming, and fraught with trial and error. Among the fruits of the past several decades of research on this topic is a group of carefully developed and tested programs that integrate these techniques into entirely doable programs that don't overly distract teachers from their main job: teaching. Several are briefly described in this and the following section.

1. A Well-Enforced Schoolwide Behavior Code

A schoolwide behavior code creates a positive school climate by clearly communicating and enforcing a set of behavioral standards. The code should consist of 5 to 7 rules—and it's essential to carefully define and provide examples of each rule. Ideally, school administrators, teachers, related services staff, students, and parents should all be involved in the development of the code. But writing the code is just the first step. Too often, teachers and others complain, a behavior code is established—and left to wither. To be effective, students must be instructed in what it means, have opportunities to practice following the rules, have incentives for adhering to it (as described in the third and fourth techniques below), and know that violating it brings consequences.

One excellent, inexpensive program for teaching the schoolwide behavior expectations reflected in a code is called Effective Behavior Support (EBS). The principal features of EBS are that all staff (administrative, classroom, lunchroom, playground, school bus, custodial, etc.) recognize and abide by the same set of behavioral expectations for all students. The behavior expectations are explicitly taught to students and they are taught in each relevant venue. In groups of 30 to 45, students are taken to various parts of the school (e.g., the bus loading zone, cafeteria, main hallway, gym, and classrooms) to discuss specific examples of behaviors that would, and would not, meet the behavior expectations. Once they have learned the expectations, they are motivated to meet them by earning rewards and praise for their good behavior.

2. Social Skills Training

As discussed earlier, many antisocial students enter school without adequate knowledge of—or experience with—appropriate social skills. These skills must be taught, practiced, and reinforced. This is the purpose of social skills training. Skills taught include empathy, anger management, and problem solving. They are taught using standard instructional techniques and practiced so that students not only learn new skills, but also begin using them throughout the school day and at home. While the training is vital for antisocial students, all students benefit from improving their social skills—especially students "on the margin" of antisocial behavior. Social skills curricula are typically taught in one or two periods a week over the course of several months and in multiple grades.

3. Adult Praise

Adult praise (from teachers, parents, or others) is a form of focused attention that communicates approval and positive regard. It is an abundantly available, natural resource that is greatly underutilized. Researchers have found that teachers do tend to praise their regular students for good behavior, but they tend not to seize opportunities to praise antisocial students when they are behaving well (Mayer & Sulzer-Azaroff, 2002). This is indeed unfortunate because praise that is behavior specific and delivered in a positive and genuine fashion is one of our most effective tools for motivating all students and teaching them important skills. Reavis et al. (1996) note that praise should be immediate, frequent, enthusiastic, descriptive, varied, and involve eye contact. We would also suggest that the ratio of praise to criticism and reprimands be at least 4:1—and higher if possible. Although antisocial students may not immediately respond to praise because of their long history of negative interactions with the adults in their lives, when paired with other incentives (such as the type of reward system described below), the positive impact of praise will eventually increase.

Funding Early Interventions

With the research reviewed here, building support for the idea of early interventions should not be difficult—but finding funds could be if you don't know where to look. One source is Title I. Schools in which at least 40 percent of the students are poor should look into using the schoolwide provision of Title I to fund universal interventions. Under Title I schoolwide, you can combine several federal, state, and local funding streams to support school improvement programs. Insofar as students are identified as emotionally disturbed, their interventions can be funded by IDEA. The federal government also provides funding to reduce behavior problems through the Safe and Drug Free Schools and Communities Act. In this case, state education agencies receive funds to make grants to local education agencies and governors receive funds to make complementary grants to community-based organizations. Schools can also partner with mental health agencies, enabling services to be covered by insurance such as Medicaid and the State Children's Health Insurance Program. Plus, most states have funding streams that could support the programs described in this article. (For more information on funding, see chapter two of *Safe, Supportive, and Successful Schools: Step by Step*, available from Sopris West for $49; order online at

www.sopriswest.com/swstore/product.asp?sku=872)

4. Reinforcement Contingencies and Response Costs

Rewards and penalties of different sorts are a common feature of many classroom management strategies. Research shows that there are specific "best" ways to arrange these reinforcements to effectively motivate students to behave appropriately. These strategies are called individual reinforcement contingencies, group reinforcement contingencies, and response costs. Individual contingencies are private, one-to-one arrangements between a teacher or parent and a student in which specified, positive consequences are made available dependent ("contingent") upon the student's performance. Earning a minute of free time for every 10 or 15 math problems correctly solved, or attempted, is an example of an individual contingency.

Group contingencies are arrangements in which an entire group of individuals (e.g., a class) is treated as a single unit and the group's performance, as a whole, is evaluated to determine whether a reward is earned, such as an extra five minutes of recess. (Note: A group can fail to earn a reward, such as an extra five minutes of recess, but should not be penalized, such as by losing five minutes of the normal recess.) This strategy gets peers involved in encouraging the antisocial student to behave better. For example, if the antisocial student disrupts the class, instead of laughing at his antics, other students will encourage him to quiet down so that they can all earn the reward. To make it easier to keep track of students' behavior, reinforcement contingencies are often set up as point systems in which students must earn a certain number of points within a certain time period in order to earn a reward.

"Response costs" are a form of penalty that is added to the package of contingencies when working toward a reward is not quite enough to change students' behavior. Teachers can increase the effectiveness of contingencies by adding a response cost so that good behavior earns points and bad behavior subtracts points—making it much harder to earn a reward. (Response costs are the basis for late fees, traffic tickets, penalties in football, foul shots in basketball, and other sanctions in public life.)

5. Time-Out

Time-out is a technique of last resort in which students are removed for just five to 15 minutes from situations in which they have trouble controlling their behavior and/or their peers' attention is drawn to their inappropriate behavior. We recommend both in-classroom time-out for minor infractions and out-of-classroom time-out (the principal's office or a designated time-out room) for more serious infractions. Students should be given the option of volunteering for brief periods of time-out when they temporarily cannot control their own behavior, but teachers should *never* physically try to force students into time-out. Finally, *in-class* time-out should be used sparingly and should *not* be used with older students. Older students who need to be removed from a situation can be sent to the principal's office or another "cool-down" room instead of having an in-class time-out.

The research foundation for these techniques is quite strong and the empirical evidence of their effectiveness is both persuasive and growing. For the past 40 years, researchers in applied behavior analysis have worked closely with school staff and others in testing and demonstrating the effectiveness of these techniques within real world settings like classrooms and playgrounds. Literally hundreds of credible studies have documented the effectiveness of each of these techniques—as well as combinations of them—in remediating the problems that antisocial children and youth bring to schooling. The research has also surfaced guidelines for the effective application of the techniques in school contexts (Walker, 1995).

IV. Effective Programs for Preventing Antisocial Behavior

In spite of huge advances in our knowledge of how to prevent and treat antisocial behavior in the past decade, the Surgeon General's Report on Youth Violence indicates that less than 10 percent of services delivered in schools and communities targeting antisocial behavior patterns are evidence-based (see Satcher, 2001). As these children move through schools without effective intervention services and supports, their problems are likely to become more intractable and ever more resistant to change. This is simply not necessary. Effective, manageable programs exist.

Effective programs require an upfront investment of time and energy, but they more than "pay for themselves" in terms of teaching time won back.

We highlight three promising interventions—Second Step, First Step to Success, and Multisystemic Therapy—as examples of, respectively, universal, selected, and indicated interventions. The coordinated implementation of these or similar programs can make a remarkable difference in the orderliness of schools and classrooms and in the lives of antisocial youth (not to mention the victims of their aggression).

Second Step, a social skills training program for K-9 students, is described in detail. It was recently rated as the number one program for ensuring school safety by a blue ribbon panel of the U.S. Department of Education. Evaluations of Second Step have found results ranging from decreases in aggression and disruption among 109 preschool and kindergarten children from low-income, urban homes (McMahon, 2000) to less hostility and need for adult supervision among over 1,000 second- to fifth-grade students (Frey, Nolen, Van Schoiack-Edstrom, and Hirschstein, 2001).

First Step, is an intensive intervention for highly aggressive K-3 students. Experimental studies with kindergartners have found great improvments in their overall classroom behavior and academic engagement, and substantial reductions in their aggression during implementation and over many years following the end of intervention (see Walker, Kavanagh, Stiller, Golly, Severson, and Feil, 1998; Epstein and Walker, 2002). Similarly, studies involving two sets of identical twins enrolled in regular kindergarten programs found that exposure to the program produced powerful behavior changes upon introduction of the intervention that were maintained throughout the program's implementation (Golly, Sprague, Walker, Beard, and Gorham, 2000). These types of positive effects have also been replicated by other inves-

tigators. The First Step program has been included in six national reviews of effective early interventions for addressing oppositional and/or aggressive behavior in school.

Multisystemic Therapy (MST) is a family-focused intervention conducted by a trained therapist. It is aimed at the most severely at-risk youth, those who have been or are about to be incarcerated, often for violent offenses. Very often, the student has already been assigned to an alternative education setting. The therapist teaches parents the skills they need to assist their antisocial child to function more effectively across a range of social contexts. Daily contact between the student and therapist is common in the early stages of MST and reduces to several times per week as the intervention progresses. Therapists periodically talk to teachers to find out about the children's behavior, attendance, and work habits. Most importantly, teachers need to let therapists know when they perceive incremental improvements in the children's behavior—the therapists use this information to guide their work with the families. According to the Blueprints for Violence Prevention Project, MST has been found to reduce long-term rates of being re-arrested by 25 to 70 percent, to greatly improve family functioning, and to lessen mental health problems (Blueprints, 2003). (To find out if MST is available in your area, visit) **www.mstservices.com**

As the research clearly shows, these three programs have the potential to prevent countless acts of aggression and positively influence both school and family functioning.

Disruptive student behavior will decrease and teaching time will increase, allowing all children to learn more. Office discipline referrals will decrease, freeing up school staff to address other school needs like supporting instruction. Effective programs do require an upfront investment of time and energy, but over the school year, and certainly over the school career, they more than "pay for themselves" in terms of teaching time won back.

An obvious subtext in the article has been that elementary schools—and especially K-3 teachers—must bear the burden of preventing antisocial behavior. This may come as a surprise since behavior problems seem so much more severe as children age. But if there's one uncontestable finding from the past 40 years of research on antisocial children, it's this: The longer students are allowed to be aggressive, defiant, and destructive, the more difficult it is to turn them around. While high schools can, and should, do what they can to help antisocial students control themselves, elementary schools can, and should, actually help antisocial children to become socially competent.

Hill M. Walker is founder and co-director of the Institute on Violence and Destructive Behavior at the University of Oregon, where he has been a professor since 1967. Walker has published hundreds of articles; in 1993 he received the Outstanding Research Award from the Council for Exceptional Children and in 2000 he became the only faculty member to receive the University of Oregon's Presidential Medal. Elizabeth Ramsey is a school counselor at Kopachuck Middle School in Gig Harbor, Wash., and a co-author of the Second Step program. Frank M. Gresham is distinguished professor and director of the School Psychology Program at the University of California-Riverside. He is co-author of the Social Skills Rating System and co-principal investigator for Project REACH. The Division of School Psychology in the American Psychological Association selected him for the Senior Scientist Award. Together, Walker, Ramsey, and Gresham wrote Antisocial Behavior in School: Evidence-Based Practices, on which this article is based.

References

Blueprints for Violence Prevention (2003). Multisystemic Therapy online at **www.colorado.edu/cspv/blueprints/model/programs/MST.html**

Burns, B. (2002). Reasons for hope for children and families: A perspective and overview. In B. Murns & K.K. Hoagwood (Eds.), *Community treatment for youth: Evidence-based interventions for severe emotional and behavioral disorders* (pp. 1–15). New York: Oxford University Press.

Caprara, G., Barbaranelli, C., Pastorelli, C., Brandura, A., & Zimbardo, P. (2000). Prosocial foundations of children's academic achievement. *Psychological Science, 11*(4), 302–306.

Catalano, R., Loeber, R., & McKinney, K. (1999). School and community interventions to prevent serious and violent offending. *Juvenile Justice Bulletin.* U.S. Department of Justice, Office of Juvenile Justice and Delinquency Prevention, Washington, D.C.

Eddy, J.M., Reid, J.B., & Curry, V. (2002). The etiology of youth antisocial behavior, delinquency and violence and a public health approach to prevention. In M.R. Shinn, H.M. Walker, & G. Stoner (Eds.), *Interventions for academic and behavior problems II: Preventive and remedial approaches,* (pp. 27–51). Bethesda, Md.: National Association for School Psychologists.

Epstein, M. & Walker, H. (2002). Special education: Best practices and First Step to Success. In B. Burns & K. Hoagwood (Eds.), *Community treatment for youth: Evidence-based intervention for severe emotional and behavioral disorders* (pp. 177–197). New York: Oxford University Press.

Frey, K.S., Nolan, S.B., Van Schoiack-Edstrom, L., and Hirschstein, M. (2001, June). "Second Step: Effects on Social Goals and Behavior." Paper presented at the annual meeting of the Society for Prevention Research, Washington, D.C.

Golly, A., Sprague, J., Walker, H.M., Beard, K., & Gorham, G. (2000). The First Step to Success program: An analysis of outcomes with identical twins across multiple baselines. *Behavioral Disorders, 25*(3), 170–182.

Gresham, F.M. (1991). Conceptualizing behavior disorders in terms of resistance to intervention. *School Psychology Review, 20,* 23–36.

Gresham, F.M., Lane, K., & Lambros, K. (2002). Children with conduct and hyperactivity attention problems: Identification, assessment and intervention. In K. Lane, F.M. Gresham, & T. O'Shaughnessy (Eds.), *Children with or at risk for emotional and behavioral disorders* (pp. 210–222). Boston: Allyn & Bacon.

Grossman, D., Neckerman, M., Koepsell, T., Ping-Yu Liu, Asher, K., Beland, K., Frey, K., & Rivara, F. (1997). Effectiveness of a violence prevention curriculum among children in elementary school: A randomized, control trial. *Journal of the American Medical Association, 277*(20), pp. 1605–1611.

Herrnstein, R. (1961). Relative and absolute strength of response as a function of frequency of reinforcement. *Journal of the Experimental Analysis of Behavior, 4,* 267–272.

Herrnstein, R. (1974). Formal properties of the matching law. *Journal of the Experimental Analysis of Behavior, 21,* 486–495.

Kauffman, J. (1999). How we prevent emotional and behavioral disorders. *Exceptional Children, 65,* 448–468.

Kazdin, A. (1993). Adolescent mental health: Prevention and treatment programs. *American Psychologist, 48,* 127–141.

Kellam, S., Rebok, G., Ialongo, N., & Mayer, L. (1994). The course and malleability of aggressive behavior from early first grade into middle school: Results of a developmental epidemiologically-based prevention trial. *Journal of Child Psychology and Psychiatry, 35*(2), 259–281.

Loeber, D. & Farrington, D. (2001). *Child delinquents: Development, intervention and service needs.* Thousand Oaks, Calif.: Sage.

Loeber, R., Dishion, T., & Patterson, G. (1984). Multiple-gating: A multistage assessment procedure for identifying youths at risk for delinquency. *Journal of Research in Crime and Delinquency, 21,* 7–32.

Loeber, R. & Farrington, D. (Eds.). (1998). *Serious and violent juvenile offenders: Risk factors and successful interventions.* Thousand Oaks, Calif.: Sage.

Loeber, R. & Farrington, D.P. (2001) *Serious and violent juvenile offenders: Risk factors and successful interventions.* Thousand Oaks, Calif.: Sage.

Mayer, G.R. & Sulzer-Azanoff, B. (2002). Interventions for vandalism and aggression. In M. Shinn, H. Walker, & G. Stoner (Eds.), *Interventions for academic and behavior problems II: Preventive and remedial approaches* (pp. 853–884). Bethesda, Md.: National Association of School Psychologists.

McMahon, S.D., et al. (2000). "Violence Prevention: Program Effects on Urban Preschool and Kindergarten Children." *Applied and Preventive Psychology, 9,* 271–281.

Patterson, G. (1982). *A social learning approach, Volume 3: Coercive family process.* Eugene, Ore.: Castalia.

Patterson, G.R., Reid, J.B., & Dishion, T.J. (1992). *Antisocial boys.* Eugene, Ore.: Castalia.

Reavis, H.K., Taylor, M., Jenson, W., Morgan, D., Andrews, D., & Fisher, S. (1996). *Best practices: Behavioral and educational strategies for teachers.* Longmont, Colo.: Sopris West.

Reid, J.B., Patterson, G.R., & Snyder, J.J. (Eds.). (2002). *Antisocial behavior in children and adolescents: A developmental analysis and the Oregon Model for Intervention.* Washington, D.C.: American Psychological Association.

Satcher, D. (2001). *Youth violence: A report of the Surgeon General.* Washington, D.C.: U.S. Public Health Service, U.S. Department of Health and Human Services.

Severson, H. & Walker, H. (2002). Proactive approaches for identifying children at risk for sociobehavioral problems. In K. Lane, F.M. Gresham, & T. O'Shaughnessy (Eds.), *Interventions for children with or at-risk for emotional and behavioral disorders,* pp. 33–53. Boston: Allyn & Bacon.

Snyder, J. (2002). Reinforcement and coercion mechanisms in the development of antisocial behavior: Peer relationships. In J. Reid, G. Patterson, & L. Snyder (Eds.), *Antisocial behavior in children and adolescents: A developmental analysis and model for intervention,* pp. 101–122. Washington, D.C.: American Psychological Association.

Snyder, J. & Stoolmiller, M. (2002). Reinforcement and coercive mechanisms in the development of antisocial behavior. The family. In J. Reid, G. Patterson, & J. Snyder (Eds.), *Antisocial behavior in children and adolescents: A developmental analysis and model for intervention* (pp. 65–100). Washington, D.C.: American Psychological Association.

Sugai, G. & Horner, R., & Gresham, F. (2002) Behaviorally effective school environments. In M. Shinn, H. Walker, & G. Stoner (Eds.). *Interventions for academic and behavior problems II: Preventive and remedial approaches* (pp. 315–350). Bethesda, Md.: National Association of School Psychologists.

Walker, H.M. (1995). *The acting-out child: Coping with classroom disruption.* Langmont, Colo.: Sopris West.

Walker, H.M., Horner, R.H., Sugai, G., Bullis M., Spraque, J.R., Bricker, D. & Kaufman, M.J. (1996). Integrated approaches to preventing antisocial behavior patterns among school-age children and youth. *Journal of Emotional and Behavioral Disorders, 4*, 193–256.

Walker, H., Kavanagh, K., Stiller, B., Golly, A., Severson, H., & Feil, E. (1997). *First Step to Success: An early intervention program for antisocial kindergartners,* Longmont, Colo.: Sopris West.

Walker, H., Kavanagh, K., Stiller, B., Golly, A., Severson, H., & Feil, E. (1998). First Step: An early intervention approach for preventing school antisocial behavior. *Journal of Emotional and Behavioral Disorders, 6*(2), 66–80.

Walker, H. & Severson, H. (1990). *Systematic screening for behavioral disorders.* Longmont, Colo.: Sopris West.

Walker, H.M., Nishioka, V., Zeller, R., Severson, H., & Feil, E. (2000). Causal factors and potential solutions for the persistent under-identification of students having emotional or behavioral disorders in the context of schooling. *Assessment for Effective Intervention, 26*(1) 29–40.

Wolf, M.M. (1978). Social validity: The case for subjective measurement, or how applied behavior analysis is finding its heart. *Journal of Applied Behavior Analysis, 11,* 203–214.

True Blue

An American educator brings her anti-bullying program to South African schools.

by M. Christine Mattise, M.Ed.

Where could she be?

"She was sad and ran away," the children reported, "and now we can't find her!"

I was aware of the recess bell ringing loudly, the crunching of many small feet on the snow. The sounds faded away slowly as I herded the classes inside, until there was only silence.

A flicker of red behind a tree caught my eye—her small rubber boot. I found her sitting there, hugging her knees and whimpering.

Her body was fine—she had been missing for less than 15 minutes—but her spirit was shattered. We talked quietly about what had happened and, in a few minutes, she uncurled and we walked inside.

As the guidance counselor at an elementary school in a small New Hampshire town, I thought I had been dealing effectively with this bullying situation, in which several children had set their sights on this one girl.

Traditional interventions (small group, individual counseling, classroom guidance, parent conferences) were obviously having little or no effect. The bullies had stuck with their project relentlessly, using snide looks, vicious whispering and a systematic plan to totally isolate one child on the playground.

The victim had suffered obediently in silence, believing what the bullies said about her—that she was unattractive, slow to learn, had a weird laugh and that no one wanted to play with her or be her friend. How did she come to accept the negative self-images? Why did she abandon her own right to be free from fear on the playground?

These children had no language or context to understand why their hurtful behaviors were so painful and damaging.

That became my goal: I would create this absent language for children in schools. I called it "Hurt-Free Schools."

Little did I realize that educators on a distant continent were involved in a similar, even more desperate, search for this new language. Far away in a land of both great beauty and great pain, other schools were struggling to stop the damages caused by bullies.

My pledge to create a language of empowerment for children led me to South Africa, a country struggling to recover from a giant among all-time bullies, apartheid. Interestingly, my journey to South Africa began in Glasgow, Scotland, at a university conference where I presented my anti-bullying program. There, I engaged in a lively discussion with a South African educator that ended with my half-humorous, utterly sincere offer to come to South Africa to teach the Hurt-Free model. I've spent the past three summers doing just that.

It didn't matter whether the school was located in Nashua or Kwa-Zulu Natal, we were both looking for the same thing: a way to teach and empower all children to claim their universal right to live in emotional, social and physical safety within a climate of peace and mutual respect.

As my work evolved, I developed the basic foundation for my vision: the positive presence of a school community that promises to work together to weave a web of emotional, social and physical safety around every child.

Of all the elements of a Hurt-Free School, I believe the most vital concept is that it is child-friendly.

I constantly remind myself of the child curled in the snow, now grown. What strategies could have made a difference for her in that bullying situation? What tools could she have used to understand her rights and to get the help she needed?

I believe that every intervention designed to build a climate of safety in school must be easily understood, developmentally appropriate and, most important, give children real tools they can use on the playground.

I chose the rainbow to embody my child-friendly vision. The "Rainbow of Safety," as I call it, meets all of my criteria: universal and protective, honoring individuality and celebrating diversity.

The words of children say it all:

It's a rainbow that goes over the whole school. Everyone is under it; no one is left out.

Even when there's a really scary storm with thunder and lightning, it makes you feel good to know that you might get to see a rainbow when the rain stops.

I don't have to be afraid to tell a bully to stop on my own because I know that other kids will come over to help me.

I know how and when to ask for help from an adult if I don't feel safe.

THE COLOR OF SAFETY

The Rainbow of Safety uses four colors to help children process decisions about their behaviors in school.

It is important to set firm guidelines regarding the use of these colors.

Children need to be reminded that the colors stand for the decisions they make about what they say or do. Young children should be reassured that choices can be changed, turning mistakes and missed opportunities into better decisions in the future.

True Blue

True Blue is the first color of our rainbow. This universal color of the sky represents the best of humankind: equity, respect, acceptance, kindness, responsibility and tolerance. True Blue is what we reach for under the Rainbow of Safety.

Again, my trip to South Africa reminded me of the universal message behind True Blue. Just as *life, liberty and the pursuit of happiness* have meaning to Americans, the word *ubuntu* has meaning to South Africans.

The Zulu word *ubuntu* describes our relationships to one another. Though difficult to define, *ubuntu* is, to me, the connection to one another that makes us uniquely human. To experience our humanity most fully, we must honor these bonds to one another, intertwining our journeys through life with mutual concern and respect.

The first time I used *ubuntu* to describe True Blue was in front of about 100 girls sitting cross-legged on the floor. The girls looked at each other, eye to eye, recognizing their mother tongue. It passed between them like a shock of electricity, leaving proud smiles and straightened shoulders.

I have adapted this word as one of the elements of the Rainbow of Safety in South Africa. *Ubuntu* in school means that we must work together if we want a safe school. If even one child is afraid to be hurt on the playground, our school is not a safe place.

When we are all watching for one another's safety, we know that:

- If you are hurt on the playground, someone will come over to see if you are all right.

- If you are alone, you are welcome to join in a game.
- If you are being teased by a bully, other children will come and tell the bully to stop.
- If you need help, ask an adult.

In real life, we know, adults struggle to reach True Blue behavior. How then can a child be expected to meet such lofty ideals?

The Rainbow of Safety uses the image of the traffic light (or robot in South Africa) to help children strive to be as Blue as possible. By using a universal image, like a real traffic light with cars approaching an intersection, children may look to the Rainbow's traffic light to guide them safely through their behavior decisions in school.

Growing Green

Growing Green is a comfortable, friendly color for most American children. It encourages them to act upon their best intentions, yet supports them if they fall short of their goals. Children are works in progress who must be given encouragement and as many successful experiences as possible.

Caution Yellow

Caution Yellow teaches children that thoughtless choices can take away others' rights and have significant impact on a school's level of safety. Children are urged to stop, think and make choices that turn Yellow behavior back to Green with words like:

I'm sorry.
I should not have said that.
I didn't mean to hurt you.
I'll try harder to pay more attention to your rights/feelings next time.

Yellow provides a concrete tool to help even the very young child grasp the subtle concepts behind social climate theory.

The Rainbow of Safety addresses the "spectator syndrome," which bullying depends upon for its ongoing survival. Choosing to look away, doing nothing or not seeking adult help when needed are unacceptable options in a Hurt-Free School. Children are taught that such choices jeopardize the safety of all and can turn Cau-

tion Yellow into Danger Red if better choices aren't made.

Danger Red

Danger Red hurts! It is never acceptable under the Rainbow of Safety. It differs from Yellow in that it represents a deliberate choice to hurt another person. Red behavior becomes bullying when it is hurtful, deliberate, repeated and continues even after the bully has been told to stop.

Our school now overflows with Rainbow of Safety language. Traffic lights are found in hallways and classrooms. Mini-traffic lights are on every student's desk, used in some cases as part of individual behavior contracts with teachers. Students use giant rainbow sunglasses, visors and teddy bears to role-play real-life behavior challenges.

If students are not listening attentively, the teacher stops and says quietly, "I will wait until your listening turns back to Green."

The morning announcements talk about True Blue with a behavior challenge such as: "Telling the truth is not as hard as it may seem. If you start to say something Yellow, stop and change it to Green."

The Rainbow of Safety offers a plan—indeed, a set of tools—to give schools the strategies they need to make every school day count for every child.

Rather than accept the hopelessness that keeps bullying alive, the Rainbow of Safety offers a neutral language that teaches all children to claim their rights to safety while respecting those of others.

So not only can you find that little girl curled up in the snow, but you can offer her tools to rejoin life, with safety and comfort, on the playground and in the classroom.

M. Christine Mattise, an elementary school guidance counselor in New Hampshire, has lectured extensively about bullying and violence-prevention character education in the U.S. and abroad. The author of several books, she can be reached through her websites: www.hurt-free-character.com or www.bullying-in-school.com.

UNIT 6

Cultural Diversity and Schooling

Unit Selections

Key Points to Consider

- What is multicultural education? To what does the national debate over multiculturalism in the schools relate? What are the issues regarding it?

- How would you define the equity issues in the field of education? How would you rank order them?

- What are the ways that a teacher can employ to help students understand the concept of culture?

- Critique the slogan, "Every child can learn." Do you find it true or false? Explain.

Student Website

www.mhcls.com/online

Internet References

Further information regarding these websites may be found in this book's preface or online.

American Scientist
http://www.amsci.org/amsci/amsci.html

American Studies Web
http://www.georgetown.edu/crossroads/asw/

National Institute on the Education of At-Risk Students
http://www.ed.gov/offices/OERI/At-Risk/

Prospects: The Congressionally Mandated Study of Educational Growth and Opportunity
http://www.ed.gov/pubs/Prospects/index.html

The concept of "culture" encompasses all of the life ways, customs, traditions, and institutions that a people develop as they create and experience their history and identity as a people. In the United States of America, many very different cultures coexist within the civic framework of a shared constitutional tradition that guarantees equality before the law for all. So, as we all have been taught, out of many peoples we are also one nation united by our constitutional heritage.

The civil rights movement in America in the 1950s and 1960s was about the struggle of cultural minorities to achieve equity: social justice before the law under our federal Constitution. The articles in this unit attempt to address some of these equity issues.

There is an immense amount of unfinished business before us in the area of intercultural relations in the schools and in educating all Americans regarding how multicultural our national population demographics really are. We are becoming more and more multicultural with every passing decade. This further requires us to take steps to ensure that all of our educational opportunity structures remain open to all persons regardless of their cultural backgrounds or gender. There is much unfinished business as well with regard to improving educational opportunities for girls and young women; the remaining gender issues in American education are very real and directly related to the issue of equality of educational opportunity.

Issues of racial prejudice and bigotry still plague us in American education, despite massive efforts in many school systems to improve racial and intercultural relations in the schools. Many American adolescents are in crisis as their basic health and social needs are not adequately met and their educational development is affected by crises in their personal lives. The articles in this unit reflect all of the above concerns plus others related to efforts to provide equality of educational opportunity to all American youth and attempts to clarify what multicultural education is and what it is not.

The "equity agenda," or social justice agenda, in the field of education is a complex matrix of gender- and culture-related issues aggravated by incredibly wide gaps in the social and economic opportunity structures available to citizens. We are each situated by cultural, gender-based, and socioeconomic factors in society; this is true of all persons everywhere. We have witnessed a great and glorious struggle for human rights in our time and in our nation. The struggle continues to deal more effectively with educational opportunity issues related to cultural diversity and gender.

The "Western canon" is being challenged by advocates of multicultural perspectives in school curriculum development. Multicultural educational programming, which will reflect the rapidly changing cultural demographics of North American schooling, is being advocated by some and strongly opposed by others. This controversy centers around several different issues regarding what it means to provide equality of opportunities for culturally diverse students. The traditional Western cultural content of general social studies and language arts curricula is being challenged as Eurocentric.

Helping teachers to broaden their cultural perspectives and to take a more global view of curriculum content is something that the advocates of culturally pluralistic approaches to curriculum development would like to see integrated into the entire elementary and secondary school curriculum structure. North America is as multicultural a region of the world as exists anywhere. Our enormous cultural diversity encompasses populations from many indigenous "First Americans" as well as peoples from every European culture, plus many peoples of Asian, African, and Latin American nations and the Central and South Pacific Island groups. There is spirited controversy over how to help all Americans to better understand our collective multicultural heritage. There are spirited defenders and opponents of the traditional Eurocentric curriculum.

The problem of inequality of educational opportunity is of great concern to American educators. One in four American children does not have all of basic needs met and lives under poverty conditions. Almost one in three lives in a single-parent home, which in itself is no disadvantage, but under conditions of poverty, it often is. More and more concern is expressed over how to help children of poverty. The equity agenda of our time has to do with many issues related to gender, race, and ethnicity. All forms of social deprivation and discrimination are aggravated by great dispar-ities in income and accumulated wealth. How can students be helped to have an equal opportunity to succeed in school?

Some of us are still proud to say that we are a nation of immigrants. In addition to the traditional minority/majority group relationships that evolved in the United States, new waves of immigrants today are again enhancing the importance of concerns for achieving equality of opportunity in education. In light of these vast sociological and demographic changes, we must ensure that we will remain a multicultural democracy.

The social psychology of prejudice is something that psychiatrists, social psychologists, anthropologists, and sociologists have studied in great depth since the 1930s. Tolerance, acceptance, and a valuing of the unique worth of every person are teachable and learnable attitudes. A just society must be constantly challenged to find meaningful ways to raise human aspirations, to heal human hurt, and to help in the task of optimizing every citizen's potential. Education is a vital component to that end. Teachers can incorporate into their lessons an emphasis on acceptance of difference, toleration of and respect for the beliefs of others, and the skills of reasoned debate and dialogue.

The struggle for optimal representation of minority perspectives in the schools will be a matter of serious concern to educators for the foreseeable future. From the many court decisions upholding the rights of women and cultural minorities in the schools over the past years has emerged a national consensus that we must strive for the greatest degree of equality in education as may be possible. The triumph of constitutional law over prejudice and bigotry must continue.

Brown at 50

Wendell LaGrand

A QUARTER CENTURY AGO, WHILE ATTEND-
ING A 25TH anniversary celebration of *Brown v. Board of
Education,* Constance Baker Motley was met at an Alabama airport by a college student who was assigned to
pick her up and take her to the event.

Now a senior U.S. district judge in New York City,
Motley had been a young lawyer on the staff of the
NAACP Legal Defense and Educational Fund Inc., the
group that litigated *Brown.*

When the student asked Motley about the conference,
she replied, "We are celebrating the 25th anniversary of
Brown."

The student responded, "Who's that?"

"And that," Motley told a conference on *Brown* this
winter, "is when I knew it was 25 years after *Brown.*" Another quarter century has passed, and yet another generation is primed for a refresher course on the landmark
case that added fire to the civil rights movement by ending legal segregation in public schools.

"*Brown* was a catalyst for forms of change in American
life and legal structures," says Louis H. Pollak, a federal
judge in Philadelphia who was part of the LDF staff in the
1950s. "It went beyond simply telling the government not
to enforce racial segregation. It put the force of law affir-
matively on the side of the promotion of equality. Without *Brown*, it's hard to see that we could have moved even
as far as we have."

Brown came at a watershed moment in American society. By the 1950s, the United States had beaten fascism
and was grappling with the communist world.

The great migration of African-Americans from the rural south led to the formation of new neighborhoods in
the industrial, urban North. The Brooklyn Dodgers'
Jackie Robinson had integrated baseball, and President
Truman had desegregated the armed forces—a key moment, according to Motley.

"That signaled a change in our nation's public policy,"
Motley told an audience at Columbia University this winter. "I feel the Supreme Court got its inspiration from Truman in 1948."

The grass roots were already pushing for change.
"Teachers organized themselves in Virginia," says Richmond, Va., lawyer Oliver Hill, also an LDF staff member.

"Prior to *Brown*, the impact of apartheid America was
felt by many of us," says LDF president Elaine Jones,
who will step down from that post in May. "I knew what
the back of the bus was like. I knew about the water
fountains—one marked white, the other marked black.
The segregation in the cafeteria, the auditoriums, even
in the courtrooms, it was a part of our natural fabric. It
was seismic. It ushered in the era of massive resistance."

Presiding over the band of LDF lawyers was Thurgood
Marshall, who masterminded the *Brown* litigation. A
larger-than-life figure, Marshall came to the National Association for the Advancement of Colored People as a
protégé of pioneering civil rights lawyer Charles Hamil-
ton Houston.

Marshall was one of the lawyers who argued the case
before the Supreme Court—which he later joined, becoming the first black justice.

Motley and Pollak were among the foot soldiers. They
burned the midnight oil at LDF's Manhattan headquarters,
dodged defiant law enforcement officers in the South, and
pressed their cases before reluctant judges. Other LDF colleagues included Hill; Robert L. Carter, now a federal
judge in New York City; William T. Coleman, now a Wash-

ington, D.C., attorney; Jack Greenberg, now a Columbia law professor; and the late James Nabrit Jr. and Spottswood Robinson.

"There could not have been anything more challenging than working with Thurgood and that group of extraordinary people," Pollak recalls. "Not only were they fine lawyers, they were fine citizens."

Volumes have since been written about Marshall, but to the young lawyers in his charge, Marshall provided focus, inspiration and leadership.

"He was an able lawyer, a leader with the most marvelous spirit about life and an extraordinary sense of humor that could deflate every pomposity," Pollak says.

"There were serious problems, both tactical and strategic," Pollak continues. "When we needed to make a decision, Thurgood made it. It taught us a lot about life."

In arguing the case before the high court, Marshall also had the task of going up against one of the most respected lawyers in history. John W. Davis was a master appellate litigator who had just scored a prominent victory in 1952 over President Truman in *Youngstown Sheet & Tube Co. v. Sawyer*, 343 U.S. 579, the steel seizure case.

Davis "was a marvelous lawyer who had to rely on the desirability of adhering to stare decisis," says Earl E. Pollock, who was a law clerk to Chief Justice Earl Warren. "That does not exactly get people's juices flowing."

"Marshall was very effective," Pollock adds. "To some extent, he had the advantage of being able to make a more emotional argument based on fairness and morality."

When the Supreme Court opinion was announced on May 17, 1954, the LDF lawyers were jubilant. But, at the same time, they realized how much of the battle was left to fight.

"The day it was announced, I was in New York," Judge Pollak says. "It was glorious news, perfectly terrific." But, he adds, "Many of us kind of naively thought the world would be transformed. We underestimated the resistance to change."

Carter, too, remembers when *Brown* was decided.

"Everyone thought [the civil rights battle] was over," Carter says. He soon realized, though, that "the problem was white supremacy" and the task to "remove the government mandate of segregation" would continue.

From *ABA Journal*, April 2004, pp. 38-39. Copyright © 2004 by American Bar Association. Reprinted by permission.

Learning To Teach in Urban Settings

Valerie Duarte and Thomas Reed

Teacher education programs throughout the United States are grappling with how to raise the achievement levels of children in diverse communities. The fact that urban schools show a downward trend in achievement levels among their student populations speaks to the gravity of the situation and brings to the forefront the need for more culturally responsive teachers in urban settings.

The challenge confronting urban schools results from a number of issues. Urban settings are historically more economically disadvantaged than suburban districts and therefore do not have the ability to offer competitive compensation packages to teachers. Urban schools also serve a student population that is characterized largely by poverty, and that is overwhelmingly minority (many non-English speaking). One of every three school-age children is from a minority background (National Center for Education Statistics [NCES], 2000), yet most are taught by white classroom teachers (National Education Association, 1997). The incongruity that exists between the student population and the curriculum being taught also speaks clearly to the need for more culturally responsive teachers (Gay, 2002). Furthermore, urban schools often experience a large turnover in their teaching staff from year to year, and so are unable to attract and retain highly qualified personnel (Oakes, Franke, Quartz, & Rogers, 2002). As a result, many urban classrooms are staffed with teachers who are new to the teaching field. Although these teachers' commitment to working with minority groups in urban settings may be strong, they often lack knowledge and understanding of the students' varied cultures (Gay, 2002; Sleeter, 2001).

Teacher candidates tend to view multicultural teaching primarily as planning "special events" outside of the everyday curriculum. For example, they might celebrate Black History Month in February by studying famous black Americans. Such a narrow view tends to distort children's understanding of culture as something separate and distinct from everyday life, reinforcing the notion that culture occurs outside of the classroom.

Teacher candidates need an understanding of urban cultures, as well as the pedagogy and skills that will help them implement a meaningful curriculum for urban students

> Teacher candidates need an understanding of urban cultures, as well as the pedagogy and skills that will help them implement a meaningful curriculum for urban students.

(Gay, 2002). They need to be more cognizant of the fact that a commitment to teach in urban settings goes beyond knowledge about the curriculum and how children learn and touches a much deeper issue—that of how to connect the curriculum to children's everyday lives. Teacher candidates need to make the classroom and the curriculum more congruent and more meaningful for children (Villegas & Lucas, 2002). A culturally responsive teacher uses the children's cultures and background experiences as instructional vehicles to make learning more effective. Research illustrates that connecting curriculum to culture can lead to improved academic achievement among diverse populations (Gay, 2002). Teachers cannot be expected to be culturally responsive in the classroom, however, if they are not adequately prepared with the necessary knowledge, skills, and dispositions.

Most universities require teacher candidates to take at least one course on multiculturalism (Artiles & McClafferty, 1998), sometimes at the beginning of the teacher education program. However, these courses may offer no more than a general awareness of the differences among cultures. It is difficult to determine accurately the impact of these courses, since studies regarding teacher candidates' particular beliefs and attitudes remain inconclusive (Sleeter, 2001). Nevertheless, it is clear that individual beliefs and attitudes are more likely to undergo change following in-depth investigation, dialogue, and continued support throughout the teacher education program. (Villegas & Lucas, 2002).

Figure 1

PURPOSE AND DESCRIPTION OF THE STUDY

In light of these challenges, the authors designed a project to address the need for more culturally responsive teachers. The teacher candidates in our program had limited background experiences in urban settings, making clear the need for a curriculum that provided a broader and more comprehensive view of what it means to teach in urban schools. In addition, candidates needed restructured field experiences, to help them decide whether or not they felt capable of meeting the challenge of teaching urban children.

Twenty early childhood education majors (18 female, 2 male; 19 white, 1 African American) enrolled in a 3-hour clinical experience conducted in a public school setting. During the fall semester, students completed an initial survey (see Figure 1) designed to reflect their attitudes, beliefs, and values towards teaching in urban settings. Upon their return in the spring semester, students were asked to volunteer for assignment in a rural school (control group) or an urban school (experimental group).

During the course of the spring semester, the students assigned at the urban school participated in two workshops given by a diversity expert in a school setting. Participants viewed, responded to, and reflected on two videos that were designed to raise social consciousness, and they read and reflected on two books covering diversity. Students assigned at the rural school received no additional training and support. At the conclusion of the semester, students in both groups revisited the initial survey.

The experimental group was assigned to an elementary school that is predominantly African American (98 percent). The school was selected for participation after researchers received a modest grant from the state

department of education for developing partnerships. Funds from the grant were used to buy books, provide the diversity speaker with a stipend, and give classroom teachers a small stipend for their participation. Many of the teachers at this school had taught there for a number of years, and therefore were experienced with the norms of the culture in this community. A strong commitment to education was evident in the large number of after-school activities and parent activities that were held at the school.

A diversity expert from a neighboring school district was asked to conduct two workshops at the school site. Since our preservice teachers were mostly white middle-class candidates, we hoped the workshops would help them become more knowledgeable regarding the impact of culture on learning, while providing them with opportunities for discussion and reflection.

The two books selected for use with the experimental group were *And Don't Call Me a Racist!* (Mazel, 1998) and *White Teacher* (Paley, 2000), both chosen for their contributions to understanding diverse issues in and out of the public school arena. Teacher candidates were asked to respond to a series of questions based on each of these books.

Two selections also were made from the video series *Teaching Children Tolerance*. Teacher candidates were asked to view and respond to "A Time for Justice" (Guggenheim, 1992) and "Starting Small" (McGovern, 1997). Again, candidates were asked to respond to a series of questions based on each of these videos.

FINDINGS

Initial Survey

Students' responses to the initial questionnaire indicated that our teacher candidates held stereotypical attitudes and beliefs regarding minority children and minority neighborhoods. Typically, they described a minority neighborhood as being low-income, and populated by people of color and people who spoke a language different from theirs. They described the children as underachievers, having behavior and learning problems, and living in homes where the parents did not care about their learning. Schools were described as old and dirty with boring classrooms, insufficient resources, and ineffective learning programs. They believed that what was being taught in the school may not be reinforced in the home. The 20 candidates' opinions mostly dovetailed, and tended to support other research findings regarding white preservice students' attitudes (Sleeter, 2001).

Almost all of the students agreed that the home played a significant role in children's learning, as it is the foundation for creating the strong positive belief system needed for achievement. Many students reported that language was another important aspect to consider. However, they offered few specifics regarding how to modify instruction to meet the urban children's needs.

When asked about the effect of children's physical and emotional needs on learning, most of the students agreed that these areas were important, but again gave no specific suggestions as to how to address these needs. The general consensus was that children's most basic needs could be met by giving hugs, offering snacks, and being loving. Most of the comments were teacher-centered and addressed a need for teachers to become more involved in those interpersonal activities with children that broaden communication. Beyond that, however, they showed little evidence of having strategies in mind that would improve instruction.

When asked about making a commitment to teaching in an urban school, about half of the respondents said they would accept a position; they reasoned that teachers can make a difference in the quality of schools and in the lives of children, and what better place to be than where they are needed. Others appeared more interested in receiving a salary and stated that teaching in an urban setting was better than not teaching at all. Some respondents said they would decline the opportunity to teach in an urban setting, citing their opinion, that the children there are poorly behaved.

When asked to identify experiences from our program that may have prepared them for teaching in an urban setting, the teacher candidates were ambivalent. Some mentioned previous practicum experiences, a course in children's literature, and language classes. At least three candidates believed that this part of their education was lacking and reported having had no learning experiences that helped prepare them for teaching diverse populations.

Responses to the Assigned Books

White Teacher. This book chronicles Vivian Paley's experiences as a white teacher in a predominantly black school. Teacher candidates were asked to read a selected chapter in the book and make a connection to their past experiences. Classroom management surfaced as a primary concern. Many students wrote of Paley's frustration regarding a perceived inability to be an effective classroom disciplinarian. The teacher candidates discussed, at some length, how children tend to carry "baggage" from home that makes it difficult to teach them and effectively manage classroom behavior. Teacher candidates also recognized that their lack of understanding of cultural terms and ethnic words and phrases contributed to the challenge of teaching.

And Don't Call Me a Racist! Teacher candidates were asked to read and respond to this book, which contains quotes (some historical) from famous and influential people regarding race. Students discussed what in the book made them angry, surprised, and proud. The comments varied widely, but many students were surprised about how often African Americans felt compelled to hide their color to get along in a white world. Many said they were impressed with the resilience, perseverance, and fortitude that African Americans exhibited in advancing the movement for racial equality.

Much of the rhetoric in this text—comments about selling slaves, blacks being inferior to whites, blacks being unable to think for themselves, the United States as a racist nation—angered the candidates. Several ideas in the readings made the candidates uncomfortable, chiefly: 1) being white affords you privileges unobtainable to minorities, 2) reverse discrimination is a way to make up for past atrocities, 3) the educated black person as a social monstrosity, and 4) some African Americans appear to suffer from a constant burden that never seems to go away. Several aspects made the candidates proud, beginning with the realization of all the gains regarding integration and equal opportunities that exist because of the civil rights movement, and that with a renewed emphasis on diversity, racism has a chance to be reduced further. Others thought that resisting old traditional viewpoints on an individual basis helped to reduce racism as a whole. However, what seemed to be most significant were the mentions of inspiring African Americans, such as Frederick Douglass, Oprah Winfrey, Colin Powell, Martin Luther King, Jr., and Maya Angelou.

Responses to the Videos

A Time for Justice. The students watched this video chronicling the civil rights movement, and were asked to respond to a questionnaire about the video and discuss it in a group. Several aspects of the video disturbed the candidates, including the images of white police officers going unpunished after beating civil rights protesters, the killing of white men who advocated for civil rights, churches being bombed, children needing the escort of the National Guard to enter public schools, and separate public facilities and restaurants for white and blacks. One candidate remarked, "I didn't know it was that bad."

Students also were asked to indicate how watching this video gave them hope. Many of the respondents were impressed by the dedication and commitment from those involved in the civil rights movement. The bus boycotts and sit-ins also impressed upon the students the importance of following through on a commitment.

Finally, students responded to questions about what they envisioned their role to be in eradicating discrimination. Candidates responded that guiding children to appreciate others and accept differences was paramount. They also mentioned the importance of teaching history and awareness of the civil rights movement as part of the curriculum, establishing a just and fair classroom, and using multicultural reading materials. The teacher as a role model seemed to be at the forefront of the students' ideas as the primary way to reduce discriminatory behavior and actions among school children.

Starting Small. The teacher candidates also viewed *Starting Small,* which shows a number of kindergarten settings around the United States where teachers are engaged in instruction focused on gaining understanding of one another's cultural differences, as well as appreciating how people are alike. Candidates responded to another questionnaire. Their discussion centered around the activities that were presented in the video and how these activities would enhance curriculum. The candidates found the video offered valuable information specific to activities that could be done in early childhood classrooms to incorporate the students' cultural backgrounds. Most of the students believed that teaching tolerance and a respect for diversity should be the foundation of the curriculum. They added that one way to accomplish this goal would be to bring speakers from the community into the classroom to discuss their cultures, and by having the children share artifacts from their home cultures that are connected to curriculum areas (e.g., a quilt from a Native American group showing mathematical patterns).

ENDING SURVEY

At the end of the spring semester, all 20 participants responded to the same questionnaire that they had been given in the fall. Their responses indicate that most had broadened their definition of what constituted an urban setting where the segment of student population was minority. Now, they recognized that all parents want the best for their children and that the circumstances of being at a low socioeconomic level do not necessarily indicate that children have poor ability or that schools are dysfunctional. At least one student indicated that some teachers have a preconceived notion regarding the achievement level of minority students that may negatively affect a teacher's expectations regarding achievement.

Control Group

When asked about the impact of culture on achievement, students from the control group seemed to confuse cultural background for socioeconomic status and they continued to believe that culture and academic success were connected; in other words, they seemed to consider that children from a lower socioeconomic base are not as likely to reach the same achievement levels as children from higher socioeconomic groups. Those from, a lower socioeconomic base are not likely to have the same knowledge foundation to build on; a lack of valuable home learning experiences and learning materials for children to use before coming to school would therefore have a negative impact on the child's ability to perform in school.

When asked about how they would meet the academic needs of children from diverse backgrounds, the control group stated that many activities should be created to address these differences, but gave no specific ideas for instructional strategies. In addition, the control group appeared more aware that trying home circumstances make it difficult for children to achieve in school, and that children might seek fulfillment through less acceptable means. The control group recognized the need for teachers to maintain a positive attitude and be approachable, and stated that teachers should be helpful and not penalize students. They suggested that lesson plans should facilitate

children's growth and development, and that seeking a one-to-one relationship with a needy child and seeking assistance from school personnel were positive steps to take.

When asked whether they would accept a position to teach in an urban school, most of the participants responded "Yes," citing that all children need someone to care for them, that they wanted to make a difference, and that it's an opportunity to have a positive impact in the lives of children. One respondent said, "Yes, I am a teacher." We viewed these responses as altruistic, stemming from the idea that a teacher is a professional who has a duty to perform. However, two respondents replied "no"; one stated, "No, [I wouldn't accept the position] unless it was the only one offered."

The control group participants believed that previous practicum programs gave them the opportunity to learn about diversity. Both settings were primarily in schools populated by African American children.

Experimental Group

Students in the experimental groups also appeared to have a much broader sense of what constituted teaching in an urban setting where the segment of the student population was minority. The respondents overwhelmingly noted that a child's background can affect achievement, and that minority children often have fewer learning experiences and less formally educated parents to help them at home. When asked about strategies needed to modify instruction, the experimental group offered clearly defined ideas, including: utilizing real-life scenarios that would make learning experiences more meaningful; presenting materials to accommodate different learning styles; utilizing multicultural and diverse literature to focus on issues supporting the minority experience; knowing more about the children and designing instruction to facilitate learning that includes their cultural background; modifying and adjusting instruction as needed; and providing one-on-one instruction and involving parents as classroom assistants, as well as keeping them informed about what is going on in the classroom. One respondent pointed out that "doing what benefits everyone" is key to any successful instructional strategy.

Most of the students agreed that children suffering from emotional distress because of their home circumstances will find it difficult to concentrate and focus on the task at hand while at school—they will be easily distracted, and may distract others as well. Teachers need to remember that when children come to school worried about family problems, their motivation to learn will be impaired. One respondent indicated that if teachers were aware of Maslow's hierarchy of needs and designed instruction to facilitate emotional development, students would be more likely to perform better.

The experimental group stated that teachers need to include activities focused on enhancing and building self-esteem among children, allowing time for talking about problems, and using play as a means to respond to problems. They mentioned safety as an important issue and stressed that children should feel safe coming to school and living in the community. They also stressed the importance of working with families by identifying community resources. Many of the suggestions centered on stressing to the family the need to seek help in solving a problem before the child is enrolled in school.

When asked about making a commitment to teach in an urban school, the experimental group reported overwhelmingly that this was what they wanted to do. This group showed a clear change in perception, expressing confidence in themselves with such comments as, "Yes, I have what it takes" and "Yes, because I expect to be the best," while the control group's support for acceptance of a position was the result of feeling it to be their responsibility as a teacher. Some respondents continued to be unsure, stating that they needed more experience, or that they felt as though they were not up to the challenge of teaching in an urban school.

The respondents credited previous methods and practicum experiences with providing them opportunities to learn about diversity issues. Even more so, they gave overwhelming credit to the workshops, mentors, and diverse activities provided through this project as a very significant part of their overall experience, and as the key to their growing confidence and desire to teach in urban settings.

DISCUSSION

In this project, the authors sought information that would serve as a guide in preparing a stronger undergraduate program for teaching in urban settings. We recognized that a well-designed teacher education program is vital for increasing the number of culturally responsive teachers in schools, and it is our goal to ensure the readiness of teacher candidates as effectively as we can. We also recognize that due to candidates' limited experiences, we need to restructure field experiences to include opportunities for candidates to grow in the strategies needed to be successful in urban settings.

At the same time, we wanted candidates to examine their own beliefs and attitudes regarding teaching in diverse settings, and to be able to refine these same beliefs. We hoped that they would identify strategies that could be incorporated into their teaching styles and enhance their ability to teach in urban settings. Ultimately, we hoped to increase the percentage of participants who would feel comfortable accepting a teaching position in an urban setting.

We believe the experimental group very clearly found themselves to be better informed due to the opportunities built into the project. Research states that merely placing promising

candidates in urban settings is not enough to ensure their success, or that their confidence and skills will grow. They also need opportunities to openly discuss their beliefs and actions with expert teachers in the classroom. The experimental group stated that they had learned more about how to deal with the community and cultural norms of the school population, citing specific ways in which children's needs should be met (e.g., providing food, keeping children safe). Their responses demonstrated a child-centered approach, whereas responses from the control group focused on teacher-centered actions (i.e., don't penalize, be positive, remember that teachers are there to be helpful).

The experimental group showed a change in perception about themselves as opposed to the control group, whose purpose was mainly the result of feeling that this was their responsibility as a teacher. The experimental group demonstrated a more sensitive disposition to the needs of children in urban settings and the project helped them make the choice to seek a position in an urban community.

References

Artiles, A., & McClafferty, K. (1998). Learning to teach culturally diverse learners: Charting change in preservice teachers' thinking about effective teaching. *The Elementary School Journal, 98*(3), 189-211.

Gay, G. (2002). Preparing for culturally responsive teaching. *Journal of Teacher Education, 53*(2), 106-117.

Guggenheim, C. (1992). *A time for justice. America's civil rights movement* [video]. Montgomery, AL: Teaching Children Tolerance.

Mazel, E. (Ed.). (1998). *And don't call me a racist!* Lexington, MA: Argonaut Press.

McGovern, M. (1997). *Starting small. Teaching tolerance: A project of the Southern Poverty Law Center* [video]. Montgomery, AL: Teaching Children Tolerance.

National Center for Education Statistics. (2000). *Digest of educational statistics.* Washington, DC: Government Printing Office.

National Education Association. (1997). The status of American public school teachers, 1995-96. Washington, DC: Author.

Oakes, J., Franke, M., Quartz, K., & Rogers, J. (2002). Research for high-quality urban teaching: Defining it, developing it, assessing it. *Journal of Teacher Education, 53*(3), 228-235.

Paley, V. (2000). *White teacher* (3rd ed.). Cambridge, MA: Harvard University Press.

Sleeter, C. (2001). Preparing teachers for culturally diverse schools: Research and the overwhelming presence of whiteness. *Journal of Teacher Education, 52*(2), 94-106.

Villegas, A. M., & Lucas, T. (2002). Preparing culturally responsive teachers: Rethinking the curriculum. *Journal of Teacher Education, 53*(1), 20-33.

Valerie Duarte and *Thomas Reed* are Associate Professors, School of Education, University of South Carolina Spartanburg.

Challenging Assumptions About the Achievement Gap

The national dialogue about the achievement gap can help policy makers and educators find ways to better serve minority students. However, school policy and practice must be founded not on perceptions of group stereotypes, Mr. Ramirez and Mr. Carpenter argue, but on knowledge about each student's needs and strengths.

AL RAMIREZ AND
DICK CARPENTER

HERE IN Colorado, snow is particularly significant. It affects our economy through winter recreation and tourism, reduces the danger of forest fires , and provides water for most residents. And while to the casual observer the snow all looks the same, Coloradans know differently. We evaluate each snowfall not only by its quantity but also by its quality, that is, how wet it is. Sometimes the moisture content of the snow is low, which sets off a rush of snowboarders and skiers to the mountains but supplies little water to the arid landscape. Other times the moisture content is high, which contributes greatly to the state's water supply. Thus differences within the general category of snow are critical to our state's health and future.

Similarly, "within-group" differences are important to recognize when we look at student achievement, particularly as it relates to race or ethnicity. Since the *Brown v. Board of Education* decision more than 50 years ago, much attention has been paid to significant "between-group" differences. This focus resulted in policies and practices designed to reduce such disparities. Yet, until quite recently, educational researchers, policy makers, and practitioners have paid far less attention to within-group differences that are probably as important as those between groups and could, in fact, help us figure out how to narrow the differences between groups.

Take, for example, Latinos, who now constitute the largest minority group in the U.S. and who are certainly well represented in the public schools.[1] As a group, Latino students share many similar characteristics that set them apart from other groups. On average, Latino students tend to be poorer, attend more segregated schools, and live in urban areas. Latino students also account for the largest number of students served in programs of English-language acquisition. While these characteristics typify the group of students we call Latinos, it would be a mistake to assume that all Latino students have similar needs or require the same type of education.[2]

Yet current policies and educational practices directed toward Latino students are built on such assumptions and have had the unintended consequence of hurting the students' futures, educational and otherwise. Among these overgeneralized policies and practices are presuming that all students with Spanish surnames need English-language-acquisition classes; creating a policy of defacto segregation by assigning Latino students only to schools with English as a Second Language (ESL) programs; and presuming Latino students are potential dropouts rather than college-bound students.

When policy makers and education professionals remain oblivious to these false assumptions, misinterpretations occur, and stereotypical thinking prevails. Indeed, our investigation of the achievement gap underscores the relative insignificance of race and ethnicity, compared to other factors that most affect student learning. Furthermore, we have found that the "achievement gap" between Latino and white students may be a "phantom gap" derived from the practice of lumping all nonwhite students into a single comparison group. In short, the importance of within-group differences eclipses the importance of between-group differences.

ACHIEVEMENT GAP RESEARCH

Research on the academic achievement gap between majority and minority students is sometimes misapplied by policy makers and practitioners, and this in turn can lead to ineffective and even counterproductive programs for students.[3] Media coverage further exacerbates this misunderstanding about the lagging academic performance of minority groups, for it oversimplifies complex data in order to fit the conventions of news reporting and to manufacture catchy headlines. Moreover, policy discussions and debates about the achievement gap have missed the mark by casting the problem as a "minority group" phenomenon, without considering the dynamic interplay of variables that affect the learning of any individual child.

Of the achievement gap research that does consider factors in addition to race or ethnicity, much of it involves such home-based variables as socioeconomic status, home language, and parent involvement or such school-based variables as school segregation and teacher quality. However, the findings are far from conclusive.

Beginning with home-based variables, much of the research indicates that the income level of a student's family is highly correlated with academic success in school, a phenomenon that is indeed true for Latino students.[4] Moreover, in some studies the effect of socioeconomic status often overwhelms the relationship between race or ethnicity and academic achievement, since minority groups tend to be overrepresented among the poor. Yet not all researchers agree about the impact of socioeconomic status on student learning, and some cite other factors as having more influence.[5]

Regarding home language, the research remains mixed and crammed with cross-cutting issues. Some researchers believe that a student's language background is central to success in school, particularly when it is related to the level of parents' education.[6] For example, the U.S. Department of Education reported that, in 1999, the percentage of Latino parents with a high school or higher education was 49% for those who spoke mostly Spanish at home and 83% for those who spoke mostly English at home. Other researchers find that maintaining Spanish as the home language enhances academic achievement when combined with other factors.[7] Still others contend that language background accounts for little in explaining student achievement.[8]

In contrast to the mixed findings on the role of language, there is general agreement among researchers on the importance of parent involvement, particularly for black and Latino students.[9] While parent involvement takes many forms, numerous researchers have concluded that the most significant type is assisting children with schoolwork at home.[10] Parent involvement also plays an important role in students' course-taking patterns. For example, James Valadez illustrates how Latino parents influence their children's enrollment in algebra and advanced mathematics courses.[11]

Turning to school-based variables, some researchers conclude that school segregation significantly affects the academic achievement of minority students. Gary Roberts describes a spiraling relationship in which student achievement and segregation interact in a negatively correlated fashion.[12] John Ogbu writes of a "cultural ecological" model in which minority students perceive ongoing patterns of discrimination and prejudice when comparing their experiences to those of their majority peers, which then inhibits academic achievement.[13] Other authors have identified what they call an "oppositional culture," which is most prevalent in schools with smaller percentages of minority students.[14] In such situations, minority student engagement, participation, and achievement all suffer, and any achievement gap is exacerbated.

Finally, although teacher quality has enjoyed attention in the literature of the achievement gap, researchers differ regarding its significance. For example, Harold Wenglinsky, Jonah Rockoff, and Peter Denner and his colleagues all find a strong relationship between teacher quality, defined in terms of training or experience, and student learning.[15] Yet Theodore Eisenberg indicates that advanced subject-matter knowledge on the part of teachers does not translate into higher levels of student learning.[16] Considering the emphasis given to this factor in the No Child Left Behind Act and the importance this law attaches to closing the achievement gap, teacher quality is a particularly salient variable.

WHAT WE STUDIED

Based on our experiences in schools and our review of the educational research on the achievement gap, we hypothesized that academic achievement for Latino students would be based on factors similar to those that affect all students. Furthermore, we hypothesized that within-group differences in the Latino student population would be much larger than the differences between white students and Latino students. In order to test these suppositions, we examined data in the National Educational Longitudinal Study (NELS:88).

NELS:88 is a comprehensive study authorized by the U.S. Congress and conducted by the National Center for Education Statistics. It is a series of cohort studies of American students that began in 1988 with eighth-grade students who were followed into high school, postsecondary education, and the work force. Follow-up studies were done in 1990, 1992, 1994, and 2000. NELS:88 uses both questionnaire data and test data for each student. In addition, NELS:88 involves questionnaires for the school principal, for two teachers, and for parents.

The sample for our study was drawn from the 12th-grade follow-up study. To determine both within-and between-group differences, we calculated effects for whites, blacks, and Latinos. Thus our sample included data on 15,618 students: 2,170 Latinos, 1,660 blacks, and 11,788 whites. We chose to look at mathematics as the measure of student achievement. While including other subjects would provide a more complete picture of achievement, idiosyncrasies of the database required that we limit our achievement measure to mathematics only.

The NELS:88 database contains many hundreds of possible variables to draw upon and combine in examining factors that could be important to student achievement. Thus it was necessary for us to identify factors that, based on other research, have been shown to influence student learning generally. Our review led us to investigate the relationship between mathematics achievement and the following variables:

- socioeconomic status,
- language other than English regularly spoken at home,
- participation at any time in an ESL program,
- time spent on homework,
- class size,
- number of minority students in the class,
- number of units of algebra taken,
- number of undergraduate courses taken by the teacher in the subject he or she teaches most frequently,
- number of graduate courses taken by the teacher in the subject he or she teaches most frequently,
- family composition (i.e., two parents in the home),
- level of parent involvement, and
- urbanicity (i.e., urban, suburban, or rural).

FINDINGS AND RECOMMENDATIONS

Our analysis discovered that the "achievement gap" really consists of "multiple gaps" that exist both between and within groups. Socioeconomic status and participation in ESL were the most significant factors for all groups of students. For the most part, white and Latino student achievement were mirror images of each other, and each was affected similarly by each of the factors we examined. But this was not the case for black students in the sample. For example, Latino and white student achievement reflected similar differences based on urbanicity, but the same did not hold true for black students. Latino students who spoke English at home, who had never been enrolled in an ESL class, who came from intact families, and who spent more time on homework demonstrated higher levels of academic achievement than Latino students who did not share these characteristics. These relationships were similar for white students.

Turning to between-group differences, none of the variables we considered revealed a statistically significant gap between whites and Latinos. Socioeconomic background, experience in an ESL class, units of algebra, and level of parent involvement had a similar impact on the achievement of both white and Latino students. How-

ever, hours of homework were not a good predictor of student achievement for Latino students, while this variable was a good predictor for both black students and white students. Finally, while the differences we found between white students and Latino students were not significant, the differences between black students and white students and between black students and Latino students were significant.

While these findings are important, a caveat is worth bearing in mind. They do not indicate a simple, straight-line relationship, in which increases or decreases in one variable affect student achievement in direct proportion. Nevertheless, our findings do clearly indicate that family income, the number of parents in the home, the number of algebra units taken, the level of parent involvement, and the level of English-language skills are significant predictors of academic achievement for Latino students. Moreover, the differences on these factors among Latinos are greater than those between Latinos and whites. And many of the same factors exert a similar effect on achievement for white students.

Our research also indicates that the achievement gap is not monolithic. Instead, it is a richly textured, complex, and nuanced framework. Our findings underscore the need to disaggregate student data into many combinations of subsets in order to understand the dynamic relationships that exist within and between groups. The practice of lumping together data from all students of color—and even data from divisions within a single group—is a mistake that is bound to produce poor policy choices and poor educational practices.

Data-driven decision making is gaining popularity with educators and policy leaders. This methodology holds much promise to help us better understand the needs of students, to evaluate the effectiveness of our education programs, and to inform parents and key stakeholders about our schools. However, we must remain wary of the allure of numbers and conscious of the destructiveness of flawed research. We must be careful about jumping to conclusions simply because we find a number that implies a difference between groups of students. We must always investigate the underlying factors that contribute to the average score for any group of students. As our research demonstrates, taking action based on limited data and analysis is professionally irresponsible. We have an ethical obligation to be thorough in our understanding of the phenomena we study in our schools.

Finally, what is evident from our investigation is that both school-based factors and home-based factors are important to the success of every child, regardless of racial or ethnic differences. School policy and practice must be founded not on perceptions of group stereotypes, but rather on knowledge about each student's needs and strengths. Thus the voices of parents, teachers, and students must be included when practitioners and policy makers seek to design better ways to serve students. The national dialogue about the achievement gap has the potential to help policy makers and educators find ways to better serve Latino and other minority students. But if we are to create such constructive policies, research and practice must be based on thoughtful reflection about what we know rather than what we assume.

References

1. Gill Griffin, "Color Change: African-Americans and Latinos Reassess Their Relationships in Wake of Changing Demographics," *San Diego Union-Tribune*, 23 February 2003, pp. 1-2.
2. Hersholt C. Waxman, Shwu-yong L. Huang, and Yolanda N. Padron, "Motivation and Learning Environment Differences Between Resilient and Nonresilient Latino Middle School Students," *Hispanic Journal of Behavioral Sciences*, vol. 19, 1997, pp. 137-56.
3. Fenwick W. English, "On the Intractability of the Achievement Gap in Urban Schools and the Discursive Practice of Continuing Racial Discrimination," *Education and Urban Society*, vol. 34, 2002, pp. 298-311; and Alejandro Portes and Rubén G. Rumbaut, *Immigrant America: A Portrait* (Berkeley: University of California Press, 1990).
4. Sampson L. Blair and Marilou C. Legazpi, "Racial/Ethnic Difference in High School Students' Academic Performance: Understanding the Interweave of Social Class and Ethnicity in the Family Context," *Journal of Comparative Family Studies*, vol. 30, 1999, pp. 539-55; and Alejandro Portes and Dag McLeod, "Educational Progress of Children of Immigrants: The Roles of Class, Ethnicity, and School Context," *Sociology of Education*, vol. 69, 1996, pp. 255-75.
5. Sharon Anne O'Conner and Kathleen Miranda, "The Linkages Among Family Structure, Self-Concept, Effort, and Performance on Mathematics Achievement of American High School Students by Race," *American Secondary Education*, vol. 31, 2002, pp. 72-95; and Sammis B. White, "Socioeconomic Status and Achievement Revisited," *Urban Education*, vol. 28, 1993, pp. 328-43.
6. Tracey Derwing et al., "Some Factors That Affect the Success of ESL High School Students," *Canadian Modern Language Review*, vol. 55, 1999, pp. 532-47.
7. David P. Dolson, "The Effects of Spanish Home Language Use on the Scholastic Performance of Hispanic Pupils," *Journal of Multilingual and Multicultural Development*, vol. 6, 1985, pp. 135-55; and Ana Celia Zentella, "Latino Youth at Home, in Their Communities, and in School: The Language Link," *Education and Urban Society*, vol. 30, 1997, pp. 122-30.
8. David Adams et al., "Predicting the Academic Achievement of Puerto Rican and Mexican-American Ninth-Grade Students," *Urban Review*, vol. 26, 1994, pp. 1-14; and Raymond Buriel et al., "The Relationship of Language Brokering to Academic Performance, Biculturalism, and Self-Efficacy Among Latino Adolescents," *Hispanic Journal of Behavioral Sciences*, vol. 20, 1998, pp. 283-96.
9. William Jeynes, "A Meta-analysis: The Effects of Parental Involvement on Minority Children's Academic Achievement," *Education and Urban Society*, vol. 35, 2003, pp. 202-18.
10. Charles V. Izzo et al., "A Longitudinal Assessment of Teacher Perceptions of Parent Involvement in Children's Education and School Performance," *American Journal of Community Psychology*, vol. 27, 1999, pp. 817-39.
11. James R. Valadez, "The Influence of Social Capital on Mathematics Course Selection by Latino High School Students," *Hispanic Journal of Behavioral Sciences*, vol. 24, 2002, pp. 319-39.
12. Gary J. Roberts, "The Effect of Achievement on Student Friendships in Desegregated Schools," *Equity and Choice*, vol. 5, 1989, pp. 31-36; Russell W. Rumberger and J. Douglas Willms, "The Impact of Racial and Ethnic Segregation on the Achievement Gap in California High Schools," *Educational Evaluation and Policy Analysis*, vol. 14, 1992, pp. 377-96; and Richard R. Valencia, "Inequalities and the Schooling of Minority Students in Texas: Historical and Contemporary Conditions," *Hispanic Journal of Behavioral Sciences*, vol. 22, 2000, pp. 445-59.
13. John U. Ogbu, *Minority Education and Caste: The American System in Cross-Cultural Perspective* (New York: Academic Press, 1978).
14. Jeremy D. Finn and Kristin E. Voelkl, "School Characteristics Related to Student Engagement," *Journal of Negro Education*, vol. 62, 1993, pp. 249-68; and Tomas D. Rodriguez, "Oppositional Culture and Academic Performance Among Children of Immigrants in the U.S.," *Race, Ethnicity, and Education*, vol. 5, 2002, pp. 199-216.
15. Harold Wenglinsky, "How Schools Matter: The Link Between Teacher Classroom Practices and Student Academic Performance," *Education Policy Analysis Archives*, vol. 10, 2002, available at http://epaa.asu.edu/epaa/v10n12; Jonah Rockoff, "The Impact of Individual Teachers on Student Achievement: Evidence from Panel Data," abstract available at http://econwpa.wustl.edu/eprints/pe/papers/0304/0304002.abs; and Peter R. Denner et al., "Connecting Performance to Student Achievement: A Generalization and Validity Study of the Renaissance Teacher Work Samples Assessment," paper presented at the annual meeting of the Association of Teacher Educators, Jacksonville, Fla., 2003.
16. Theodore A. Eisenberg, "Begle Revisited: Teacher Knowledge and Student Achievement in Algebra," *Journal for Research in Mathematics Education*, vol. 8, 1997, pp. 216-22.

AL RAMIREZ *is an associate professor in the Department of Educational Leadership & Policy Studies, University of Denver.* ***DICK CARPENTER*** *is an assistant professor in the Department of Leadership, Research, and Foundations, University of Colorado, Colorado Springs.*

The Challenge of Diversity and Choice

Charles Glenn

More than twenty years ago, an urban superintendent in Massachusetts lamented to me that he was being asked to encourage differences among the schools in his district. For decades he had sought to ensure that all the schools in his district were as similar as possible, that it wouldn't matter where a student was assigned. Now, to help parents choose out-of-neighborhood schools and thus facilitate voluntary racial integration, he was being asked in the name of "educational equity" to undo what he had devoted his career to doing—also in the name of educational equity. Wouldn't helping schools become distinctive create new inequalities and injustices? he asked.

It was a good question—one that I found myself answering frequently in twenty-one years of directing the state's educational-equity efforts. On the one hand, I told administrators, educators should work to eliminate differences in educational quality, as measured both by inputs of schooling (the training and experience of teachers, for example, and the quality of facilities and other resources) and by outputs of instruction (performance on standardized tests, persistence in education). Those battles are far from won, even after the past thirty or forty years of massive spending and other efforts in the name of equal educational opportunity. In particular, the gap in educational effectiveness among schools in different communities is inexcusably large—in fact, larger than in other Western democracies with diverse populations.

On the other hand, schools of equal educational quality need not be identical, and the recent trend toward increased choice and diversity in American schooling has if anything made the system more equitable for children who previously had no choice but to attend poorly performing schools. That is not to say that all forms of school choice are good public policy: as I will suggest, choice can have positive or negative effects, depending upon the policy framework that guides it.

First, though, a quick overview of what I mean by choice and diversity: In 1970, when I began my career as a state education official, American public schools varied widely in both quality and curricula, but it was essentially an unacknowledged variation, the guilty secret behind what I would later call "the myth of the common school." In most cases, local officials assigned students to public schools according to where they lived. Parents dissatisfied with assignments often enrolled their children in tuition-charging private schools (if they lived in a city, usually Roman Catholic schools) or moved to different districts; in a few cases

local policies allowed them to transfer their children on a space-available basis. (In fact, when my division of the Massachusetts Department of Education set out to achieve racial desegregation of the Boston public schools, it found that some 7,000 white students had taken advantage of open enrollment to flee their neighborhood schools in racially changing parts of the city.)

By contrast, parents and students in Boston today can access a bewildering menu of educational opportunities. There are now numerous moderately priced private schools, either non-Roman Catholic or nonsectarian and nonreligious (although fewer Roman Catholic schools are available). More significant, there is a choice process for public school enrollment. Parents indicate their school preferences through parent information centers, and school assignments seek to fulfill those preferences, with random selection for oversubscribed schools.

The first such methods of "controlled choice," pioneered in Cambridge and then adopted in a dozen other Massachusetts cities, were intended not only to increase racial and social class integration but also to allow the staff of each school to develop distinctive educational identities that would satisfy some parents very much rather than barely satisfy many. Nonetheless, policymakers and parents soon discovered that the inflexibility of the school systems limited the schools' distinctiveness. Thus Massachusetts (like two-thirds of all states) adopted charter school legislation that has fostered dozens of new public schools, each approved by the state for its distinctive approach. In response, the Boston Public Schools adopted its own program of distinctive pilot schools freed from some local requirements and went on to break up high schools into smaller units, each with its own flavor and mission.

My oldest grandson, whose family lives in Boston, entered first grade this fall; his parents spent months considering all the alternatives available. Elsewhere, many parents have even more alternatives, including cyberschools, whose students never meet their teachers or one another, and in three states voucher programs, with others on the way.

Americans have good reason to welcome this evolution, though there are dangers. Those who urge expanded parental choice in U.S. schools advance four primary arguments; most advocates employ all four, though generally one or another is emphasized:

1. The liberty to shape the education of one's children through school choice is a fundamental matter guaranteed by international human rights covenants.

2. Publicly funded school choice is especially a matter of justice for poor parents because more-affluent parents already have their choice of schools.

3. Market pressures, freedom from bureaucracy, and the opportunity to focus on a clearly defined mission will make schools more effective educationally.

4. Variety in the forms of schooling is inherently a good thing, given that pupils have differing strengths and needs and respond well to different approaches—the implication, after all, of Howard Gardner's theory of multiple intelligences.

Correspondingly, four primary arguments are raised against school choice—usually without mentioning the ways in which choice threatens the educational status quo.

1. School choice may lead to increased racial and social class segregation.

2. Choice will lead to (further) degradation of the public educational system (or, in the case of choice limited to public schools, to the schools that are already least successful), and thus to inferior education for those who do not participate.

3. Choice will lead to new injustices since the poor will not be able to participate on equal terms.

4. Choice will lead to Balkanization of American society and further conflict by exposing various groups to divisive influences, rather than the socialization provided by the common public school.

Most thoughtful advocates of expanded school choice concede—certainly I do—that all those possibilities are real and serious unless choice is organized effectively, and some thoughtful opponents concede that it is possible to organize choice to prevent negative effects. The dispute often, therefore, comes down to whether the positive effects of choice can be enjoyed and the negative ones prevented once choice is widely available.

Several years ago Joe Nathan of the University of Minnesota and I, longtime allies in working for school reform, spent a day together identifying our agreements and disagreements about parental choice of schools. Dr. Nathan opposes supporting religious schools with public funds (either directly or with vouchers), funding single-sex schools, and allowing schools to set admissions requirements related to their educational mission; I support all three under some circumstances. The result was agreement on the principles any acceptable school choice policy must reflect (see accompanying table).

It will be obvious from this extensive list that neither of us is a libertarian, willing to "let the market rip" or "let the devil take the hindmost." Instead, though we differ on whether some forms of educational diversity, such as schools with a religious character, should be eligible for public support, we agree that school choice

should operate within a solid framework of policies and public accountability to ensure that all children benefit.

* * * * *

This article could go on at length about what form policies friendly to parental choice should take: just last year I published, with a European colleague, a two-volume study of how twenty-six different countries have regulated the provision of schooling in order to balance school autonomy and public accountability. Here, however, I'd like to warn of a danger that can be addressed effectively only by educators, not by government. A painstakingly designed system of public school diversity and choice might allow teachers and other educators to design the schools of their dreams and allow parents to choose among those schools based on solid information about each, all within a framework of protection and accountability—yet the resulting schools might largely prove uninspired carbon copies produced by educators lacking the foggiest idea of how to do anything differently.

I first contemplated that possibility in the late 1980s, when the Boston Public Schools' new "controlled choice" policy required schools to attract pupils without relying on attendance zones to provide a guaranteed clientele. Each school had unprecedented flexibility to redesign its programs and to use external funding to support its distinctive mission. Any school that was not attracting enough applications received generous paid planning time after school and over the summer, as well as a budget for outside consultants of its choosing, to develop attractive programs. A state-federal task force I headed scoured the country for alternative models of effective urban education that schools could adopt.

In some cases, the response from individual teachers or from whole groups of teachers was gratifying, and many schools underwent significant changes. In most cases, though, teachers were reluctant to identify meaningful aspects of the school that required change: "more parking for the teachers" was the only result of one school's planning process! In some cases, the action plans were concerned more with improving the image of the schools than with improving their instructional programs.

There is probably a more basic issue, too: public schools have long practiced a sort of defensive teaching designed not to offend any parent —in effect, "the bland leading the bland." As my book *The Myth of the Common School* shows, urban public schools with large immigrant enrollments came under pressure in the 1850s to remove textbooks that offended Roman Catholics; in the 1970s, my office required every school district in Massachusetts to review all its materials for "sex-role stereotyping" and any failure to reflect the diversity of American society. The courts are frequently the first resort of parents offended by this or that their children experience in school.

Such concerns are often legitimate, and a system of mandatory schooling must be extremely careful not to indoctrinate children or offend their consciences. But the cumulative impact upon public schools has too often led

A Model School Choice Policy

School choice must:

a. Provide better education for poor children and more effective involvement for their parents (the bottom-line criterion for judging whether a school choice policy is acceptable)

b. Provide for more accountability for validly measurable educational outcomes than now provided by public schooling based upon a local monopoly

c. Be based upon clear standards for the educational outcomes that every pupil should achieve at every level in order to participate effectively in our society, political order, and economy

d. Forbid discrimination in admission to schools, or in employment at those schools, on the basis of race

e. Make effective provision for outreach to parents, especially low-income and language-minority parents, to ensure that they are well informed about the choices available and how those can be matched with the strengths, needs, and interests of their children, and with their own hopes and beliefs about education

f. Ensure that geography and the availability of affordable housing do not prevent low-income families from having access to the full range of opportunities, including help with transportation

g. Ensure that no participating school lacks adequate safeguards for treating pupils and teachers fairly and respectfully

h. Ensure that the interests of pupils with special needs, limited proficiency in English, or other conditions requiring additional assistance are met adequately and, so far as possible, while safeguarding their parents' opportunity to make choices about their education

i. Ensure that the resources available to pupils in different schools—teachers and other staff as well as facilities and materials—are adequate and are not based upon their parents' wealth

j. Bar the participation of schools that teach hatred or disrespect for any racial, religious, ethnic, or sexual group

k. Ensure that there are real choices available and that meeting the criteria listed above does not impose a drab uniformity of curriculum, school life, or teaching style

l. Ensure autonomy to make staffing and budgetary decisions at the school level (in order to protect the distinctive character of schools among which parents can choose, based upon clarity of mission and a shared understanding of education)

m. Ensure that reform efforts are applied in a context in which any school that receives public funding, including a "regular" public school, bears the same responsibility as charter schools either to improve its educational results (as measured by standardized tests and other valid indicators over a three-to five-year period) or to be closed

to lowest-common-denominator education, so apprehensive of offending anyone that it fails to engage students in their own education or to expose them to the strongly held and well-argued positions that could provide them with models as they develop their own—often very different—convictions.

That, I suggest, is an additional reason we should do everything possible to develop schools that are truly distinctive—not simply different in some superficial way, but distinctive because the individuals who work in them share a clear set of educational ideas that will ordinarily be based upon a common understanding of human nature and the goals of human development.[1] That characteristic, more than any organizational arrange-

ment, is surely the reason for the repeatedly documented effectiveness of Roman Catholic schools in educating African-American youth and, in other countries, for the similar effectiveness of schools with a clearly defined educational mission.

By the same token, educators are free to create such distinctive schools only if well-informed parents are free to choose or reject them. The more that such schools come into existence, the more that prospective parents will need accurate, reliable information about each school's educational criteria. Yet even the best-designed system of parental choice, with all the bells and whistles of accountability, parent information, and protections against discrimination, will prove ineffective not only if it lacks significant choices but also if they are made (as happens all too often) according to socioeconomics or to minority enrollments. School choice promotes equity only if it provides parents with better reasons than those to choose a particular school.

It is by no means necessary that the distinctive school's mission be religious, though I suppose that every coherent way of understanding the world is in some sense religious, but its mission must be more than a bag of tricks picked up here and there and lacking any common theme. Kieran Egan has written,

> It's not the lack of a research base of knowledge about development and learning that is hindering educators' wider success; rather, our main problem is our poverty in conceptions of education. . . . It is always easier and more attractive to engage in technical work under an accepted paradigm than do hard thinking about the value-saturated idea of education.[2]

* * * * *

I want to challenge those who would improve American public education to "hard thinking about the value-saturated idea of education." If we are to have schools that are distinctively excellent, we must have schools that are different because of hard thinking, thinking that grapples with complicated and delicate questions.

Too much discussion among educators is about how to do things; not nearly enough is about what is worth doing. We are afraid that we will discover basic disagreements, and that it will be impossible for us to work together. But it is precisely around those basic disagreements that—always courteously, always respectfully—we can build a diverse educational system.

Am I proposing that we abandon the goal of a common school that can meet the needs of every student and that teaches them to appreciate one another? Yes and no. Certainly it is past time that we recognize that no one school can be good for every student or satisfy every parent, and we can no longer assume that involuntary assignments, which thirty years of experience have proved ineffective, are the only means of achieving racial and other forms of integration in schools. Instead, we should be seeking what, in one of my annual reports to the Massachusetts Board of Education, I called the "new common school": the school freely chosen by parents and by teachers and, as a result, free to translate a shared vision of education into the thousand details of classroom and school life. Such a policy allows schools to function within a policy framework that stresses outcomes and leaves the ways and means up to those most directly engaged with the process of education and the lives of individual children and youth. As noted earlier, Massachusetts and other states have begun to implement such a framework, with accountability for results and increased autonomy at the school level.

The recent evidence shows that there is still a long way to go. Around the country, constraints—all sorts of limits upon the freedom of charter schools and others to organize instruction, staffing, and accountability —are creeping back. My challenge to those who would improve American public education, though, involves more than technical adjustments at the margins of school choice, however important that task may be. The true challenge is in undertaking what policymakers can only permit and encourage: developing models of educational effectiveness that embrace Egan's "hard thinking about the value-saturated idea of education." Real education will always involve helping to form the person; it will always be "value-saturated" and rest upon consequential choices no research design can make. Parents, educators, and policymakers alike need to rediscover the distinction, so much more emphasized in other languages, between "instruction" and "education": consider the resonance of the words *Bildung* in German, or *éducation* in French, describing the lifelong enterprise of becoming a fully realized human being. Those called "educators" should recognize the moral weight of that description; Horace Mann said that the teacher at his desk has a calling more sacred than the minister in his pulpit. Do we dare think of ourselves in that way? Do we dare take our calling any less seriously?

It will require imagination and a willingness to think through the implications of different means of teaching and of organizing schools and curricula—thinking based, though, not on mere technical efficiency, but on how such means correspond to and advance a coherent vision of education.

Doing so will lead us—will lead you—along different paths, often parallel, sometimes crossing, at other times diverging widely. It is essential that you not lose nerve because of those differences simply because someone you respect reaches different conclusions about how, and why, education should be provided. It is the richness and the promise of the present moment in education that we are free to create distinctive schools—each a "common school" for those who choose it—without fear that we are somehow betraying the mission of schooling in a democracy.

Free and distinctive schools, created by the hard thinking and hard work of imaginative educators, will not betray the mission of democratic education, but will rather fulfill it as never before in American life.

Notes

1. See Gary R. Galluzzo, "Moving to the Margins," *Educational Horizons* 82:4 (Summer 2004), for a discussion of the school as "a school of thought."
2. Kieran Egan, *Getting It Wrong from the Beginning* (New Haven, Conn.: Yale University Press, 2002): 180f.

Charles Glenn, the author of *The Myth of the Common School, served for two decades as the Massachusetts state education official responsible for urban education. He was selected to write the article on school choice in the* International Encyclopedia of Education *(2nd Edition).*

UNIT 7
Serving Special Needs and Concerns

Unit Selections

34. **Rethinking Inclusion: Schoolwide Applications**, Wayne Sailor and Blair Roger
35. **Self-Efficacy: A Key to Improving the Motivation of Struggling Learners**, Howard Margolis and Patrick McCabe
36. **Vouchers For Parents: New Forms of Education Funding**, Lamar Alexander

Key Points to Consider

- What can schools do to encourage students to read during the summer months? What can teachers do to encourage reading for pleasure throughout the school year?

- Describe life in an American suburban high school. What concerns do you have about student experience of this setting? If possible, use your own experiences as a guide.

Student Website

www.mhcls.com/online

Internet References

Further information regarding these websites may be found in this book's preface or online.

Constructivism: From Philosophy to Practice
http://www.stemnet.nf.ca/~elmurphy/emurphy/cle.html

National Association for Gifted Children
http://www.nagc.org/home00.htm

National Information Center for Children and Youth With Disabilities (NICHCY)
http://www.nichcy.org/index.html

People who educate serve many special needs and concerns of their students. This effort requires a special commitment to students on the part of their teachers. We celebrate this effort, and each year we seek to address special types of general concern.

People learn under many different sets of circumstances which involve a variety of educational concerns both within schools and in alternative learning contexts. Each year we include in this section a variety of special topics that we believe our readers will find interesting.

The general literature thematically varies from year to year. Issues on which several good articles may have been published in one year may not be covered well in other years in professional and trade publications. Likewise, some issues are covered in depth every year such as articles on social class, education, or school choice.

We also look at rethinking the concept of inclusion, which is the development of heterogeneous classrooms rather than tract classrooms, and a school wide approach is discussed involving guiding principles and features relating to how to develop a heterogeneous classroom environment. A school-wide applications model and how it can be applied in classrooms is discussed.

The next article in this unit deals with the development of self efficacy. Efficacy can mean self-confidence, and they make several good suggestions as to how to do this. The concept of motivation is also discussed in this article, and how it relates to developing students self confidence. The authors speak about how helping students regain or gain more self confidence can help them to improve the likelihood that their struggle to learn will be successful.

The next article is a discussion by Lamar Alexander of how vouchers for parents can develop new forms of education funding by allowing students and parents to develop clear choices as to where they will go to school. There is also a discussion of first year teaching, as arduous under the best of circumstances, as well as the elementary and secondary education act known as the No Child Left Behind Act of 2001, which requires that anyone teaching a core academic subject at the secondary level must be highly qualified.

There are well and long recognized reasons to build good relationships between schools and the families which they serve. The students of a school or school system can benefit both academically and in other ways if partnerships between schools and communities can be encouraged.

Since first issued in 1973, this ongoing anthology has sought to provide discussion of special social or curriculum issues affecting the teaching and learning conditions in schools. Fundamental forces at work in our culture during the past several years have greatly affected millions of students. These social, cultural, and economic pressures on families have produced several special problems of great concerns to teachers. Serving special needs and concerns requires greater degrees of individualization of instruction, and greater attention paid to the development and maintenance of healthier self concepts by students.

Rethinking Inclusion:

Schoolwide Applications

"Inclusion" is usually regarded as the placement of special education students in general education settings. But Mr. Sailor and Ms. Roger present a new vision of integrated education, in which previously specialized adaptations and strategies are used to enhance the learning of all students.

WAYNE SAILOR AND BLAIR ROGER

As A FIELD, special education presents an excellent case study of the paradox of differentiation and integration, wherein we seek solutions through increased specialization but, in so doing, we redefine a problem in terms of discrete parts at the expense of the whole. As Thomas Skrtic pointed out more than a decade ago, a large and ever-widening gap exists between the purpose of special education—to provide needed supports, services, adaptations, and accommodations to students with disabilities in order to preserve and enhance their educational participation in the least restrictive environment—and its practice.[1] And that practice has evolved over three decades into a parallel and highly differentiated educational structure, often with only loosely organized connections to the general education system.[2]

Having disengaged from general education early on, special education began to undergo a process that, at times, has seemed to mimic cell division. At one point in its ontogeny, the field could list some 30 distinct eligibility categories for special education services (e.g., learning disabilities, behavioral disorders, severe disabilities, autism, and so on).[3] Many of these early categories further subdivided, with autism, for example, splitting into a host of subcategories lumped under "autism spectrum disorders."[4]

How has all of this come about? The paradox of differentiation and integration—with its tensions in practice and contradictions in policy—offers a reasonable hypothesis. In our efforts to better meet the educational needs of specific identifiable groups, we have promoted differentiation at the expense of integration. If such a policy produced exemplary outcomes, the only remaining questions would concern how to direct scarce resources to meet the needs of a few individuals, and the values underlying special education would no doubt resolve the tension in favor of customization and differentiation. But the positive outcomes don't seem to be there.[5]

In its early days, special education embraced the diagnostic/prescriptive model characteristic of modern medicine, and disability was viewed as pathology. Psychology, with its partner the test industry, became the "gatekeeper" for special education. Students referred by teachers and parents were diagnosed in one of the categories of disability and tagged for separate (highly differentiated) treatment. Indeed, special education policy handbooks at the district level came to resemble the *Diagnostic and Statistical Manual* of the American Psychiatric Association.

Then in the 1980s, the U.S. Department of Education began to advance policy reforms designed to slow the growth in the number of special education categorical placements and practices. These initiatives occurred against a backdrop of publications citing positive outcomes from integrated practices and a corresponding barrage of studies associating separate classrooms and pullout practices with negative outcomes.[6]

The first of these reforms was called the Regular Education Initiative and was designed to stimulate the provision of special education supports and services in general education classrooms. It generated enormous controversy within special education. Indeed, a special issue of the *Journal of Learning Disabilities* was devoted entirely to an attempt to refute the research underlying the policy.[7] Framing the reform of special education policy as general education policy ("regular" education initiative) failed completely within the community of special education.

More recently, federal policy has advanced "inclusion" as recommended practice and has expended significant funds for training, research, and demonstration purposes. This initiative, too, has failed to significantly change special education placement and service configurations, over about a 15-year period. Again, the policy has drawn fire from within special education and has failed to attract interest and enthusiasm from general education.[8]

The No Child Left Behind (NCLB) legislation, for all its problems, does offer special education an opportunity to pursue once again the pathway to integration. First, NCLB makes clear that *all children* in public education are general education students. Second, the law is firmly anchored in accountability, even going so far as to define "evidence" and to restrict scientific inquiry to approved methodologies. If students identified for special education are placed in general education settings and provided with specialized services and supports, and if evidence for academic and social outcomes is to be evaluated according to approved methodologies, then there is an opportunity to achieve a measure of integrated education policy. And the sum of available evidence overwhelmingly supports integrated instructional approaches over those that are categorically segregated,[9] regardless of the categorical label or severity of the disability.[10]

A SCHOOLWIDE APPROACH

That inclusion policy has failed to garner much support from general education can be partially attributed to the way "inclusion" has been defined. Virtually all definitions begin with a general education classroom as the unit of interest and analysis for the provision of supports and services. The problem with a general-classroom-based model is that it doesn't seem credible to the general education teacher, whose job is usually seen as moving students as uniformly as possible through the curriculum. Students whose disabilities impede them from progressing at the expected rate and who, as a result, fall whole grade levels behind their classmates on various components of the curriculum seem to belong elsewhere. Special education has usually been there to oblige with separate categorical placements, particularly when "inclusion" has been tried and has "failed."

Alternatively, when inclusion is a core value of the school program, students with IEPs (individualized education programs) who cannot function in various components of the classroom curriculum often find themselves at tables, usually in the back of the classroom, with paraprofessionals who, in a one-on-one approach, work with

them on "something else." This practice not only segregates special education students within the general education classroom but also creates a distraction that has a detrimental effect on general and special education students alike.[11]

But does inclusion need to be tied to a classroom-based model? If the objective is to avoid separate, categorical placements as the chief alternative to general education placements, then can we shift the unit of analysis from the classroom to the school? So if Joey is a student who, because of his disabilities, cannot progress at grade level in the third grade, then we can ask, For those portions of the third-grade curriculum that Joey cannot successfully engage, even with support, where should he be? With whom? And doing what? The problem then becomes one of scheduling, personnel deployment, and the use of space, not one of alternative placement.

A schoolwide approach is not a variation on the older "pull-out" model. Under emerging schoolwide models, students with IEPs are not removed from general education classrooms to receive one-on-one therapies and tutorials or to go to "resource rooms." Following the logic of integration, all services and supports are provided in such a way as to benefit the maximum number of students, including those not identified for special education. Indeed, in recent years, special education has developed evidence-based practices that have been shown to work for general education students as well. Learning strategies, positive behavior support, and transition planning are three excellent examples.[12] Here's a good summary of this new kind of thinking:

> In a transformed urban school, then, learning and other educational supports are organized to meet the needs of all students rather than historical conventions or the way the rooms are arranged in the building. Creative reallocation of even limited resources and innovative reorganization of teachers into partnerships and teams offer ways to break old molds and create the flexibilities needed to focus on student learning and achievement. Previously separate "programs," like special education, Title I, or bilingual education, come together to form a new educational system that delivers necessary additional supports and instruction in the same spaces to diverse groups of students. The new system anchors both organizational and professional effort in student content, performance, and skill standards that are owned by local communities and families while informed by national and state standards, curriculum frameworks, and effective assessment strategies.[13]

The Individuals with Disabilities Education Act (IDEA) contains language in its "incidental benefits" section that encourages applications of special education that hold promise for general education students. This approach enables special educators to support students with special needs by means of integrated arrangements.

Three decades of comprehensive special education have produced an extraordinary wealth of pedagogical adaptations and strategies to enhance learning. This unique set of conditions came about through the provision of set-aside funds for research under IDEA, and much of that research has focused on problem-solving strategies that can benefit any hard-to-teach students. Today, NCLB exhorts us to teach all students to the highest attainable standards. Special education has designed instructional enhancements that can facilitate this outcome, but for these research-based enhancements to benefit all students, special education needs to be integrated with general education. Emerging schoolwide approaches and the call for a "universal design for learning"[14] represent early efforts in this direction.

When a schoolwide approach is applied to "lower-forming" schools, such as those sometimes found in isolated rural settings or in inner-city areas affected by conditions of extreme poverty, mounting evidence suggests that integrated applications of special education practices can yield positive outcomes for all students. For example, when fully integrated applications of learning strategies designed originally for students with specific learning disabilities have been implemented, scores on NCLB-sanctioned accountability measures for all students have increased. Where social development is at issue, the use of schoolwide positive behavior support has led to higher standardized test scores for general education students in low-performing schools.[15]

SAM

To illustrate how an integrated model works in practice, we describe below our own version of such an approach, called SAM for Schoolwide Applications Model, which is being implemented and evaluated in eight California elementary and middle schools and in one elementary school in Kansas City, Kansas. We describe this model in terms of six "guiding principles," which can be broken down into 15 "critical features." Each feature can be evaluated over time using SAMAN (Schoolwide Applications Model Analysis System), an assessment instrument designed to enable schools themselves to link specific interventions to academic and social outcomes for all students. While this approach can appear to mimic comprehensive school reform in some ways, it is specifically designed to be integrated into the existing values and culture of each individual school. In other words, under SAM, a school that wishes to unify its programs and resources is presented with the 15 critical features and instructed to use team processes to implement them according to its own culture and time lines. Across our nine research sites, we are seeing great diversity and creativity on the part of school teams.

GUIDING PRINCIPLES AND CRITICAL FEATURES

Guiding Principle 1. General education guides all student learning. As a fully integrated and unified model, SAM proceeds on the key assumption that all student learning is guided by a district's framework for curriculum, instruction, and assessment and is thus aligned with state standards. Four critical features support this principle: 1) all students attend their regularly assigned school; 2) all students are considered general education students; 3) general education teachers are responsible for all students; and 4) all students are instructed in accordance with the general education curriculum.

Most teacher training programs today continue to encourage general education teachers to expect special education teachers to assume primary responsibility for students with IEPs. Special education departments at colleges and universities reinforce this notion by training special education teachers in self-contained classrooms and by having little overlap with general education departments, such as departments of curriculum and instruction.[16] An integrated schoolwide model, on the other hand, essentially requires teachers to see their role differently. At SAM schools, the general education teacher is the chief agent of each child's educational program, with support from a variety of others. Using SAM, general education teachers have primary responsibility for all students, consider themselves responsible for implementing IEPs, and collaborate with special education professionals to educate students with disabilities.

Furthermore, this guiding principle encourages schools to avoid such alternative placements as special schools for students who need extensive services and supports. Through SAM, schools welcome these students and configure any funding that comes with them to benefit a variety of students through integrated applications.

At our research sites, it is school policy to encourage parent participation and involvement, and parents are given extensive information about the schoolwide model. In those rare cases when parents feel strongly that their child requires a separate, self-contained placement —and the district concurs—the student may be referred to a comparable non-SAM school that offers self-contained classes for students with disabilities.

SAM does not allow for separate classes for students with disabilities at the school site, so the challenge is to focus on how such students can be supported in the general education classroom, how they can be supported in other environments, and how specialized therapies and services can be provided. The use of space, the deployment of support personnel, and scheduling issues become significant. At SAM schools, very little attention is focused on the existence of disabilities among some students. Every effort is made to foster friendships and positive relationships among students with and without disabilities.

SAM differs from traditional inclusion models by ensuring that students with IEPs are pursuing goals and objectives matched to and integrated with the curriculum being implemented in the general education classroom. Under SAM, no student with disabilities would be found at the rear of a classroom, engaged with a paraprofessional on some task that is unrelated to what the rest of the class is doing. If the class is engaged in a higher level curricular activity, say, algebra, and a student with disabilities cannot engage that material with measurable benefit, then that student might be assigned to an integrated grouping outside of the classroom for that period. In that case, instruction in remedial math would take place with general education students who are also operating at the same curricular level.

There are times, of course, when one-on-one instruction is appropriate in the general education classroom, but this option would be available to any student who could benefit rather than restricted solely to students identified for special education. For example, any child who needs intensive instruction in reading might receive a 30-minute tutorial session in the school's learning center while the rest of the class is engaged in a reading exercise.

Guiding Principle 2. All school resources are configured to benefit all students. Three critical features support this principle: 1) all students are included in all activities; 2) all resources benefit all students; and 3) the school effectively incorporates general education students in the instructional process.

In traditional schools, students in special education often do not accompany general education students on field trips; attend sporting events, assemblies, performances, and after-school programs; or take part in specialized reading, math, and science programs or enrichment programs in the arts. SAM schools seek to overcome such barriers to inclusion in all regular school events. All students with IEPs are members of age-appropriate, grade-level classrooms, and they attend all non-classroom functions with their classmates.

The trick is to enable all school personnel to contribute to the mission of the school.

Large SAM schools, particularly secondary schools, also make use of small-group arrangements at the classroom level and small learning communities at the school level. Cooperative learning groups, student-directed learning, peer tutorials, peer-mediated instructional arrangements, and so on can greatly enhance outcomes for all students in integrated instructional settings. In addition, particularly in large middle schools and high schools, teams of general and support teachers skilled in math or literacy can use learning centers to support any student's needs. The learning center becomes flexible space for tutorial services offered by teachers or volun-

teer members of the National Honor Society, as well as a place to make up tests, complete homework with assistance, see a missed film, find resources for a paper or project, and so forth.

Guiding Principle 3. Schools address social development and citizenship forthrightly. A single critical feature undergirds this principle: the school incorporates positive behavior support (PBS) at the individual, group, and schoolwide levels. PBS was originally developed as specialized instruction in social development for students with behavioral disabilities. But it has demonstrated its efficacy for all students, particularly those in schools challenged by urban blight and poverty.[17] SAM schools incorporate schoolwide PBS as a comprehensive intervention package to help meet the social development needs of all students.

Guiding Principle 4. Schools are democratically organized, data-driven, problem-solving systems. Four critical features support this principle: 1) the school is data-driven and uses team processes; 2) all personnel take part in the teaching/learning process; 3) the school employs a noncategorical lexicon; and 4) the school is governed by a site leadership team.

SAM schools are encouraged to upgrade district software to enable the leadership team to make use of all available databases that affect the social and academic performance of students. Through a process called schoolcentered planning, SAM schools use a variety of performance data fields, disaggregated at the district level, to make decisions regarding priorities related to school improvement.

SAM schools recognize that all salaried personnel at a school can contribute to the teaching/learning process. A custodian may have hidden talents for vocational training, or a speech therapist may be skilled in musical composition. The trick is to enable all school personnel to contribute to the primary mission of the school and not to be completely constrained by bureaucratic specifications of roles. SAM schools also seek to move away from such categorical descriptors as "learning disabilities," "inclusion," "specials," and so on. There are just two kinds of teachers in a SAM school: classroom teachers and support teachers.

A site leadership team is established at each SAM school. It represents all school personnel and may include parents and members of the local community. This team undertakes the process of school-centered planning to evaluate data related to student academic and social performance, to prioritize specific interventions to improve outcomes, and to advance the mission of the school through full implementation of SAM.

Guiding Principle 5. Schools have open boundaries in relation to their families and communities. Two critical features support this guiding principle: 1) schools have working partnerships with their students' families; and 2) schools have working partnerships with local businesses and service providers.

SAM schools go beyond the traditional structure of parent/teacher organizations and solicit the active participation of family members in the teaching/learning process. Some SAM sites have made the establishment of a family resource center at the school a top priority. Some have even created a "parent liaison" position.

SAM schools also reach beyond the "business partnership" relationship that has characterized some school reform efforts. Schools undertake a "community mapping" process to understand their respective communities. Under many circumstances, the school community may not be geographically defined. But the point is to engage the school's constituents in the life of the school.

Furthermore, effective community partnerships set the stage for meaningful service-learning opportunities and open up possibilities for community-based instruction for any student. Students with IEPs, for example, who cannot engage a secondary-level, classroom-based math curriculum, might take part in "community math" in real-life applied settings such as banks and stores. Other students who are chronically unmotivated by school may reconnect with the learning process through community-based learning opportunities.

Guiding Principle 6. Schools enjoy district support for undertaking an extensive systems-change effort. Just one critical feature is necessary here: schoolwide models such as SAM that offer a significant departure from traditional bureaucratic management and communication processes must have district support . One way to garner such support is to set up pilot projects with the understanding that expansion to additional sites is contingent on documented gains in measured student academic and social outcomes. District-level support may be expected to increase following successful demonstrations and sharing results across schools over time.

MEASUREMENT STRATEGIES

Each SAM school employs a package of psychometrically established instruments with which to assess progress related to the priorities that were established through the school-centered planning process. These instruments include a schoolwide evaluation tool to assess support for positive behavior,[18] SAMAN to assess the 15 critical features of SAM, and EVOLVE to assess the training of paraprofessionals and the ways they are deployed.[19]

Districts are encouraged to use the COMPASS Data Analyzer[20] as an adjunct to the districtwide data system to enable each SAM school to receive feedback about its own priorities and specific data of interest. The program also facilitates reporting to the other teams and committees at the school.

STRUCTURAL ELEMENTS OF SAM

SAM is a fully integrated and unified approach to the education of all students. As a process, it is intended to enable schools to engage in collaborative, team-driven decision making that is focused on interventions de-

signed to enhance academic and social outcomes for students. The process of educating all students together presents both challenges and opportunities. The SAM approach requires certain structural elements to be in place. As touched upon earlier, two elements, a site leadership team and school-centered planning, must be present at the school level. And two more elements, a district leadership team and a district resource team, must be present at the district level.

Site leadership team. The SLT, usually with between eight and 12 members, evaluates schoolwide data on student progress; sets priorities, goals, and objectives for each school term; and networks with and reports to the other teams and committees that function at the school. The principal is usually a member of the SLT but does not need to be its chair. Membership on SLTs is usually determined by a combination of internal teacher nominations, with elections for one-year renewable terms; principal appointments; and invitations to specific parents and community members. Expenses incurred by parent and community participants, the cost of substitutes for participating teachers who attend out-of-class meetings, the cost of supplies, and so on, can become budget items for SLTs. SLTs follow strict team procedures with regard to agenda, floor time, minutes, and so on, so that precious time is not wasted. SLTs meet at least biweekly and undergo full-day "retreats" at least twice a ye a r, prior to the beginning of each new term. The school-centered-planning process takes place during these retreats.

School-centered planning. The SCP process is patterned after empowerment evaluation.[21] Using this process, a facilitator, supplied by the district or arranged through a university partnership, assists the SLT to begin with a vision for why the school decided to become a SAM school. A set of goals is derived to make the vision real, and a set of specific objectives for the coming term is spelled out for the various school/community personnel. Measurement strategies are identified for each objective so that subsequent planning and objective setting can take account of data on pupil performance that are linked to specific measurable processes. The SLT holds interim meetings to review progress in the implementation of each SCP action plan for the term.

District leadership team. The DLT consists of district personnel with an interest in implementing SAM. The superintendent may well be a member but usually will not be the chair. DLTs are frequently chaired by the head of curriculum and instruction, since SAM processes are driven primarily by general education. Other members of the DLT typically include the head of pupil support services, the special education director, the Title I director, and the director of programs for second-language learners. The superintendent may appoint other members as needed. The DLT usually meets three or four times a year to review SAM school-site plans and to consider requests for approval of policy and budget items arising from these plans.

District resource team. The final structural component is the DRT. This team is usually made up of district-level staff members who work closely with the schools, such as regional special education personnel, grade-level specialists, the parent support coordinator, and transportation officials. The function of the DRT is to help the DLT consider requests for resources from each school site for the coming term. If, for example, a SAM site requests two additional paraprofessionals to implement one or more objectives on its plan for the coming term, the DRT will consider the request, balance the needs of that site against the collective needs of all district schools, and make recommendations to the DLT. Typically, DRTs with several SAM sites in the district will meet on a fairly frequent basis to help the district stay ahead of the curve of systems change.

The Schoolwide Applications Model is a work in progress. It represents an effort to integrate all aspects of comprehensive school reform with a new and innovative approach to the delivery of special education supports and services. Research must continue if we are to determine whether the premise of SAM holds: namely, that dedifferentiated educational practices can support personalized learning—in and outside of classrooms—while creating a sense of unity and a culture of belonging in the school.

Notes

1. Thomas M. Skrtic, *Behind Special Education: A Critical Analysis of Professional Culture and School Organization* (Denver: Love Publishing, 1991).

2. Steven J. Taylor, "Caught in the Continuum: A Critical Analysis of the Principle of the Least Restrictive Environment," *Journal of the Association for Persons with Severe Handicaps,* vol. 13, 1988, pp. 41-53.

3. Wayne Sailor and Doug Guess, *Severely Handicapped Students: An Instructional Design* (Boston: Houghton Mifflin, 1983).

4. Johnny L. Matson, *Autism in Children and Adults: Etiology, Assessment, and Intervention* (Pacific Grove, Calif.: Brookes/Cole, 1994).

5. See for example, Wayne Sailor, testimony before the Research Agenda Task Force of the President's Commission on Excellence in Special Education, 18 April 2002.

6. See, for example, Diane Lea Ryndak and Douglas Fisher, eds., *The Foundations of Inclusive Education: A Compendium of Articles on Effective Strategies to Achieve Inclusive Education,* 2nd ed. (Baltimore: TASH, 2003), available at www.tash.org; and Margaret Wang, Maynard C. Reynolds, and Herbert J. Wahlberg, eds., *Handbook of Special Education: Research and Practice Vol. 1: Learner Characteristics and Adaptive Education* (Oxford: Pergamon Press, 1987).

7. See *Journal of Learning Disabilities,* vol. 21, 1988.

8. James M. Kauffman, Kathleen McGee, and Michele Brigham, "Enabling or Disabling? Observations on Changes in Special Education," *Phi Delta Kappan,* April 2004, pp. 613-20; and Larry M. Lieberman, "Special Education and Regular Education: A Merger Made in Heaven?," *Exceptional Children,* vol. 51, 1985, pp. 513-16.

9. An exception can be made for students with a hearing problem. Some recent research suggests that instruction delivered in American Sign Language results in better academic outcomes than interpreted instruction in general education classrooms.

10. Wayne Sailor and Kathy Gee, "Progress in Educating Students with the Most Severe Disabilities: Is There Any?," *Journal of the Association for Persons with Severe Handicaps,* vol. 13, 1988, pp. 87-99.

11. Michael F. Giangreco and M. B. Doyle, "Students with Disabilities and Paraprofessional Supports: Benefits, Balance, and Band-Aids," *Exceptional Children,* vol. 68, 2002, pp. 1-12.

12. Sailor and Gee, op. cit.; George Sugai and Rob H. Homer, "Including Students with Severe Behavior Problems in General Education Settings: Assumptions, Challenges, and Solutions," in Alice J. Marr, George Sugai, and Gerald A. Tindal, eds., *The Oregon Conference Monograph 6* (Baltimore: Paul H. Brookes, 1994), pp. 102-20; and Mary Morningstar, Jeannie Kleinhammer-Tramill, and Dana Lattin, "Using Successful Models of Student-Centered Transition Planning and Sevices for Adolescents with Disabilities," *Focus on Exceptional Children,* vol. 31, no. 9, 1999, pp. 1-19.

13. Dianne L. Ferguson, Elizabeth B. Kozleski, and Anne Smith, "Transformed, Inclusive Schools: A Framework to Guide Fundamental Change in Urban Schools," National Institute for Urban School Improvement: The Office of Special Education Programs, August 2001, available from www.inclusiveschools.org/publicat.htm#transformed.

14. Cynthia Curry, "Universal Design: Accessibility for All Learners," *Educational Leadership,* October 2003, pp. 55-60; "Principles of Universal Design," Center for Universal Design, North Carolina State University, 1997, available at www.design.ncsu.edu/cud; James Rydeen, "Universal Design," available at http://industryclick.com//magazinearticle.asp?magazinearticleid=33035&mode=print; and David H. Rose, Sheela Sethuraman, and Grace J. Meo, "Universal Design for Learning," *Journal of Special Education Technology,* vol. 15, no. 2, 2000, pp. 56-60.

15. Steve R. Lassen, Michael M. Steele, and Wayne Sailor, "The Relationship of School-wide Positive Behavior Support to Academic Achievement in an Urban Middle School," manuscript in preparation.

16. Claude Goldenberg, "School-University Links: Settings for Joint Work," in *Successful School Change* (New York: Teachers College Press, 2004), pp. 138-62.

17. Cheryl Utley and Wayne Sailor, eds., *Journal of Positive Behavior Interventions*, vol. 4, 2002.

18. Robert H. Horner et al., "The School-wide Evaluation Tool (SET): A Research Instrument for Assessing School-wide Positive Behavior Support," *Journal of Positive Behavior Interventions*, vol. 6, 2004, pp. 3-12.

19. Giangreco and Doyle, op. cit.

20. Robert Harsh, "COMPASS Data Management System," available at http://sbiweb.kckps.org:2388/common/ default.asp.

21. David M. Fetterman, "Empowerment Evaluation: An Introduction to Theory and Practice," in idem, Sakeh J. Kafterian, and Abraham Wandersman, eds., *Empowerment Evaluation: Knowledge and Tools for Self-Assessment and Accountability* (Thousand Oaks, Calif.: Sage, 1997), pp. 1-46.

WAYNE SAILOR is a clinical psychologist, a professor of special education, and an associate director of the Beach Center on Disability, University of Kansas, Lawrence. **BLAIR ROGER** is an educational consultant based in Oakland, Calif. They wish to thank the administrators, teachers, staff, students, and families of the Ravenswood (Calif.) School District, East Palo Alto, and of USD 500, Wyandotte County, Kansas City, Kan. The authors also thank Leonard Burrello of Indiana University, Bloomington, and the Forum on Education (www.forumon-education.org) for initiating a forum on the paradox of differentiation, which led to this article. Preparation of this article was supported, in part, by the National Center on Positive Behavior Interventions and Supports (Grant no. 113265980003).

From *Phi Delta Kappan,* March 2005, pp. 503-509. Copyright © 2005 by Phi Delta Kappa International. Reprinted by permission of the publisher and author.

Self-Efficacy

A Key to Improving the Motivation of Struggling Learners

HOWARD MARGOLIS and PATRICK P. McCABE

Self-efficacy . . . influence[s] task choice, effort, persistence, and achievement. Compared with students who doubt their learning capacities, those who have a sense of efficacy for [particular tasks] participate more readily, work harder, persist longer when they encounter difficulties, and achieve at a higher level. . . . Students do not engage in activities they believe will lead to negative outcomes. (Schunk and Zimmerman 1997, 36)

Many struggling learners resist academics, thinking that they lack the ability to succeed, even if they expend great effort. In other words, these struggling learners have low rather than high self-efficacy for academics. It is widely believed that without sufficiently high self-efficacy, or the belief that they can succeed on specific academic tasks like homework, many struggling learners will not make the effort needed to master academics. They will give up or avoid tasks similar to those previously failed (Baker and Wigfield 1999; Bandura 1993; Casteel, Isom, and Jordan 2000; Chapman and Tunmer 2003; Henk and Melnick 1995; Jinks and Morgan 1999; Lipson and Wixson 1997; Lynch 2002; Pajares 1996; Pintrich and Schunk 2002; Schunk and Zimmerman 1997; Walker 2003).

A key to reversing this perspective—getting struggling learners with low self-efficacy to invest sufficient effort, to persist on tasks, to work to overcome difficulties, to take on increasingly challenging tasks, and to develop interest in academics—is for teachers to systematically stress the development of high self-efficacy. Fortunately, research suggests that teachers can often strengthen struggling learners' self-efficacy by linking new work to recent successes, teaching needed learning strategies, reinforcing effort and persistence, stressing peer modeling, teaching struggling learners to make facilitative attributions, and helping them identify or create personally important goals (Ormrod 2000; Pajares 2003; Pajares and Schunk 2001; Pintrich and Schunk 2002; Schunk 1999; Zimmerman

2000a). For these strategies to be effective, however, struggling learners with low self-efficacy must succeed on the very type of tasks they expect to fail. This strongly suggests that classwork must be at their proper instructional level, and homework at their proper independent level (Culyer 1996; Lipson and Wixson 1997). Work should challenge rather than frustrate them (Strickland, Ganske, and Monroe 2002). It should strengthen expectations of success rather than failure. To achieve this, teachers need to (a) give struggling learners work at their proper instructional and independent levels, and (b) adhere to instructional principles likely to improve self-efficacy.

Frustration, Instructional, and Independent Levels

Perhaps the most important academic decision teachers make for struggling learners is determining the levels at which to instruct them. Swanson's (1999) findings support this contention. As part of a larger meta-analysis assessing the effectiveness of interventions for students with learning disabilities, he identified the instructional components that best predicted outcomes. Two of the more important components were controlling task difficulty and sequencing tasks from easy to difficult. His findings reflect recommendations that reading specialists have made for decades—instruct students at their proper instructional and independent levels and avoid the frustration level (Leslie and Caldwell 2001; McCormick 2003; Newcomer 1986).

Criteria for instructional, independent, and frustration level tasks are often defined by objective measures (e.g., the percent of words correctly identified in oral reading) and are influenced by each struggling learner's unique perceptions about what is frustrating or anxiety provoking. What one struggling learner finds challenging, another, with the same skills, can find frustrating and nightmarish. Challenge is also influenced by such factors as a struggling learner's ability to organize, initiate, monitor, and sustain activities. A task that one struggling learner has little difficulty structuring and organizing can overwhelm and frustrate another at the same academic level.

For struggling learners with expectations of failure, teachers should avoid tasks the learners find frustrating or anxiety provoking. If frequently encountered, such tasks will provoke dysfunctional but understandable avoidance reactions: refusal to start or complete work; off-task dawdling; unthoughtful, careless responses; distractibility and fidgetiness. Little learning will occur, and motivation will plummet. As Newcomer (1986) noted: "Continuing to expect a child to read material at his or her frustration level can create serious achievement and emotional problems" (26).

Although perceptions are personal and teachers may need to adjust instructional and independent level criteria for particular struggling learners, teachers should follow well-established guidelines for determining instructional and independent levels. In most cases, these guidelines set the stage for success.

For materials to be at a student's instructional reading level, students should quickly and correctly read aloud 90 to 95 percent of words in context and understand 70 to 89 percent of the text. Instructional level assumes that teachers will work with students, teaching vocabulary, skills, and strategies; monitoring and guiding practice; and structuring independent practice. For independent level materials, which students should find easier than instructional level materials, students should quickly and correctly read aloud 96 percent or more of the words in context and understand 90 percent or more of the text (McCormick 2003). Whenever students work by themselves, at their desks or at home, materials should be at their independent level. Giving instructional level homework to struggling learners is equivalent to giving them frustration level materials, as their independent work habits and skills are often poor and teachers are not there to teach, supervise, and support them.

Commercial informal reading inventories (IRIs) can help identify a struggling learner's instructional, independent, and frustration reading levels (Lipson and Wixson 1997; McCormick 2003). Although such IRIs are easy to administer, and some are supported by extensive validity data (Leslie and Caldwell 2001; McCabe and Margolis 1999), they lack the specificity of Curriculum-Based Assessment (CBA) for determining and monitoring struggling learners' reading levels in specific curriculum (Fewster and Macmillan 2002; Idol, Nevin, and Paolucci-Whitcomb 1999). One CBA strategy for identifying struggling learners' instructional and independent reading levels is to individually administer a hierarchical series of 100-word selections from the books the learners will likely read (Idol, Nevin, and Paolucci-Whitcomb 1999). By having learners read three different selections from each prospective book that matches their estimated reading abilities and comparing each learner's median performance for accuracy (number of words correctly read), rate (correct words per minute) and comprehension (percent of questions correctly answered) to locally derived norms, teachers can get relatively reliable indications of the challenge these books present (Idol, Nevin, and Paolucci-Whitcomb 1999; Fewster and Macmillan 2002).

Teachers also can use the cloze procedure to quickly estimate the learners' ability to understand specific reading materials. The procedure, which has learners silently read passages of 250 to 300 words, can be administered to individual students or whole classes. Unlike the materials from which the cloze passages were copied, the cloze passage replaces every fifth word with a blank space of even length (Lipson and Wixson 1997; Spinelli 2002). Students write in the missing words. Materials on which students accurately identify 44 to 56 percent of the missing words (synonyms are counted as incorrect) represent their instructional level, 57 percent or more their independent level, and 43 percent or less their frustration level (Spinelli 2002). These guidelines can help teachers identify materials that struggling learners can successfully read.

Instructional and independent levels are different for tasks and assignments that do not stress the fluent identification of words in context. Salvia and Ysseldyke (2001) consider correct response rates of 85 to 95 percent challenging and less than 85 percent "too difficult." They caution for "students with severe cognitive handicaps, rates of correct response of less than 90 percent may indicate that the material is too challenging for guided practice" (25).

By adhering to these guidelines and, when they're too demanding, reducing them and the length, complexity, and abstractness of the work to reflect struggling learners' actual difficulties, perceptions of difficulty, and feelings of anxiety, teachers can often strengthen learners' self-efficacy for academics. One strategy for determining the adaptations needed is FLIP (Schumm and Mangrum 1991), which asks students to evaluate materials for friendliness (F), language (L), interest (I), and prior knowledge (P). By using FLIP, or adapting it to different subject matter, materials, and assignments, teachers can design instruction that increases the probability of success.

Whenever instructional or independent level data are unclear and teachers have to choose between more or less difficult levels, they should choose the less difficult. As struggling learners' moderate efforts produce high rates of success, more challenging materials and tasks should replace easier ones. Otherwise, they will have little opportunity to learn anything new, may get bored, and may think that teachers have little confidence in their abilities.

Instructional Principles

Frequently Link New Work to Recent Successes

To effectively link new work to recent successes requires many recent successes. To create many, teachers need to "stack the deck for success" by adhering to the struggling learners' proper instructional and independent levels, "stimulating recall of prerequisite learning" (Borich 2000, 159), shortening and simplifying work, and limiting the number and length of assignments. The key is giving learners moderately challenging work they can succeed at, if they make a moderate effort.

One way to help assure that struggling learners get tasks likely to produce high rates of success is to systematically employ CBA and to continually monitor learners' success rates

FLIP question: "How difficult is the language in my reading assignment?"

Possible student responses:

- Many new words; complicated sentences

- Some new words; somewhat complicated sentences

- No new words; clear sentences

Source: Schumm and Mangrum 1991, 122.

FIGURE 1. Sample FLIP question and possible responses.

(Rieth and Evertson 1988). By administering brief CBA probes several times a month, to assess progress in learners' areas of difficulty (e.g., reading, writing, spelling), and designing instruction and assignments to match their achievement and readiness to handle similar or increasingly challenging tasks, teachers can increase the learners' probability of success (Alper, Ryndak, and Schloss 2001; Galagan 1985; Spinelli 2002).

Once struggling learners have recent successes to draw on, teachers can help them link new work to their previous successes by explicitly showing and asking them how the new work resembles those past successes and then reminding them of what they did to succeed. Examining prior successes also provides teachers an excellent opportunity to employ one or several other self-efficacy enhancing strategies: teaching struggling learners to evaluate their work and chart their successes; teaching them to attribute success to controllable factors like effort, persistence, and correct use of strategies; having them review and annotate portfolios of successful work; helping them identify or develop specific, short-term, realistic goals; and persuading them to keep trying (Henk and Melnick 1998; Ormrod 2000; Pintrich and Schunk 2002; Schunk 2003; Walker 2003).

Teach Needed Learning Strategies

Characteristically, struggling learners do not know how to approach academic tasks. They do not know what learning or cognitive strategies to use or how to use them (Ellis and Lenz 1996; Vaughn, Gersten, and Chard 2000). Thus, teachers need to explicitly and systematically teach them the secrets of learning—the strategies that produce success (Swanson 2000).

Explicit, systematic instruction involves sequencing materials and tasks from easy to difficult; modeling and explaining to struggling learners, in a simple step-by-step fashion what they need to do; providing feedback about what they are doing right and what they need to do differently; providing abundant opportunities for guided practice, with task-specific feedback about how to correct errors; and, when they have achieved a high degree of proficiency (e.g., 96 percent word recognition in context for reading [McCormick 2003] and 85 percent on non-word recognition tasks, such as subtraction problems [Joyce and Weil 1996]), having them practice independently. As

Vaughn, Gersten, and Chard (2000) concluded: "Teaching students how to apply a particular strategy should be overt, and students should have multiple opportunities to practice the strategy under quality feedback conditions before they are expected to use the strategy on their own" (105).

In addition to sequencing, modeling, explicit step-by-step directions, feedback, correction, and practice (Pintrich and Schunk 2002; Swanson 2000), teachers might increase struggling learners' expectations of success by involving them in cooperative learning activities which are well within their ability to achieve. They know they will discreetly get whatever help they need, and they view their group as friendly and internally noncompetitive (Alderman 1999; Henk and Melnick 1998; Schunk and Zimmerman 1997; Vermette 1998). Teachers might also increase struggling learners' expectations of success by giving them strategy reference cards to use whenever they want (Casteel, Isom, and Jordon 2000). Reference cards present and illustrate each step of a strategy in ways struggling learners can readily comprehend. If they use reference cards when learning a strategy, they are apt to feel comfortable with them. Because they determine when to use the cards, they can dispense with them when they want. By putting struggling learners in control of using the cards and modeling the use of the cards themselves, teachers can eliminate any stigma associated with them.

For struggling learners who believe they lack the ability to succeed and who avoid more than superficial involvement in schoolwork, explicit, systematic strategy instruction may lack the power to involve them in meaningful, engaging ways. In such situations, teachers (and in some cases, parents) need to provide extrinsic, age-appropriate reinforcers (e.g., stickers, small toys, free time, computer time) that struggling learners are willing to work for until they become interested in the work and develop a strong, sustaining belief that with moderate effort, they can succeed. To prevent extrinsic reinforcement from backfiring and to reduce or eliminate it within a few months, teachers need to adhere to several basic principles of reinforcement and instruction:

- Use the smallest, most natural reinforcers for which struggling learners will work.

- Vary reinforcers to avoid boredom; change reinforcers that no longer work.

- Start by reinforcing struggling learners every time they correctly apply the strategy; briefly explain why they earned the reinforcer.

- Gradually thin out the frequency of extrinsic reinforcement by reinforcing fewer instances of correct strategy application. Go slow—do not reduce reinforcement too quickly.

- From the beginning, pair tangible, extrinsic reinforcers with common social and verbal reinforcers (e.g., smiles, task-specific praise).

- Reinforce struggling learners in all environments and situations in which they should use the learning strategy and correctly use it (e.g., with different teachers or in different classes, reinforce correct strategy use).

- Listen to struggling learners to learn about their personal goals, values, interests, and problems and link schoolwork to these.

- Stress work that struggling learners find important, interesting, or curiosity arousing.

Reinforce Effort and Persistence

Social cognitive theory predicts that many struggling learners, students who have suffered countless academic difficulties and failures, will have low self-efficacy for academics (Henk and Melnick 1998; Jinks and Morgan 1999; Schunk and Zimmerman 1997; Walker 2003; Zimmerman 2000a). Consequently, they are less prone than successful learners to tackle tasks they perceive as difficult, invest significant effort in such tasks, persist in the face of difficulty, and perform at high levels (Bandura 1997; Ormrod 2000; Pajares 1996; Schunk 1999; Zimmerman 2000a).

To strengthen struggling learners' self-efficacy, teachers need to select tasks well within struggling learners' abilities, sequence tasks from easy to difficult, help struggling learners realize they have the skills to succeed, provide them with help and encouragement whenever needed, show them how to correct their mistakes, and introduce "difficult" tasks only when they are no longer difficult—when struggling learners have mastered the prerequisites on which success depends (Rosenshine 1983; Salvia and Ysseldyke 2001; Swanson 2000). In such situations, resistance will often evaporate, creating legitimate opportunities to reinforce effort and persistence.

Resistance, however, will not evaporate if the initial tasks are too lengthy, too complex, or too difficult. Thus, to create opportunities to reinforce effort and persistence, initial assignments should be challenging but well within the struggling learners' abilities. Success should require reasonable, moderate effort—not Herculean. Struggling learners should view tasks as doable, not impossible.

Doable tasks that struggling learners can successfully complete with moderate effort makes "effort feedback" credible and can enhance self-efficacy, motivation, and achievement (Schunk 2001). Effort feedback, however, can backfire, if struggling learners are frequently reinforced for the effort invested in repeating the same task. They may "doubt their capacities and wonder why they still have to work hard to succeed" (Schunk 2001, 139).

Stress Peer Modeling

Although teacher modeling is highly effective (Swanson 2000), peer models may be particularly effective in strengthening self-efficacy (Alderman 1999; Pajares and Schunk 2001; Schunk 1999, 2003). Fortunately, teachers who give students interesting work at their proper instructional and independent levels usually have several peer models to choose from, as such work encourages proper behavior.

Peer models can be mastery or coping models. Peer coping models have the advantage of showing struggling learners how other students, similar to them, make and overcome mistakes in acquiring and applying new skills and learning strategies. This fosters the belief, "She's like me. If she can do it, I can" (Schunk 2001).

To improve the effectiveness of peer coping models, teachers should

- choose an important skill or strategy that is likely to challenge but not frustrate models and struggling learners;

- break complicated skills and strategies into manageable components;

- select models who resemble the struggling learners and who they respect;

- have models explain their actions, in a simple step-by-step manner, while they work to learn and apply the skill or strategy;

- have models correct their mistakes and verbally attribute failures to controllable factors (e.g., poor effort) and successes to controllable factors (e.g., correctly using a strategy) and ability (e.g., "I read well enough to use the Multipass strategy");

- have struggling learners observe models reinforced, in a variety of appropriate situations, for correctly using the targeted skill or strategy; and

- reinforce struggling learners, in a variety of appropriate situations, for correctly using the targeted skill or strategy.

Teach Students to Make Facilitative Attributions

Attributions are people's explanatory beliefs about why things happen to them. They explain success and failure and influence future actions, including effort, persistence, and choices (Bandura 1997; Pajares and Schunk 2001; Zimmerman 2000b).

> The attributions that people assign to the things that happen to them . . . guide their future behavior.... [Students] may attribute their school successes and failures to ...aptitude or ability (how smart or proficient they are), effort (how hard they tried), other people (how well the teacher taught or how much their classmates like them), task difficulty (how "easy" or "hard" something is), luck, mood, illness, fatigue, or physical appearance. . . . If students erroneously attribute their failures to stable and uncontrollable causes, they are unlikely [emphasis added] to change their future behaviors in ways that will lead to greater success. (Ormrod 2000, 497-98)

To counteract the effects of erroneous attributions that destroy self-efficacy—reducing struggling learners' willingness to try, to make reasonable efforts, and to persist—teachers need to stress accurate, facilitative attributions throughout the day and teach struggling learners to do the same.

Facilitative attributions associate successes with controllable factors, such as effort, persistence, and the correct use of learning or cognitive strategies. They stress what students did (Composite explanation: "I succeeded because I tried very hard.... I stuck to it.... I followed the steps on my cue cards"). Similarly, they attribute poor performances and failures to the same controllable factors, but stress what students did not do (Composite explanation: "I failed because I didn't try hard enough.... I didn't stick to it.... I didn't follow the steps on my cue cards").

Facilitative attributions also link successes to ability, such as learned intelligence (e.g., "I'm smart about that now. I learned how to use Multipass to understand the tough parts of my science book"). In contrast, they divorce poor performance or failure from ability.

Many experts have recommended combining attribution statements with cognitive strategies (Borkowski, Weyhing, and Carr 1988; Chapman and Tunmer 2003; Fulk 1994; Mushinski Fulk and Mastropieri 1990; Pintrich and Schunk 2002; Schunk and Rice 1993; Shelton, Anastopoulos, and Linden 1985). In a sense, it provides the best of both by giving struggling learners the formula, the secret for achieving success—the strategy—and teaches them to take credit for using and sticking with the strategy. Mushinski Fulk and Mastroprini (1990) designed a model for integrating strategy and attribution instruction.

Help Students Create Personally Important Goals

Perhaps nothing is more motivating than combining personally important goals with the belief that with reasonable effort, they are achievable (Pintrich and Schunk 2002; Schunk 2001; Zimmerman 2000b). But not every goal is motivating. Not every goal will improve low self-efficacy. For goals to positively influence self-efficacy and motivation, they need to be personally important to struggling learners, short-term, specific, and achievable (Alderman 1999; Bandura 1997; Schunk 1999; Stipek 1998). Moreover, to sustain motivation, struggling learners need credible feedback that they are making substantial progress toward achieving their goal (Alderman 1999; Bandura 1997; Pajares and Schunk 2001; Schunk 1999, 2003).

Personally important goals are goals that students want to achieve, goals they think will make an important difference in their lives. Struggling learners are far more likely to work to achieve goals that are important to them (Slavin 1999), and which they think they can achieve, than goals they view as unimportant and beyond their abilities.

Short-term goals (e.g., "Get a B+ on next week's social studies test") work hand in hand with long-term goals (e.g., "Pass social studies so I'm eligible for the hockey team"). Long-term goals, goals that will take months or years to attain, express students' dreams, students' hopes. Short-term goals are subgoals; they are intermediate steps between the present and long-term goals. Struggling learners need short-term goals to prevent loss of motivation, caused by the remoteness of long-term goals. Without frequent, explicit, visible feedback that they are making progress on short-term goals, struggling learners often get discouraged, retreating from academics. Frequently noting progress improves self-efficacy and motivation (Schunk 1999, 2001).

Specific, short-term goals are easily measurable, allowing struggling learners and teachers to frequently evaluate progress against a clear standard. For example, struggling learners can easily judge whether they met these specific, short-term goals:

- Write two compositions that earn a "B" on the class writing rubric.

- Try out for the band.

Step 1: *Explain purpose.* Explain the purpose of the strategy. Make sure the student understands how the strategy will help her. Relate the purpose to the student's frame of reference so she sees value in learning the strategy.

Step 2: *Discuss effort.* Discuss with the student how she controls her own effort and the critical role effort plays in producing successful outcomes.

Step 3: *Model examples.* Apply the strategy correctly and incorrectly. Label the examples correct and incorrect.

Step 4: *Model attributions.* Model controllable attributions while engaging in the strategy (e.g., "I got the right answer because I first skimmed the chapter, read all the headings and subheadings, and tried hard. . . . I got the wrong answer because I rushed and didn't skim the whole chapter. I didn't try hard.")

Step 5: *Provide guided practice.* Give the student ample opportunity to practice the combined strategy-attribution sequence with timely task-specific feedback until she routinely gets the right answer, makes positive attributions about her efforts, and appears comfortable with the strategy (e.g., "Kelly, that's great. You got the right answer because you first skimmed the chapter and worked hard. You told yourself that putting the effort in improves your understanding.").

Step 6: *Provide independent practice.* Give the student ample opportunity to use the combined strategy-attribution sequences by herself. Monitor student behavior and offer task-specific feedback as needed (e.g., "Nice job Kelly. You worked hard and gave yourself credit for skimming the chapter before reading it. Your effort made a difference.").

Step 7: *Conduct formative evaluation.* Assess the student's progress and modify teaching strategies if difficulty is apparent (e.g., if Kelly has trouble skimming full chapters of some twenty pages, reduce skimming to a more manageable fraction and provide more frequent feedback).

Step 8: *Introduce a new strategy.* Once the student routinely uses the strategy correctly and takes credit for making adequate effort and using it correctly, introduce a slightly different strategy appropriate for the student's instructional level. Re-institute attribution retraining sequence with step 1.

Note: Adapted from B. M. Mushinski Fulk and M. A. Mastropieri 1990.

FIGURE 2. General steps for combined attribution retraining and strategy instruction.

Scene: The teacher reads a paragraph aloud to his class. The paragraph, on Martin Luther King's assassination, is projected onto a screen, from an overhead projector. As the teacher reads aloud, he illustrates the Paraphrasing Reading Strategy (Ellis 1996) by saying:

- I'm using the RAP strategy.

- The three steps are "R" for Read a paragraph, "A" for Ask yourself what the paragraph was about, and "P" for Put the main idea and two details in your own words.

- I read the paragraph. I'll check the "R" on my checklist.

FIGURE 3. A teacher think-aloud for a learning strategy checklist.

Although many struggling learners can monitor and evaluate their work, some cannot. Teachers can teach struggling learners to monitor their work by frequently demonstrating think-alouds when evaluating struggling learners' work (Tierney and Readance 2000; Walker 2003; Wilheim 2001), and teaching them to use simple self-evaluation forms, rubrics, learning strategy reference cards, and learning strategy checklists (Casteel, Isom, and Jordan 2000; Lipson and Wixson 1997; Walker 1997, 2003). Figure 3 illustrates how teachers might use a think-aloud with a learning strategy checklist.

Realistic goals, goals that struggling learners can achieve with moderate effort, are more motivating than excessively difficult or excessively easy goals. Excessively difficult goals lead to resistance or despair because struggling learners believe them impossible to achieve. In contrast, excessively easy goals offer no challenge. They are boring; when achieved, struggling learners do not feel more competent. One instance in which excessively easy goals may be appropriate, but only temporarily, is when struggling learners are reeling from sustained difficulty and failure and need successful experiences to begin restoring confidence.

If struggling learners lack personally important goals, or they are vague, teachers should help them formulate precise, personal goals. Otherwise, it is more difficult to meaningfully involve them in academics. Fortunately, many struggling learners appreciate the activity, as they, like most people, want something. The two keys are finding out what struggling learners want and helping them express it in explicit, visible, concrete terms.

One way to get the information needed to help struggling learners formulate personally important goals is to ask them to complete an interest inventory. Another, more personal way is to listen empathetically to them about anything they want to discuss. Teachers can then meet with them and use this information to collaboratively write down the struggling learners' long-term and related short-term goals. One strategy to better understand their goals, and to help them better understand their own goals, is for teachers and struggling learners to circle, discuss, illustrate, and define vague words—words that are difficult to visualize and describe. If the opportunity to help struggling learners develop personally important goals is unavailable, teachers might ask guidance counselors for assistance.

Once struggling learners have defined personally important, specific, realistic, short-term goals, and understand their relationship to their long-term goals and schoolwork, teachers and struggling learners need to frequently assess progress toward achieving these goals (Schunk, 2001). If struggling learners are making good progress, teachers and learners should discuss what they are doing to produce success; if progress is poor, how to improve the situation. Typically, as learners note progress, their self-efficacy and enthusiasm for learning improves.

Incorporate Other Motivational Factors

Motivation, or the willingness to initiate and sustain goal directed activity, is influenced by self-efficacy (Bandura 1993; Henk and Melnick 1998; Jinks and Morgan 1999; Pajares and Schunk 2001; Pintrich and Schunk 2002; Schunk and Rice 1993; Schunk and Zimmerman 1997; Zimmerman 2000b; Zimmerman and Martinez-Pons 1990). "If," as an old saying goes, "people don't think they can, they won't." The converse, however, is not true. Just because people think they can do something, does not mean they will. However, they will likely invest in activities they find interesting or valuable, if their environment is safe and supportive, and if difficulties do not lead to embarrassment or comparisons with more successful peers. Thus, attempts to increase self-efficacy must take place within emotionally safe, secure classes that emphasize motivational principles that create or nurture a desire to learn and achieve. Such classes are usually taught by enthusiastic, optimistic teachers who

- run well-organized classes;

- encourage students to use well-organized, well-stocked learning centers and libraries;

- treat students with respect;

- show interest in students;

- give students choices;

- relate curriculum to students' lives and interests, in and out of school;

- radiate interest in their lessons;

- stimulate and maintain curiosity;

- engage students in collaborative learning activities, such as cooperative learning and peer tutoring;

- encourage sharing;

- use a variety of teaching approaches, appropriate to lesson objectives;

- make expectations clear and realistic;

- provide help, whenever needed, in socially appropriate ways, that avoid student embarrassment;

- compare students' achievements to their past achievements, rather than to other students';

- stress cooperative rather than competitive activities;

- provide frequent, immediate, task-specific feedback, including corrective comments and justified praise;

- ensure that students have the prerequisite knowledge and skill to master new topics and assignments;

- emphasize what is right about students' work; and

- challenge rather than frustrate students.

Caveats

As Linnenbrink and Pintrich (2003) noted, "Psychology and educational psychology are probabilistic sciences. . . . [Because they examine] what occurs, on average, across situations, there may be . . . situations where the principles do not apply. . . . [Thus,] it is important that teachers use psychological research as a guide …rather than a prescriptive device" (134). Consequently, teachers who employ this article's suggestions need to monitor their effects on struggling learners and continue to use and refine those suggestions that work and modify or abandon those that don't. More important than any single suggestion is addressing struggling learners' self-efficacy in informed, systematic ways.

Because self-efficacy is task-specific (e.g., affected by the level and complexity of the task and the social and physical context in which it must be completed), attempts to strengthen it need to focus on the specific task or academic subject in which struggling learners feel incompetent. It is quite possible, for example, that they feel highly confident in one subject (e.g., mathematics) and inadequate in another (reading). The distinction is often finer. In reading, some have confidence in their comprehension abilities with second grade materials but none in their second grade word recognition skills.

No one knows how high self-efficacy must be to improve poor effort, persistence, and academic performance. High self-efficacy, however, is not always good. Overconfident or cocky students may not invest the effort needed to do well (Zimmerman 2000b). Therefore, they need intrinsically interesting tasks that, within reason, challenge their abilities. If they are overconfident and uninterested in tasks, teachers need to link reinforcement to both effort and accomplishment (Pajares 2003; Pintrich and Schunk 2002).

To succeed, struggling learners often need teachers' assistance. If materials and tasks are at the learners' proper instructional and independent levels, the help needed should be minimal. If learners need excessive help, or have to invest a Herculean effort, the task is at their frustration level. In such situations, teachers need to modify tasks so struggling learners need only minimal help.

If teachers often give more help than struggling learners need, they may interpret this as a sign that teachers think they are incompetent (Schunk 2001). Thus, teachers need to carefully assess the amount of help needed and give struggling learners the least amount of help needed to achieve success.

Often, struggling learners' low self-efficacy is part of larger, more complex problems. Although the suggestions in this article can often improve self-efficacy, they will probably be most effective if incorporated into a comprehensive program that systematically addresses the struggling learners' priority needs. Moreover, some struggling learners have had so much failure in their lives, and have so many other problems, that efforts to improve self-efficacy will take a long time and an informed, coordinated, skilled effort on the part of teachers, related service personnel, and parents. Not addressing struggling learners' self-efficacy needs, however, is likely to impede educational progress (Bandura, 1993), as "students' self-beliefs about academic capabilities . . . play an essential role in their motivation to achieve" (Zimmerman 2000a, 89).

Conclusion

For students to meaningfully involve themselves in learning for sustained periods, sufficient self-efficacy is required. Understandably, many struggling learners believe that academics mean failure and frustration—they have low self-efficacy for academics.

To reverse this, teachers must recognize that low self-efficacy is not an immutable, global trait. Rather, it is a modifiable, task-specific set of beliefs derived largely from frequent failures. By matching task difficulty to struggling learners' instructional and independent levels, linking new work to recent successes, teaching them strategies that produce success, reinforcing effort and persistence, using peer models, stressing and teaching facilitative explanations for successes and failures, and helping them understand how schoolwork can help them achieve personally important goals, teachers can often strengthen struggling learners' self-efficacy. By doing so, teachers increase the likelihood that struggling learners will become more motivated, more involved, more persistent, and more successful learners.

REFERENCES

Alderman, M. K. 1999. *Motivation for achievement: Possibilities for teaching and learning.* Mahwah, NJ: Lawrence Erlbaum Publishers.

Alper, S., D. L. Ryndak, and C. N. Schloss. 2001. *Alternative assessment of students with disabilities in inclusive settings.* Boston: Allyn and Bacon.

Baker, L., and A. Wigfield. 1999. Dimensions of children's motivation for reading and their relations to reading activity and reading achievement. *Reading Research Quarterly* 34 (4): 452-57.

Bandura, A. 1993. Perceived self-efficacy in cognitive development and functioning. *Educational Psychologist* 28 (2): 117-48.

Bandura, A. 1997. *Self-efficacy: The exercise of control.* New York: Freeman.

Borich, G. D. 2000. *Effective teaching methods.* 4th ed. Merrill: Upper Saddle River, NJ.

Borkowski, J. G., R. S. Weyhing, and L. A. Carr. 1988. Effects of attributional retraining on strategy-based reading comprehension in learning-disabled students. *Journal of Educational Psychology* 80:46-53.

Casteel, C. P., B. A. Isom, and K. F. Jordan. 2000. Creating confident and competent readers: Transactional strategies instruction. *Intervention in School and Clinic* 36 (2): 67-74.

Chapman, J. W., and W. E. Tunmer. 2003. Reading difficulties, reading-related self-perceptions, and strategies for overcoming negative self-beliefs. *Reading and Writing Quarterly: Overcoming Learning Difficulties* 19 (1): 5-24.

Culyer, R. C. 1996. Making homework work. *Education Digest* 61(9): 52-53.

Ellis, E. S. 1996. Reading strategy instruction. In *Teaching adolescents with learning disabilities: Strategies and methods,* 61-125. Ed. D. D. Deshler, E. S. Ellis, and B. K. Lenz. 2nd ed. Denver: Love Publishing.

Ellis, E. S., and B. K. Lenz. 1996. Perspectives on instruction in learning strategies. In *Teaching adolescents with learning disabilities: Strategies and methods,* 9-60., ed. D. D. Deshler, E. S. Ellis, and B. K. Lenz. 2nd ed. Denver: Love Publishing.

Fewster, S., and P. D. Macmillian. 2002. School-based evidence for the validity of curriculum-based measurement of reading and writing. *Remedial and Special Education* 23 (3): 149-56.

Fulk, B. M. 1994. Mnemonic keyword strategy training for students with learning disabilities. *Learning Disabilities Research and Practice* 9 (3): 179-85.

Galagan, J. 1985. Psychoeducational testing: Turn out the light, the party's over. *Exceptional Children* 52:288-99.

Henk, W. A., and S. A. Melnick. 1995. The reader self-perception scale (RSPS): A new tool for measuring how children feel about themselves as readers. *Reading Teacher* 48:470-82.

———. 1998. Upper elementary-aged children's reported perceptions about good readers: A self-efficacy influenced update in transitional literacy contexts. *Reading Research and Instruction* 38 (1): 57-80.

Idol, I., A. Nevin, and P. Paolucci-Whitcomb. 1999. *Models of curriculum-based assessment: A blueprint for learning.* 3rd ed. Austin, TX: Pro-Ed.

Jinks, J., and V. Morgan. 1999. Children's perceived academic self-efficacy: An inventory scale. *The Clearing House* 72 (4): 224-30.

Joyce, B., and M. Weil. 1996. *Models of teaching.* 5th ed. Boston: Allyn and Bacon.

Leslie, L., and J. Caldwell. 2001. *Qualitative Reading Inventory-3.* NY: Longman.

Linnenbrink, E. A., and P. R. Pintrich. 2003. The role of self-efficacy beliefs in student engagement and learning in the classroom. *Reading and Writing Quarterly: Overcoming Learning Difficulties* 19 (2): 119-38.

Lipson, M. Y., and K. K. Wixson. 1997. *Assessment and instruction of reading disability: An interactive approach.* 2nd ed. NY: Longman.

Lynch, J. 2002. Parents' self-efficacy beliefs, parents' gender, children's reader self-perceptions, reading achievement and gender. *Journal of Research in Reading* 25 (1): 54-67.

McCabe, P., and H. Margolis. 1999. Developing reading programs: How the Qualitative Reading Inventory II can help consultants. *Journal of Educational and Psychological Consultation* 10 (4): 385-93.

McCormick, S. 2003. *Instructing students who have literacy problems.* 4th ed. Englewood Cliffs, NJ: Merrill.

Mushinski Fulk, B. M., and M. A. Mastropieri. 1990. Training positive attitudes. *Intervention in School and Clinic* 26 (2): 79-83.

Newcomer, P. L. 1986. *Standardized Reading Inventory* (manual). Austin, TX: Pro-Ed.

Ormrod, J. E. 2000. *Educational psychology: Developing learners.* 3rd ed. Upper Saddle River, NJ: Prentice Hall.

Pajares, F. 1996. Self-efficacy beliefs in academic settings. *Review of Educational Research* 66 (4): 543-78.

Pajares, F. 2003. Self-efficacy beliefs, motivation, and achievement in writing: A review of the literature. *Reading and Writing Quarterly: Overcoming Learning Difficulties* 19 (2): 139-58.

Pajares, F., and D. H. Schunk. 2001. Self-beliefs and school success: Self-efficacy, self-concept, and school achievement. In *Perception,* 239-66., ed. R. Riding and S. Rayner. London: Ablex Publishing.

Pintrich, P. R., and D. H. Schunk. 2002. *Motivation in education: Theory, research, and applications.* 2nd ed. Englewood Cliffs, NJ: Prentice Hall.

Rieth, H., and C. Evertson. 1988. Variables related to the effective instruction of difficult-to-teach children. *Focus on Exceptional Children* 20 (5): 1-8.

Rosenshine, B. 1983. Teaching functions in instructional programs. *Elementary School Journal* 83:335-51.

Salvia, J., and J. E. Ysseldyke. 2001. *Assessment.* 8th ed. Boston: Houghton Mifflin Company.

Schumm, J. S., and C. T. Mangrum II. 1991. FLIP: A framework for content area reading. *Journal of Reading* 35 (2): 120-24.

Schunk, D. H. 1999. Social-self interaction and achievement behavior. *Educational Psychologist* 34 (4): 219-27.

———. 2001. Social cognitive theory and self-regulated learning. In *Self-regulated learning and academic achievement: Theoretical perspectives,* 125-51., ed. B. J. Zimmerman and D. H. Schunk. Mahwah, NJ: Lawrence Erlbaum Associates.

———. 2003. Self-efficacy for reading and writing: Influence of modeling, goal setting, and self-evaluation. *Reading and Writing Quarterly: Overcoming Learning Difficulties* 19 (2): 159-72

Schunk, D. H., and J. M. Rice. 1993. Strategy fading and progress feedback: Effects on self-efficacy and comprehension among students receiving remedial reading services. *Journal of Special Education* 27:257-76.

Schunk, D. H., and B. J. Zimmerman. 1997. Developing self-efficacious readers and writers: The role of social and self-regulatory processes. In *Reading engagement: Motivating readers through integrated instruction,* 34-50., ed. J. T. Guthrie and A. Wigfield. Newark, DE: International Reading Association.

Shelton, T. L., A. D. Anastopoulos, and J. D. Linden. 1985. An attribution training program with learning disabled children. *Journal of Learning Disabilities* 18 (5): 261-65.

Slavin, R. E. 1999. *Educational psychology: Theory and practice.* 6th ed. Boston: Allyn and Bacon.

Spinelli, C. G. 2002. *Classroom assessment for students with special needs in inclusive settings.* Upper Saddle River, NJ: Merrill.

Stipek, D. 1998. *Motivation to learn: From theory to practice.* 3rd ed. Boston: Allyn and Bacon.

Strickland, D. S., K. Ganske, and J. K. Monroe. 2002. *Supporting struggling readers and writers: Strategies for classroom intervention 3-6.* Newark, DE: International Reading Association.

Swanson, H. L. 1999. Instructional components that predict treatment outcomes for students with learning disabilities: Support for a combined strategy and direct instruction model. *Learning Disabilities Research and Practice* 14 (3): 129-40.

Swanson, H. L. 2000. What instruction works for students with learning disabilities? Summarizing the results from a meta-analysis of intervention studies. In *Contemporary special education research: Synthesis of the knowledge base on critical instructional issues,* 1-30. ed.

R. Gersten, E. P. Schiller, and S. Vaughn. Mahwah, NJ: Lawrence Erlbaum Associates.

Tierney, R. J., and J. E. Readence. 2000. *Reading strategies and practices: A compendium.* 5th ed. Boston: Allyn and Bacon.

Vaughn, S., R. Gersten, and D. J. Chard. 2000. The underlying message in LD intervention research: Findings from research syntheses. *Exceptional Children* 67 (1): 99-114.

Vermette, P. J. 1998. *Making cooperative learning work.* Upper Saddle River, NJ: Merrill.

Walker, B. J. 1997. Discussions that focus on strategies and self-assessment. In *Lively discussions: Fostering engaged reading,* 183-204, ed. L. B. Gambrell and J. F. Almasi. Newark, DE: International Reading Association.

Walker, B. 2003. The cultivation of student self-efficiency in reading and writing. *Reading and Writing Quarterly: Overcoming Learning Difficulties* 19 (2): 173-87.

Wilheim, J. D. 2001. *Improving comprehension with think-aloud strategies.* New York: Scholastic Professional Books.

Zimmerman, B. J. 2000a. Self-efficacy: An essential motive to learn. *Contemporary Educational Psychology* 25:82-91.

———. 2000b. Attaining self-regulation: A social cognitive perspective. In *Handbook of self-regulation,* 13-39, ed. M. Boekaerts, P. R. Pintrich, and M. Zeidner. San Diego: Academic Press.

Zimmerman, B. J., and M. Martinez-Pons. 1990. Student differences in self-regulated learning: Relating grade, sex, and giftedness to self-efficacy and strategy use. *Journal of Educational Psychology* 82:51-59.

Howard Margolis is a professor of special education at Queens College of the City University of New York in Flushing. Patrick P. McCabe is an associate professor in the Graduate Literacy Education Program at St. John's University in Jamaica, New York.

From *The Clearing House,* July/August 2004, pp. 241-249. Reprinted by permission of the Helen Dwight Reid Educational Foundation. Published by Heldref Publications, 1319, Eighteenth St., NW, Washington, DC 20036-1802. Copyright © 2004.

VOUCHERS FOR PARENTS
New Forms of Education Funding

LAMAR ALEXANDER

In 1990, as the new president of the University of Tennessee, I was trying to understand what had made American colleges and universities the best in the world. I asked David Gardner, then the president of the University of California, why his university has such a tradition of excellence. "First," he said, "autonomy. The California constitution created four branches of government, with the university being the fourth. The legislature basically turns over money to us without many rules about how to spend it.

"The second is excellence. We were fortunate, at our beginning, to have a corps of faculty dedicated to high standards. That tradition has continued. And third, generous amounts of federal—and state—money have followed students to the schools of their choice. That has increased opportunity for those who couldn't afford college, created choices that make good fits between the student and the school, and stimulated competition that encouraged excellent programs."

Autonomy. High standards. Government dollars following students to the schools of their choice. That was the formula for the GI Bill, passed by Congress in 1944. The program gave World War II veterans scholarships redeemable at any accredited institution, public or private. Those veterans who didn't hold a diploma could even use the scholarships at Catholic high schools. With these scholarships came few federal rules, thus preserving the universities' autonomy. And by allowing students to choose their college, the GI Bill encouraged excellence and discouraged weak programs.

Not all university leaders welcomed the program. "It will create a hobo's jungle," warned legendary University of Chicago president Robert Hutchins. Instead, the GI Bill became the most successful piece of social legislation Congress ever enacted. It became the model for the federal grants and loans that today follow 58 percent of America's college students to the schools of their choice. In 1972, when Congress debated whether future federal funding for higher education should go directly to institutions or be channeled through students, the model of the GI Bill helped carry the day for the latter approach, which was surely the right one. Pell Grants (named

for Sen. Claiborne Pell, D-R.I.), Stafford Loans, and other forms of financial assistance to students followed. This year the federal government will spend nearly $17 billion on grants and work-study programs and will provide an additional $52 billion in student loans.

BANG FOR THE BUCK

Rarely has the federal taxpayer gotten so much bang for the buck. These federal vouchers trained the "greatest generation" and made it possible for a greater percentage of Americans to continue into higher education than in any other country. At the time of the GI Bill's passage in 1944, only about 6 percent of Americans held a four-year college degree. Today that figure stands at 26 percent.

Moreover, these scholarships have strengthened public institutions. At the end of World War II, 50 percent of American college students were attending public institutions. Today 76 percent choose to attend public colleges and universities. So many foreign students want to attend American universities that some institutions impose caps in order to make room for lower-achieving homegrown students. British prime minister Tony Blair is overhauling his nation's system of higher education because he sees a growing gap between the quality of American and British universities. Likewise, former Brazilian president Fernando Henrique Cardoso recently told a small group of U.S. senators that the most important thing he would remember about his residency at the Library of Congress is "the uniqueness, strength, and autonomy of the American university."

Meanwhile, federal support for elementary and secondary education has taken just the opposite approach—with opposite results. Instead of allowing tax dollars to follow students to the schools of their parents' choice, the federal government gives $35 billion directly to the schools themselves (or to the states, which then give it to schools). In addition, thousands of pages of federal and state regulations govern how these funds are spent, thereby diminishing each school's autonomy. Measured by student learning, rarely has the taxpayer gotten so little bang for so many bucks. In 1999, 8th-grade students in this country were ranked 19th in math and 18th in science compared with 38 other industrialized nations. The National Assessment of Educational Progress, known as the nation's report card, shows other alarming trends. For example, between 1996 and 2000, the gap between affluent and poorer U.S. students actually widened in seven out of nine key indicators—like reading, math, and science. Two out of every three African-American and Hispanic 4th graders could barely read. Seventy percent of children in high-poverty schools scored below even the most basic level of reading.

ENHANCING LOCAL CONTROL

It is time to try a different funding approach, and Pell Grants, the college scholarships offered to low-income students, provide a useful model. Congress should enact "Pell Grants for Kids," which would provide a $500 scholarship to each middle- and low-income child in America. Children could use these scholarships at any public or private school or for any educational program, such as private tutoring. Homeschooled children would also be eligible for the scholarship, as long as the money was spent on an accredited educational program. Overall, the grant would be available to about 60 percent of America's 50 million primary and secondary school students, those whose families earn $53,000 or less. It would put the parents of approximately 30 million children directly into the education marketplace, each of them armed with a $500 grant, thereby encouraging choice and competition.

This idea has a distinguished lineage. In the late 1960s, Theodore Sizer, then at the Harvard Graduate School of Education, proposed a "Poor Children's Bill of Rights" that would have supplied scholarships of $5,000 per child to the poorest half of children in the United States, for use at any accredited school, public or private. In 1992, while I was serving as secretary of education under President George H.W. Bush, the president asked Congress to appropriate a half billion dollars to create a pilot "GI Bill for Kids." The program would have awarded $1,000 scholarships to 500,000 children in states and cities that wanted to try the idea, but the Democrat-controlled Congress refused to enact it.

The most important point to make here is that most of this new scholarship money is likely to be used at the public schools that nine out of ten students now attend. I believe parents are likely either to give the money to their school to meet its general needs or to seek the school's advice on how best to spend the money to help their child. Surveys show that while many Americans are discouraged about the state of education generally, most parents support their own child's public school. Parents in affluent school districts regularly augment their schools' budgets with contributions for extra programs, particularly in the arts. Pell Grants for Kids would give children of low- and middle-income parents the same opportunity.

Pell Grants for Kids would provide more federal dollars for schools while also encouraging more local control—I mean more control by parents and teachers—over how

that money is spent. Once parents make the decision about *where* the $500 will be spent, the principal and teachers in that school or program decide *how* it will be spent. For example, in a public middle school with 600 students, if two-thirds of the children are eligible for the grant, that's $200,000 in new federal dollars each year following those children to that school. This would be manna from heaven for schools, many of which engage in time-consuming charity sales to net $500 or $1,000 for needed programs and projects. Enterprising principals surely would design programs to attract parents' investment—perhaps an after-school program, an extra math teacher, or an intensive language course. And if they didn't, parents would have the option to spend the money on another accredited educational program that suited their child's needs, such as tutoring.

NARROWING GAPS

Aside from stimulating competition, these new federal funds would help to narrow the gaps in spending between wealthy and poor districts and make more real the promise that no child will be left behind. For example, in Bryan, Texas, property values average about $128,000 per student. Next door is College Station, home of Texas A&M University, where property values are $305,000 per student. As a result, College Station is able to collect far more in property taxes and its schools thus spend twice as much per student as those in Bryan. Last year Herman Smith, superintendent of schools in Bryan, told me, "College Station is talking about *cuts* in programs and personnel that we could only dream of."

About 90 percent of Bryan's 13,500 students would be eligible for the $500 Pell Grants for Kids, putting more than $6 million in new federal dollars into the hands of Bryan parents. They could then provide more funds to Bryan's public schools, as is likely, or use the scholarship to help pay for enrichment programs or private school tuition. Bryan would still have fewer dollars to spend than College Station, but the gap would narrow.

OVERCOMING OBJECTIONS

Let's consider some questions and criticisms that might accompany the Pell Grant for Kids proposal:

- *In a time of tight budgets, can the nation afford to offer $500 scholarships to 30 million schoolchildren?* If it were enacted today, Pell Grants for Kids would cost $15 billion a year. A number of measures could be taken to ease the burden. First, implement the program gradually, providing $500 scholarships only to kindergarten and 1st graders in the initial year. This would cost just $2 billion. Second, over the next several years, devote most of the new appropriations for K–12 education (not related to children with disabilities) to Pell Grants for Kids. Done this way, it would not take many years to fully fund the scholarships while staying within a reasonable budget. For instance, if Congress had allocated two-thirds of all new federal spending (non–disability related) on K–12 education since 1992 to this program, $10 billion would have been available for scholarships this year—enough to provide full $500 scholarships to all middle- and low-income children in kindergarten through the 8th grade.

Or consider this: In just the first two years of the current administration, Congress appropriated $4.5 billion in new dollars for K–12 education (not counting another $3 billion more for children with disabilities). That $4.5 billion would have been enough to fully fund $500 scholarships for all nine million low- and middle-income children in kindergarten through 3rd grade.

- *Aren't K–12 schools and colleges so different that the Pell Grant analogy is invalid?* It is true that schools and colleges sometimes emphasize different public purposes. For example, schools are asked to teach children what it means to be an American, to inculcate moral values, and to make up for poor parenting. Universities have research and public service missions that schools don't share. But the core mission of both schools and colleges is the same: teaching and learning. Most high schools teach some college courses. Most community colleges teach some high-school students. That is why it is so odd that the way the federal government funds K–12 education is so different from the way it funds colleges.

- *Aren't you overlooking some real problems that colleges have?* No doubt universities have significant problems. Some college students don't pay back their loans. Some for-profit institutions are shams. Some courses are weird. Some tenured faculty members are worthless. In the context of rising tuition costs, there is too little interest in creating a less leisurely university calendar, in proposals such as requiring professors to work over the summer. Such abuses are the price of institutional autonomy and choice. Overall, however, American colleges and universities are by far the best in the world—and therefore useful models for how to improve our other educational institutions.

- *Can we trust middle- and low-income parents to spend $500 wisely on their child's education?* I would remind those who make this condescending argument that Congress currently appropriates $8 billion each year to provide childcare vouchers to 2.3 million low-income parents. These parents may use the voucher at any licensed center, public, private, or religious. Likewise, 9.5 million low-income students may spend their federal student aid dollars at any accredited college. If Congress trusts low-income citizens to choose childcare and higher education providers for themselves, why not trust them to spend $500 on K–12 education programming for their children? In addition, because of our experience using established accredit-

ing agencies to monitor Pell Grants for colleges, it should be relatively easy to create a similar system to make sure that Pell Grants for Kids are not spent on fly-by-night operations.

- *Will more federal funding mean more federal control over education?* Pell Grants for Kids would actually reduce federal control over education. The current funding process dictates how federal dollars are to be spent and imposes heavy regulations on local schools. Letting federal dollars follow children to the school of their parents' choice would put control back into the hands of parents and teachers.

CHURCH AND STATE

- *Would Pell Grants for Kids violate the principle of separation of church and state?* Federal grants have followed students to parochial colleges since World War II and to parochial daycare centers since 1990.

- *Will giving individual schools so much autonomy leave some mired in mediocrity?* Autonomy need not mean a lack of accountability. The No Child Left Behind Act requires states to establish tough academic standards and to measure students' and schools' performance on an annual basis. With these accountability systems in place, the argument for choice is that much stronger. Parents will have the knowledge of school performance to make informed choices about where to spend their new federal dollars. For this reason, students who decide to use their $500 scholarships at private schools would still be required to participate in their state's testing program.

- *Why not let all Title I money follow children to the schools of their choice?* For now, I believe a gradual approach is warranted. The nation should begin by letting parents control how most, not all, of newly appropriated federal dollars for K–12 education are spent. Let's monitor parents' spending patterns and school performance for a while and then evaluate whether to expand the program.

- *But private school tuition costs far more than $500.* Correct. So those who worry that vouchers will hurt public schools should relax. But six hundred parents armed with $500 each can exercise $300,000 in consumer power at a public middle school. Five hundred dollars can also help pay for language lessons or remedial help. At Puente Learning Center in South Los Angeles, Sister Jennie Lechtenberg teaches students of all ages English and clerical skills at an average cost to the center of $500 per year.

TOWARD BETTER SCHOOLS

Of course by themselves Pell Grants for Kids would not create the best schools in the world. As David Gardner said, it took autonomy and high standards in addition to generous funding following students to schools of their choice to help create the finest university system in the world. To increase schools' autonomy, Congress should provide generous support to the charter school movement, offer waivers from federal rules to successful school districts, and use its oversight power to simplify federal laws and regulations. To help schools aspire to the excellence most colleges enjoy, Congress needs to give schools more flexibility in administering the mandates of No Child Left Behind. To make it easier for schools to pay teachers more for teaching well, just as colleges do, Congress should encourage the National Board for Professional Teaching Standards and other efforts to reward outstanding teachers. These organizations, in turn, must make the measure of students' progress a key ingredient in a teacher's evaluation.

It is a mistake to expect that merely switching to the higher education model for funding is all Congress needs to do to help transform public schools. To help children arrive at school ready to learn, Congress should heed President Bush's challenge to strengthen Head Start by improving coordination, emphasizing cognitive skills, increasing accountability, and involving governors. So that state and local governments can remain financially sound enough to support good schools, Congress should keep its promise to end unfunded federal mandates. So that children can learn what it means to be an American, Congress should help states put the teaching of American history and civics back in its rightful place in school curricula.

BETTER PARENTING

Finally, no plan for better schools is complete without better parenting. In his research James Coleman found that, until a child is 14, parents are twice as important as school for the child's learning. Yet the United States has gone from a society that values the job of being a parent to one that has been waging a war on parents. Liberal divorce laws and the diminished importance of marriage, higher taxes, poor schools, trash on television, unsafe streets, uncontrolled illegal drugs, and inflexible work arrangements have all made it harder for parents raising children. No part of American society has paid a higher price for this than our schools. Giving every middle- and low-income child a $500 scholarship to help encourage choice within education is a start, but only a start, toward putting government and society squarely on the side of parents raising children.

Nonetheless, enacting Pell Grants for Kids should be the next central thrust of federal efforts to improve the nation's schools. For the past half century, the United States has actively supported the expansion and improvement of higher education through a generous funding system that encourages autonomy, choice, and competition. Our institutions of higher education have helped produce the research that has been responsible for creating half our new jobs since World War II. They have sculpted an educated leadership and citizenry that have made our democracy work and made it possible to defend our freedoms. It is past time to take the formula that has worked so well to help create the best colleges in the world and use it to help create the best schools for our children.

Mr. Alexander is a U.S. senator (R-TN). From "Putting Parents in Charge," by Lamar Alexander, *Education Next, Summer 2004, pages 39–44*

UNIT 8

The Profession of Teaching Today

Unit Selections

Key Points to Consider

- What is "expertise" in teaching? Be specific and use examples.

- Describe the learning needs of new teachers in terms of curriculum, instruction, assessment, management, school culture, and the larger community. How important is maintaining order?

- How would a teacher education program that is based on the premise of developing novice teachers as "transformative" urban educators place student teachers in urban classrooms?

- Why do teachers leave the profession? What can be done to solve schools' staffing problems?

Student Website
www.mhcls.com/online

Internet References
Further information regarding these websites may be found in this book's preface or online.

Canada's SchoolNet Staff Room
http://www.schoolnet.ca/home/e/

Teachers Helping Teachers
http://www.pacificnet.net/~mandel/

The Teachers' Network
http://www.teachers.net

Teaching with Electronic Technology
http://www.wam.umd.edu/~mlhall/teaching.html

The task of helping teachers to grow in their levels of expertise in the classroom falls heavily on those educators who provide professional staff development training in the schools. Meaningful staff development training is extremely important. Several professional concerns are very real in the early career development of teachers. Level of job security or tenure is still an issue, as are the concerns of first-year teachers and teacher educators. How teachers interact with students is a concern to all conscientious, thoughtful teachers.

There are numerous external pressures on the teaching profession today from a variety of public interest groups. The profession continues to develop its knowledge base on effective teaching through ethnographic and empirical inquiry about classroom practice and teachers' behavior in elementary and secondary classrooms across the nation. Concern continues about how best to teach to enhance insightful, reflective student interaction with the content of instruction. We continue to consider alternative visions of literacy and the roles of teachers in fostering a desire for learning within their students.

All of us who live the life of a teacher are aware of those features that we associate with the concept of a good teacher. In addition, we do well to remember that the teacher/student relationship is both a tacit and an explicit one—one in which teachers' attitude and emotional outreach are as important as students' response to our instructional effort. The teacher/student bond in the teaching/learning process cannot be overemphasized. We must maintain an emotional link in the teacher/student relationship that will compel students to want to accept instruction and attain optimal learning. What, then, constitutes those most defensible standards for assessing good teaching?

The past decade has yielded much in-depth research on the various levels of expertise in the practice of teaching. We know much more now about specific teaching competencies and how they are acquired. Expert teachers do differ from novices and experienced teachers in terms of their capacity to exhibit accurate, integrated, and holistic perceptions and analyses of what goes on when students try to learn in classroom settings. We can now pinpoint some of these qualitative differences.

As the knowledge base of our professional practice continues to expand, we will be able to certify with greater precision what constitutes acceptable ranges of teacher performance based on more clearly defined procedures of practice, as we have, for example, in medicine and dentistry. Medicine is, after all, a practical art as well as a science—and so is teaching. The analogy in terms of setting standards of professional practice is a strong one. Yet the emotional pressure on teachers that theirs is also a performing art, and that clear standards of practice can be applied to that art, is a bitter pill to swallow for many. Hence, the intense reaction of many teachers against external competency testing and any rigorous classroom observation standards. The writing, however, is on the wall: The profession cannot hide behind the tradition that teaching is a special art, unlike all others, which cannot be subjected to objective observational standards, aesthetic critique, or to a standard knowledge base. The public demands the same levels of demonstrable professional standards of practice as are demanded of those in the medical arts.

Likewise, we have identified certain approaches to working with students in the classroom that have been effective. Classroom practices such as cooperative learning strategies have won widespread support for inclusion in the knowledge base on teaching. The knowledge base of the social psychology of life in classrooms has been significantly expanded by collaborative research between classroom teachers and various specialists in psychology and teacher education. This has been accomplished by using anthropological field research techniques to ground theory of classroom practice into demonstrable phenomenological perspectives. Many issues have been raised—and answers found—by basic ethnographic field observations, interviews, and anecdotal record-keeping techniques to understand more precisely how teachers and students interact in the classroom. A rich dialectic is developing among teachers regarding the description of ideal classroom environments. The methodological insight from this research into the day-to-day realities of life in schools is transforming what we know about teaching as a professional activity and how to best advance our knowledge of effective teaching strategies.

Creative, insightful persons who become teachers will usually find ways to network their interests and concerns with other teachers and will make their own opportunities for creative teaching in spite of external assessment procedures. They acknowledge that the science of teaching involves the observation and measurement of teaching behaviors but that the art of teaching involves the humanistic dimensions of instructional activities, an alertness to the details of what is taught, and equal alertness to how students receive it. Creative, insightful teachers guide class processes and formulate questions according to their perceptions of how students are responding to the material.

To build their aspirations, as well as their self-confidence, teachers must be motivated to an even greater effort for professional growth in the midst of these fundamental revisions. Teachers need support, appreciation, and respect. Simply criticizing them while refusing to alter social and economic conditions that affect the quality of their work will not solve their problems, nor will it lead to excellence in education. Not only must teachers work to improve their public image and the public's confidence in them, but the public must confront its own misunderstandings of the level of commitment required to achieve teacher excellence. Teachers need to know that the public cares about and respects them enough to fund their professional improvement in a primary recognition that they are an all-important force in the life of this nation. The articles in this unit consider the quality of education and the status of the teaching profession today.

First-Year Teaching Assignments

A Descriptive Analysis

BYLLIE D'AMATO ANDREWS and ROBERT J. QUINN

My first day as a first-year teacher in 1969 began with a breakfast for new teachers followed by independent work at my school. I had no idea where to start, what to do, or who to ask. As the last teacher hired, I was the "floater." I did not have a classroom of my own. I taught in other teachers' classrooms during their respective prep periods. At some point during that first day, I realized that I would probably need some books and supplies to teach my students. All of the more experienced teachers were busy in their classrooms, and for some reason, the principal was thoroughly involved in helping the new PE teacher round up equipment. Finally, someone showed me where the books were stored and let me borrow a cart to put them on. The other teachers had already raided the book room. There were almost enough books for my two advanced eighth-grade math classes and just enough books to make one classroom set for my two regular eighth-grade math classes. But the classes were in different rooms, and it took several days to obtain a cart I could call my own to transport the books from room to room. In addition, I found one set of eighth grade science books that were supposed to stay in the science classroom. I was not certified to teach science, but my principal assured me that it was not a problem.

My experience is still the norm in many schools. In 1989, Huling-Austin et al. (1989) wrote the following about the experience of first-year teachers:

> Beginning teachers are often given teaching assignments that would challenge even the most skillful veteran teachers. Such assignments can take several forms: teaching in a subject area for which the teacher is not certified; having too many class preparations; "floating" from classroom to classroom; working with low-ability, unmotivated, or disruptive students; or being responsible for demanding or time-consuming extracurricular activities. (42)

Secondary teachers still are given unreasonable teaching assignments (Brock and Grady 2001; Feiman-Nemser et al. 1999; Johnson and Carey-Webb 1999; Wise et al. 1987). For example, Donaldson (1999) writes about her first-year teaching experience during 1997-98: "My second surprise materialized in October. … Traveling between four rooms to teach five classes, I struggled to locate and retain enough desks and textbooks for all my students and enough chalk for myself" (49-50). Darling-Hammond (1998) further explains:

> Most U.S. teachers start their careers in disadvantaged schools where turnover is highest, are assigned the most educationally needy students whom no one else wants to teach, are given the most demanding teaching loads with the greatest number of extra duties, and receive few curriculum materials and no mentoring. After this hazing, many leave. Others learn merely to cope rather than to teach well. (10)

First-year teachers still float, still are assigned the most educationally needy students, and still are assigned demanding extra duties. One of my former students, whose student teaching I supervised in fall 1998, was hired in fall 1999 to teach in a high school in the school district in this study. Not only was she a floater, but she also was assigned to teach two proficiency reading classes and given the extra duty of serving as an advisor to the cheerleading squad. She taught for two years, then took maternity leave. She is uncertain if she will return to teaching. Another former student, whose student teaching I supervised in fall 2000, was hired at the same high school in fall 2001. She only teaches drama classes. She was responsible for putting on two productions during her first year. She also was required to advise the cheerleading squad. New teachers in secondary schools frequently face such demands (Brock and Grady 2001; Darling-Hammond, Gendler, and Wise 1990; Donaldson 1999; Wise et al. 1987).

Novice teachers often are given the same responsibilities as their experienced colleagues, despite that learning to teach is a continuum of experience over a period of time rather than something first-year teachers can learn all at once.

Novice teachers often are given the same responsibilities as their experienced colleagues (Brock and Grady 2001; Feiman-Nemser et al. 1999), despite that learning to teach is a continuum of experience over a period of time rather than something first-year teachers can learn all at once (Mager 1992). To compound their daily dilemmas and uncertainties, they often receive the most difficult assignments or are assigned to teach subjects for which they have little or no preparation (Feiman-Nemser et al. 1999; Wise et al. 1987). The tasks that a beginning teacher must assume are not added sequentially as the beginner gradually increases his or her teaching skills and knowledge. Instead, the beginner teacher must learn while he or she is performing the full complement of teaching duties (Lortie 1975).

Purpose

Although previous studies have raised important issues regarding first-year teachers floating, teaching outside of their area of expertise, and teaching too many different classes, most of the evidence they provide is anecdotal. This study seeks to quantify the extent to which these practices occur at the middle and high school levels.

Methodology

Survey

A ten-question survey was used to gather information for this study (see Appendix). The first two questions were demographic in that they asked for the respondent's age and gender. Questions 3 and 4 gathered specific information regarding the level and subject area the respondent taught. Questions 5 through 7 addressed an area directly related to the purpose of the study. Question 5 sought to determine the number of teaching preparations. Question 6 attempted to determine if first-year teachers were teaching outside the area of their field. Question 7 gathered information regarding the practice of floating. Questions 8 through 10 sought to determine the types of support and/or mentoring first-year teachers received. For the purposes of this article, the responses of secondary teachers to the first seven questions were used.

Population

All first-year middle school and high school teachers in a K-12 school district were asked to participate in this study. Some of these teachers teach in schools with high-achieving, high socioeconomic populations, while others teach in schools comprised of at-risk populations. The school district has an overall student population of almost 60,000 and includes eleven middle schools and thirteen high schools.

The youngest respondent was twenty-three years old and the oldest was fifty-nine. Almost 70 percent of the respondents were between twenty-three and thirty-three years old. Three respondents were over fifty years old. Table 1 provides a more detailed breakdown of the ages of the respondents.

In the sample population, 34 respondents (66.7 percent) were female and 17 respondents (33.3 percent) were male.

TABLE 1. Age Breakdown of Respondents

Age	Number of respondents	Percent
24 or younger	5	9.8
25-29	22	43.1
30-34	8	15.7
35-39	4	7.9
40-44	7	13.7
45-49	2	3.9
50-54	0	0.0
55 or older	3	5.9
Total	51	100

TABLE 2. Subject Area Taught by Secondary Teachers

Subject area	Number of respondents
Mathematics	8
Science	6
Math and Science	2
English/Language Arts	9
History/Social Studies	6
Special Education	9
Physical Education	2
Foreign Language	2
Music	1
English/Language Arts/Alternative Education	1
English as a Second Language	1
Other	4
Total	51

Question 3 asked the respondents to circle the grade level he or she taught at the time of the survey. Twenty-two were middle school teachers, 20 were high school teachers, 6 were special education middle school teachers, and 3 were high school special education teachers.

Most of the middle school special education teachers provided additional detail regarding their work. Two described their assignments as being a self-contained resource. One of these individuals added that they were involved in the "SIP" (social intervention program). Three other middle school special education teachers indicated that they engaged in "pushing-in" to regular education classrooms, as well as teaching one or two self-contained subjects. Of the three high school special education teachers, there were a resource teacher, a developmental English teacher, and a teacher who taught comprehensive life skills and a community-based class.

Subject Areas

Question 4 asked the respondents to circle all subject areas that applied. The last choice was "Other" and included space for the respondents to list any subjects that were not given. Table 2 provides the subject area breakdown for secondary teachers.

TABLE 3. Class Preparations for Secondary Teachers	
Preparations	Number of respondents
1	7
2	22
3	12
4	3
5	3
6	1
Missing	3
Total	51

Preparations

Question 5 asked the respondents to give their number of teaching preparations. The results are provided in table 3. Twenty-nine (60.4 percent) of the secondary teachers had only one or two classes for which to prepare. Nineteen out of forty-eight (59.6 percent) secondary first-year teachers were assigned three or more class preparations. Three secondary first-year teachers made no comments on this item. In his October 2002 president's speech, "Supporting New Teachers," Johnny Lott, former president of the National Council of Teachers of Mathematics, suggested that first-year secondary mathematics teachers "be given fewer preparations than experienced teachers—two at the most" (3). Twelve secondary teachers indicated they had three different class preparations and seven indicated they had four or more preparations.

Teaching out of Area of Expertise

Question 6 asked the responding first-year teachers if they taught only in the area of their university training. Fifteen teachers reported that they were teaching one or more classes that were not in the area of their university training. One of these was actually teaching English, which was her minor and, thus, not considered out of area. Two of the secondary teachers were in the Options Program. This program allows teachers who are not certified to teach special education to obtain a provisional special education endorsement while taking university courses toward a special education certification. These teachers have three years to obtain their special education certification (personal communication with Human Resources Office, October 23, 2002). Thus, twelve out of fifty-one secondary teachers actually taught out of their area.

Floating

Question 7 asked respondents if they had their own classroom. Twenty of the fifty-one teachers responded that they did not have their own classrooms. Fourteen of these teachers taught in other teachers' classrooms during the other teachers' preparation period. Four were special education teachers who shared classrooms with other special education teachers and/or "pushed in" to general education classrooms. The other two sec-

ondary teachers were physical education teachers; one taught dance in a dance room and one taught PE in the gym.

Discussion and Recommendations

This study confirmed that the phenomena of floating, teaching out of area of expertise, and having too many preparations, often reported anecdotally in the literature, still occur for secondary first-year teachers in this district. The results of this study provide baseline quantitative data for each of these phenomena. In the district studied, 39.2 percent of first-year secondary teachers are floating, 39.6 percent have three or more classes for which to prepare, and 25.5 percent teach outside their area of university preparation.

Efforts should be made to give every first-year teacher a reasonable teaching assignment. First-year teachers' responsibilities should be limited. Although almost two-thirds of first-year teachers have two or fewer preparations, we find that having approximately one-third of our first-year teachers teaching three or more preparations is unacceptable. We also feel that having roughly two out of every five first-year secondary teachers float is unacceptable. If possible, first-year teachers should be given their own classroom or, at the very least, they should not have to travel more than the veteran teachers in their schools.

Finally, the Elementary and Secondary Education Act (ESEA), known as the No Child Left Behind Act of 2001, requires that anyone teaching a core academic subject at the secondary level must be highly qualified. Highly qualified means that the teacher must be fully certified by the state to teach in that subject area. Consequently, many of the secondary first-year teachers in this study who teach out of their area of expertise would cause their schools to be out of compliance with this law. Therefore, colleges of education should encourage capable candidates to enter high-need content areas so that more schools can hire sufficient numbers of highly qualified teachers to teach their core courses.

The first year of teaching is arduous under the best of circumstances. The practices described in this study exacerbate an already difficult situation and must be eradicated. Further research that better informs administrators, combined with recent legislation, may lead to critical improvements that will benefit teachers as they begin their careers.

REFERENCES

Brock, B. L., and M. L. Grady. 2001. *From first-year to first-rate: Principals guiding beginning teachers.* 2nd ed. Thousand Oaks, CA: Corwin.

Darling-Hammond, L. 1998. Teacher learning that supports student learning. *Educational Leadership 55* (5): 6–11.

Darling-Hammond, L., T. Gendler, and A. Wise. 1990. *The teaching internship: Practical preparation for a licensed profession.* Santa Monica, CA: Rand.

Donaldson, M. I. 1999. Teaching and traditionalism: Encounters with "the way it's always been." In *Reflections of first-year teachers on school culture: Questions, hopes, and challenges,* ed. M. I. Donaldson and B. Poon, 47–58. San Francisco: Jossey-Bass.

Feiman-Nemser, S., C. Carver, S. Schwille, B. Yusko. 1999. *A conceptual review of literature on new teacher induction.* Washington,

APPENDIX

Survey

1. Age _____

2. Gender (circle only one)
   a. Male
   b. Female

3. Grade level now teaching (circle only one)

   Elementary
   a. Primary K-3
   b. Intermediate 4-6
   c. Special Education K-6

   Secondary
   d. Middle School
   e. High School
   f. Special Education 7-8
   g. Special Education 9-12

- If your answer was c, f, or g, please describe your teaching assignment (i.e., self-contained classroom, resource teacher, etc.) below.

Special education assignment description: _____
_____
_____
_____

- If your answer was d or e (you are a middle or high school teacher), please answer questions 4, 5, and 6.
- If your answer was a or b (you are an elementary school teacher), proceed to question 7.

Comments: _____
_____
_____
_____

4. Subject Area (circle all that apply):
   a. Math
   b. Science
   c. English/Language Arts
   d. History/Social Studies
   e. Physical Education
   f. Foreign Language
   g. Occupational Education
   h. Music
   i. Other(s) _____

Comments: _____
_____
_____

5. How many different preparations do you teach? _____ Explain:_____
_____
_____

6. Are you teaching only in the area of your university training? _____ If no, please explain: _____
_____
_____
_____

(Appendix continues)

APPENDIX *(continued)*

7. Do you have your own classroom? (Are all of the classes you teach held in the same classroom, and no other teacher uses this classroom?)
   a. Yes
   b. No

   If you answered b, please explain your particular situation (i.e., you teach in five different classrooms, you teach in two classrooms because you teach two sections of science and need to be in a lab, etc.): _____
   _____
   _____
   _____
   _____

8. Type of new teacher induction (e.g., explanations about policies and procedures, use of available resources, school calendar, obtaining a substitute, sick days, etc.).
   a. District orientation. Check only one.
   ___ One-half day of district orientation
   ___ One day of district orientation
   ___ More than one day of district orientation

   b. Building orientation. Check all that apply.
   ___ One-half day building orientation with other new staff
   ___ One day building orientation with other new staff
   ___ More than one day building orientation with other new staff
   ___ Building tour with other new staff
   ___ Individual building tour by principal or other staff member

   c. Other orientations. Check all that apply.
   ___ Orientation as part of total staff meetings
   ___ Curriculum explanation
   ___ Explanation of district procedures
   ___ Assignment of a mentor or partner teacher
   ___ Individual meeting with principal

   Comments on any part of question 8: _____
   _____
   _____
   _____
   _____

9. I received a teacher handbook with the school district's and/or my school's policies at the beginning of the school year.
   a. Yes
   b. No

Comments on question 9: _____
_____
_____
_____
_____

10. I have a mentor either assigned to me by my principal or through the school district's Mentor Teacher Program.
    a. Yes
    b. No

DC: National Partnership for Excellence and Accountability in Teaching. ERIC, ED 449147.

Huling-Austin, L., S. J. Odell, P. Isher, R. S. Kay, and R. A. Edeldelt. 1989. *Assisting the beginning teacher.* Reston, VA: Association of Teacher Educators.

Johnson, J. K., and A. Carey-Webb. 1999. Sometimes things just don't work out. *English Journal* 88 (6): 19–22.

Lortie, D. C. 1975. *Schoolteacher: A sociological study.* Chicago: University of Chicago Press.

Lott, J. W. 2002. Supporting new teachers. *National Council of Teachers of Mathematics News Bulletin* 29, no. 3 (October): 3.

Mager, G. M. 1992. The place of induction on becoming a teacher. In *Teacher induction and mentoring: School-based collaborative programs,* ed. G. P. DeBolt, 3–33. Albany: State University of New York Press.

Wise, A. E., L. Darling-Hammond, B. Berry, and S. P. Klein. 1987. *Licensing teachers: Design for a teaching profession.* Santa Monica, CA: Rand.

Byllie D'Amato Andrews is an adjunct instructor and **Robert J. Quinn** is an associate professor, both in the Department of Curriculum, Teaching, and Learning at the University of Nevada, Reno.

From *The Clearing House,* November/December 2004, pp. 78-83. Reprinted by permission of the Helen Dwight Reid Educational Foundation. Published by Heldref Publications, 1319, Eighteenth St., NW, Washington, DC 20036-1802. Copyright © 2004. www.heldref.org

Nurturing Passionate Teachers:
Making Our Work Transparent

Randall Wisehart

At the beginning of the school year the first year teachers and student teachers I will be working with will hear this typical statement from the principal of our high school: *We need to get those test scores up. We want our school to look good. Our goal is to increase the percentage of students passing the state test by 10% this year and another 10% next year. I expect all of us to be working toward this challenging goal.*

I don't even have to ask. I know what they're thinking. "Is this what teaching is about now, raising test scores? This isn't why I became a teacher. I'm not approaching my first year of teaching excited about the possibility of getting my students from a 465 (just below the cut score) to a 475 (just over the cut score). I can't imagine arriving at school each morning pumped at the idea of raising those test scores. I want to inspire students to become lifelong learners. I want to be a passionate teacher; I want to help students use their minds well. But I still want to be able to pay my rent. Help me. I'm confused. Do I build relationships with students or focus on raising those test scores?"

I have been a teacher in public schools for over 25 years. Over the last few years I have also taught students from Earlham College as well as mentoring beginning teachers. During 2002-2003, in my capacity as a mentor teacher, I worked with over a dozen beginning teachers and student teachers and got from them lots of feedback about what was helping them and what wasn't. They were very clear about what helped:

- seeing me demonstrate lessons;
- asking me questions as I reflected on a lesson;
- sharing specific strategies and activities and discussin possibilities;
- reflecting with them after I watched *them* teach.

Most important they said, was having me share what was going on in my mind as I taught, asked questions, did professional reading, talked to my peers about what I was thinking and reflected on how it might impact my practice. When I was able to make my thinking transparent to them, they saw possibilities for themselves (Fullan, 1993). When I posed questions to them, they could see applications for their own practice. When they tried things in their own classrooms, they came back to me and I tried to help them make their own teaching, in turn, transparent

(Schon, 1987). They were learning how, in a world focused on standardized testing, to become passionate teachers (Fried, 2001).

I believe strongly that the numbers and letters in our grading systems get in the way of what is important in classrooms (Guskey, 2001b). When we reduce learning in our students' eyes to numbers and letters, we lose passion, we lose complexity, we lose fun, we lose depth, we lose the essence of learning (Meier, 2002).

I do believe it is important that we learn specific classroom strategies that help students construct meaning, and that we analyze classroom data so students can understand what they do well and how they need to improve. I also want students to look at their scores on standardized tests as one way of understanding themselves as learners. However, I want them to be able to put that standardized test score in a context of learning that also includes rich classroom assessments, careful documentation of goals accomplished, and thoughtful self-assessments. What we seem to have lost is the scope of how students learn. This is what I want beginning teachers and student teachers to reflect on as they enter the profession of teaching (Stiggins, 1999; Wiggins, 1998b).

Anyone who works with new teachers must let them know that they should not have to make a choice between bringing up test scores or promoting lifelong learning. Mentor teachers must show beginning teachers how to be "passionate teachers," which I define as living a life as a reflective educator, making it a priority to build positive relationships with students, creating a classroom community in which students share responsibility for their own learning and the learning of their peers, nurturing a climate that focuses on learning rather than rules, developing strategies that grow from students' emerging strengths as learners rather than by dwelling on learning deficiencies (Sizer, 1992).

Becoming a passionate teacher means more than merely being passionate about skills, content, and the habits of mind we may wish to engender in our students. First and foremost, it means making a commitment to recreating oneself as an educator—and continuing that regenerative process throughout a career. As I work with beginning teachers and student teachers, I try to demonstrate the habits of a reflective practitioner—living a life of inquiry, reading the research, analyzing my practice to make more of an impact on student learning. I must invite beginning teachers in by making my reasoning transparent so they can examine how I make decisions as a passionate teacher. We must discuss what excites us, what scares us, and what options they have as they begin to work in their own classrooms (Barth, 2001).

Challenging the Game of School

During in-class workshop time, my 9th grade students are either finishing drafts of writing or doing independent reading. I have brief conferences with students as three college students look on.

"Matt, what have you been doing well in the class over the last grading period?"

"I dunno."

"What about reading? What are you reading on your own time?"

"I'm still reading *IT* by Stephen King."

"Right. Well, how's that going?"

"I dunno."

I know from past conferences that Matt is often reluctant to be reflective, but I plunge ahead hoping that today will be the day I break through and get him to talk in specifics about what he is doing well and where he needs to improve in terms of Indiana English/language arts standards.

"Well, are you confused by anything or interested in any certain part?"

"The dialogue and description."

Finally, I have something to work with. "So you get lost in the descriptive passages and prefer the sections where there is more dialogue? How do you vary your reading strategies when you're reading the descriptive passages, then?"

"No, you've got it backwards. I like the descriptive part. I get confused by the dialogue."

When I debriefed this interaction, my college student observers asked if it was frustrating, and I said of course it is. But conferencing is a cornerstone activity in nurturing dynamic relationships. Most of the kids in Matt's class are not confident readers. They all missed the cut score on the 8th grade state exam and had come to my class for extra help with literacy. At this point in the year, they hadn't learned yet to articulate what they do well and what they need to do better. It takes months to get reluctant learners there. Even my stronger students are so used to playing the game of "guess what the teacher wants me to do, and do that and nothing more" that an open honest discussion about their learning doesn't come easy (Bomer, 1993; Burke, 2003).

I want to tell beginning teachers how to create a community of learners in their classrooms, in stark contrast to the "game of school" (Fried, 1995) that most students are used to. I want to help them engage students in honest discussion about learning. I want them to see their students as co-learners who have much to offer, rather than as people with deficiencies. Passionate

teaching isn't about correcting mistakes (although that is often part of it); it's about honoring what students bring to the classroom; it's about helping students demonstrate what they are learning and produce quality work; it's about showing students how to reflect on their work and continue to improve.

Lessons From the Classrooms of Passionate Teachers

Of course, one can be an impassioned lecturer, but passionate teachers remember that, ultimately, teaching is about building relationships. Dealing with content, skills, and habits of mind must come after teachers and students feel comfortable together. As with Matt, I try to model for newer teachers some specific strategies and practices that are more conducive to becoming a passionate teacher. I emphasize Socratic seminars,[1] collaboration with students about most major classroom decisions, helping students relate what we're learning to state standards, and student self-assessment. This all sounds good, the beginning teachers and student teachers tell me, but how do we get students to do the work? Do we give lots of points to them if they "try"? Do we give separate grades for "effort"? How do kids even know what "quality work" is?

I invite them to watch me at work. I ask my 9th grade students:

1. If you could talk to the author of this book, what would you say or ask?
2. What has the author done to help you enjoy the book so far?
3. What has surprised you most about a character?
4. What other author does this book remind you of?

One student's uncorrected response:

1. I would ask why would people give their lives up to save someone else;
2. He made the book adventeres;
3. They would go out to the ocean and save someone;
4. This book reminds me of tears of a tiger because they both try and save someone.

This does not show much depth of thought. I could have put a large red "F" on the paper since the student did not adequately respond to the prompts. Instead, as I read more and more responses, I reflected. Yes, I had made a gallant effort to model reading techniques while we read together, showing them my own responses and asking them to reflect on what could be added to make them better, etc.

I showed the first year teachers and student teachers samples of the reading responses. I shared with them my plan. I decided to revise a rubric based on the criteria I had already given out (Goodrich-Andrade, 2000; Stiggins, 2001; Wiggins, 1998a). I had already established that students could "redo" their work at any time and receive "full credit" for their revised work if it was better than the original. After handing out the revised rubrics and my feedback to their responses, I met with some students and left others to work from my written comments. Following is the revised version of the student's response, albeit done only after a rather vehement protest:

1. This book reminds me of when I had to try out. I was nervous just like Mike was. Mike was scared that the coach was mean or something. I think it is scary to try out for a basketball team.

2. The author made this book joyful because it made me think. It almost feels like it is a true story. He tells a lot of good details and ideas.

3. Yes, because they felt scared when it came down to tryouts. A real person would feel that way too. I would be scared not to make the team.

4. I like the section where the coach was picking the players when he got to the last player he made it look like he was going to pick someone else. Instead, he picked Mike. He told some jokes as he picked the players. Everyone cheered for one or the other.

This is still not exemplary work, as I reminded the first year and student teachers. However, if my questioning during student conferences can help students, like Matt, who are labeled "at risk" or "below standard" according to test scores take small but significant steps to improve the quality of their work, I will help them get that much closer to being able to produce work that will help them continue to make progress as learners—and come closer to passing that high stakes test.

Passionate teachers continually reflect on the interplay of standards, student motivation, student learning and grades. Given the current emphasis on standards and high stakes tests, more and more teachers wonder about giving "credit" for effort.[2] A passionate teacher wants students to achieve the standards and produce quality work, to complete their assignments but also to understand the importance of developing good habits of mind and habits of work.

If I give students "credit/points/grades" for effort, irrespective of performance, what I am really communicating is, "If you will be quiet and not bother me, I will give you a minimal passing grade or enough points for effort that it will make up for substandard work." If I do this, I am not helping students; I am perpetuating school as a game with minimal expectations. Instead, I show new teachers how to give students feedback on dispositions or habits of mind. A passionate teacher can explicitly discuss with students concepts such as "persistence" and describe what it looks like. Teachers and students could then collaboratively develop a rubric and use it to give students feedback on developing and sustaining qualities of persistence. In this case, giving students "credit" for persistence or effort takes on an entirely different tone (Guskey, 2003).

This is a lot for a new teacher to think about, especially if her own K-12 experience has been a traditional one. My challenge as a mentor teacher is to keep showing her examples and to continue to share what I think of as I teach—how this lesson relates to state standards; how that observation connects with students' past performance; whether or not to give immediate feedback or let the student work on; should a student redo something or move to something else and come back to this later; whether to ask another question or simply listen to the student for a bit; what to do about other students who need my assistance; whether to intervene in an issue on the other side of the room; how to respond to the administrator who just walked into my room to ask if I have taken attendance yet? And these are all questions to address within a span of about 30 seconds. Welcome to my world.

The Passionate Teacher Researcher: Stories and Test Scores

Working with first year teachers and student teachers means doing a lot of demonstrating and reflecting, as well as sharing stories such as this:

A few years ago I had finally begged and bribed nineteen eighth graders to pilot an exhibition system in which they would present their humanities portfolios to a committee for feedback. At the last minute Tammy, my teaching partner, asked me to add Christy, who had come to our eighth grade humanities class in February, from an alternative school, and had recently had her baby taken away by the legal system. She had missed all of our foundational work from the first semester. Christy had been in and out of alternative schools for years and had a history of failure. She was an angry girl with loads of problems.

Over the course of the winter and spring, students in the pilot program were given extra class time to work on their portfolios and prepare work for public presentation. As her classmates revised their written work and planned how to best demonstrate their growth as learners, Christy kept writing and revising drafts of her poems.

When the time came for students to present, Christy did not show the poise or insight of most other students. She did not make the connections to other subject areas and did not have nearly as much written work in her portfolio. She was, however, justifiably pleased with the poetry she had written about her baby.

After all twenty students had presented, they displayed their portfolios in booths for parents, other students, and other teachers (Meier, 1995; Sizer, 1984). Christy's mom came to see Christy's booth. She was dressed nicely and brought a camera as well as a few young children in tow.

"This is the first time in five years that Christy has finished a school year without being expelled. She actually wanted to come to school. Before she was always ditching." The look of pride in her mother's face shone like a medal.

I believe that Christy didn't give up because we were willing to scaffold her as she came closer to producing quality work. Christy didn't give up in part because we helped her set realistic goals and let her know that we expected her to do well. She knew Tammy would not give up on her. Something clicked for Christy in a positive way that we hope she can build on. The rest is up to her.

What did I learn from telling this story to beginning teachers? Christy clearly was not performing up to "standard" on most measures of academic performance. She had trouble writing grammatically correct sentences even after several revisions. What did she learn? She learned to persist, to adjust her work to come closer to standards, to organize, to express her thoughts and feelings. That was clearly documented.

It isn't always easy to draw a direct correlation between passionate teachers and the standardized test scores of their students. The documented experiences of students such as Christy help to show the impact passionate teachers can have. As a passionate teacher who works with new teachers, I must show them how to tell their own stories and how to put into practice what they learn from their stories.

"All right," the beginning teachers and student teachers tell me. "We can see some use of anecdotes. But what about those test scores?"

For the entire school year of 2001-2002, I told them, I continued to teach my high school freshmen as I always had—lots of writing workshop time, Socratic seminars each week, response journals rather than questions at the end of chapters, projects and performance rather than traditional tests, minilessons and lots of revising/proofreading of their own writing rather than lessons on parts of speech, grammar, and usage, and lots of conferences on how their work was (or was not) measuring up to state standards (Burke, 1999; Strickland, 2002).

I was anxious to see how my students did on the high stakes test in the fall following their year with me. I had a wide range of students, including roughly as many highly at-risk students as other teachers. (I had 145 students out of the 485 in the entire 9th grade.) My students beat the grade/average by nearly ten percentage points, with 69% scoring above the cut compared to 59% of their fellow students who had had more traditional instruction in their freshman year.

This seemed to impress the beginning teachers. They were often told by others that the only way to bring those test scores up was for schools to reject "innovative" methods in favor of traditional instruction, to use more worksheets, to focus on discrete facts and isolated skills, to stay close to the suggested curriculum framework and follow the text book chapter by chapter. My stories and reflections balanced what they were hearing from other teachers, an argument for learner-centered classrooms even in this era of standardized testing (Fried, 2001; Meier, 2002).

As a year of working with beginning teachers and student teachers came to an end, I realized that wherever they went to teach, they would have to find a support network or else they would gradually slip into traditional practices and view passionate teaching as impractical if idealistic in today's schools.

If we believe that teachers, acting on their own, can create and maintain classrooms of passionate learning when isolated behind closed doors, we are kidding ourselves. A passionate teacher, for her own survival, must reach out to others, share her questions and inquiries, try to keep the professional conversation on teaching and learning (Barth, 2001; Fullan, 1999).

I have encouraged several student teachers and their mentors this year to engage in an inquiry project and share what they are learning. I believe that all passionate teachers should engage in some form of an inquiry cycle as an integral part of their teaching. Passionate teachers should pose important questions about teaching and learning, collect data from their classrooms to help them reflect, do professional reading to inform their inquiry, and share with colleagues what they are learning and how

they are adjusting their practice based on their inquiry. The more I work with beginning teachers, the more I believe that when teachers engage in inquiry about their practice, they are modeling the characteristics of lifelong learners.

The questions beginning teachers ask themselves are crucial. They must ask questions that help them navigate the dangerous terrain between being true to their students and focusing mainly on achieving higher test scores. Those of us who are veteran passionate teachers routinely recreate ourselves through our questions, our observations, our adjustments, our failures, our successes. Our gift and our responsibility to beginning teachers is to make our passionate teaching transparent. We must show them how building genuine relationships with students helps them score better on tests. Only with our support can beginning teachers hold onto the passion that brought them to this work.

Notes

1. See Dennis Gray. Putting minds to work. *American Educator,* Fall 1989, pp. 16-25 and Art Costa and Bena Kallick, *Discovering and exploring habits of mind* (Alexandria, VA: Association for Supervision and Curriculum Development, 2000).

2. Thomas Guskey. How classroom assessments improve learning. *Educational Leadership,* February 2003, pp. 6-11)

References

Barth, R. *Learning by heart.* San Francisco: Jossey-Bass, 2001.

Bomer, R, *A time for meaning.* Portsmouth, NH: Heinemann, 1993.

Burke, J. *The English teacher's companion.* Portsmouth, NH: Heinemann, 1999.

Burke, J. *Writing reminders.* Portsmouth, NH: Heinemann, 2003.

Costa, A. & Kallick, B. *Discovering and exploring habits of mind.* Alexandria, VA: Association for Supervision and Curriculum Development, 2000.

Fried, R. *The passionate learner.* Boston: Beacon Press 2001.

Fried, R. *The passionate teacher.* Boston: Beacon Press, 1995.

Fullan, M. *Change forces* (Philadelphia: Palmer Press, 1993.

Fullan, M. *Change forces: The sequel.* Philadephia: Palmer Press, 1999.

Goodrich Andrade, H. Using rubrics to promote thinking and learning. *Educational Leadership,* February 2000.

Gray, D. Putting minds to work. *American Educator,* Fall 1989.

Guskey, T. How classroom assessments improve learning. *Educational Leadership,* February 2003.

Guskey, T. *Developing grading and reporting systems for student learning.* Thousand Oaks, CA: Corwin Press. 2001a.

Guskey,T. High percentages are not the same as high standard. *Phi Delta Kappan,* March 2001b.

Meier, D. *The power of their ideas.* Boston: Beacon Press, 1995

Meier, D. *In schools we trust.* Boston: Beacon Press, 2002.

Schon, D. *Educating the reflective practitioner.* San Francisco: Jossey-Bass, 1987.

Sizer, T. *Horace's compromise.* Boston: Houghton Mifflin, 1984.

Sizer, T. *Horace's school.* New York: Houghton Mifflin, 1992.

Stiggins, R. Assessment, student confidence, and school success. Phi Delta Kappan, November 1999.

Stiggins, R. *Student-involved classroom assessment.* Upper Saddle River, NJ: Prentice Hall, 2001.

Strickland, J., & Strickland, K. *Engaged in learning: Teaching English 6-12.* Portsmouth, NH: Heinemann, 2002.

Wiggins, G. *Educative assessment.* San Francisco: Jossey-Bass, 1998a.

Wiggins, G. *Understanding by design.* Alexandria, VA: Association for Supervision and Curriculum Development, 1998b.

Randall Wisehart *is an English teacher and teacher leader at Richmond High School, Richmond, Indiana.*

Becoming a Teacher as a Hero's Journey:
Using Metaphor in Preservice Teacher Education

Lisa S. Goldstein

Becoming a teacher is hard work. A sizable body of research indicates that student teaching internships or other field-based practica are a particularly difficult part of this process. Many preservice teachers have misconceptions about the work of teachers and teaching (Cole & Knowles, 1993); when they begin their field placements they often feel disillusioned by the contrast between their idealized images and the realities of the profession. As they experience the myriad challenges of classroom life, preservice teachers often call into question the ideas and skills they were taught in their university coursework (Zeichner & Tabachnick, 1981). Further, the numerous stressors linked with student teaching—expectations, role clarification, conformity, time, evaluation, assignments, peer discussions, feedback (MacDonald, 1993)—contribute to making field experiences arduous and overwhelming.

One of our tasks as teacher educators is to create educational contexts and opportunities that support and sustain our students as they navigate these difficult times. One successful strategy toward this end is the use of metaphor (Bullough, 1991; Bullough & Stokes, 1994; Carter, 1990; Connelly & Clandinin, 1988; Dickmeyer, 1989; Marshall, 1990; Provenzo, Mc-Closkey, Kottkamp & Cohn, 1989; Stofflett, 1996; among others). In this article, I share the results of a recent study that explored the ways in which the hero's journey metaphor offered support to a cohort of preservice elementary school teachers during their first field placement experience. Because "the hero is a universal ideal that helps people think about their lives in a more profound and creative way" (Noble, 1994, p. 30) and because the hero's journey's emphasizes transformation and growth, the hero's journey is an appropriate and potentially powerful metaphor for nascent teachers.

This study revealed that the hero's journey metaphor was helpful to the students in a range of ways. However, I also found that many participants who enjoyed thinking of their experience as a hero's journey were resistant to the image of the hero. I will describe the benefits my students experienced as a result of using the hero's journey metaphor as a way to view their field placement experience, examine the contradictions in the students' responses to this metaphor, and conclude by discussing implications of these findings for teacher education program development.

Using Metaphor in Preservice Teacher Education

For several years I taught an elementary classroom organization and management course at a large research university in the Southwestern United States. In conjunction with this practicum course, which met weekly and covered topics such as classroom environments, discipline, lesson and unit planning, professionalism, and so on, my students would spend 20 hours per week as interns in elementary school classrooms (grades 1-5) in a socio-culturally diverse urban school district for a period of 10 weeks. Concurrent with this practicum and internship, the students were enrolled in four other methods courses.

This was always a demanding and difficult semester for my students: they faced the daunting task of transforming themselves from college students into professionals as they simultaneously learned teaching strategies and dealt with the practical and logistical challenges of field placements. In an attempt to support my preservice teachers during their challenging internship semester, in the Spring of 1999 I elected to modify my classroom organization and management class to take advantage of the power of metaphor. Because metaphor allows preservice teachers to "create meaning in ambiguous, complex situations" such as those commonly found in classrooms (Provenzo, McCloskey, Kottkamp & Cohn 1989, p. 52), I expected that metaphor would offer my students a powerful way to understand their field experiences and to explore their roles in those experiences.

The body of scholarship on the role of metaphor in teacher education indicates that metaphor can be a useful tool for supporting novice teachers (Bullough, 1991; Bullough & Stokes, 1994; Carter, 1990; Connelly & Clandinin, 1988; Dickmeyer, 1989; Marshall, 1990; Provenzo, McCloskey, Kottkamp & Cohn, 1989; Stofflett, 1996). Metaphor is seen as "a means for assisting beginners to articulate who they think they are as teachers" (Bullough & Stokes, 1994, p. 220) and as a way to help preservice teachers to "grasp intellectually systems that operate in ways quite mysterious to [them]" (Dickmeyer, 1989, p.152). Because metaphor impacts the way we perceive situations and events, it can be used to redescribe reality (Provenzo, McCloskey, Kottkamp & Cohn, 1989) and "to encourage reconceptualization of problem situations" (Marshall, 1990,

p. 129) such as those encountered by preservice teachers in their field placements.

Although the literature clearly highlights the contribution metaphor can make to preservice teacher education, the research also indicates that the challenge of finding their own working metaphors can be very difficult for some students (Bullough, 1991; Bullough & Stokes, 1994). Further, Grimmett and MacKinnon (1992) suggest that the process of developing metaphors "might … appeal only to the more linguistically inclined student teacher" (p. 434). These limitations might compromise the potential impact metaphor offers.

In order to make the most of the power of metaphor and to sidestep these limitations, I offered my students a pre-selected metaphor. I elected to modify my practicum course by incorporating the metaphor of the hero's journey, a frequently occurring trope in Western literature and film, both because of the inherent power of the theme and because of its strong parallels to the process of becoming a teacher. Class sessions and course assignments linked to the hero's journey metaphor were spread across the semester, and efforts were made to link the metaphor to the central academic content and professional skills presented in the course.

Teacher Education and the Hero's Journey

Using the hero's journey with preservice teachers allowed me to draw not only on the power of metaphor, but also on the broad and deep power of myth. Joseph Campbell, the scholar most readily associated with modern interpretation of mythic themes, argues that myth carries the human spirit forward, offering symbols, themes and images that enable and support growth and transformation, in contrast to other kinds of stories and experiences that cause fear and limit growth (Campbell, 1949). Given that the driving purposes for modifying my classroom organization and management course were to reposition the semester's experience in ways that would combat negativism, provide inspiration and support, and enable the students to see themselves as successful student teachers, using the mythic hero's journey metaphor seemed like an ideal solution.

The hero's journey unfolds following a set pattern (Campbell, 1949, p. 245- 246). The hero is called to awaken and to begin her journey. She[1] meets a helper who encourages her to go forth and who gives her tools and gifts to assist her on her journey. Then she proceeds to a threshold where she leaves behind her previous life and enters new realms of experience. At this point the hero meets a presence who guards the passage into the new realms; she must successfully negotiate with this gatekeeper in order to gain entry and continue on her journey.

Once she passes over the threshold, the hero enters a period of initiation where she meets unfamiliar forces, some of which threaten her and some of which offer magical aid. Successful negotiation of these trials leads our hero to personal transformation, growth, and illumination. The hero then returns to the world to share what she has learned.

Even in this brief description, there are many parallels to the teacher education process. Although some have always wanted to be a teacher and others felt a call later in life (Ayers, 1995),

as the deadline for declaring the education major or applying to begin the professional development course sequence approaches, the student responds to the call to awaken and embarks upon her journey to become a teacher. She begins her specialized methods coursework, where she meets helpful professors and teaching assistants who offer her encouragement, knowledge, teaching skills and other tools necessary for success in the field.

Next the student proceeds to the threshold of her field placement classroom, where she encounters her cooperating teacher, a presence who guards the passage; each hero must negotiate her relationship with the threshold guardian in order to gain entrance to this new realm of experience. The threshold guardian plays a crucial role in the hero's journey: the student cannot begin her initiation until she has crossed the threshold.

Unlike the ever-helpful ally or the always-dangerous dragon, the threshold guardian is generally a complex character with motivations and behaviors that are often unclear and unstable. For preservice teachers the cooperating teacher can appear both as friend and foe, be supportive or intimidating, easy to approach or challenging, and often takes on all these personas (Borko & Mayfield, 1995; Graham, 1999).

Once she has crossed the threshold, the student begins her initiation period. In her placement classroom the student encounters unfamiliar forces of all kinds; she must find new allies, face a range of trials, and call on her inner resources and her untapped strengths in order to be successful. The close connections between student teaching and the hero's initiation period are explored in great depth in literature focused on student teaching as a rite of passage (Berman, 1994; Eddy, 1969; White, 1989).

For student teachers, there are many potential allies on this journey: other student teachers, the children in the placement classroom, the children's parents, the cooperating teacher or other teachers on the faculty, the principal, the fieldwork supervisor. However, these people also have the potential to be dragons, testing and challenging the preservice teacher. And, as is the case for all who embark on a hero's journey, often the fiercest dragons will be found within the student herself.

Facing dragons—external and internal—is the heart of the journey. Successfully battling the dragons and enduring the trials are the source of the transformation that is the reward of the hero's journey: in teacher education our hero begins as a college student and ends as a novice teacher, ready to go out into the world and share what she has learned.

I felt that using the hero's journey as a metaphor for their first internship semester would offer my students an alternative way of thinking about their experience, perhaps providing a more positive perspective. This study was designed to allow me to determine if using the mythic hero's journey as a metaphor could reposition the challenges of the fieldwork experience, thereby serving as a source of support and encouragement to these students during this difficult yet essential professional transformation.

Using *Star Wars* in Teacher Education

Although the hero's journey is a well-known mythic theme, I felt it necessary to discuss the hero's journey with my students in the context of a familiar story. I opted to use the *Star Wars* trilogy of films—*Star Wars* (Lucas, 1977); *The Empire Strikes Back* (Lucas, Brackett & Kasdan, 1980); and *The Return of the Jedi* (Lucas & Kasdan, 1983)—as a mediating force to help the students see and forge the connections between the mythic hero's journey cycle and their nascent teaching lives.

I chose *Star Wars* for many reasons. George Lucas, creator of the *Star Wars* galaxy, very deliberately crafted the trilogy using the standard mythic figures and themes of the hero's journey: he stated, "I wanted to take all the old myths and put them into a new format that young people could relate to" (Lucas, cited in Bouzereau, 1997, p. 27). Joseph Campbell buttresses Lucas's claim, stating "*Star Wars* is a very old story in a very new costume" (Campbell, 1988, p. 179). *Star Wars*, familiar and easily accessible, formed a natural bridge between the ancient hero's journey cycle and the contemporary culture in which my students' teaching experiences take place.

Using the *Star Wars* films in this study allowed me to avoid one of the problems discussed in the research literature on the uses of metaphor in preservice teacher education. Using film as a vehicle for illustrating and communicating the hero's journey metaphor was a way to broaden the appeal of thinking non-literally about the process and experience of becoming a teacher beyond those linguistically inclined student teachers in the cohort, thereby avoiding the limitations mentioned by Grimmett and MacKinnon (1992).

Finally, the decision to use the *Star Wars* films to connect my students to the hero's journey theme was also a decision to connect them to me. Gleefully and effortlessly quoting from *Star Wars* films at every opportunity, I am what my sons call "a *Star Wars* geek." My deep knowledge of *Star Wars* enabled me to see the connections between Luke Skywalker's journey and that of my students, and my deep passion for these films enabled me to convince my students to trust me long enough to try something unexpected in our practicum class.

Rethinking the Hero

It is important to note that it was "the hero's journey" and not "the hero" that was presented and offered to the students as a metaphor for their experience. Students were encouraged to think of the process of becoming a teacher as a hero's journey, but they were never encouraged to see themselves—or any other teachers—as heroes; the term *hero* has many troubling associations.

In the world of comic books and cartoons, a hero is faster than a speeding bullet, more powerful than a locomotive, and able to leap tall buildings in a single bound. I did not want my students to feel any sense that they would be expected to live up to some unreachable expectations or standards. Further, I was worried about the stereotypical image of the hero/superhero as an independent, solitary figure. Applying this vision of the hero to teaching would communicate to the preservice teachers an image of the teacher as an isolated individual, someone who closes her classroom door and works alone in an insular setting.

Another potential problem with linking the term hero and the teaching profession is that hero is commonly used—particularly

in films and in the popular media—to describe super-teachers who go above and beyond the normal expectations of their jobs, or to describe savior-teachers who rescue their students from administrative cruelty, gangs, poverty, or ignorance. I did not want my students to envision their professional lives along these problematic and unreasonable lines.

My hope was that the students would remain focused on the journey aspect of the metaphor, rather than on the hero aspect. However, I suspected that it might be impossible to offer the hero's journey as a metaphor for the teacher education process without implying that the students on this journey were heroes. So I took preventive measures at the outset and attempted to draw an alternative portrait of the hero that students could build on when envisioning themselves on a hero's journey.

Using *Star Wars* helped alleviate some concerns about using the term hero in relation to the process of becoming a teacher. One of the enduring beauties of the *Star Wars* trilogy is the particularly flawed and imperfect character of its central protagonist. Luke Skywalker—impatient, impetuous, immature—is on a hero's journey, yet still he makes mistakes, gets scared, and needs help as he journeys toward his future. It was this particular spirit of the hero's journey that I hoped would sustain and support the students in the cohort as they began their professional lives. Like Luke, they would make mistakes, get scared, and need help on their journeys toward their future careers and, also like Luke, they would succeed despite their apparent weaknesses.

Although it is considered the classic scholarship on the subject, I avoided the work of Joseph Campbell (1949) when teaching the introductory lessons about the hero's journey metaphor because it reinforces the stereotypical representations of the hero. Instead, I drew heavily upon Kathleen Noble's (1994) feminist reinterpretation of the hero in an effort to interrupt those stereotypical images. Noble points out that the term hero has a different meaning in myth than in everyday usage. She states that the heroes of mythology are known

> ...for their great capacity for life and for pursuing higher goals. They are expected to develop their resilience, autonomy and self-reliance, and to approach the challenges in their lives with intelligence and creativity, and to act with integrity in all endeavors. Their quests challenge them to roam in the inner or outer worlds in search of new knowledge and to use that knowledge to serve their fellow creatures. (Noble, 1994, p. 6)

This working definition of hero is well aligned with my aspirations for my students and for their professional lives, and portrays a vision of teaching that is worthy of pursuit.

Study Procedures

Data for this study comprised several of the papers and activities assigned as course requirements in my classroom organization and management class in Spring 1999. As an initial assignment in the course, students watched the *Star Wars* trilogy films using a guided viewing packet I developed for this study in order to help them attend carefully to Luke Skywalker's hero-journey. The packet was organized around the stages of the hero's journey and drew on the image of the mythic hero developed by Kathleen Noble and discussed extensively in class.

Each section of the viewing packet—call to awaken, initiation, allies/helpers, trials/dragons, and transformation and return—had space for note-taking, a set of questions designed to focus the students' thinking about the details of the films in specific relation to Luke's hero's journey, and a set of questions designed to structure students' reflections on their own lives as aspiring teachers. My intent was that thinking about Luke's experiences would become a springboard for examination and reflection of the students' lived experiences and would therefore shed light on their own hero-journeys.

As the semester progressed and field placements began, students often mentioned Luke Skywalker and other *Star Wars* characters in class discussions. Questions that had been raised in the viewing guide or in our initial discussions of *Star Wars* and the hero's journey, scenes from the films that had been highlighted as representations of important moments in Luke's hero journey, and new insights, connections, parallels, and "a-ha!" moments were brought up by students on a regular basis. The students' field placements were revealing new meanings in the films and, more importantly, it seemed that the films were helping the students make sense of their experiences in the field.

The students wrote two papers for the course that were linked to the hero's journey theme. One paper focused on their call to awaken; in this assignment students were asked to reflect on and discuss their decision to become a teacher. The other hero's journey paper was centered around the students' initiation process; intended as an opportunity for the students to consider and begin to interpret their experiences over the semester, this paper required students to discuss the various allies and dragons they encountered, to detail the trials they weathered, and to describe any transformations that may have occurred. The viewing packets and both of these papers were data sources for this study. In addition, data were drawn from one free-write done in class intended for formative evaluation of the course and of the study, and the students' comments on an informal summative evaluation tool which covered the course as a whole.

Participation in this study was open to all students enrolled in the class; all of the students in the cohort—14 Anglo females in their early to mid-twenties—elected to participate in the study and had their papers and evaluative materials considered as data for this project.[2]

Finally, students were given the option of participating in focus group discussions held 6 months after the completion of the course: at this point in time the students had almost finished their student teaching placements and were able to look back on the ways that the hero's journey metaphor contributed to their professional experiences after the study ended. Nine students participated in these focus group discussions. To accommodate their schedules, I held three different focus group sessions, each of which covered the same topics and issues.

Manual and computer-assisted data analysis strategies were employed to examine and code all of the student writings. First, I read and coded all students' responses to each assignment in the order in which they were completed—I read all the viewing guides, all the call to awaken papers, all the freewrites, then all the initiation papers and informal course evaluations. My goal here was to develop an overall sense of the progression of the class's experiences, attitudes, and perceptions over the duration of their field placement and to identify general themes common to all the participants. Next I looked at each individual, reading the complete portfolio of data written by each participant. This analysis strategy revealed the development of each preservice teacher's thoughts, concerns, and attitudes over the course of the field placement period and enabled me to engage in case and cross-case analysis.

As I read and re-read these data, I used sticky notes to mark any statements that (1) directly addressed the hero's journey metaphor, (2) discussed or critiqued the utility of the word hero, (3) drew connections between the hero's journey metaphor and the students' lives or experiences in their field placement, and (4) mentioned characters or constructs from the *Star Wars* films. My next phase of analysis involved engaging in repeated readings and considerations of the marked entries, looking inductively for any patterns in the data. I developed working interpretations of these patterns, and attempted to warrant them with evidence pulled from the data set.

The patterns I had identified and my working interpretations of those patterns were used to generate the central questions posed to the focus groups. Rooted in Pamela Moss's work on the use of the hermeneutic circle in warranting knowledge claims (Moss, 1994), the focus groups played a central role in shaping the next phase of my data analysis.

Moss describes the hermeneutic circle as a means for arriving at interpretations of data "that seek to understand the whole in light of its parts, that privilege readers who are most knowledgeable about the context … and that ground those interpretations not only in textual and contextual evidence available, but also in a rational debate among the community of interpreters" (Moss, 1994, p. 7). This process involves an iterative cycle that begins with an initial interpretation of the data, followed by critical dialogue among a group of knowledgeable individuals committed to an "ethic of disciplined, collaborative inquiry that encourages challenges and revisions to initial interpretations" (Moss, 1994, p. 7). The participants in the focus groups served as my community of interpreters, testing and challenging my working interpretations of their experiences. Focus group discussions were audiotaped, transcribed, and used as an additional data source.

Following the focus group meetings, I returned to the data searching for evidence confirming and disconfirming my revised interpretations. Going back into the data with this focus, looking specifically for particular issues, allowed me to uncover relevant information that I had overlooked in my earlier readings.

Once I felt confident that I had constructed a trustworthy and believable account of the situation, I began to write up my findings. I invited the participants to read drafts of this manuscript, hoping to continue the hermeneutic process of input, feedback, critique and re-interpretation. Unfortunately, none of the participants were able to continue participation; the new school year had begun and most of them were busy facing the challenges of their induction year.

Findings

The hero's journey metaphor, looked at in isolation, served all of the students well. However, I found that in the specific context of this study the hero's journey never existed in isolation. I had assumed that it would be possible to separate the hero's journey from the image of the hero, but the data indicate the students did not perceive the metaphor in this way. Students' connection with the hero's journey metaphor forced them into an inevitable relationship—comfortable or uncomfortable—with the term hero.

For some students there was no distinction between being on a hero's journey and being a hero; they were part of the same metaphorical package. These students took strength from thinking about themselves as heroes, and found the hero's journey metaphor to be beneficial to their experience. As Amber said, "I like thinking of myself as a hero on a journey. It gives meaning, purpose, and humor to my life." For other students, though, the connection between the hero's journey and the hero image was not seamless. These students encountered cognitive dissonance: they loved the hero's journey metaphor, but did not like to think of themselves as heroes.

Being on a Hero's Journey

As I had hoped, structuring my classroom organization and management course around the theme of the hero's journey had a positive impact on the individual preservice teachers' experiences. Most fundamentally, asking students to write about their calls to awaken and their initiation experiences led them to reflection and discovery. Although any reflective writing activity might have had the same beneficial effect (Cole & Knowles, 1993; Gore & Zeichner, 1991; Schon, 1983; van Manen, 1977), the students' comments suggest that the hero's journey allowed them to see their own lives from a different angle and to make new connections. For example, Jane said:

> Writing the papers on why I decided to become a teacher and on the dragons and allies really was very helpful because I had never thought about any of that before…. I couldn't believe that I had gotten that far without thinking about why I wanted to be a teacher. I mean, I never ever thought about it. And that was really beneficial to me.

Many of the participants expressed similar sentiments, grateful both for the opportunity to reflect on their experiences and for the structure offered by the hero's journey framework. In her initiation paper handed in at the end of the semester, Ashley wrote the following:

> As the semester comes to a close, it is nice to reflect back on what transformations I have made. [In my viewing guide] I wrote about Luke, "After his Jedi training he had discipline, faith, deeper understanding, dedication, and powers of mind control. He had a no-

ble purpose." Likewise I feel my training and quest has instilled in me stronger discipline, faith, understanding, and dedication.

Along similar lines, some participants found that using the hero's journey as a metaphor for their teacher education experience led to powerful personal insights. Thanks to the hero's journey, Micki wrote, "I have found strengths in myself that I never knew existed and weaknesses that aren't as weak as I had perceived them to be." Amber, too, had a new understanding of herself at the end of the semester. Considering the contributions made by the hero's journey metaphor, she explained:

> The true purpose and gift of this process [has been] to really look at myself as a person and as a teacher…. Viewing this venture as a heroic journey has enabled me to work for what I want and what I believe in…. Through this process I have come to learn that my greatest ally is my own zeal for teaching and my greatest dragon is my own self-doubt. I had no idea that these two parts has been at work all along. This has not only been a journey to teaching, but more importantly, a journey to myself.

Other students used the image of the hero's journey as a source of "inspiration and momentum" (Alexis), as a way to "get my thoughts and emotions back on track" (Erin), or as a reminder that "I am learning things all the time and not to get too frustrated when I'm not perfect" (anonymous course evaluation).

The students' end-of-course evaluations displayed a great deal of enthusiasm for the hero's journey metaphor. Here are several of the students' anonymous responses to the question, *"When I teach the course next year, should I continue to use the hero's journey metaphor as an organizing theme? Why or why not?"*:

> Definitely! The hero's journey that the [*Star Wars*] characters go on is so similar to ours. It is a fun and exciting way to look at this process.

> Yes, it is a fun but meaningful way to help students cope with the pressures of the [professional development sequence course] block. You should continue to use it.

> Yes, I think the connection is helpful to many people. I think it is so unique and I really felt like you shared so much of yourself with us.

> Yes—it applies well to the journey of becoming a teacher.

> Yes, because it was helpful for me to view my last year of school as a journey. It made me realize that I am learning things all the time and not to get too frustrated when I'm not perfect.

The hero's journey metaphor was powerful for the students. I had hoped that it would provide support and encouragement during a difficult semester, and the data indicate that it did so.[3]

Being a Hero

A small number of students reported drawing directly on the hero image as a source of support and strength. Christy told her focus group that she had been nervous before an interview for a teaching position; in order to calm down she recalled telling herself, "I am a hero and I can do this. I need to go in there and be confident and be a hero."

Alexis also found strength in her image of herself as a hero. In recalling her experience receiving pointed critical feedback from her cooperating teacher, Alexis wrote, "I appreciated her for that because, after all, I am a hero. I believe my ability to handle this type of feedback made me feel more heroic."

Amber used the hero image to put her classroom struggles into perspective. She wrote:

> My last observation time was very chaotic and stressful for me. I thought to myself how horrible it was going and then I thought to God to give me strength. Then HERO popped into my mind and I smiled. Suddenly it seemed not so stressful and almost laughable.

It is not clear whether the students were drawing on Noble's powerful and inspirational understanding of the term hero or on more stereotypical images. Regardless, the idea of being a hero offered these particular students strength, confidence, resilience, and perspective when they needed it most. So, despite my concerns about the term hero, some of the students found it useful.

Noble's feminist reinterpretation of the hero made an important contribution to the students' experience in our course and in their field placements. In contrast to the solitary figure of the hero, Noble's view highlights the crucial importance of allies. She writes:

> Many of us grow up believing that heroes must accomplish their goals by relying solely upon their own wits…. But a careful reading of these tales reveals that heroes are aided by allies at critical junctures all along the way and that without such help their quests could not possibly succeed. (Noble, 1994, p. 109)

When presented in this light, the hero's journey metaphor can be a way to create connections rather than reinforce isolation.

This image of the hero as an individual linked closely to a network of allies resonated strongly for the students. Candy, a focus group participant, reported that thinking of themselves as a group of heroes on a transformative journey "always cheered everybody up" and allowed each student to offer and request support as needed. Further, Christy reported that the hero's journey metaphor offered a form of shorthand communication among the group: "We all had this same knowledge base and started at square one so it was really easy to describe how you were feeling." Using Noble's feminist definition of hero allowed for the development of community among the students, thereby avoiding the problem of forced isolation and independence that I had associated with the term.

Not Being a Hero

Although the students found the hero's journey a useful metaphor that enriched their thinking about themselves and their experiences in their first practice teaching placement, the data revealed a strong undercurrent of discomfort with the word hero. For example, one student who wrote in her anonymous course evaluation about the ways in which she benefited from the hero's journey metaphor concluded the evaluation by stating, "However, I never really considered myself to be a hero." Another student wrote: "I liked the hero metaphor but I don't necessarily feel like a hero."

I explored this curious tension further in the focus group discussions. I was confronted by tremendous contradiction: on one occasion Christy stated "I was totally agreeable with the [hero's] journey… but I never thought of myself as a hero," and then minutes later told a story of calming her pre-interview jitters by telling herself, "I am a hero and I can do this." Although Christy's inconsistency was the most notable, almost all of the focus group participants expressed satisfaction with the hero's journey metaphor and ambivalence about the word hero.

As we talked about the hero's journey in class throughout the semester, we returned frequently to Noble's vision of the mythic hero. All of the focus group participants recalled our class discussions about the difference between Noble's understanding of the word hero and the typical definition of the term, and were able to describe those differences. But it appeared that our classroom discussions about these nuances of meaning did little to counteract the cumulative effect of a lifetime of experience with the word. Carrie made a statement that summed up the situation well: "It's hard to get past that stereotype of what a hero is."

The most obvious concerns with the hero label were related to gender. As Christy said:

> This image of a hero, really, stereotypically, is a male. With a sword. Strong, fights for the heroine, wins. So it is really hard after being bombarded with that image for your entire life, to think Oh, I'm a hero. I'm 5 foot 1[inch]; blonde hair, female, I don't have any weaponry [pause] I think that's what's hard for me. I think I'm not a hero. A hero has to be some ripped guy who is killing people.

Despite my efforts to use Noble's work to undercut the stereotypes, the hegemony of macho male heroism perpetuated by popular culture was robust and powerful in my students' thinking about the hero's journey.

I believe that my decision to use *Star Wars* as a bridge between my students and the hero's journey metaphor contributed to this problem. Although it could be argued that Princess Leia, the only female character of any importance in the original *Star Wars* trilogy, is on a hero's journey, the films' central focus is on Luke Skywalker and his transformation from a frustrated farm boy on a dusty planet at the outer rim of the galaxy to Jedi Knight and galactic leader. Had I used *The Wizard of Oz* or another hero's journey film that features a female in the hero role, I might have been better able to disrupt the association of images of the heroic with typical male behaviors.

In responses that typify the loss of strength and self-confidence that accompany females' adolescence (Pipher, 1994), some of the preservice teachers in this study felt "too ordinary" to be heroes. These responses appear to be shaded by self-doubt and uncertainty:

> I'm too ordinary and just like every other teacher in the school … why should *I* be the hero? (Carrie)

> Hero is just something that seemed too strong of a word for what we were doing…. there are so many people doing it that it doesn't seem heroic because you're not standing out. And heroes are thought of, in my mind, as people who are standing out because they're doing something amazing. (Jane)

> For me a hero is like someone who saves lives, or gets the Congressional Medal of Honor. (Micki)

Along similar lines, Erin suspected that the pleasure she and her classmates took from teaching disqualified them from heroism: "I wonder if we can't look at the hero part because we all chose education for ourselves, not for the kids we're going to teach. So that's kind of a selfish reason; you can't really be a hero while you're being selfish."

Research by scholars examining the lives of young women offers some insight into these attitudes and beliefs. For example, Mary Pipher's work on adolescent girls' loss of clarity and vitality would suggest that my participants—all females in the tail end of their adolescence—were unable to accept an image of themselves as powerful and competent, and so they rejected hero as a result (Pipher, 1994). In contrast to Pipher's view, Carol Gilligan and her colleagues (Gilligan, Lyons & Hanmer, 1990) point out that maintaining connection and relationship is a crucial part of the social world of adolescent women; perhaps my participants presented themselves as "ordinary" and "not standing out" from their fellow teachers in an effort to maintain a sense of shared experience and community.

Another explanation for their resistance to the label hero relates to my participants' lack of professional experience. As novice teachers, my participants may have felt unready for the leadership and visibility heroism seems to demand; perhaps they hoped that rejecting the term hero would provide them the safety and anonymity they desired.

The participants' inexperience may have contributed to their resistance to the term hero in another way, namely, allowing them to hold unchallenged, mistaken impressions of teachers' working lives. In her book *Eve's Daughters: The Forbidden Heroism of Women,* Miriam Polster (1992) points out that "women's quiet but profoundly courageous acts simply go unremarked, submerged in a subsidiary world of attachment and service" (Polster, 1992, p. 9). This may have been happening at the preservice teachers' field placement sites. Preoccupied with successfully navigating their own experiences in the field, the participants may have been very unaware of the depth and intensity of the commitment brought to the classroom by their mentor teachers, all of whom were female.

The preservice teachers in this study who loved being on a hero's journey but disliked the term hero may also have been influenced by society's negative images of teachers and teaching. Although these women were actively pursuing careers in teaching, they nevertheless saw teaching as unspectacular work. The participants positioned teaching as a profession too mundane and common to warrant association with heroism. Further, many of the participants in this study had been challenged and criticized by their family and friends when they elected to pursue a career in teaching, because the low pay and low status afforded to our profession made it seem an unappealing, poor choice. These preservice teachers may have internalized these negative messages about teaching and therefore were not able to apply the word hero to a teacher.

Comments made in the focus groups reflect the preservice teachers' resistance to seeing teaching as a profoundly demanding and significant profession. For example, Carrie said, "It seems like it's almost just a conceited kind of a label. 'Yeah, I'm HEROIC, what are you?' You feel silly, kinda. Too small to be saying that." Jane echoed that sentiment, asserting, " It's just hard to call yourself a hero. I mean, you feel heroic if you get through a lesson?" And Micki argued, "I'm just a regular person and this is what I have chosen to do with my life…. I just don't think of myself as doing this great thing. And I don't think of teaching as such a noble profession. I just like being around kids all day long."

My participants' discomfort with being a hero was not surprising: I too had concerns with the word hero and with the idea of heroism in teaching. What I found surprising, however, were the understandings of teaching and teachers that informed their resistance to the term hero. To this group of preservice teacher education students, teachers were ordinary and teaching was no great thing.

Implications For Teacher Education

Despite my participants' discomfort with the word hero, the data indicate that using the metaphor of the hero's journey helped support my students as they navigated the challenges of their field placement experience. The hero's journey metaphor offered these preservice teachers guidance and encouragement, allowed them to tap into hidden strengths within themselves, helped put their frustrations and setbacks into perspective, and provided them with membership in a community of support and encouragement.

Although the commonplace hero-imagery of western culture was hegemonic and difficult to overcome, the preservice teachers were able to disrupt at least one of their preconceptions about heroes. Their ability to incorporate Kathleen Noble's feminist view that "heroes are aided by allies at critical junctures all along the way and that without such help their quests could not possibly succeed" (1994, p. 109) allowed them to move through their field placement experience as part of a community of supportive allies.

This suggests that the hero's journey metaphor works on two levels: it simultaneously offers support to each individual and offers means for the creation of a network of personal and professional connection within the cohort group. A hero's journey-inspired teacher education program could be a way to prepare students for collective action, for running classrooms and schools in egalitarian ways, and for engaging in equitable forms of communication, but only if the stereotypical male image of the hero can be minimized.

That my participants loved the hero's journey but did not love the idea of being a hero illustrates that even a powerful metaphor offers only partial connection. Teaching is a complicated endeavor and teachers are required to fill many different roles in their professional capacity; no single metaphor could perfectly capture all facets of a teacher's experience. This is an important reminder to teacher educators hoping to use metaphor with their students: because no metaphor is going it be a perfect fit, it is important to give preservice teachers space and flexibility as they think figuratively about their work with children.

Though I intended to keep our metaphorical focus on the hero's journey and away from being a hero, I see now that this was an unrealistic expectation. Once the students bought into seeing themselves as being on a hero's journey, they inevitably cast themselves as heroes. Although most of my students found the hero role uncomfortable, this does not mean that the hero's journey metaphor should be discounted entirely as a tool for teacher education.

Although my explicit goal in incorporating the hero's journey metaphor into my classroom organization and management course was to support and sustain the students during a notoriously challenging semester, I also saw the metaphor as a means for enriching their thinking, broadening their understanding of teaching, and enhancing their sense of what they were capable of achieving personally and professionally. Using the students' discomfort with and disconnection from the hero metaphor as a starting place for inquiry and critical reflection would be a way to encourage the students to think more deeply about themselves and probe and question their underlying conceptions of themselves as teachers.

I believe that my participants' resistance to the term hero is the aspect of this study that has the most to contribute to teacher education. Their comments offer powerful insight into the ways in which a typical group of preservice elementary teachers think about themselves and about the profession of teaching. Knowing that preservice teachers may view teachers and teaching in ways that downplay their importance and minimize their significance suggests that teacher education coursework and field experiences must be structured and organized in ways to shift these perceptions. Maxine Greene offers useful words of guidance as we begin this process:

> All we can do is speak with others as passionately and eloquently as we can; all we can do is to look into each other's eyes and urge each other on to new beginnings. Our classrooms ought to be nurturing and thoughtful and just all at once; they ought to pulsate with multiple conceptions of what it is to be human and alive. They ought to resound with the voices of articulate young people in dialogues always incomplete because there is always more to be discovered and more to be said. We must want our students to achieve friendship as each one stirs to wide-awakeness, to imaginative ac-

tion, and to renewed consciousness of possibility. (Greene, 1995, p. 43)

Modifying assignments to include more opportunities for dialogue and deep reflection; creating reading lists that balance attention to nuts-and-bolts practical issues with opportunities to engage with challenging, powerful, and beautiful ideas; restructuring field experiences to nurture more meaningful commitments in the relationship between the preservice teacher, the cooperating teacher, and the university fieldwork supervisor; and reorganizing taken-for-granted institutional arrangements and creating new partnerships are all viable options.

Preservice teachers must learn to see teaching as a moral and intellectual endeavor of the most profound importance. There are innumerable ways to accomplish this, and each teacher educator and teacher education program would need to work diligently to create new possibilities for their students. Perhaps the hero's journey metaphor can play a role in this process.

Notes

1. Because all of the participants in this study were women, I will use the female pronoun when discussing the hero.
2. Students were assured that their decision to participate or to abstain from participation in this study would not affect their workload for the course, their grade, our evaluation of their work, or their future relationships with the university. All of the students enrolled in the cohort chose to participate in the study; all of the data are presented here with the students' permission.
3. In order to accommodate changes in our teacher education program, I stopped teaching the Classroom Organization and Management course after this study was completed. Had I continued with the course I would have taken my students' advice and used the hero's journey metaphor as a central feature of the class.

References

Ayers, W. (Ed.) (1995). *To become a teacher*. New York: Teachers College Press.

Berman, D.M. (1994). Becoming a teacher: The teaching internship as a rite of passage. *Teaching Education, 6* (1), 41-56.

Borko, H. & Mayfield, V. (1995). The roles of the cooperating teacher and university supervisor in learning to teach. Teaching & *Teacher Education, 11* (5), 501-18.

Bouzereau, L. (1997). *Star wars: The annotated screenplays*. New York: DelRay Books.

Bullough, R.V., Jr. (1991). Exploring personal teaching metaphors in preservice teacher education. Journal of Teacher Education, *42* (1), 43-51.

Bullough, R.V., Jr. & Stokes, D.K. (1994). Analyzing personal teaching metaphors in preservice teacher education as a means for encouraging professional development. *American Educational Research Journal, 31* (1), 197-224.

Campbell, J. (1949). *The hero with a thousand faces*. Princeton, NJ: Princeton University Press.

Campbell, J., with Moyers, B. (1988). *The power of myth*. New York: Anchor Books.

Carter, K. (1990). Meaning and metaphor: Case knowledge in teaching. *Theory into Practice, 29* (2), 109-115.

Cole, A. L. & Knowles, J.G. (1993). Shattered images: Understanding expectations and realities of field experiences. *Teaching & Teacher Education, 9* (5-6), 57-71.

Connelly, F.M & Clandinin, D.J. (1988). *Teachers as curriculum planners.* New York: Teachers College Press.

Dickmeyer, N. (1989). Metaphor, model, and theory in education research. *Teachers College Record, 91* (2), 151-60.

Eddy, E.M. (1969). *Becoming a teacher: The passage to professional status.* New York: Teachers College Press.

Gilligan, C., Lyons, N.P. & Hanmer, T.J. (1990). *Making connections.* Cambridge, MA: Harvard University Press.

Gore, J.M., & Zeichner, K.M. (1991). Action research and reflective teaching in preservice teacher education: A case study from the United States. *Teaching & Teacher Education, 7* (2), 119-136.

Graham, P. (1999). Powerful influences: A case of one student teacher renegotiating his perceptions of power relations. *Teaching & Teacher Education, 15* (5), 523-40.

Greene, M. (1995). *Releasing the imagination: Essays on education, the arts, and social change.* San Francisco: Jossey-Bass.

Grimmett, P.P. & MacKinnon, A.M. (1992). Craft knowledge and the education of teachers. In G. Grant (Ed.), *Review of research in education: Vol. 18* (pp. 385-456). Washington, DC: American Educational Research Association.

Lucas, G. (Screenwriter) (1977). *Star wars.* 20th Century Fox.

Lucas, G., Brackett, L. & Kasdan, L. (Screenwriters) (1980). *The empire strikes back.* 20th Century Fox.

Lucas, G. & Kasdan, L. (Screenwriters) (1983). *The return of the jedi.* 20th Century Fox.

MacDonald, C.J. (1993). Coping with stress during the teaching practicum: The student teacher's perspective. *Alberta Journal of Educational Research 39* (4), 407-18.

Marshall, H.H. (1990). Metaphor as an instructional tool in encouraging student teacher reflection. *Theory into Practice, 29* (2), 128-32.

Moss, P.A. (1994). Can there be validity without reliability? *Educational Researcher, 23* (2), 5-12.

Noble, K. (1994). *The sound of a silver horn: Reclaiming the heroism in contemporary women's lives.* New York: Ballantine Books.

Pipher, M. (1994). *Reviving Ophelia: Saving the selves of adolescent girls.* New York: G.P. Putnam's Sons.

Polster, M.F. (1992). *Eve's daughters: The forbidden heroism of women.* San Francisco: Jossey-Bass.

Provenzo, E.F., McCloskey, G.N., Kottkamp, R.B. & Cohn, M.M. (1989). Metaphor and meaning in the language of teachers. *Teachers College Record, 90* (4), 551-73.

Schon, D. (1983). *The reflective practitioner: How professionals think in action.* New York: Basic Books.

Stofflett, R.T. (1996). Metaphor development by secondary teachers enrolled in graduate teacher education. *Teaching & Teacher Education, 12* (6), 577-89.

van Manen, M. (1977). Linking ways of knowing with ways of being practical. *Curriculum Inquiry, 6* (3), 205-228.

White, J.J. (1989). Student teaching as a rite of passage. *Anthropology and Education Quarterly, 20* (3), 177-195.

Zeichner, K.M. & Tabachnick, B.R. (1981). Are the effects of university teacher education "washed out" by school experience? *Journal of Teacher Education, 32* (3), 7-11.

Lisa S. Goldstein *is an associate professor and director of early childhood teacher education with the Department of Curriculum and Instruction at the University of Texas at Austin, Austin, Texas.*

From *Teacher Education Quarterly,* Winter 2005, pp. 7-24. Copyright © 2005 by Caddo Gap Press. Reprinted by permission.

UNIT 9

For Vision and Hope: Alternative Visions of Reality

Unit Selections

Key Points to Consider

- What might be the shape of school curricula by the year 2020?

- What changes in society are most likely to affect educational change?

- How can schools prepare students to live and work in an uncertain future? What knowledge bases are most important? What skills are most important?

- What should be the philosophical ideals for American schools in the twenty-first century?

Student Website

www.mhcls.com/online

Internet References

Further information regarding these websites may be found in this book's preface or online.

Goals 2000: A Progress Report
  http://www.ed.gov/pubs/goals/progrpt/index.html
Mighty Media
  http://www.mightymedia.com
Online Internet Institute
  http://www.oii.org

T here are competing visions as to how persons should develop and learn. Yet there is great hope in this competition among alternative dreams and specific curriculum paths which we may choose to traverse. In this, all conscientious persons are asked to consider carefully how we may make more livable futures for ourselves and others. This is really an eternal challenge for us all. We will often disagree and debate our differences as we struggle toward what we become as persons and as cultures.

Which education philosophy is most appropriate for our schools? This is a complex question, and we will, as a free people, come up with alternative visions of what it will be. Let us explore what might be possible as more students go on the Internet and the wonder of the cyberspace revolution opens to teachers and students. What challenges can we expect in using the technology of the cyberspace revolution in our schools? What blessings can we hope for? What sorts of changes need to occur in how people go to schools as well as in what they do when they get there?

The breakthroughs that are developing in new learning and communications technologies are really quite impressive. They will definitely affect how human beings learn in the very near-term future. While we look forward with considerable optimism and confidence to these educational developments, there are still many controversial issues to be debated in the early years of the twenty-first century; the "school choice" issue is one. Some very interesting new proposals for new forms of schooling, both in public schools and private schools, are under development. We can expect to see at least a few of these proposals actually tried.

Some of the demographic changes and challenges involving young people in the United States are staggering. Ten percent of all American teenage girls will become pregnant each year, the highest rate in the developed world. At least 100,000 American elementary school children get drunk once a week. Incidence of venereal disease has tripled among adolescents in the United States since 1995. The actual school dropout rate in the United States stands at 30 percent.

The student populations of North America reflect vital social and cultural forces at work to destroy our progress. In the United States, a massive secondary school dropout problem has been developing steadily through the past decade. The next decade will reveal how public school systems will address this and other unresolved problems brought about by dramatic upheavals in demographics. In the immediate future, we will be able to see if emergency or alternative certification measures adopted by states affect achievement of the objectives of our reforms.

At any given moment in a people's history, several alternative future directions are open to them. North American educational systems have been subjected to one wave after another of recommendations for programmatic change. Is it any wonder that change is a sensitive watchword for persons in teacher education on this continent? What specific directions it will take in the immediate future depend on which recommendations of the reform agenda are implemented, which agencies of government (local, state/provincial, and federal) will pay for the very high costs of reform, and which shifts in perceived national educational priorities by the public will occur that will affect fundamental realignments of our educational goals.

Basic changes in society's career patterns should also be considered. It is estimated that in the United States the average nonagricultural worker now makes a major job change about five times in his or her career. The schools will surely be affected, indirectly or directly, by this major social phenomenon. Changes in the social structure due to divorce, unemployment, and job retraining efforts will also have an impact. Educational systems are integral parts of the broader social systems that created them; if the larger social system experiences fundamental change, this is reflected in the educational system.

In the area of information science and computer technologies applicable for use in educational systems, the development of new products is so rapid that we cannot predict what technological capacities may be available to schools 20 years from now. We are in a period of human history when knowledgeable people can control far greater information (and have immediate access to it) than at any previous time. As new information-command systems evolve, this phenomenon will become more and more meaningful to all of us.

The future of education will be determined by the current debate concerning what constitutes a just, national response to human needs in a period of technological change. The history of technological change in all human societies since the beginning of industrial development clearly demonstrates that major advances in technology and breakthroughs in the basic sciences lead to more rapid rates of social change. Society is on the verge of discoveries that will lead to the creation of entirely new technologies in the dawning years of the twenty-first century. All of the social, economic, and educational institutions globally will be affected by these scientific breakthroughs. The basic issue is not whether schools can remain aloof from the needs of industry or the economic demands of society but how they can emphasize the noblest ideals of free persons in the face of inevitable technological and economic changes. Another concern is how to let go of predetermined visions of the future that limit our possibilities as free people. The schools, of course, will be called upon to face these issues. We need the most enlightened, insightful, and compassionate teachers ever educated by North American universities to prepare the youth of the future in a manner that will humanize the high-tech world in which they live.

Building a Community of Hope

Hopeful school communities clearly articulate their articles of faith and then create realistic structures to translate faith into action.

Thomas J. Sergiovanni

Archimedes once said, "Give me a lever long enough ... and I shall move the world." In many schools, the lever that can make difficult situations manageable and challenging goals attainable is *hope*. Placing hope at the core of our school community provides encouragement and promotes clear thinking and informed action, giving us the leverage we need to close the achievement gap and solve other intractable problems.

The evidence suggests that hope can be a powerful force. We know that sick people who belong to groups that provide encouragement, prayer, or other forms of support get healthier and stay healthier than do sick people who lack the benefit of this hopeful support. According to Roset,

> Medical researchers find that a sense of hopefulness, from an increased sense of control, is connected with biological changes that enhance physical, as well as mental, health. (1999, p. 7)

But too often, hope is overlooked or misunderstood. Modern management theory tells us that the only results that count are those you can see and compute—not those you can feel. According to this theory, we must be objective; look at hard evidence before we dare to believe, think, or judge; and in other ways blindly face reality. "If it can't be measured," the saying goes, "it can't be managed."

Why tie our hands and discourage our hearts when we know that hope can make a difference? Educators can be both hopeful and realistic as long as the possibilities for change remain open. Being realistic differs from facing reality in important ways. Facing reality means accepting the inevitability of a situation or circumstance; being realistic means calculating the odds with an eye toward optimism.

Hope and Wishful Thinking

Hoping is often confused with wishing. But hope is grounded in realism, not in wishful thinking. Menninger, Mayman, and Pruyser write about *realistic hope*, which they define as

> the attempt to understand the concrete conditions of reality, to see one's own role in it realistically, and to engage in such efforts of thoughtful action as might be expected to bring about the hoped-for change. (1963, p. 385)

The activating effect of hope makes the difference (see fig. 1). Some education communities engage in wishful thinking but take no deliberate action to make their wishes come true. Hopeful education communities, in contrast, take action to turn their hopes into reality.

Hope and Faith

Hope and faith go together. Faith comes from commitment to a cause and strong belief in a set of ideas.

> Hope is so closely linked to faith that the two tend to blend into one.... No matter what we put our faith in, when faith goes, hope goes with it. In some ways, hope is faith—faith with our eyes on possibilities for the future. (Smedes, 1998, p. 21)

Leaders of hopeful school communities recognize the potential in people and in situations.

This quotation brings us closer to an understanding of how hope works to help schools become effective learning communities. Organizations often communicate faith as a set of assumptions. By publicly articulating and endorsing our key assumptions, we make them come alive

FIGURE 1 Wishful Leaders/Hopeful Leaders

Wishful leaders	Hopeful leaders
↓	↓
passive reaction	active reaction
↓	↓
"I wish these kids would behave."	"I hope these kids behave. What can I do to help?"
↓	↓
no faith to back up wishes	faith in assumptions and ideas
↓	↓
no pathways to action	pathways to action
↓	↓
no action	action
↓	↓
no change	change

and give them the power to stir others to action. We might have faith, for example, that

- All students can succeed if given appropriate support.
- Under the right conditions, both students and teachers will take responsibility for their own learning.
- Schools can transform themselves into caring learning communities.
- Given the opportunity and the training, all parents can be effective partners in the education of their children.
- Under the right circumstances, all teachers can become leaders if the issues are important to them.

These assumptions suggest pathways that bring faith and action together. For example, our faith that all students can succeed will remain wishful thinking unless we transform it into hope by providing the necessary support to ensure that all students *do* succeed.

School leaders have an important responsibility here. They need to guide the school community in developing and articulating its articles of faith, thereby creating a powerful force of ideas. These ideas provide the basis for becoming a community of hope, and they fuel the school's efforts to transform hope into reality. Developing a community of hope elevates the work of leadership to the level of moral action.

Schools Built Around Hope

The following examples show how faith fuels hope and how hope can transform a school.

A Framework for Hope

In 1995, test scores at Wyandotte High School in Kansas City, Kansas, were among the lowest in the state, threatening the school's accreditation. "Even at their worst, other schools in the district could always guarantee that they were 'at least better than Wyandotte'" (Stewart, 2004, p. 75).

Instead of closing the school, the district made a last-ditch effort to improve it. Wyandotte administrators were hopeful that the school could succeed, but they recognized that their hope needed to be embedded in ideas that they trusted. A framework of reform called First Things First, developed by the Institute for Research and Reform in Education and adopted districtwide in Kansas City, provided the key to building a new community of hope at Wyandotte. School staff committed to this framework, which identified seven crucial conditions for school improvement (Institute for Research and Reform in Education, n.d.).

Four features specifically applied to students. The school would

- Provide continuity of care by forming Small Learning Communities that keep the same group of professionals and students together for extended periods during the day and across multiple school years.
- Set high, clear, and fair standards for academics and conduct that clearly define what all students will know and be able to do by graduation and at key points along the way.
- Reduce student-adult ratios to 15:1 or lower during core instructional periods, primarily by redistributing the professional staff.
- Provide enriched and diverse opportunities for students to learn, perform, and be recognized.

Three features specifically applied to teachers and administrators. The school would

- Equip, empower, and expect all teaching staff to implement standards-based instruction that actively engages all students in learning by giving teaching teams the authority to make instructional decisions, creating opportunities for continual staff learning, and specifying clear expectations about what good teaching and learning look like.
- Give Small Learning Communities the flexibility to quickly redirect resources (time, money, people, and space) to meet emerging needs.
- Ensure collective responsibility for student outcomes by providing collective incentives and consequences for teaching teams based on improvements in district performance.

As the Wyandotte staff worked toward faithful implementation of the First Things First framework, staff members increasingly committed to aligning their practice with the framework. Each of the school's eight Small

Learning Communities pairs a team of 10 teachers with a group of 150-200 students, who remain together throughout their high school experience. Mutual commitment to and belief in the framework have created a greater sense of community among school staff members. Teacher study groups have emerged, and peer coaching has become an established practice, further helping to develop a collaborative culture.

In a sense, moving from an ordinary school to a community of hope is a kind of psychological magic.

Ample evidence exists that the Wyandotte of today has been remarkably successful in improving student learning as measured by a variety of tests and other indicators. Perhaps most telling, however, is that "families used to stand in line to have their child transferred from Wyandotte. Now families are asking to transfer their child to Wyandotte" (Stewart, 2004, p. 82).

Pathways to Success

Samuel Gompers Elementary School in Detroit, Michigan, houses approximately 350 students in an economically distressed urban neighborhood.[1] More than 90 percent of the students live at the poverty level. Students come to Gompers with basic needs for food, clothing, shelter, and security. Many have never visited a dentist or received their basic health immunizations before coming to school. Yet the school espouses an ambitious goal: to ensure "that our students have the skills to become contributing members of a global society." To achieve that goal,

> Our school will successfully educate all students in a clean, safe, and healthy learning environment. We will meet the needs of the whole child through the developmental pathways: cognitive-intellectual, physical, social-interactive, speech and language, moral, and psycho-emotional. (Samuel Gompers Elementary School, 2000, p. 9)

The developmental pathways that provide the structure to turn Gompers's hopes into reality are components of the Comer process—officially known as the School Development Program. This approach to school improvement rejects the belief that low-income parents cannot adequately prepare children for school and that low-income children cannot perform well in school. Instead, the Comer process assumes that teachers, principals, and other members of the school community are willing and able to ensure that students succeed. It also assumes that schools are concerned with the whole child—that fulfilling students' needs and providing a supportive climate create the essential conditions for academic learning (Comer, 1980).

In 1993, Gompers Elementary School committed to the assumptions underlying the Comer process. The staff put its faith into action through Corner's developmental pathways, which provide a research-based strategy for improvement.

- The *cognitive-intellectual pathway* emphasizes the ability to understand and use information and the ability to understand and change the environment. The school pursues this core pathway through hands-on teaching and learning, metacognitive learning, academic clubs, and after-school tutoring. One out of every three students received tutoring during the 2001-2002 school year. Students who fall behind attend a required Summer Learning Academy.

- The *physical pathway* stresses that each student will receive proper nutrition, be physically fit, and enjoy good health. Gompers ensures that its students have warm and clean clothes to wear. Groups such as the local post office and the National Association of Women Business Owners have supplied almost all students with new coats each winter (McDonald, 2003). The hum of a washing machine and dryer in the school is nearly continuous. Students are given "safe route" maps to follow in getting to school and back home again. Breakfast is served to all students in their classrooms.

- The *social-interactive pathway* emphasizes students' ability to be empathetic, to communicate in relationships, and to interact with others who differ from them. The school provides a full complement of sports, extracurricular clubs, peer mentoring, cross-age reading parties, and other opportunities that encourage cooperative learning.

- The *speech and language pathway* emphasizes building communication skills across the curriculum. The school also addresses this pathway through a daily morning assembly, a variety of school productions, and speech and language workshops. The school invites parents with 2- and 3-year-old children to attend workshops designed to help them support their children's growing language skills.

- The *moral pathway* emphasizes respect for the rights and needs of others and addresses additional character development issues. For example, a weekly "Efficacy" class for 3rd, 4th, and 5th graders helps students make choices that respect the rights and interests of others.

- The *psycho-emotional pathway* addresses self-esteem issues and the ability to express emotion while respecting others. In an enriched co-curricular program, the school provides both intervention programs—such as anger management and living with ADHD—and enrichment programs, such as dance, art, and drama.

Hope at Gompers does not occur by accident; the school staff nurtures hope through a carefully planned, sustained school improvement effort. The developmental pathways outlined by the Comer process provide practical and successful means to address problems and improve conditions. Faith in the assumptions underlying the pathways gives Gompers staff members hope.

And their hope has become a reality. Gompers students have consistently improved their Metropolitan Achievement Test scores. In 2000, Gompers ranked 221 of 2,013 Michigan schools on the Michigan Educational Assessment, earning the highest scores in the state among schools in its size category (School Development Program, 2001). Test scores aside, the school earned the U.S. Department of Education's 1996 National Title I School Recognition Award for outstanding progress in compensatory education and was listed in 1995 as one of the 10 best schools in Detroit. The Department of Education selected Gompers as a Blue Ribbon School in 2000-2001.

From Hope to Action

Other schools have high hopes, too, but are not succeeding because they have no systematic process for transforming hope into action. As Snyder and colleagues (1991) write,

> Individuals with high hope possess goals, find pathways to these goals, navigate around obstacles, and develop agency to reach their goals.

The process of turning hope into reality requires that we answer the following questions:

- What are our goals? (What do we hope for?)
- What are our pathways? (What routes will we take to realize our hopes?)
- What obstacles do we face?
- How committed are we to actually doing something to realize our hopes?
- Is efficacy present in sufficient strength? (Do we believe strongly enough that we can make a difference?)
- If our school's efficacy is low, how can we strengthen it?

Educators can be both hopeful and realistic as long as the possibilities for change remain open.

The question of efficacy is crucial. The jury is still out on which view of human nature will prevail—optimistic or pessimistic. But I believe that leaders of hopeful school communities recognize the potential in people and in situations. To these hopeful leaders,

> what people can achieve, or aspire to, is just as surely part of human nature, just as surely summoned by the

human condition, as are more negative traits and dimensions. (Selznick, 2002, p. 70)

In a sense, moving from an ordinary school to a community of hope is a kind of psychological magic. But we can make this magic happen by identifying and committing to our key articles of faith, by establishing structures that translate our hopes into action, and by providing the context for both the school and the individual members of the school community to realize their potential.

Note

1. Except where otherwise noted, the Gompers story is drawn from the school's 2000-2001 Blue Ribbon Program Application.

References

Comer, J. P. (1980). School power: *Implications of an intervention program*. New York: Free Press.

Institute for Research and Reform in Education. (n.d.). *First things first: An introduction*. Philadelphia: Author. Available: www.irre.org/pdf_ffiles/FTF_Intro.pdf

McDonald, M. (2003, Jan. 22). School succeeds with some help from its friends. *The Detroit News* [Online]. Available: www.detnews.com/2003/detroit/0301/29/s04-64852.htm

Menninger, K., Mayman, M., & Pruyser, P. (1963). *The vital balance: The life process in mental health and illness*. New York: Penguin Books.

Roset, S. M. (1999). *Exploring hope: Implications for educational leaders*. Master of Education Thesis, Department of Educational Administration, University of Saskatchewan, Canada.

Samuel Gompers Elementary School. (2000). *2000-2001 Blue Ribbon Schools Program application*. Detroit, MI: Author.

School Development Program. (2001). Selected achievement by SDP schools [Online]. Available: http://info.med.yale.edu/comer/about/achievements.html

Selznick, P. (2002). On a communitarian faith. *The Responsive Community*, 12(3), 67-74.

Smedes, L. (1998). *Standing on the promises: Keeping hope alive for a tomorrow we cannot control*. Nashville, TN: Thomas Nelson.

Snyder, C. R., Harris, C., Anderson, J. R., Holleran, S. A., Irving, L. M., Sigmon, S. T., et al. (1991). The will and the ways: Development and validation of an individual-differences measure of hope. *Journal of Personality and Social Psychology*, 60(4), 570-585.

Stewart, M. (2004). An urban high school emerges from chaos. In *Breaking ranks II Strategies for leading high school reform* (pp. 75-82). Reston, VA: National Association of Secondary School Principals.

Thomas J. Sergiovanni is Lillian Radford Professor of Education at Trinity University, San Antonio, Texas; tsergiov@trinity.edu. His forthcoming book, *Strengthening the Heartbeat: Leading and Learning Together* (Jossey-Bass, fall 2004) discusses in more detail how hope, trust, and other virtues can help build effective learning communities.

Mission and Vision in Education

by Edward G. Rozycki

Happy talk, keep talking happy talk,
Talk about things you'd like to do,
You gotta have a dream, if you don't have a dream,
How you gonna have a dream come true?

—Rodgers and Hammerstein, *South Pacific*

Junk Food

Like all sweet things, happy talk risks being addictive. Our educational institutions, responding to public pressure for the upbeat and the heart-warming, have become intellectually obese with happy talk: sweet slogans that enervate clear definition of goals, that obscure inquiry into their achievability, and that have provoked the "fad diets" of standardized testing, teacher accountability, and lockstep curriculum.

A recent vogue has been to introduce another layer of happy talk on top of the timeworn expatiation on missions and goals: statements of vision. Theoretically, we might say that vision statements justify leadership claims on resources. A non-academic might ask, "Just what do you do to earn your salary?" "Provide vision," comes the answer. Absent critical examination, however, there may be precious little difference between vision and delusion, if by "statements of vision" we mean verbal concatenations mistaken for causal analyses.

As generally conceived, vision statements provide the impetus for missions. And mission statements provide the targets for goal statements. We might find the relationships easy to understand with this simple illustration:

Vision statement: We'll have pie in the sky by and by.
Mission statement: We'll bake something that flies.
Goal statement: We'll make some dough.

Unfortunately, as the history of American education so vividly attests, once this goal has been reached, the missionaries absent themselves from the educational scene with alacrity. The point here is not to ridicule visions or missions, but to suggest they be tempered with a sense of proportion, a knowledge of resources available, and cool evaluation of the likelihood of success. Above all else, it is important to stop sacrificing the Good to pursuit of a Vision of the Best.

Mission and Vision Statements: The GIGO Effect

Much criticism has it that teachers are ill prepared in college for the reality of their jobs in schools. Little attention has been paid, however, to how teachers are subjected, once they have been hired, to group-think processes of indoctrination, usually called "staff development." Staff development works not infrequently to increase their credulity, stultify their normal critical abilities, and undermine their capacity for reasoned judgment. Much staff development in education is dedicated to examining mission and vision statements.

Here is a mission statement from an affluent school district just outside Philadelphia: *Empower each student to succeed in life and contribute to society.* There is perhaps no more certain indicator of the depth to which our society has been secularized than in the mission statements of those who arrogate to themselves heretofore Divine attributes of Omnipotence and Omniscience. Imagine educators in a middle or high school knowing that they have empowered their students to succeed in life—or perhaps that is merely hyperbole for teaching the students to be literate and minimally mathematical. Are we, then, to imagine that educators are so ego-deficient that someone must routinely, grandiosely, recast their humble yet important achievements of basic schooling as feats of historical significance?

Another nearby community has its schools profess: *The mission of the X School District is to ensure that every student is inspired and prepared to be a passionate lifelong learner and a productive, invested participant in the local and global communities.* (Can one even say this aloud without hyperventilating?) Weeks of faculty time are spent cooking this mission down into supposedly operational goals. On the surface, the issue is this: how are teachers to bring the mission into their day-to-day pursuits? Instruction time is forgone as teachers meet to pursue this will-o'-the-wisp. In their committees they find out that the surface is only to be polished: hardly ever scratched. Insightful or possibly critical questions are deflected during the group-think process by the school's resident lickspittle, who cajoles those assembled into "preserving a collegial atmosphere" and "keeping everyone on task"—an insinuation that probing inquiry is "out of place" or "not quite professional." Whatever scatterbrained confabulations the staff generates are taken as answers, solemnly recorded and duly acceptable to local, state, and regional accrediting agencies. As they say in the computer-programming world, GIGO—garbage in, garbage out.

Such activity wastes time, spirit, and intellect—ask any educator (in private)—because the mission statement is never subjected to careful scrutiny prior to attempts to "operationalize" it: "Our vision is yadda, yadda. Our mission, therefore, is blah, blah, blah. What does this mean for your classroom?" "For me it means glug, glug, glug!" "Excellent! We'll definitely meet our accreditation requirements now."

Mission and Vision Statements: Organizational Sporks

Unless you have dealt with preschoolers, you may not have encountered a Spork. Sporks are plastic spoons with a few dull tines molded into their tips so they can work somewhat like forks to pick up food. Sporks are for novices—those too inexperienced to handle spoon and fork expertly on their own. We also give children Sporks if we do not trust them to use them as we want, e.g., as eating utensils rather than as swords for dueling or shovels for digging, or whatever fertile imagination may dream up. Sporks are safe. But they are hardly precision instruments.

The primary use of mission or vision statements is as dull utensils of publicity and persuasion: they are slogans intended to motivate people to selected ends and to obscure the real differences of opinion normally found in school communities. Clever staff-development processes invite all members of the school community to "contribute" to the formulation of mission statements but leave the authority for interpreting those vague residues of concern in the hands of the few. That's why probing questions are discouraged. When authority and control of resources are the real issues, educators are invited to keep talkin' happy talk.

Educator Dementation

I work with doctoral students in education. Most of them are principals, superintendents, or other school administrators. They are intelligent, dedicated, hard-working people. But they are so involved in the political environment of the schools that they confuse the language appropriate to such an environment with that necessary to delineate a research problem carefully. They imagine that visions, missions, and goals automatically relate as causes and effects. They believe that ideas which are articulable are variables which are measurable; that voices which are ignored are voices of assent.

When I talk to my students about non-educational matters, I notice that they have not lost their capacity for careful judgment; they have a clear sense of costs and benefits and of the likelihood of achieving them. They have a normally developed conception of cause and effect. And they know how to deliberate on ethical issues as well as anyone. But when the discussion wanders into the field of education, their common sense suddenly shrivels: they treat their general knowledge, their life's wisdom, as nothing. That, I believe, is the consequence of the indoctrination they have received as educators. That is what is wrong with the pre-service training of teachers, not some lack of technical expertise or content-area knowledge. In-service staff development—in particular, the perpetual blather about visions, missions, and goals—just reinforces their intellectual, psychological, and moral lobotomy.

Assessing Visions and Missions

So I train my students to ask questions. I assure them it is legitimate to subject the dogmas and slogans of their profession to the same kind of scrutiny that they do other concerns of life. In particular, I teach them to consistently formulate two kinds of questions: critical questions, and criteria questions.

Critical questions worry the causal assumptions of a vision or mission statement. They may also look to uncover alternatives to the means-ends relationships alluded to. Criteria questions ask how we identify items mentioned in a mission or vision.

For example, let's examine the mission mentioned earlier:

The Mission of the X School District is to ensure that every student is inspired and prepared to be a passionate lifelong learner and a productive, invested participant in the local and global communities.

Critical questions are:

1. How does what happens to students during the time they are in X School District cause them to be lifelong learners? Are there later important influences? How can we ensure that outcome?
2. Need they be passionate about it?
3. Is inspiration necessary or sufficient to have that effect?
4. How does what happens to students during the time they are in X School District cause them to be productive participants in either the local or global community? Are there later important influences?
5. Need it be both local and global communities?
6. Will we not be satisfied if they are not "invested"?

Criteria questions hammer away at two points: what are the criteria for identifying important terms, and how will we know at any given time that those criteria have been met? Some examples are:

7. What are the criteria for being a lifelong learner? How can we tell whether an eighth-grader will meet those criteria at age forty-five, or if he will be "passionate" about it?
8. Does a successful, compulsive gambler count as a passionate lifelong learner?
9. What do we mean by a "productive, invested participant"?
10. What kind of participation counts as being in the local, or global, community?

My students who undertake analyses of vision or mission statements find this activity easy, once they get over the shock that I am inviting them to think along these lines. They burst out frequently in gleeful laughter yet insist that they will never have the opportunity to ask such questions on the job.

I ask them, "Why is that, do you suppose?"

I get many variations on the same answer: "You ask questions like that and they'll take you for a trouble-maker."

Then I get down to the moral of the lesson: Be assertive. Tell your potential critics that you are coming at the vision and mission statements from a research and implementation perspective. If they will not or cannot answer your critical and criteria questions, then all the visioning and missioning in the world will not amount to anything more than wishful thinking and wasted time.

Edward G. Rozycki is a twenty-five-year veteran of the school district of Philadelphia. He is an associate professor of education at Widener University, Widener, Pennsylvania.

Beyond the Book

Electronic Textbooks Will Bring Worldwide Learning

Parker Rossman

Future learners will have access to the rapidly proliferating world of knowledge and ideas, thanks to new technologies. With ELTIS—the proposed Electronic Learning Tutorial Instrument System—learners also will have personal avatars to help them navigate tomorrow's "Cosmopedia" of ever-evolving information resources.

Textbooks have long been crucial to education, because they organize information and make it convenient and manageable for learners. But the traditional printed book is not only expensive but hard to update. Textbooks have grown ever larger and added features such as full-color illustrations, often making them too heavy for youngsters to carry in their backpacks and expensive for the world's impoverished people who desperately need more and better learning aids.

New information is being added to human knowledge so rapidly that a new textbook may be out of date by the time it appears in print. Clearly, traditional printed textbooks alone will not be adequate to meet the world's education needs in the long-range future. Fortunately, powerful new technologies are going to greatly overcome those limitations, enabling educators to focus their skills on helping individual students.

The Emerging Digital E-Book

Many possibilities for new kinds of textbooks arise from the convergence of content such as print, video, sound, film, and graphics with a variety of delivery media, including cell phones, digital radio, TV, and the Internet. Personalized avatars or cyber assistants may someday guide learners through the vast intelligent grid that will emerge as the Internet evolves into a true "Cosmopedia" linking all the world's online resources, big and small, from electronic encyclopedias and databanks to blogs and instant messaging.

The rich kids of the world already have many excellent options available. But what about learners in the developing world who might benefit even more from low-cost, high-tech learning resources? One answer could be what I call ELTIS, an online Electronic Learning Tutorial Instrument System. Experiments with e-books are an important step toward the development of ELTIS.

One early e-book experiment was MIT Dean Thomas J. Mitchell's *City of Bits*, which was published both online and as a printed book with attached CD-ROM. In the online version, readers could enter an electronic "agora," or meeting place, and go to any section of the text, adding their own comments or read the comments left by others. Readers appreciated having both the physical and the online editions, each useful for different purposes. The print-on paper text was convenient for rapid reading; for serious study, the online version offered links and other helpful aids. Clicking on a reference to Aristotle's *Politics*, for example, provided immediate access to the relevant passage in both English and the original Greek. Footnotes of the online edition were linked to Web pages, and readers were invited to add the Web addresses of still other relevant links.

Two major problems were encountered during this experiment. The first was that, because Web sites often change, it required constant monitoring to replace links that moved or became inactive. Special software can help with that chore. The second problem was the graffiti (such as advertisements and irrelevant comments) that piled up in the agora. In future e-textbooks, special passwords may limit access to the discussion area to people who are registered in a class or otherwise authorized to take part.

The publishers of printed textbooks have been experimenting with different ways to use computer technology. Some textbooks now add a CD containing spoken text, music, pictures, film clips, and/or links to supplemental sources on the Internet. For example, on CDs accompanying biology textbooks, readers can click on a photograph of the heart and be jumped to an animation where a model human heart can be virtually examined and dissected. John R. Campbell's textbook *Animal Sciences* (McGraw-Hill, 2003) offers links to 20 recorded lectures, and still more CD features are available in international editions published in several languages. Rapid progress in computerized translation is also bringing close the time when a text can be accurately and cheaply translated into other languages.

Hundreds of e-books are now available from major publishers. Most, however, simply reproduce existing printed texts and fail to exploit the educational potential of incorporating other media and technologies. It might be better to expand our concept of the book to include anything that can be read, viewed, or otherwise obtained using a booklike "reading appliance." Such handheld book-shaped instruments could have built-in Internet connections to download notes, revisions, and background materials. They might even read themselves aloud while you are exercising, driving, waiting in line, or lying in bed. They will certainly have enough memory to include dictionaries, encyclopedias, and perhaps even a whole personal library. A future e-book on history might feature built-in multimedia elements, such as animated maps to show how national boundaries changed over time or video sequences showing reenactments of battles or other major events.

So long as many people prefer reading text from a printed page rather than a video screen, future books will likely appear in both print and electronic editions. Some textbook publishers already encourage professors to create their own online anthologies by selecting material from many different sources—so long as they pay the appropriate royalty to each source. Publishers can build in controls to make sure such custom-made e-books cannot be recopied. Some even build in controls that erase the text entirely on the date when the class for which it was created ends.

Soon, however, even these flexible e-books will be outmoded by still more powerful technologies. It would be a big mistake to judge the potential future of electronic learning solely by what is available or on the drawing boards today. The ultimate purpose of ELTIS is to create a system of learning modules on the Internet that can be updated easily and available at low cost to nearly everyone in the world.

One exciting possibility for ELTIS is for online textbooks to become more like video games and enable students to evolve their own best learning practice. *Joystick Nation* author J.C. Herz and others have shown how computer games can radically transform learning strategies. Herz tells of one online game that attracted a million players who immediately began to improve and enlarge the rules, even though that was technically illegal. As is now true of many gamers, ELTIS users will continue to develop and expand it. If even 1% of a million learners become interested enough in an online textbook to contribute to innovation in the product, that makes 10,000 people doing the research and development. [*Ed. note:* For more on potential use of technologies in education and learning, see the October-November 2004 issue of the online journal INNOVATE, www.innovateonlineinfo.]

Learning Systems Tailored To the Individual

Physicist Alfred Bork has developed an automated online tutor that could be made cheaply available to learners all over the world. Bork's "skilled tutor" can communicate in a student's native language and provide meaningful interactions every 20 seconds, such as replying in free-form fashion to a student's question. Learning units allow individual pacing and different learning strategies. Additional help is available within the program so that all motivated students, regardless of gender, race, economic status, handicaps, or other factors, can master a subject. Such automated tutors might even include a built-in ombudsman to help students deal with government and institutional bureaucracy.

Experimental packages that operate on Bork's automated tutor are available today for 25 introductory or remedial courses offered by most colleges. For a French course, the automated tutor conducts grammar and pronunciation drills and enables students to explore French history, culture, literature, etc.—either alone online or interacting with students in France who are studying English. Similarly, the tutor module for accounting guides students through routine procedures, freeing class time for a human instructor to discuss ethics and other application related issues at a level that was once available only to students in professional seminars at top graduate schools.

Media professor Jay David Bolter of Georgia Tech has suggested that future e-books might "change for each reader and each reading." Sometimes a learner will want to skim the highlights from a vast reservoir, as one now browses in a library. For more in-depth learning, the same material might be reformatted into a digital textbook organized around a learner's current priorities. Instead of presenting only one static set of text and photographs, ELTIS can expand or contract the amount of detail to match any level of mastery in a subject. This will allow users to skim a subject or concentrate on details just as the human mind does. Ideally, ELTIS should be able to automatically translate from other languages, identify quotations, interpret pictures, explain symbols, define scientific and mathematical

formulas, or turn printed musical

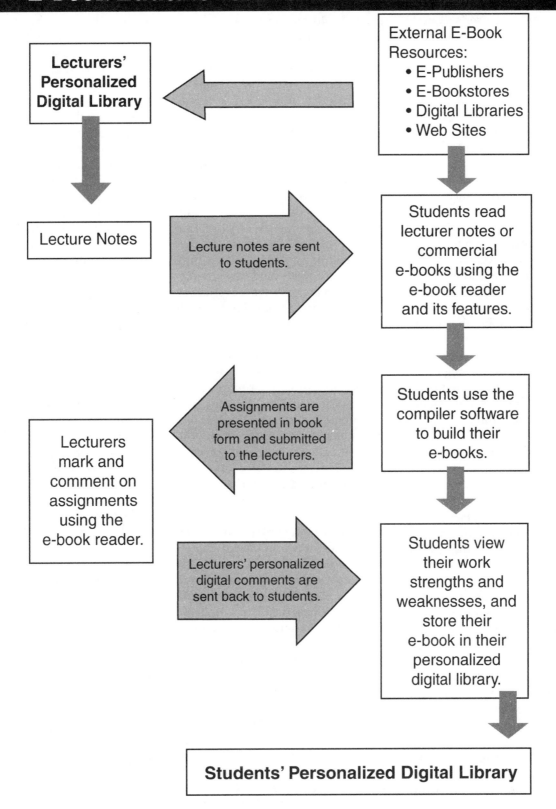

E-Book Educator-Student Interaction Model

Lecturers' Personalized Digital Library

External E-Book Resources:
- E-Publishers
- E-Bookstores
- Digital Libraries
- Web Sites

Lecture Notes

Lecture notes are sent to students.

Students read lecturer notes or commercial e-books using the e-book reader and its features.

Lecturers mark and comment on assignments using the e-book reader.

Assignments are presented in book form and submitted to the lecturers.

Students use the compiler software to build their e-books.

Lecturers' personalized digital comments are sent back to students.

Students view their work strengths and weaknesses, and store their e-book in their personalized digital library.

Students' Personalized Digital Library

How e-learning flows: This model for how learning flows to students from teachers and electronic texts was developed by computer and information science researchers Norshuhada Shiratuddin, Monica Landoni, and Forbes Gibb (University of Strathclyde) and Shahizan Hassan (University of Newcastle Upon Tyne). See their paper "E-Book Technology and its Potential Applications in Distance Education," published in the *Journal of Digital Information* (Volume 3, Issue 4), Article No. 160, 2003-02-19; accessible online at jodi.ecs.soton.ac.uk/Articles/v03/i04/Shiratuddin/.

notes into sounds at a user's request.

Computer and communications technology can increasingly be embedded in tools, clothing, furniture, and even the walls that people pass by. At the Sony Computer Science Laboratory in Tokyo, Rekimoto Jun'ichi is working on a system that uses a terminal known as a NaviCam to pick up signals from a monitor nearby and respond by downloading data from a network such as the Internet. A computer circuit might be placed, for example, inside the wall next to an exhibit at a museum. When any visitor carrying the NaviCam approached, the device would respond to a signal from the nearby wall and pick up a recorded lecture about the exhibit, then guide the visitor along to the next exhibit. Wearing a virtual-reality headset, a learner with a NaviCam might approach a chunk of crystal and immediately see a large, 3-D scale model of its molecular structure.

Teacher-Guided Technology

One key component of the ELTIS idea is that, instead of accepting what vendors produce and then deciding how to make use of new technologies, educators must decide first what learners around the world most need and then work with manufacturers to create tools specifically designed to achieve these priority goals. ELTIS should help learners organize their thoughts and develop learning projects to match their current interests or address crucial issues in society. In the last century, you could view the videotape of a lecture and replay any section you did not understand. This proved especially useful in learning a foreign language. Using ELTIS, you will be able to consult an expert adviser, access dictionaries to define any word or idea, or obtain additional background information in many forms from the future Cosmopedia.

Bork, "the physicist who developed the automated tutoring system, argues convincingly that mastery of any subject is now possible for all students. Bork's own experiments have involved teaching science. Instead of just telling students about important scientific principles, his automated science tutor allows students to work as scientists themselves, creating, testing, and applying scientific laws. A program for discovering Mendelian genetics, for example, enables even young children to draw and test conclusions from their own discoveries.

This suggests a new kind of textbook within ELTIS. A single online math "book," for example, might begin with modules suitable for pre-school children, then seamlessly move up through multiplication and division, algebra, calculus, and beyond as each step is mastered. Explanations, streaming video, and graphic illustrations can provide practical demonstrations and real-world examples appropriate to each age group and skill level. For grading and assessment, the system would constantly probe to find what the learner knows, as part of a seamless process. Learners do not "fail" when they are slow to comprehend. Instead, they are automatically offered additional help, showing them their mistakes and how to correct and understand them before moving on. Bork proposes testing such learning modules on large numbers of users in class, at home, and in various informal environments.

In time, the electronic tutor aspect of ELTIS will give learners much more control over their education. Using a learning system continually connected to the Internet, you will have access to everything needed for a course—all recommended lectures (available as printed text, audio, or video), lists of frequently asked questions, opportunity to join Internet chat discussion-seminars, movies as illustrations, and navigation maps to help you move through vast amounts of optional material. Guided by the course outline, syllabus, proposals for discussion sessions, and regular announcements, the automated tutor can test you to make sure you are mastering the essentials and even provide evaluations and assign grades.

While studying in ELTIS, you can freely add your own highlighting and annotations to a text. You can also create personal indexing terms to supplement the built-in index. By accessing your personal computerized profile, the system can select or even customize any learning module to match your current needs, learning style, and existing knowledge. Computers already have enough capacity to store most of what an individual has learned in an electronic memory where it can later be retrieved whenever the learner needs it. If you come upon a foreign word, you can touch or highlight it on screen and immediately see the word translated. If the definitions offered are not satisfying, you can bring onto that page an encyclopedia paragraph with more detailed and graphic explanations and links to further sources.

Although you can move a quotation, paragraph of text, photo, or graphic into a term paper you are writing, plagiarism will be difficult because each source will be automatically cited through the use of metadata tags that identify authors. On the other hand, if you find an appealing new idea that you don't immediately need, you can add it to a personal electronic notebook or memory system. While reading, you can insert any ideas or questions that occur to you directly into a seminar Web page and thus have this material available for a class presentation or discussion.

Avatars Will Boost Creativity

The technology supporting ELTIS can be easy to use and almost invisible. This technology may be as different from today's computers as a bicycle is from a spaceship. One especially exciting possibility is a program called an avatar, an electronic personal assistant.

An avatar program specifically designed for an individual learner can stay on the job 24 hours a day. This "virtual self" can search a million Web pages, organize the information it finds, and put it exactly where you

Connected to Learning: Two Scenarios

In 2012, "Gustavo," a 16-year-old aspiring poet in Colombia, is poor and has no way to reach a school. He has tried correspondence courses, with lessons sent back and forth by mail, but the postal service is slow and unreliable. Bought new, a single textbook might cost more than his family's income for an entire month. Such realities would have been deeply discouraging were it not for ELTIS—the Electronic Learning Tutorial Instrument System—connecting Gustavo with a high school in Cartagena, as well as several Spanish universities guiding him through a special course on Cervantes.

"Kira" is 14 and lives in South Los Angeles. Despite efforts by government, businesses, and community groups, polluted air is still a problem here. For days at a time, the smog can be so bad that Kira, who suffers from asthma, can't open her house door without triggering a serious attack. Once, this might have kept her from school, or even forced her family to move to another city. But now, thanks to ELTIS, Kira's illness is actually

helping to advance her education by motivating her to make the best use of the resources available to her.

For both Gustavo and Kira, access to a world of learning through ELTIS has been life altering.

Linked together through the Internet, Kira and her "classmates" (including kids' from other schools in distant cities) learn about biology by developing their own personal health profile programs. Guided by their teacher, they measure and record each other's heartbeat, lung capacity, and height weight ratio, then score their individual fitness levels by the norms and goals in a national database. Monitoring fitness is a good habit to develop, and applying math skills to practical problem solving helps make the work fun. Also, by frequently comparing herself with other real kids, short and tall, fat and thin, healthy and sickly, Kira is learning how wide a range of physical conditions are really "normal." This makes her less likely to set unrealistic models of perfection for herself, or to be unfairly biased against people with

body type or physical abilities noticeably different from her own.

Gustavo uses ELTIS to not only finish his high-school education, but also to do research on the life of Cervantes, who wrote Don Quixote while in prison. This inspires him to become more politically involved, and he decides to use his writing skill to help work toward peace. ELTIS connects him with the work of several human-rights groups, and he applies for a virtual internship with the International Peace Research Institute in Stockholm.

For both Kira and Gustavo, learning is fully integrated into their life despite not being in a classroom. Their teachers apply the available technologies of education in appropriate ways. Interactive games and computer access facilitate team-learning activities and socialization. But teachers also recognize and build upon each student's individual strengths and motives. The successful teacher knows how to custom-mix different modes of education to make each student's learning endeavors individually meaningful.

need it. An avatar will also be able to draw on information collected in previous courses or from personal reading, as well as from books, films, and other materials in your personal electronic library collection. The avatar can even direct your attention to unanswered questions and areas requiring more research. Perhaps more than any other single component of ELTIS; a learner's personal avatar can enable creative work at a greater depth than today's students can even imagine. As ELTIS evolves, students and teachers, amateurs, and professionals, will be able to collaborate meaningfully in original research

projects conducted locally or spanning continents.

Emerging software can even help learners do better thinking by improving the mental models they use to draw conclusions and make decisions. The pictures of reality that people carry around in their heads often differ greatly and can be deeply flawed by ignorance or bias. For example, our judgment of a person may be faulty because we do not know enough about him or her. Through conversation and other methods of gaining background information we can modify and correct our opinions. ELTIS will use computer simulation and modeling

technology to correct faulty reasoning by making learners aware of what their mental models may be leaving out.

All this suggests that human learning capacity can indeed be increased. Already we can dimly see the possibilities ELTIS holds for making education more dynamic, modifiable, and much more under the learner's control than is possible with today's printed textbooks.

Some Current Experiments

Many higher education institutions and vendors of educational media have projects under way that suggest how ELTIS may develop. Here are just a few examples.

- Nokia offers a cell phone that a teacher can use to quickly download a film from a satellite and project it for the class.

- TAKS, an online tool developed by the University of Texas, helps high-school students take practice tests that measure their comprehension of various subjects. Also available are interactive tutorials that include multimedia learning materials. Students enjoy using them because they are self-paced and offer immediate feedback.

- "Moodle" is an evolving, free, open-source learning appliance available in 34 languages for teachers at all levels, from kindergarten on up. It offers an astonishing variety of features that an instructor can adapt and change online.

- The University of Virginia, Microsoft, and Thomson Learning are collaborating on a system to "reinvent traditional approaches to learning" in ways that will extend the classroom beyond its four walls. The project will design and deliver rich digital course content based on new insights into how students learn.

Much more is sure to come. Perhaps ELTIS will incorporate a fantasy amplifier/imagination stimulator of the kind envisioned by imagineer Alan Kay at Disney. It has long been Kay's dream to equip learners of all ages with an enhanced imagination device to use in exploring the world of knowledge on their own.

To accomplish such visionary objectives, the Oxygen project at MIT is actively working on several key delivery vehicles. MIT's Enviro21 is designed to link all existing information networks and appliances, so that "all the written knowledge in the world" can be in every schoolchild's pocket. Oxygen also aims to create concept maps that will help users navigate and organize information. At the heart of the Oxygen system will be a collaboration editor to facilitate work with others and to keep track of routine details such as document versions and files. Customization to each individual user's needs will be possible in every part of the system, which is to be made available free to everyone everywhere.

Most fascinating is the idea that every element in the Oxygen system, from enormous supercomputers to microchips so small as to be nearly invisible, might be linked together. In time, tiny chips or "smart dust" can be built into literally anything, giving it a unique cybernetic identity. This would give every object and machine the ability to communicate and cooperate, thereby freeing human beings from the tedium of many routine maintenance tasks while enlarging our creative capacities. When everyone and everything is interconnected, the potential will exist to break down age-old cultural, social, and linguistic barriers, enabling humans to perceive and explore our universe and ourselves in ways never possible before.

Starting Today

Until an ELTIS-type system is available, CD-ROMs and other kinds of e-textbook packages can be the first step toward a worldwide electronic learning system. Before the neighborhood school becomes a "community learning tele-center" with wireless Internet connections, it can have an extensive library of CD-ROMs and download inexpensive teaching videos.

Yet, however powerful its self-teaching tools become, ELTIS can only supplement, never replace, the human teacher-counselor-tutor-coach-guide. Tomorrow's educators will be challenged to use all these new technologies appropriately to broaden opportunities for learners of every age, background, and income level. In the process, they must reconceptualize their own jobs away from being primarily fact presenters and drill masters to becoming intellectual role models, posers of intriguing problems, patient advisers, motivators, and inspirers.

Parker Rossman *is former vice president of the Global/ Pacific Electronic University Consortium. He is the author of the free, online three-volume textbook The Future of Higher (Lifelong) Education (http://ecole-con.missour.edu/globalresearch/index.html).*

His previous article for THE FUTURIST was "Cosmopedia: Tomorrow's World of Learning," May-June 2004. His address is 3 Lemmon Drive, Columbia, Missouri 65201. E-mail g.p.ross@mchsi.com; Web site ecole-con.missour.edu/global research.

For additional resources related to this article, please visit www.wfs.org/rossmanresource.htm.

An Emerging Culture

RUDOLF STEINER'S CONTINUING IMPACT IN THE WORLD

by Christopher Bamford and Eric Utne

Beginning at the end of the 19th century, a relatively unknown Austrian philosopher and teacher began to sow the seeds of what he hoped would blossom into a new culture. The seeds were his ideas, which he sowed through extensive writings, lectures, and countless private consultations. The seeds germinated and took root in the hearts and minds of his students, among whom were individuals who would later become some of the best known and most influential figures of the 20th century. Since the teacher's death in 1925, a quiet but steadily growing movement, unknown and unseen by most people, has been spreading over the world, bringing practical solutions to the problems of our global, technological civilization. The seeds are now coming to flower in the form of thousands of projects infused with human values. The teacher, called by some "the best kept secret of the 20th century," was Rudolf Steiner.

Steiner, a truly "Renaissance man," developed a way of thinking that he applied to different aspects of what it means to be human. Over a period of 40 years, he formulated and taught a path of inner development or spiritual research he called "anthroposophy." From what he learned, he gave practical indications for nearly every field of human endeavor. Art, architecture, drama, science, medicine, economics, religion, care of the dying, social organization—there is almost no field he did not touch.

> **"My meeting with Rudolf Steiner led me to occupy myself with him from that time forth and to remain always aware of his significance. We both felt the same obligation to lead man once again to true inner culture. I have rejoiced at the achievements his great personality and his profound humanity have brought about in the world."**
>
> Albert Schweitzer

Today, wherever there is a human need you'll find groups of people working out of Steiner's ideas. There are an estimated ten thousand initiatives worldwide—the movement is a hotbed of entrepreneurial activity, social and political activism, artistic expression, scientific research, and community building. In this report we limit our investigation to a tiny, representative sampling of these initiatives, primarily from North America.

Waldorf Schools

EDUCATION FOR THE HEAD, HANDS, AND HEART

Waldorf education is probably the most widespread and mature of Steiner's many plantings. There are more than 150 Waldorf schools in North America and over 900 worldwide, double the number just a decade ago, making it possibly the fastest growing educational movement in the world. Steiner's interest in education was lifelong. As a young man, he earned a living as a tutor, starting at 14 helping fellow students. Then, from the age of 23 to 29, he lived in Vienna with the family of Ladislaus and Pauline Specht, undertaking the education of their four sons, one of whom, Otto, was hydrocephalic. At the age of 10, Otto could hardly read or write. His parents were uncertain whether he could be educated at all. Steiner took responsibility for him. Believing that, despite appearances, the boy had great intellectual capacities, Steiner saw his task as slowly waking the boy up and bringing him into his body. To do this, he knew he first had to gain the child's love. On this basis, he was able to awaken his dormant faculties. He was so successful that Otto went on to become a doctor.

Waldorf students create their own "main lesson books" for each subject.

For Steiner, Otto was a learning experience. As he says in his *Autobiography:* "The educational methods I had to adopt gave

Lao Tsu (604-531 BC) Tao Te Ching, Chapter 42

The Tao begot one.
One begot two.
Two begot three.
And three begot
the ten thousand
things.

Dear Reader,

Over the last 30 years I've encountered Rudolf Steiner's ideas in a number of different venues: as an active parent of four Waldorf-educated boys; as a natural foods merchant distributing Biodynamic® foods (grown according to Steiner's indications); as a truth seeker, struggling unsuccessfully to understand Steiner's dense and, for me, impenetrable writings; as a former architecture student intrigued by Steiner's contributions to 20th-century art and architecture; and, more recently, as the seventh and then eighth grade class teacher at City of Lakes Waldorf School in Minneapolis.

Despite all this exposure to the manifestations of his philosophy, I didn't begin to fathom Steiner's own thinking until several years ago when I began reading his writings in earnest. His language suffered from translation, was often time- and culture-bound, and frequently filled with archaic and new-agey references. Yet, as I kept at it, his ideas soon became more accessible and increasingly meaningful to me. After I "graduated" with my class in June 2002, I decided to meet some actual people whose lives had been touched by Steiner's ideas. Last summer, my 17-year-old son Oliver and I traveled 2,500 miles around Europe, visiting centers of Steinerian activity. In Järna, Sweden, we participated in an international youth conference for some 200 Waldorf-educated 16- to 30-year-olds from every race and 40 countries. In Dornach, Switzerland, we met the leadership of the worldwide General Anthroposophic Society, founded by Steiner. In other places we met people who have been involved in various aspects of Steiner's work for two or three generations. Since returning, I've been taking similar people-meeting excursions to the East and West Coasts.

What I've found is fascinating and heartening to me, and I wanted to share it with you. So I went to see the folks at the Rudolf Steiner Foundation and asked them to underwrite the costs of researching, writing, and publishing a special section on the continuing legacy of Rudolf Steiner. They turned around and raised the funds from private donors. My co-author of this section is Christopher Bamford, who has written widely on a variety of topics, including the recently published *What Is Anthroposophy?* (Anthroposophic Press, Great Barrington, Massachusetts) and "An Endless Trace: The Passionate Pursuit of Wisdom in the West" (Codhill Press, New York).

As you read the section I think you'll agree that the people influenced by Steiner's ideas are at least as interesting as the ideas themselves. Like the rest of society, they are a diverse lot. Some are well-scrubbed and impressively accomplished, like the actresses Jennifer Aniston and Julianna Margulies, and American Express president and CEO Kenneth Chenault, all of whom are Waldorf educated. Others, like me, are rather wacky, basically inept, unreconstructed idealists and malcontents. But then, I never had a Waldorf education!

The people involved in Steiner's ideas that I find most compelling are working within the framework of communities, in Waldorf schools, Biodynamic® farms, anthroposophical medical clinics, Camphill Villages for the handicapped, early childhood and elder-care centers, and artistic collaboratives. They're not isolated and alienated, stuck in institutions inhospitable to their values. They're developing the social skills necessary to form real, viable communities. If they study anthroposophy, Steiner's nonreligious path to self-knowledge, they're struggling to learn what we all sign on for in this human life—they're learning how to love.

There are an estimated ten thousand initiatives around the world that trace their lineage to Steiner and his ideas. These initiatives add up to an insurgent movement today that just may be the seedbed of a new, more just and humane emerging culture—the alternative that so many of us have been searching for all our lives. I believe these people, the heirs to Rudolf Steiner's legacy, are building, in our midst, a truly viable template for a greener and kinder world.

—Eric Utne

me insight into the way that the human soul and spirit are connected with the body. It became my training in physiology and psychology. I came to realize that education and teaching must become an art, and must be based upon true knowledge of the human being."

As with everything Steiner did, his curriculum for Waldorf education began with a question. In 1919, in the chaos following the First World War, Emil Molt, director of the Waldorf Astoria Cigarette Company, asked Steiner to help with the creation of a school for his workers. Four months later, the first Independent Waldorf School opened in Stuttgart, Germany. From that spontaneous beginning arose the now worldwide Waldorf School Movement.

Waldorf Education: It's All in the Curriculum

Whenever he visited a Waldorf school, Rudolf Steiner's first question to the students was always, "Do you love your teacher?" Similarly, he would ask the teachers, "Do you love your students?" The class teacher accompanies the children from first grade through eighth grade, i.e., from childhood into the beginning of adolescence. Children and teacher grow together. Making and doing, creating beauty, and working with one's hands—knitting, crocheting, painting, drawing, and woodworking—are an integral part of the educational and developmental process. Besides teaching manual dexterity and training eye-hand coordination, the work with color, form, and different materials develops an aesthetic sense, which permeates all other activities. Coordinated physical movement, learning through the body, accompanies all stages of development. The practice of Eurythmy—Steiner's art of movement, which makes speech and music visible through action and gesture—allows the child to develop a sense of harmony and balance. Rhythm is an important component of all these activities. Rhythm (order or pattern in time) permeates the entire school day, as well as the school year, which unfolds around celebrating festivals drawn from different religions and cultures.

"I loved school. I hated being sick because I didn't want to miss anything. I felt teachers cared about me so much, it gave me confidence. Now I feel there's nothing I can't do."

Jessica Winer '80,
artist

The curriculum is based upon an understanding of the developing child. From birth through ages six or seven, children absorb the world through their senses and respond primarily through imitation. As they enter the primary school years, they are centered more in feeling and imagination. Then, as they continue their journey into the middle school, rational, abstract thinking begins to emerge. The curriculum respects this developmental process and gives it substance. Based on the idea that "ontogeny recapitulates phylogeny," that a developing child goes through the phases of human cultural evolution, children at different ages study what is appropriate to their development. Thus they learn reading by first "becoming" the letters, through physical gesture. In their "main lesson" books that are their textbooks, crayoned pictures of mountains and trees metamorphose into the letters M and T, and form drawings of circles and polygons become numbers.

Most Waldorf kids actually like school and develop a real love of learning.

Movement, music, and language (including foreign languages) begin in first grade. They hear fables and stories of the holy ones of different cultures. They learn to knit and crochet and play the recorder. Leaving the "paradise" of the first two grades, they encounter the sacred teachings of their culture. For example, in North America, the stories of the Old Testament are taught. In Japan, ancient Shinto stories are told. Farming, gardening, house building, measurement, and grammar now enter the curriculum. They memorize poems and begin to play stringed instruments.

With the fourth grade comes mythology, embroidery, zoology, geography, and geometric drawing. Mathematics and languages become more complex; art becomes more representational. In the fifth grade, history enters; they recite poems, begin botany, learn to knit with four needles, and start woodworking. And thus it continues, each grade providing more wonders.

Rather than pursuing several subjects at a time, the Waldorf curriculum unfolds in main lesson blocks of three or four weeks. The students create their own texts, or "main lesson books" for each subject. This enables students to live deeply into the subject. In this age of distraction, Waldorf children learn to be able to concentrate and focus.

Students learn the alphabet by first discovering the forms of the letters in nature

With high school, the mood changes in harmony with the tremendous developmental changes occurring at this time. Students no longer have a class teacher, but specialists in different fields who teach the various blocks and encourage dialog and discussion. Exact observation and reflection are prized. The aim is to engage students in the present and build on the confidence and ability to think for oneself that developed in the lower grades.

Waldorf Schools in North America

Waldorf education in America developed almost imperceptibly. The first school was founded in New York in 1928 and, over the next 20 years, only six more schools were founded. But something had germinated and slowly began to spread. Looking back, the growth was steady. The number of schools more or less doubled every decade. The reasons for this success are not hard to find. Waldorf schools appeals to parents seeking a truly holistic, child-centered, loving, artistic, practical, and wonder-filled education.

An Example:
The Green Meadow Waldorf School

The Green Meadow Waldorf School in Spring Valley, New York, founded in 1950, is one of the oldest Waldorf schools in North America. As you approach the wooded suburban enclave you realize that this is a different kind of school. The several buildings are clustered around a courtyard, forming a little campus, which in turn is surrounded by mature oaks and white ash. Gardens, large climbing logs and stones, and sculpture abound. Each building has its own character and form, yet the entire assemblage works as a whole. The colors are warm and natural, not bright. There's no graffiti. The roofs are shingled and gently sloped. Many of the walls are set at softer, more oblique angles. Even many of the windows have their rectangular shapes softened with another edge, making them five- or six-sided instead of just four-sided.

There is something peaceful in the air. The impression intensifies as you enter. Warmth pervades the space. Your senses begin to dance. Beauty, color, and natural flowing forms surround you. Children's paintings adorn the walls. Muffled sounds filter through the classroom walls and doors as you walk down a corridor. You can hear musical instruments, singing, children reciting a poem, the calm voice of a class teacher. And the smells! Bread baking in the kindergarten, fragrant plants and nontoxic paints. When you enter a classroom, the impression is confirmed—this is what a school ought to be. The children are happy, they are learning, they seem to love their teachers and each other.

"My parents... felt that the Waldorf school would be a far more open environment for African Americans.... I think the end result of Waldorf education is to raise our consciousness.... It taught me how to think for myself, to be responsible for my decisions. Second, it made me a good listener, sensitive to the needs of others. And third, it helped (me) establish meaningful beliefs."

Kenneth Chenault,
President & CEO,
American Express Corporation,
Waldorf alumnus

The Green Meadow School is home to a veritable United Nations of religious diversity. Of the 388 students (K–12) in Green Meadow, more than 60 are of Jewish descent, approximately 25 are the children of members of the nearby Jerrahi Islamic Mosque, and the rest come from Protestant, Catholic, Buddhist, agnostic, atheistic, and who-knows-what other religious traditions. Waldorf schools are sometimes assumed to be Eurocentric because of their European origins, yet the curriculum turns out to have universal appeal, adapting well in cultures as diverse as the *favelas* (slums) of Sao Paolo, Brazil, the black settlements of South Africa, rural Egypt and urban Israel, Eastern Europe, India, Southeast Asia, Australia, Japan, and the Pine Ridge Lakota Indian reservation in South Dakota.

Waldorf Graduates

Parents considering Waldorf want to know "What will become of my child?" According to Harm Paschen from the University of Bielefeld, Germany, studies of European Waldorf high school grads show that Waldorf graduates do very well indeed. Kids who go to Waldorf schools are as likely, or more likely, to attend college as students from public and other private schools. And after college, they are more likely to be employed than non-Waldorf grads. They are disproportionately well represented in teaching, the arts, business, medicine, and the social services professions. Similar research with North American grads is clearly needed.

On a recent college visit, Donna Badrig, associate director of undergraduate admissions for Columbia University, told one student, "We love Waldorf kids. We reject some students with 1600s on their SATs and accept others based on other factors, like the creative ability Waldorf students demonstrate." Similar enthusiasm for Waldorf grads was heard from admissions officers at Wesleyan University. City of Lakes Waldorf School (K–8) and Watershed High School (a new Waldorf charter school), both in Minneapolis, have seen their students go to such colleges at Sarah Lawrence, Juilliard, Wellesley, Hampshire, Wesleyan, and MIT, among others. But not all Waldorf grads go to college after high school. Many take a break from study to travel or do volunteer work before getting a job or going on to higher education.

Waldorf education is possibly the fastest growing educational movement in the world.

From our own observations, Waldorf students seem to share certain common characteristics. They are often independent and self-confident self-starters. They have genuine optimism for the future. They also tend to be highly ethical and are compassionately intelligent. They keep their sense of wonder about learning and the interdisciplinary sense that everything is connected. They seem to have a very healthy measure of what author Daniel Goleman calls "emotional intelligence," a much more reliable predictor of "success" in life, by any definition, than IQ or SAT scores. Generally speaking, they are both artistic and practical. They seem to know intuitively how to do many things.

Waldorf grad Paul Asaro, an architect, says: "I still draw upon the problem-solving skills that were nurtured... during my adolescent years." Other graduates stress independent thinking, imagination, and the relationships they developed and enjoyed with faculty and fellow students. "That's what's so wonderful about Waldorf education," says actress Julianna Margulies. "You're exposed to all these different ideas, but you're never given one view of it. You're encouraged to think as an individual." Rachel Blackmer, a veterinarian, writes: "Waldorf education is learning in its purest form. It is learning to think, to feel, and to act appropriately and with conscience." Mosemare Boyd, president and CEO, American Women Presidents, adds: "At Waldorf, we were taught to see things from the perspective of others. We saw that doing things together... was always more fun.... We learned to love learning."

Behind the Scenes

According to the Association of Waldorf Schools of North America (AWSNA), in the United States there are currently 56 full member Waldorf Schools, 15 sponsored Waldorf Schools (on their way to full membership), 69 developing Waldorf Schools, and 29 Waldorf Initiatives affiliated with AWSNA. Besides this there are a number of Waldorf-inspired or Waldorf method charter schools, as well as other Waldorf-related initiatives in the public schools.

"A Steiner education teaches you to think differently from the herd. I've found that independent ideas can be very valuable in the investment world."

David Nadel '87,
managing director,
Bear Stearns

Trained, qualified Waldorf teachers are much sought after. In North America each year, schools hire a combined total of between 300 and 400 new teachers, yet the various teacher-training centers graduate less than half that number. Many of the teachers are parents making a mid-life career change, perhaps seeking new challenges or a way to contribute to society. Robert Amis, who sold a successful equipment leasing company and took early retirement at 46, found himself accepting an offer to become a class teacher at City of Lakes Waldorf School in Minneapolis. "It's the hardest work I've ever done," he says. "I feel like I'm in a crucible, much the same as my students; and we're all wondering what changes are being wrought."

Side by Side, a leadership development program of Sunbridge College, trains 17-to 23-year-old youth who then facilitate weeklong arts and environmental overnight camps for underserved children ages 8 to 12 in New York and Los Angeles.

There are five full teacher-training centers: Rudolf Steiner College in Sacramento, California; Waldorf Institute of Southern California in Northridge, California; Center for Anthroposophy/Antioch Graduate School in Keene, New Hampshire; Sunbridge College in Spring Valley, New York; and Rudolf Steiner Center in Toronto, Ontario. In addition, there are two sponsored centers, one in Eugene, Oregon, and one in Detroit; and five developing centers—in Duncan, British Columbia; Sausalito, California; Honolulu; Chicago; and Seattle. And the Rudolf Steiner Institute, a summer school for adults and children, presently located at Thomas College in Waterville, Maine, provides a strong introduction to Waldorf education.

Waldorf in the Public Schools

According to George Hoffeker, former principal of the Yuba River Charter School in Nevada City, California, "Waldorf methods are so exciting and enlivening for all children that they shouldn't be reserved just for those who can afford it." Mary Goral, a professor at St. Mary College in Milwaukee and director of its early childhood education program, echoes this sentiment. She says, "I truly believe that what is needed in public schools is something much more like Waldorf, something that engages the whole child—body, soul, and spirit."

The first move in this direction began in September 1991 when the Milwaukee Urban Waldorf School opened—with 350 students, more that 90 percent of them African American—as part of the Milwaukee Public School System. Robert Peterkin, then superintendent of schools, had seen the need for a healthy education to serve the special needs of children in educationally deprived areas. Public school leaders, Waldorf educators, public school teachers, and scholars all worked together to found a school that would bring the integrated artistic, intellectual, and developmental Waldorf curriculum into the heart of an American city. Under the direction of Ann Pratt, an experienced Waldorf teacher, the experiment pioneered the development of an intensive teacher-training program for public school teachers. The result: reading scores increased and attendance stabilized. The school became a safe, quiet, well-ordered, attractive place to learn. A visitor recounted a telling anecdote. Waiting to see the principal, the visitor found himself seated opposite a student who was also waiting. According to the visitor, the student was, "threateningly large and had clearly committed some infraction. But there he sat outside the principal's office, quiet and self-composed, knitting."

Some publicly funded Waldorf schools are currently in transition. The Milwaukee experiment is still regrouping since losing founding principal Dorothy St. Charles to promotion. St. Charles' departure, combined with the school's move to "the worst zip code in Milwaukee," led to the loss of half its certified Waldorf teachers. The school, under the leadership of new principal Cheryl Colbert, is working with Cardinal Strich College to develop a teacher-training program to fill the need for certified Waldorf teachers. And the Sacramento school district, which operates a Waldorf-method magnet school, and the Twin Ridges Elementary School District of North San Juan, California, which operates seven Waldorf-inspired charter schools, including the first charter school in the United States to use Waldorf methods—the Yuba River Charter School—are in the midst of a court battle. The plaintiff's suit asserts that Waldorf education is religious in nature and that the two school districts are therefore in violation of the U.S. and California constitutional separation of church and state. The district court dismissed the suit, but on appeal, the circuit court gave the case new life, sending it back to district court.

"Society tells you that there is only one way to do things. Steiner students learn to create their own initiative and to be can-do thinkers."

Deborah Winer '79,
playwright

Opponents of Waldorf education, which is based on Steiner's insights into child development, equate the curriculum with anthroposophy, which they claim to be a religion. Waldorf advocates respond that Rudolf Steiner's anthroposophy is determinedly nonreligious and isn't taught in Waldorf schools anyway. The Waldorf curriculum stands on its own, they say, no matter what else Steiner taught or believed. "Anthroposophy is a founding philosophy, not a curriculum," says John Miller, a teacher at Watershed High School in Minneapolis. "Look at John Dewey, the educational reformer. Did anyone accuse his followers of teaching 'Deweyism'? No, because they just used a methodology he developed."

Critics also point to Steiner's early involvement in the Theosophical Society and to his more controversial views, such as his references to the lost continent of Atlantis. Several racist-sounding comments are often quoted to paint him as a racist. Waldorf's defenders say they reject racism out of hand. They say that Steiner was a person very much of his times, that his comments were made at the turn of the century, taken out of context, and are completely at odds with the vast preponderence of his statements having anything to do with race. They point out that many of Steiner's most reputable contemporaries shared beliefs with him that may appear today to be suspect or downright silly (Mahatma Gandhi was a member of the Theosophical Society, and Albert Einstein believed that Atlantis was a historical reality).

Despite the controversy, Waldorf-inspired charter schools are popping up all over the country. It is difficult to say just how many charter schools there are. Conservative estimates put the number at about 20 and growing. Though some fear a watering down of Steiner's principles, Donald Bufano, chairman of AWSNA, says, "Parents, and especially children at Waldorf or Waldorf-methods schools can enjoy the benefits of the education without commitment to its foundations just as one can enjoy Biodynamic® food or anthroposophic medicine whether or not they know how they work or where they come from."

Early Childhood Initiatives

The Waldorf approach to education is not limited to school-age kids. Recent students have pointed repeatedly to the critical importance of the nurturing children receive in early childhood, when infants and children are especially at risk. The combination of the breakdown of the family, the need for two working parents, and the growing number of single-parent families has left caregivers, whether at home or in daycare, uncertain how to care for children. Activities that were once natural and instinctive, like what to eat and how to bring up a baby, must now be learned consciously.

"Children," says Cynthia Aldinger, "are like sponges. They drink in everything and everyone around them." It is not only a question of the physical surroundings. What we say and do around a child, even how we think, is critical. A grassroots organization growing out of the Waldorf Early Childhood Association, Life Ways is devoted to the deinstitutionalization of child care. Founded in 1998, Life Ways provides courses and training in parenting and child care and is expanding to establish child care homes, centers, and parenting programs throughout North America.

A related effort is Sophia's Hearth in Keene, New Hampshire. Taking its name from the ancient goddess of wisdom, Sophia's Hearth works with "the art of becoming a family." As founder Susan Weber puts it, "Our work supports families in creating an atmosphere of loving warmth, joy, and respect for their infants and young children, while at the same time nurturing each parent."

The Caldwell Early Life Center at Rudolf Steiner College acts as a center for these and similar initiatives. Only two years old, but with a prestigious advisory board including naturalist Jane Goodall, well-known authors and researchers Jane Healy and Joseph Chilton Pearce, and education and child advocate Sally Bickford, it is halfway through raising the $2.5 million needed to complete a building to house its activities. These will cover the full range of early childhood needs, from working to reduce stress and isolation for families in ethnically and economically diverse neighborhoods to the creation of a demonstration daycare component.

Another Example:
The Wolakota Waldorf School

In the early 1990s a group of Lakota Sioux educators began to look for a better education for their children and discovered Waldorf education. They found that it paralleled their own wisdom traditions in many ways. Their hope was to create not only a school but also eventually a model community. In 1993 they created the Wolakota Waldorf Society as a nonprofit organization.

The Wolakota School is located on 80 acres of the Pine Ridge Reservation, near Oglala Lakota College, in Shannon County, South Dakota, the poorest county in the United States. Pine Ridge, the site of the Wounded Knee massacre, has been home to many famous Native American leaders, including Black Elk, Chief Red Cloud, and Fool Crow. The school serves 24 Lakota children. Among Waldorf schools it is unique, depending entirely on donations. There are only two teachers, Susan Bunting and Chris Young, who do everything from cooking breakfast and lunch to transporting children. If funds and space can be found, Edwin Around Him, Sr., will be hired next year as the school's third teacher. This year Edwin teaches Lakota and operates the van, when it's working.

Sponsored by Rudolf Steiner Foundation and Utne Magazine

Index

Index

Test Your Knowledge Form

We encourage you to photocopy and use this page as a tool to assess how the articles in *Annual Editions* expand on the information in your textbook. By reflecting on the articles you will gain enhanced text information. You can also access this useful form on a product's book support Web site at *http://www.mhcls.com/online/*.

NAME: DATE:

_____

TITLE AND NUMBER OF ARTICLE:

_____

BRIEFLY STATE THE MAIN IDEA OF THIS ARTICLE:

_____

LIST THREE IMPORTANT FACTS THAT THE AUTHOR USES TO SUPPORT THE MAIN IDEA:

_____

WHAT INFORMATION OR IDEAS DISCUSSED IN THIS ARTICLE ARE ALSO DISCUSSED IN YOUR TEXTBOOK OR OTHER READINGS THAT YOU HAVE DONE? LIST THE TEXTBOOK CHAPTERS AND PAGE NUMBERS:

_____

LIST ANY EXAMPLES OF BIAS OR FAULTY REASONING THAT YOU FOUND IN THE ARTICLE:

_____

LIST ANY NEW TERMS/CONCEPTS THAT WERE DISCUSSED IN THE ARTICLE, AND WRITE A SHORT DEFINITION:

We Want Your Advice

ANNUAL EDITIONS revisions depend on two major opinion sources: one is our Advisory Board, listed in the front of this volume, which works with us in scanning the thousands of articles published in the public press each year; the other is you—the person actually using the book. Please help us and the users of the next edition by completing the prepaid article rating form on this page and returning it to us. Thank you for your help!

ANNUAL EDITIONS: Education 06/07

ARTICLE RATING FORM

Here is an opportunity for you to have direct input into the next revision of this volume.
We would like you to rate each of the articles listed below, using the following scale:

1. **Excellent: should definitely be retained**
2. **Above average: should probably be retained**
3. **Below average: should probably be deleted**
4. **Poor: should definitely be deleted**

Your ratings will play a vital part in the next revision.
Please mail this prepaid form to us as soon as possible.
Thanks for your help!

RATING	ARTICLE
	1. The Biology of Risk Taking
	2. Parents Behaving Badly
	3. Metaphors of Hope
	4. Pell Grants Vs. Advanced Placement
	5. How Smart Is AP?
	6. Sobriety Tests Are Becoming Part of the School Day
	7. Spinning the Message on NCLB
	8. Choice Struggles On
	9. The 36th Annual Phi Delta Kappa/Gallup Poll of the Public's Attitudes Toward the Public Schools
	10. Tradeoffs, Societal Values, and School Reform
	11. Teaching Against Idiocy
	12. School Accountability: An Alternative to Testing
	13. Distance Education in High Schools
	14. How Schools Sustain Success
	15. A Case for School Connectedness
	16. No Child Left Behind: The Illusion of School Choice
	17. Charters "Yes!" Vouchers "No!"
	18. Intuitive Test Theory
	19. No Flower Shall Wither; or, Horticulture in the Kingdom of the Frogs
	20. Why Students Think They Understand—When They Don't
	21. Seven Worlds of Moral Education
	22. Pathways to Reform: Start with Values
	23. The Employment of Ethical Decision-Making Frameworks in Educational Change
	24. The Missing Virtue: Lessons From Dodge Ball & Aristotle

RATING	ARTICLE
	25. The Key to Classroom Management
	26. Reach Them to Teach Them
	27. Dealing with Rumors, Secrets, and Lies: Tools of Aggression for Middle School Girls
	28. Heading Off Disruptive Behavior
	29. True Blue
	30. Brown at 50
	31. Learning to Teach in Urban Settings
	32. Challenging Assumptions About the Achievement Gap
	33. The Challenge of Diversity and Choice
	34. Rethinking Inclusion: Schoolwide Applications
	35. Self-Efficacy: A Key to Improving the Motivation of Struggling Learners
	36. Vouchers For Parents: New Forms of Education Funding
	37. First-Year Teaching Assignments: A Descriptive Analysis
	38. Nuturing Passionate Teachers: Making Our Work Transparent
	39. Becoming a Teacher as a Hero's Journey: Using Metaphor in Preservice Teacher Education
	40. Building a Community of Hope
	41. Mission and Vision in Education
	42. Beyond the Book
	43. An Emerging Culture

(Continued on next page)

BUSINESS REPLY MAIL
FIRST CLASS MAIL PERMIT NO. 551 DUBUQUE IA

POSTAGE WILL BE PAID BY ADDRESEE

McGraw-Hill Contemporary Learning Series
2460 KERPER BLVD
DUBUQUE, IA 52001-9902

ABOUT YOU

Name

Date

Are you a teacher? ☐   A student? ☐
Your school's name

Department

Address   City   State   Zip

School telephone #

YOUR COMMENTS ARE IMPORTANT TO US!

Please fill in the following information:
For which course did you use this book?

Did you use a text with this ANNUAL EDITION? ☐ yes ☐ no
What was the title of the text?

What are your general reactions to the *Annual Editions* concept?

Have you read any pertinent articles recently that you think should be included in the next edition? Explain.

Are there any articles that you feel should be replaced in the next edition? Why?

Are there any World Wide Web sites that you feel should be included in the next edition? Please annotate.

May we contact you for editorial input? ☐ yes ☐ no
May we quote your comments? ☐ yes ☐ no